T0301695

GERMAN MERCHANTS IN THE NINETEENTH-CENTURY ATLANTIC

This study brings to life the community of transatlantic merchants who established strong economic, political, and cultural ties between the United States and the city-republic of Bremen, Germany, in the nineteenth century. Lars Maischak shows that the success of Bremen's merchants in helping make an industrial-capitalist world market created the conditions of their ultimate undoing: the new economy of industrial capitalism gave rise to democracy and the nation-state, undermining the political and economic power of this mercantile elite. Maischak argues that the experience of Bremen's merchants is representative of the transformation of the role of merchant capital in the first wave of globalization, with implications for our understanding of modern capitalism in general.

Lars Maischak is a lecturer in the history department at California State University, Fresno. This study is based on his dissertation, for which the Friends of the German Historical Institute awarded him the Fritz Stern Prize for the best dissertation in the field of German-American History in 2006.

PUBLICATIONS OF THE GERMAN HISTORICAL INSTITUTE

Edited by
Hartmut Berghoff with the assistance of David Lazar

The German Historical Institute is a center for advanced study and research whose purpose is to provide a permanent basis for scholarly cooperation among historians from the Federal Republic of Germany and the United States. The institute conducts, promotes, and supports research into both American and German political, social, economic, and cultural history; transatlantic migration, especially in the nineteenth and twentieth centuries; and the history of international relations, with special emphasis on the roles played by the United States and Germany.

Recent Books in the Series

Hartmut Berghoff, **Jürgen Kocka**, and **Dieter Ziegler**, editors, *Business in the Age of Extremes*

Yair Mintzker, *The Defortification of the German City, 1689–1866*

Astrid M. Eckert, *The Struggle for the Files: The Western Allies and the Return of German Archives after the Second World War*

Winson Chu, *The German Minority in Interwar Poland*

Christof Mauch and **Kiran Klaus Patel**, *The United States and Germany during the Twentieth Century*

Monica Black, *Death in Berlin: From Weimar to Divided Germany*

John R. McNeill and **Corinna R. Unger**, editors, *Environmental Histories of the Cold War*

Roger Chickering and **Stig Förster**, editors, *War in an Age of Revolution, 1775–1815*

Cathryn Carson, *Heisenberg in the Atomic Age: Science and the Public Sphere*

Michaela Hoenicke Moore, *Know Your Enemy: The American Debate on Nazism, 1933–1945*

Matthias Schulz and **Thomas A. Schwartz**, editors, *The Strained Alliance: U.S.-European Relations from Nixon to Carter*

German Merchants in the Nineteenth-Century Atlantic

LARS MAISCHAK

California State University, Fresno

GERMAN HISTORICAL INSTITUTE
Washington, D.C.

and

CAMBRIDGE
UNIVERSITY PRESS

University Printing House, Cambridge CB2 8BS, United Kingdom

One Liberty Plaza, 20th Floor, New York, NY 10006, USA

477 Williamstown Road, Port Melbourne, VIC 3207, Australia

314-321, 3rd Floor, Plot 3, Splendor Forum, Jasola District Centre, New Delhi - 110025, India

103 Penang Road, #05-06/07, Visioncrest Commercial, Singapore 238467

Cambridge University Press is part of the University of Cambridge.

It furthers the University's mission by disseminating knowledge in the pursuit of education, learning and research at the highest international levels of excellence.

www.cambridge.org
Information on this title: www.cambridge.org/9781107017290

© Lars Maischak 2013

First published 2013
First paperback edition 2015

A catalogue record for this publication is available from the British Library

Library of Congress Cataloging in Publication data
Maischak, Lars, 1970– author.
German merchants in the nineteenth-century Atlantic / Lars Maischak.
 pages cm. – (Publications of the German Historical Institute)
Includes bibliographical references and index.
ISBN 978-1-107-01729-0
1. Hanseatic League – History – 19th century. 2. Merchants – Germany – History – 19th century. 3. Merchants – United States – History – 19th century. 4. Germany – Commerce – United States. – History – 19th century. 5. United States – Commerce – Germany. – History – 19th century. I. Title.
HF458.M25 2013
382.0943´073–dc23 2012033797

ISBN 978-1-107-01729-0 Hardback
ISBN 978-1-107-56699-6 Paperback

Contents

List of Tables, Graphs, and Maps

TABLES

MAPS

Glossary

Bremische Bürgerschaft	See *Bürgerschaft*.
Bürgerkonvent	Name of the *Bürgerschaft* until 1848.
Bürgerschaft	"Citizenry," legislative organ of Bremen.
corporation	1. In the context of Bremish politics: a public organ, often enjoying political and juridical privileges, representing a group the membership of which is defined by status and/or economic activity. For example, a guild.
	2. In the context of German and American law: a private business enterprise enjoying the legal status of a natural person.
corporatism	The ideas and institutions that uphold an *economic* order based on corporations (1).
estate	A body of people defined by their function in the general division of labor of a society, often enjoying political and juridical privileges, membership in which may be inherited (e.g., in the case of the Prussian nobility) or granted by the sovereign (e.g., in the case of the Bremish mercantile estate).
estatism	The ideas and institutions that uphold a *political* order based on estates.
Handelskammer	"Chamber of commerce," corporate body representing Bremen's mercantile estate.
Hanseat	Here, a long-distance, wholesale merchant from the Hanseatic City of Bremen. Generally, a person from a Hanseatic City.
Last	"Load," a Bremish volume measure for a ship's loading capacity.
	1 Last = about 1.5 Register-Tons.
Nationalverein	"National Association," movement organization of German nationalism founded in 1859 by bourgeois notables.
Rat	Name of the *Senat* until 1822.
Senat	Executive organ of Bremen. All italicized derivations (*Senator*, etc.) refer to this organ.

Senate	American legislative body. All derivations in regular type (Senator, etc.) refer to this organ.
Zollverein	Customs Union.

Acknowledgments

It would have been impossible to write this book without the help of many friends and colleagues who generously gave their time and thoughts to make this a better work. To all of them I feel the deepest gratitude. Some particular individuals, whose efforts have left more of a trace on the following pages than those of others, should not remain unmentioned.

My doctoral advisor, Ronald G. Walters, supported me with invaluable advice and infinite patience. His rare gift of knowing at every point when to leave the candidate alone, and when to nudge him into producing work, laid the foundation of an efficient and productive cooperation. His stringent editorial help and his conscientious engagement with the often-idiosyncratic arguments advanced by this author are largely responsible for what little clarity might emerge from this product. Ron Walters went beyond what one can reasonably expect from an academic advisor not just in his care for this author's intellectual development, but also in his care for his physical well-being: frequent trips to Binkert's butcher shop ensured that his advisee's fridge remained well-stocked with essential German meat products.

Other members of the History Department of Johns Hopkins University have in similar ways left an impression on the work of this author. Vernon Lidtke introduced me to the world of German nineteenth-century thinkers whom I had thus far ignored in my pursuit of American history. Michael Johnson opened to me the strange country that is the antebellum South. Peter Jelavich, Paul Kramer, Lou Galambos, and Toby Ditz gave their time for discussing with me several key segments of this study. Even where my Northern German stubbornness rejected their constructive criticism, I hope that they will nonetheless discover on these pages the traces of my engagement with their objections and suggestions.

Among the scholars who influenced this work, David Harvey had an early and formative impact on my thinking. His assistance in guiding me toward an understanding of the role of merchant capital in the nineteenth century gave a decisive impulse for the direction of my further research and writing. The late Giovanni Arrighi, as a teacher, and Erica Schoenberger and Siba Grovogui, as members of my dissertation committee, likewise inspired me to think through the material rendered here in clearer and more thorough ways.

Christine Weideman, Assistant Head Archivist of the Manuscripts and Archives Division of Yale University Library, generously allowed me to have photocopies made of substantial portions of the letters contained in MSS 434, the John

Christopher Schwab Family Papers. As a result, I was able to complete much of my research in the comfort of my own study. Without the active help of many other archivists and their staff in Bremen, Baltimore, and New York, much of the source material that was indispensable for the completion of this project would have remained out of my reach. I am particularly indebted to Dorothea Breitenfeldt, curator for family and business papers at the Staatsarchiv Bremen, who not only pointed me to the papers of obscure merchants that turned out to be mother lodes of evidence, but also was a confidence-inspiring guide through the maze of the ancient and archaic structure of this venerable institution.

Catherine Molineux and Dirk Bönker sacrificed valuable time in reading and criticizing an early draft of this study. Even more importantly, their true and loyal friendship of many years sustained me through the trials and tribulations of graduate student life. Without them, it is safe to say that I would have thrown in the towel at some point.

Among scholars of the Hanseatic world, Heide Gerstenberger's work has been an inspiring example to my own. Her criticism of my own attempts at writing maritime history has disabused me of many a received idea that had kept me from seeing the fleet for the masts. Lydia Niehoff, Jan Oberg, and Jan Martin Lemnitzer have selflessly shared with me their insights on Bremen's merchants and have allowed me to cite the evidence that their own labors had excavated from the archives. Without their help, this Americanist would often have been lost in the bewildering landscape of a nineteenth-century German hometown.

In a chance encounter with one of the capacities in the study of German-American exchanges, Professor Dirk Hoerder, he revealed himself to me as one of the hitherto anonymous reviewers of this manuscript for Cambridge University Press. His generosity in commenting on my imperfect work and the extensive, thoughtful critique of my approach he offered in his review and in a subsequent conversation were crucial in making this study into something possibly fit for publication. The second reviewer, who remains anonymous, also deserves my gratitude for a great many enlightening insights. Naturally, any remaining errors of fact and reasoning are my responsibility alone.

No scholarly work is exclusively an academic achievement. Miami, the cat, reminded me of the importance of getting enough food and sleep as she tolerated my presence in her apartment. She is sorely missed. My parents, Ursula and Uwe Maischak, have each in their own way made possible my completion of this work. Their love and support over many years of study, along with their keen sense of narrative and humor have been the source of enduring motivations. It was not granted to my father to live to see this work published, but I take consolation in the knowledge that he shared many years of intellectual exchanges with me, the traces of which still greet me from these pages.

Bethanie Mills, my wife, has sustained me with her love and support, as well as with a generous amount of patience. As she and I had reason to celebrate the birth of our son, Henry Russell Mills Maischak, in the summer of 2011, I had to ask leave from the changing of diapers on more occasions than anyone should be allowed to. I dedicate this book to Henry, in wishing him a world of love and wonder.

Prologue

GLOBALIZATION AND ITS ENEMIES

The end of the Cold War brought the spread of free trade and globalization at the same time that it reinvigorated nationalism.[1] Rather than seeing a universal victory of liberal, Western democracy, we found ourselves bracing for the attacks of fundamentalists who advocated an authoritarian social order. In one narrative, this fundamentalist attack is a matter of an antimodernist rebellion by those who lost in the process of modernization.[2] From the mountainous heartlands of Afghanistan and Appalachia, Chechnya and Thuringia, self-styled defenders of the authenticity and purity of the people and its beliefs set out to battle the incursions of modernization. In the minds of these crusaders, global commerce is the conduit for the seed of corrosion that threatens a local morality and way of life. In their view, the city and its archetypical representative, the merchant, bear responsibility for the subjection of the simple farmers and workers to the dictates of the market and the subversion of their ethos by a commercial culture devoid of a higher calling.[3]

The longer we live under these conditions of global strife, however, the clearer it becomes that a fundamentalist critique of Western liberalism is just as attractive to urban professionals as it is to disgruntled provincials. The biographies of recent suicide attackers

---

[1] See, e.g., Barber, Benjamin, *Jihad vs. McWorld: How Globalism and Tribalism Are Reshaping the World*, New York, 1995. For the term *globalization*, and the debate over its meanings, see Altvater, Elmar, and Birgit Mahnkopf, *Grenzen der Globalisierung: Ökonomie, Ökologie und Politik in der Weltgesellschaft*, Münster, 2007; Altvater, Elmar, ed., *Der Sound des Sachzwangs – Der Globalisierungs-Reader*, Berlin, 2006; O'Rourke, Kevin H., and Jeffrey G. Williamson, *Globalization and History: The Evolution of a Nineteenth-Century Atlantic Economy*, Cambridge, MA, and London, 1999; Osterhammel, Jürgen, and Niels P. Petersson, *Globalization: A Short History*, Princeton, NJ, and Oxford, 2005.

[2] While this term will be used on the pages of this study to describe the political program of actors who perceived a need for their respective societies to "catch up" to the leading industrial and commercial powers, it is treated with caution. Following the argument made by Geoff Eley and David Blackbourn in *The Peculiarities of German History* (Oxford and New York, 1984), we should be aware that democratization, or even a liberal political stance, is not necessarily contained in a "package" of modernization. E.g., Eric Hobsbawm (*Nations and Nationalism since 1780: Programme, Myth, Reality*, Cambridge and New York, 1992) has shown that modernizers' political and social views varied, in a continuum ranging from a full embrace of "Western freedom" to authoritarianism.

[3] See, e.g., Huntington, Samuel P., *The Clash of Civilizations*, New York, 1996; Buruma, Ian, and Avishai Margalit, *Occidentalism: The West in the Eyes of Its Enemies*, New York, 2004; and Sardar, Ziauddin, *Postmodernism and the Other: The New Imperialism of Western Culture*, London and Chicago, 1998. The last is an example of the views criticized here.

are replete with university degrees and urban lifestyles. Likewise, a closer look at the presumed backwoodsmen reveals a high degree of participation in global commerce. Whether we consider opiates from Afghanistan or auto parts from Appalachia, we find that even the most remote regions of the world are tied into the world market. There are no authentic places left that have been untouched by the incursions of modernization. Local, particularist traditions that pose as deeply rooted customs are really inventions already suffused with an engagement with the outside world. In either case, global liberalism and fundamentalism appear not as ideologies that respectively promote and oppose modernity, but as ideological poles within modernity.[4]

Since the 1990s, intellectuals in the United States have perceived the newly globalized world as presenting both dangers and opportunities. Transnational history has been one reflex to the epochal changes at the turn of our century. This new branch of historical scholarship has been mining the past for traces of our direct ancestors: men and women who lived through periods of intense changes that affected the entire world, and who went beyond their local origins to craft a worldview from the experiences collected in exchanges with other countries. Transnational historians have discovered a variety of such ancestors, mostly in the Progressive Age at the turn of the twentieth century. Here they found reformers who, knowing that their local intellectual traditions and political institutions inadequately equipped them to respond to rapid industrialization and urbanization, turned abroad to look for better answers. Here they also found conquerors and colonizers who went to foreign shores as rulers, looking to spread their own, local ideas and practices in the guise of a universal civilization, an American Empire.[5]

No matter the intent of those who were driven abroad by local concerns, transnational exchange is always a two-way street. In formulating this insight, transnational historians stand in the tradition of scholarship on the Atlantic World of the eighteenth century. The subculture of sailors and merchants who built the European colonial empires of that era, as well as the novel commodities they introduced into the societies along the Atlantic's shores, remade the everyday life and the worldview of the colonizer and the colonized, even if neither ever left his home.[6]

[4] Hobsbawm, Eric J., and Terence Ranger, *The Invention of Tradition*, Cambridge and New York, 1983.
[5] Bender, Thomas, *A Nation among Nations: America's Place in World History*, New York, 2006; Rodgers, Daniel, *Atlantic Crossings: Social Politics in a Progressive Age*, Cambridge, MA, and London, 1998; Howe, Daniel W., *American History in an Atlantic Context: An Inaugural Lecture Delivered before the University of Oxford on June 3 1993*, Oxford, 1993; Kramer, Paul, *The Blood of Government: Race, Empire, the United States, and the Philippines*, Chapel Hill, NC, 2006; Tyrrell, Ian, "American Exceptionalism in an Age of International History" (1031–55) and "Ian Tyrell Responds" (1068–72), and McGerr, Michael, "The Price of the 'New Transnational History'" (1056–67) in *American Historical Review* 96, no. 4 (1991).
[6] Bailyn, Bernard, and Patricia L. Denault, eds., *Soundings in Atlantic History: Latent Structures and Intellectual Currents, 1500–1830*, Cambridge, MA, 2009; Rediker, Marcus B., and Peter Linebaugh, *The Many-Headed Hydra: Sailors, Slaves, Commoners, and the Hidden History of the Revolutionary Atlantic*, Boston, 2000; Gilroy, Paul, *The Black Atlantic: Modernity and Double Consciousness*, Cambridge, MA, 1993; idem, *There Ain't No Black in the Union Jack: The Cultural Politics of Race and Nation*, London, 1987; Bolster, W. Jeffrey, *Black Jacks: African American Seamen in the Age of Sail*, Cambridge, MA, and London, 1997; Kelly, Robin D. G., "How the West Was One: The African Diaspora and the Re-Mapping of U.S. History," in *Rethinking American History in a Global Age*, ed. Thomas Bender, Berkeley, CA, 2002, 123–47; Molineux, Catherine, "The Peripheries Within: Race, Slavery, and

Even nationalism, the political ideology of local particularism, owes its emergence to transnational exchanges. Romantic landscape painting that wanted to demonstrate the rootedness of a people in its natural environment was the application of a visual language forged in the cooperation between painters from different countries who converged on Rome, Munich, or Düsseldorf to become proficient in their art, while the leaders of national liberation movements were schooled in a way of thinking that imagines nations as historical subjects in the universities of Paris, London, or Berlin.[7]

Thanks to Atlantic and transnational history, we know that at the beginning of the modern era, there was a world in which identities were in flux; and that by the end of the nineteenth century it had been replaced by a world of nation-states imagined as self-contained units, albeit one permeated by – friendly and competitive – transnational connections. One hope of transnational history has been to break nation-states' hold on peoples' political imagination. As history is always a narrative that defines the self-image of contemporaries, transnational history has been offering the adequate narrative for an American population that can no longer afford to ignore the rest of the world. It could become an updated national history of America, just as it could become a critique of American imperial ambition, or of globalized markets, now and in the past.

When the term *transnational history* was first coined in the 1990s, its proponents were engaged in a broader debate over the meaning of *globalization*. This contested term was the subject of an intellectual exchange involving not just scholars from different disciplines, but also of the public in general, in a public sphere made truly global by the emergence of the worldwide web. Transnationalists seemed intent on liberating the historical discipline from the epistemological fetters it acquired at the time of its professionalization, when it came into being as national history – not just the history of nations as historical subjects, but also history as a justification and legitimization of particular nations, their claims to power, and the nationalist ideologies that underwrote projects of nation-state–making.[8]

At its outset, transnational history was the adaptation of globalism to the historical profession – not just a methodological innovation or a new approach to complement the business as usual, but a promise to change the terms of historical inquiry. In spite of this ambitious reach, it remained hampered by its enthusiasm for globalism – what Elmar Altvater defined as the complex of attitudes and ideas that embrace a cosmopolitan existence and condition. Invoking images of jet-setting scholars assembling in Italian villas, and American hipsters in Japanese dance clubs ironically

Empire in Early Modern England," PhD diss., Johns Hopkins University, 2005; O'Rourke and Williamson, *Globalization and History*.

[7] Anderson, Benedict, *Imagined Communities: Reflections on the Origin and Spread of Nationalism*, London and New York, 1983; Andree, Rolf, and Ute Rickel-Immel, *The Hudson and the Rhine. Die amerikanische Malerkolonie in Düsseldorf im 19. Jahrhundert*, Kat. Ausst. [Exhibition Catalog], Düsseldorf, Kunstmuseum, 1976; Buruma and Margalit, *Occidentalism*; Flacke, Monika, ed., *Mythen der Nationen. Ein Europäisches Panorama*, Munich and Berlin, 1998; Groseclose, Barbara S., *Emmanuel Leutze, 1816–1868: Freedom Is the Only King*, Exhibition Catalog, National Collection of Fine Art, Smithsonian Institution, 1976, Washington, DC, 1976.

[8] Novick, Peter, *That Noble Dream: The "Objectivity Question" and the American Historical Profession*, Cambridge and New York, 1988.

appraising Afro-French trance techno and fusion cuisine, globalism is the restless pursuit of exchange.[9]

As such, it remains oblivious to the dark underbelly of this high-powered world of transcended boundaries – the conditions of production that feed commodified authenticity into a global marketplace, the deprivations these conditions cause, and the discontent they feed. Globalism is the ideology befitting a globalized, capitalist marketplace. To criticize the nation and its accompanying ideas as insufficiently globalized is to insist on the validity of the current mode of capital accumulation against the past one.

In that transnational history shares with globalism a rosy view of a world of exchanges, it is not concerned with the reasons for the nation-state. As far as transnational history is concerned, if the nation-state is an anachronism, today, the reasons for its emergence can never have been compelling. Just as the nature of globalized capitalism does not enter into the project of transnational history, so the nature of nation-states as containers of industrial capitalism engaged in worldwide competition eludes it.

The aggressively disembedded global marketplace that "flattens" the world and the reactionary backlash against cultural homogenization we are witnessing today are not novel. Their mutual dependence on each other follows a long-established pattern, a dialectic of modernization and traditionalism, or universalism and particularism.[10] This study is an investigation of this dialectic. This investigation is conducted in the example of nineteenth-century German merchants who engaged in long-distance trade with the United States.

THE POLITICAL ECONOMY OF GLOBALIZATION

To understand the role of merchants in the world economy, this study makes use of the work of Karl Marx. In *Capital*, Marx describes "the history of the fall of Holland as the dominant mercantile nation ... [as] the history of the subsumption of merchant capital under industrial capital."[11] Sven Beckert uses this concept of the "subsumption of merchant capital under industrial capital" to theorize the *sociological, political*, and *cultural* processes that led to the formation of a national bourgeoisie in the United States.[12] Here, we employ Marx's concept to explain the *economic* changes in world trade that occurred in the nineteenth century.

What, exactly, does this concept of "subsumption" entail? After all, merchants are the economic agents with the longest history, and their role can appear to have

---

[9] Altvater, Grenzen. In its embrace of a universal, mutual, cultural exchange, this globalist vision is akin to Immanuel Kant's hope for a "perpetual peace" in a world of republics, whose citizens engage in peaceful exchanges for their mutual betterment. Kant, Immanuel, *Zum ewigen Frieden* (1795), in Akademieausgabe, Werke, vol. 8.

[10] Adorno, Theodor W., and Horkheimer, Max, *Dialektik der Aufklärung. Philosophische Fragmente*, Frankfurt, 1969 (New York, 1944); Barber, *Jihad vs. McWorld*; Friedman, Thomas L., *The World Is Flat: A Brief History of the Twenty-First Century*, New York, 2005; Mensching, Günther, *Das Allgemeine und das Besondere. Der Ursprung des modernen Denkens im Mittelalter*, Stuttgart, 1992.

[11] Marx, Karl, *Capital*, 3 vols. (Karl Marx and Friedrich Engels, Werke, vols. 23–5), vol. 3, Berlin, 1979 [1894], here vol. 3, 346. Translations by the author of this study.

[12] Beckert, *Metropolis*, throughout.

changed little from Renaissance Venice through twentieth-century New York to postmodern Singapore. Marx argues that this appearance is deceiving. He regards modern, industrial capitalism as fundamentally distinct from earlier, commercial capitalism. In *Capital*, he is not concerned with the latter, but analyzes the former.

By capitalism, Marx understands fully developed capitalist relations of production and exchange, where wage labor is the universal form of commodity production. Earlier stages of commercial capitalism, and even early pockets of industrial production, do not satisfy all of these criteria. What distinguishes capitalist modes of production from earlier ones is the universality of the creation of surplus value in commodity production.

For most of its history, merchant capital was capital *par excellence*. With the emergence of industrial capital, it lost this special place. In a fully developed capitalist society, merchant capital is a "distinct sphere of capital investment," "externally independent" from, yet "internally dependent" on industrial capital. At the heart of this "internal dependence" is the reliance of mercantile profit on surplus value generated in production. The merchant sells his commodities at their value, that is, at the price of production, and buys them from the producer below this price. In this manner, a share of surplus value "devolves on" merchant capital.[13]

The amount of mercantile profit, that is, the difference between the price the merchant pays to the producer and the price he receives from the buyer, is determined by an averaging-out of profits across all capitals in society, whether employed in production or circulation. Hence, on the one hand, the lower the share of merchant capital among all capital in a given society, the higher the average profit on any capital invested. On the other hand, a given productive capital requires for its reproduction a particular minimum of capital engaged in circulation.[14]

This requirement is a source of the "external independence" of modern merchant capital. The circulation of productive capital is never complete without realizing the surplus value embodied in the commodity produced. The realization of surplus value depends on circulation, the transformation into money of the commodity that exits the process of production (C'–M'), and the subsequent transformation of money back into commodities, namely, labor and means of production, for another cycle of production (M–C(MP/L)).[15]

The individual industrial capitalist will often have an interest in not concerning himself with the sale of the commodities produced by him. The turnover time of capital equals the time of production plus the time of circulation. While the merchant is not concerned with the former, his service may shorten the latter on a social scale, or reduce it to zero for the individual capitalist, if he buys his finished product straight from the factory, and pays him in cash. In the latter case, for the individual industrial capitalist, the valorization of his capital is complete, and he can immediately replace his means of production (e.g., buy supplies and hire laborers).[16]

There is, however, no systematic necessity for the producer to rely on a merchant for the sale of his product. The producer could market it. In this sense, too, the

---

[13] Marx, *Capital*, vol. 3, 316.
[14] Ibid., vol. 3, 290–303.
[15] Ibid., vol. 1, 161–70, vol. 2, 151–3, and vol. 3, 335–49.
[16] Ibid., vol. 2, 124–35 and vol. 3, 283–306.

merchant is "internally dependent" on the producer. Yet, the benefits of specialization have often enabled (externally) independent merchants to undertake the
distribution of commodities more efficiently. Only at a large scale of production,
can the producer dispose of the merchant and organize distribution in a model of
the "vertical integration" of production and distribution stretching from raw
materials to retail trade. This was the case with the American oil industry since
the 1890s, when Standard Oil enjoyed a near monopoly on petroleum.[17]

What, then, was the role of merchant capital in its heyday, before industrial
commodity production became the universal norm? In these former times – say, in
Renaissance Venice – mercantile profit was based on selling commodities above
their value and, more often than not, buying them below their value. Merchants
could do this because their trade linked societies not yet, or not fully, capitalist.[18]

Merchant capital inaugurated the simple form of capital circulation, "buying in order
to sell" (M–C–M'). Mercantile profit *then* – that is, *before* industrial capital became the
dominant form – sprang from differences in price between different locations. The
merchant "bought cheap, and sold dear." He bought goods that constituted a surplus for
economies not yet capitalist in nature, and turned them into commodities.[19]

The existence of merchant capital was a necessary, but not sufficient, precondition
for the emergence of capitalist production for five reasons. First, the accumulation of
capital necessary for investment in industrial production took place in the hands of
merchants. Second, trade is presupposed for capitalist production. It is by definition
production for exchange, rather than use, and requires at least a regional market for its
output. Third, the mercantile view of the product as a commodity encourages
producers to transform production into commodity production. Fourth, by establishing
continuous trading links, merchant capital first engendered the formation of an average
rate of profit, albeit one that averaged-out merely mercantile profits, not yet capitalist
profits across the board. Fifth, in a dialectic move, merchant capital, though operating
on the basis of an exchange that is not the exchange of equivalents, established a
measure of commensurability in the form of the price, and thus helped bring about a
general exchange of equivalents.[20]

Although in many ways merchant capital paved the way for modern capitalism,
its former role differed decisively from its modern one. Yet, Marx observed, the
notion that capital as such lived off fraud and plunder – nonequivalent exchange –
had survived into modern times. This notion he wished to dispel, mainly by
emphasizing that modern, industrial capitalism relies on the exchange of equivalents
at all stages of circulation and production.[21]

For the purpose of exploring the relation between industrial and merchant
capital, Bremen is a suitable example, because here we find merchant capital as a
distinct and self-conscious class, firmly in power in a city-state, taking issue with the
larger political and economic development in the emerging "nation" and in the

---

[17] Cf. Chandler, Alfred D., Jr., *Strategy and Structure: Chapters in the History of the American Industrial
Enterprise*, Cambridge, MA, 1962.
[18] Marx, *Capital*, vol. 3, 336–42.
[19] Ibid., vol. 2, 282–7.
[20] Ibid., vol. 3, 339–43.
[21] Ibid., vol. 1, 161–78.

larger world. We can understand this continuing independent role of German merchant capital as an expression of the otherwise underdeveloped state of the German economies, because "the independent development of merchant capital stands in reverse relation to the general economic development of society."[22]

THE POLITICS OF GLOBALIZATION

So far, the historical period that most resembled our own, and in which the persistent dichotomies of our own era were first fully formed, has evaded close attention from transnational historians. The decades between the Congress of Vienna and the Paris Commune were the formative years for the world we know. They saw the rise of industry outside of Britain and the acceleration of global communication by steam power and telegraphs on land and across oceans. By 1871, these processes had resulted in the creation of a modern, industrial world market, and of the strengthened, increasingly unitary, territorial states that based their legitimacy on nationality and their fiscal and military might on industry and that mediated competition and cooperation on the world market.

The new ease of communication, and the opportunities and disruptions caused by industrialization, set in motion an unprecedented number of migrants. Never before had such a high percentage of the world's population had the chance to form an image of foreign countries from firsthand experience. For those who lacked this chance, the proliferation of print media exploded the amount of information about the world available even in its farthest provincial corners. At the same time as they acquainted them with foreign events, newspapers made citizens into armchair participants in a bloody game of geopolitics whose logic culminated in World War I. The smaller and the more interdependent the world became, the more people's habits of perception were shaped by categories like nation and race.

Our world, with its dialectic of world market and nation-state, cosmopolitanism and parochialism, universalism and particularism, liberalism and fundamentalism, technological progress and barbarian regression, has its roots in the nineteenth century. It is for this reason that Marx's and Engels's account of globalization and creative destruction in the *Communist Manifesto* rings so contemporary to our ears:

The bourgeoisie has through its exploitation of the world-market given a cosmopolitan character to production and consumption in every country. All old-established national industries ... are dislodged by new industries whose introduction becomes a life and death question for all civilized nations; ... industries whose products are consumed, not only at home, but in every quarter of the globe.... In place of the old local and national seclusion and self-sufficiency, we have intercourse in every direction, universal interdependence of nations.[23]

Yet, the Communists' hope that "national one-sidedness and narrow-mindedness become more and more impossible" has not borne out. From the outset, this ever-shrinking, ever-accelerating, ever-changing world has bred a wish to recapture the

---

[22] Ibid., vol. 3, 340.
[23] Marx, Karl, and Friedrich Engels, "Manifesto of the Communist Party," in *The Marx-Engels Reader*, ed. Robert Tucker, New York and London, 1978, 473–500, here p. 476.

"feudal, patriarchal, idyllic relations" Marx and Engels had hoped were forever lost to it. Modernity has been constantly shadowed by its dark sibling, reactionary antimodernism. More often than not, its rejection of the political and philosophical foundations of modernity has been accompanied by an enthusiasm for its material blessings. Bin Laden would have been impossible to conceive without his satellite phone.[24]

In the shadow of recent events, the deep historical roots of the dialectic of modern world-society, and America's entanglement with this dialectic, are more clearly visible than in the spotlight of national history. In America, and not just among its enemies, the march of technological progress and the course of empire were from the beginning accompanied by a wish to hold back the clock of democracy, liberalism, and individual rights. Between America and Europe, some of the most active promoters of a capitalist world market were among those most skeptical toward its purported companion, the liberal-democratic society.

PIONEERS OF GLOBALIZATION

The German merchants who dominated trade between the United States and Germany through much of the nineteenth century shared the sense that the boundaries between land and ocean were being blurred by modern commerce. America and the ocean appeared as metaphors for commodity exchange in the words of Johann Georg Kohl, a merchant from Bremen:

Poseidon is, most of all, a shaker of the Earth.... Like mighty springs, America and the Ocean drive and spur the whole great machinery of our modern life. America grows abundantly in all our gardens and fields; and the Ocean pushes with its currents and tides into the most secluded channels of the hinterland.[25]

As a cosmopolitan community equally rooted on both sides of the ocean, and equally engaged in the political and economic life of multiple societies, Bremen's merchants allow us to place the antebellum United States in its international context. Their history illuminates the essential contribution to the making of an industrial-capitalist world market, and of American participation in it, of men and women deeply committed to tradition and fiercely opposed to liberalism and democracy.

Acknowledging the importance of these cosmopolitan conservatives and their American collaborators for bringing the United States into the world market, means to question the account of America as the undisputed domain of liberalism. Trading with America, these German merchants found in the New World like-minded men and women whose qualms about the dangers of unfettered market relations matched their own, yet with whom they also shared a wish to "improve" the world through the blessings of global communication and commerce.

Together, these German merchants and their American friends represent, not an alternative path to capitalism, but its mainstream. If their exertions resulted in a world increasingly characterized by liberal-democratic nation-states, it was not what they had envisioned or desired when they had set out to improve the older world they knew.

---

[24] Ibid., 475, 477.

[25] Cited by Engelsing, Rolf, "England und die USA in der bremischen Sicht des 19. Jahrhunderts," in *Jahrbuch der Wittheit zu Bremen*, vol. 1, 1957, 33–65, here pp. 55–6 (1861).

Introduction

AMERICA AND BREMEN

The group of merchants who are the subject of this work were based in the Free Hanseatic City of Bremen, an independent city-republic until 1867 that today is a part of Germany. In 1852, this group included 776 adult men in Bremen, in a population of eighty thousand.[1] Between the centers of their activities – Bremen, New York, and Baltimore – these Hanseats formed one transatlantic community. They remained linked to each other through trade, intermarriage, friendship, shared religious and political beliefs, and a reliance on the infrastructure of consulates and trade treaties that rested on Bremen's sovereignty. The boundaries that defined the group under consideration here crossed through cities, nations, and oceans. At the same time, Hanseats helped level boundaries between continents through their trade.

Within Bremen, inclusion in this group was defined by economic activity and legal status. Only holders of the Greater Privilege, the highest rank of citizenship in Bremen, were legally entitled to conduct long-distance trade there.[2] As a self-conscious elite, these merchants saw themselves in the tradition of the medieval Hanseatic League. Bremen was one of three cities appointed to represent the Hansa after its decline in the seventeenth century, hence its official designation as a state as the "Free Hanseatic City of Bremen."[3]

To approach the antebellum period of American history through a foreign port, the German city of Bremen, opens a different gaze on the American past than could be gained from a vantage point on the shore. Without America, Bremen would

---

[1] Schwarzwälder, Herbert, *Geschichte der Freien Hansestadt Bremen*, 4 vols., Hamburg, 1987, is the standard general history of Bremen. See vol. 2, 217–18, for demographic data.

[2] The *Bürgerrecht* in *Großes Bremisches Bürgerrecht* appears best translated as *privilege*, rather than *citizenship*, because the concept of citizenship implies a single status of citizen. Both the *Großes Bürgerrecht* – allowing its holder to engage in foreign trade – and the *Kleines Bürgerrecht* – required for many other occupations – had to be bought. Marschalek, Peter, "Der Erwerb des bremischen Bürgerrechts und die Zuwanderung nach Bremen um die Mitte des 19. Jahrhunderts," in *Bremisches Jahrbuch*, vol. 66 (1988), 295–305.

[3] The others were Hamburg and Lübeck, whose merchants likewise could refer to themselves as Hanseats. As I am dealing exclusively with Bremish merchants, I use the term *Hanseat* synonymously with *Bremish merchant*, unless specifically noted. The Hanseatic League received international recognition as a state-like entity with the Peace of Westphalia, at a moment when its economic and political importance was all but gone.

have remained a provincial backwater. With America, it became a center of world trade. But what did Bremen do for America?

During the mid-third of the nineteenth century, when the United States was presumably busy finding its national identity, we find strong traces of both an earlier, Atlantic World and of a later, transnational world.[4] The American economy depended on the exportation of cotton and other staples of slave labor and on the importation of immigrants, who provided manpower and capital for the market revolution and capitalist production. Without an armada of merchant vessels, and an army of merchants in the commercial centers, King Cotton would have been about as powerful as your average Polish country squire. These merchants and mariners, however, were largely foreigners.

Sven Beckert has found that in mid-1850s New York, 26 percent of the elite were foreign-born. By 1870, this share had risen to 44 percent.[5] The political influence of this particular "foreign element" in America has long been ignored. We know the economic history of foreign trade and foreign traders. We also know the history of immigrants and of the ethnic politicians who spoke in their name. But we do not know the names of the foreign merchants and bankers who spoke for themselves when they advocated their commercial and political interests in club-rooms and legislative lobbies. We know the process by which immigrants discovered their "national" identity after they had come to the United States – for example, of Württembergers and Bavarians becoming "Germans" only in their adoptive country. But we know very little about the politics of the cosmopolitan elites whose trade interests linked them with peers on both sides of the Atlantic.[6]

Economically, Hanseats were essential for facilitating the commerce on which the growing nation depended. Politically, they served as conduits for ideas between the old and new worlds. Their engagement with political and cultural ideas across the Atlantic World shows the essentially transnational character of the central political debates of the time.

The related challenges of capitalist modernization and democracy were not limited to America. Hence, it is not surprising that here as elsewhere, elites responded to both processes in similar ways. The freedom of labor, the role of

---

[4] See notes to the Prologue to this study for literature.

[5] Beckert, Sven, *The Monied Metropolis. New York City and the Consolidation of the American Bourgeoisie, 1850–1896*, Cambridge, MA, 2001, 31, 147. The share of Germans was 6% in 1855 and 23% in 1870. Beckert included in his samples taxpayers assessed on real and personal wealth of $10,000 or more in 1855 and of $15,000 or more in 1870.

[6] Archdeacon, Thomas, *Becoming American: An Ethnic History*, New York and London, 1983; Hidy, Ralph W., *The House of Baring in American Trade: English Merchant Bankers at Work, 1763–1861* (Harvard Studies in Business History, vol. 14), Cambridge, MA, 1949; Perkins, Edwin J., *Financing Anglo-American Trade: The House of Brown, 1800–1880*, Cambridge, MA, 1975; Porter, P. Glenn, and Harold C. Livesay, *Merchants and Manufacturers: Studies in the Changing Structure of Nineteenth-Century Marketing*, Baltimore, 1971; Echternkamp, Jörg, "Emerging Ethnicity: The German Experience in Antebellum Baltimore," *Maryland Historical Magazine* 86, no. 1 (Spring 1991), 1–22; Trefousse, Hans L., *Carl Schurz: A Biography*, Knoxville, TN, 1982; Hoerder, Dirk, and Jörg Nagler, eds., *People in Transit: German Migrations in Comparative Perspective, 1820–1930*, Washington, DC, 1995; Kamphoefner, Walter D., and Wolfgang Helbich, eds., *German-American Immigration and Ethnicity in Comparative Perspective*, Madison, WI, 2004; Trommler, Frank, and Joseph McVeigh, eds., *America and the Germans: An Assessment of a Three-Hundred-Year History*, Philadelphia, 1985.

religion in public life, and the rise of the working class as a political force occupied elites throughout the industrializing world.[7]

In developing their political ideas, and in building the institutions of the state of Bremen, Hanseats negotiated contradictory desires: to preserve a traditional politics of deference and to make Bremen's institutions efficient tools for facilitating world trade. The ideological and institutional framework they developed was capable of containing these contradictions and of realizing both these conflicting desires.

With Hegel, we can understand the form in which contradictions can move toward a synthesis as a dialectical relation.[8] With Marx, we can add an awareness that this relation depends on particular social and economic conditions.[9] The form that allowed Hanseats to criticize and, at the same time, to realize modern, capitalist social relations, including a capitalist world market – and the form that allowed them simultaneously to deny and affirm the traditional, communal values of an early-modern hometown – was modern conservatism. Hanseats' intense trading ties to the Atlantic World, and their exposure to its political ideas, added a cosmopolitan dimension to this form, resulting in a peculiar brand of cosmopolitan conservatism.[10]

As participants in U.S. politics, Bremen's merchants contributed to the trans-atlantic scope of this brand of modernization. Although, at first sight, Hanseatic politics may appear as stubbornly local and particularistic, it was part of a trans-national bourgeois alternative to liberalism and democracy, drawing its inspirations from Burke rather than Rousseau, preferring Adam Müller to Hegel, and having more in common with John C. Calhoun than with John Stuart Mill.[11]

In engaging with Whigs, Democrats, and Republicans, these merchants reveal that elites on all shores of the Atlantic shared political idioms that made possible a recognition of shared interests and concerns. Socially, Hanseats partook in a global, Victorian culture, at the same time that they were rooted in local, German traditions and as they absorbed the aesthetic of romantic nationalism in both its American and German formulations. In all these ways, they resembled their American and German contemporaries, while forming a group self-consciously apart from both. Ultimately, if we give proper weight to the transnational influences on the United States during the antebellum era, we find that the country was not as markedly distinct from Europe as the difference in the form of government

---

[7] See note 2.

[8] Hegel, G. W. F., *Elements of the Philosophy of Right*, trans. H. B. Nisbet, Cambridge, 1991.

[9] Marx, Karl, "Theses on Feuerbach," in *The Marx-Engels Reader*, ed. Robert C. Tucker, New York and London 1978, 143–45.

[10] Engelsing, Rolf, "England und die USA in der bremischen Sicht des 19. Jahrhunderts," in *Jahrbuch der Wittheit zu Bremen*, vol. 1, 1957, 33–65, here p. 47, cites Heinrich Smidt, son of Burgomaster Smidt, as saying that the commercial relations between Bremen and the United States were a step toward the fulfillment of the "as yet unrealized ideals of the cosmopolitans." On cosmopolitanism as an ideal of world peace through exchange, cf. Kant, Immanuel, *Zum ewigen Frieden* (1795), in Akademieausgabe, Werke, vol. 8; and Meinecke, Friedrich, *Weltbürgertum und Nationalstaat* (Hans Herzfeld, Carl Hinrichs and Walther Hofer, eds., Friedrich Meinecke, Werke, vol. 5), Munich 1962 (1911).

[11] Johann Smidt, Bremen's arch-conservative burgomaster, saw the cities "friendship" with the United States as a possible source of support for maintaining the city's independence. See Engelsing, "England und die USA," 46–7.

might suggest, and was tied into the international flow of people, ideas, and commodities as much as any European nation.[12]

In North America, especially in New York and Baltimore, Hanseats settled to facilitate trade with their hometown. After humble beginnings in the 1790s, there was a boom in the trade relations between Bremen and the United States until 1810. This first golden age of transatlantic trade was cut off by the Napoleonic Wars and the continental blockade.[13] After peace had returned in 1815, Hanseats slowly but steadily rebuilt their connections to America. Hanseatic historians have identified 1831 as the takeoff point, after which Bremen became an ever more serious presence in the United States. By the time the Civil War began, Bremen's merchants were carrying an impressive share of the United States' export trade, and brought an ever-greater share of European immigrants to New York, Baltimore, New Orleans, and Galveston.[14]

In Baltimore and New York, Hanseats were part of a larger mercantile class that was characterized by a cosmopolitan composition. Hanseats were linked to other members of this class through joint membership in clubs, as neighbors in the same upscale parts of town, as fellow board members of banks, as business partners, and sometimes as spouses. Hanseats resembled that larger mercantile class in many of their business practices. The ethos of honor and credibility was common to all merchants, whether they were from Bremen, the United States, or other foreign countries.[15] The way in which Hanseats organized their business partnerships was not exceptional either. A tight cooperation between different firms, often tied to each other by blood relations or intermarriage, was just as common among American or British merchants as it was for Hanseats; though the rapid expansion of the American business world probably resulted in a higher number of firms not tied into preexisting networks of old money and old names.[16]

In spite of these many similarities, Bremish merchants formed a distinct group within this broader class. Those qualities that set them apart were also factors

---

[12] For parallels to the English world of merchant capitalists, cf. Chapman, Stanley D., *The Rise of Merchant Banking*, London, 1984; idem, *Merchant Enterprise in Britain from the Industrial Revolution to World War I*, Cambridge, 1992.

[13] Mustafa, Sam A., *Merchants and Migrations: Germans and Americans in Connection, 1776–1835* (Aldcroft, Derek H., ed., Modern Economic and Social History Series, unnumbered vol.), Aldershot, UK, 2001.

[14] Armgort, Arno, *Bremen-Bremerhaven-New York. Geschichte der europäischen Auswanderung über die Bremischen Häfen (A history of European emigration through the ports of Bremen)*, Bremen, 1991, is a bilingual edition; Engelsing, Rolf, *Bremen als Auswandererhafen, 1683–1880* (Karl H. Schwebel, ed., Veröffentlichungen aus dem Staatsarchiv der Freien Hansestadt Bremen, Bd. 29), Bremen, 1961; Beutin, Ludwig, *Bremen und Amerika. Zur Geschichte der Weltwirtschaft und der Beziehungen Deutschlands zu den Vereinigten Staaten*, Bremen, 1953; Struve, Walter, *Germans & Texans: Commerce, Migration and Culture in the Days of the Lone Star Republic*, Austin, TX, 1996.

[15] Ditz, Toby, "Shipwrecked; or, Masculinity Imperiled: Mercantile Representation of Failure and the Gendered Self in Eighteenth-Century Philadelphia," *Journal of American History* 81, no. 1 (June 1994), 51–80; Hancock, David, *Citizens of the World: London Merchants and the Integration of the British Atlantic Community, 1735–1785*, Cambridge and New York, 1995; Lee, Robert, ed., *Commerce and Culture: Nineteenth-Century Business Elites* (Modern Economic and Social History, unnumbered vol.), Farnham, UK, 2011.

[16] Beckert, *Monied Metropolis*; idem, "Merchants and Manufacturers in the Antebellum North," in *Ruling America: A History of Wealth and Power in a Democracy*, ed. Gary Gerstle and Steve Fraser,

contributing to the extraordinary stability and success of their group. First, Hanseats maintained a conservative approach to business, eschewing "speculation" and putting the welfare of the family and the estate above a logic of pure profit maximization (Chapters 1 and 2). Second, dense ties of intermarriage, and the financial and ideological commitment they entailed, connected Hanseats in Bremen, Baltimore, and New York with each other, establishing in a transnational space a degree of mutual obligations comparable to those found among elites in "hometowns" like Bremen (Chapter 2). Third, the political ideology that Hanseats had constructed for themselves in Bremen gave them a shared worldview.

Their agreement on fundamental political values further bound the members of the network to each other. The content of this ideology, a selective embrace of liberalism paired with an insistence of maintaining social hierarchy and a politics of deference, placed them in a peculiar position on one side of an ideological divide. Running across the Atlantic and the countries that bordered it, it parted the proponents of a capitalist social order in two camps: radicals, who believed in democracy and the Enlightenment, and modern conservatives, who wished to uphold social distinctions and Christian morality (Chapters 3–5 and 9).

Fourth, Bremen was an independent state, with a foreign policy of its own. The network of consulates and trade treaties that rested on the city's status formed the groundwork of Hanseats' business enterprise. This consular network further tied merchants' interests to the city, and through it, to each other. The state of Bremen was the agent through which Hanseats shaped the development of world trade by extending the infrastructure that intensified and regularized exchange relations across the ocean (Chapters 4–6 and 8).[17]

Understanding the state of Bremen as a political entity is important not only because it provided a source of coherence to Hanseats who were active in different parts of the world, by representing their shared interest and their common beliefs, but also because to acknowledge the deeply traditionalist nature of its political structure means to avoid the trap of characterizing Hanseats as liberals, by way of a short-circuited conclusion that assumes that liberalism, capitalism, and cosmopolitanism form a package deal under a label of *modernization*.

The apprehension Bremen's mercantile elite felt in the face of growing public participation in politics was evident when Bremen's burgomaster, Arnold

---

Cambridge, MA, 2005, 92–122; Hobsbawm, Eric, *The Age of Capital, 1848–1875*, London, 1975, 241. The latter lists examples of family- and clan-based businesses in both the industrial and mercantile sectors. See also note 37. The broader, emerging middle class took many cultural cues from the mercantile elite of the Atlantic World. Hence, it is not surprising to find that both groups shared many features. See, e.g., Davidoff, Leonore, and Catherine Hall, *Family Fortunes: Men and Women of the English Middle Class, 1780–1850*. rev. ed., London and New York, 2002.

[17] Following the definition of the term by Jürgen Osterhammel and Niels P. Petersson, Hanseats formed a network. Osterhammel and Petersson list as criteria for considering a social formation a network: 1) the "social interaction between more than two people"; 2) the "longevity" of these interactions; and 3) their reinforcement by institutions. The availability of "new information technology" lends to networks "the same stability [that characterizes] hierarchical organizations." Osterhammel, Jürgen and Niels P. Petersson, *Globalization: A Short History*, Princeton, NJ, and Oxford, 2005, esp. pp. 21–7; quotes on pp. 22–3. Hanseats met these criteria. The specific, shared ideologies they held added a further dimension to their interactions and gave an additional source of stability to their network.

Duckwitz, witnessed the campaign for the Northern German Reichstag in 1867. This was the first election in the Hanseatic city since 1850 that was conducted under the rules of universal, equal, male suffrage. Duckwitz remarked disapprovingly that "this election business here is becoming American."[18]

To emphasize the traditionalist content of Bremen's system of government, but also to avoid confusion, this study uses the German original in referring to most Bremish institutions. The government of Bremen was commonly called the *Senat*. The body that represented the mercantile estate of the city, politically and economically, was known as the *Handelskammer*. For this institution, as well, this study employs the German original, because the correct translation – chamber of commerce – fails to convey the sense of a traditional estate carried by the German. Membership in this *Kammer* was mandatory for long-distance wholesale merchants, and its role in the city was that of an integral part of the constitutional system of governance and legislation. Any English translation would fail to convey this corporatist connotation. For that reason, Gothic script might even be in order.

Economically, socially, culturally, and politically, Hanseats had things in common that they did not share with their non-Hanseatic mercantile peers in Germany or the United States. At the same time, their engagement in trade, and their commitment to conservative religious and political values, gave them manifold occasions to cooperate with other groups in the United States and Germany.[19]

The distinctness of Hanseats within the larger, American mercantile class was not a function of ethnicity. Bremish merchants mingled with other elite Germans in German Societies, or in Baltimore's Germania Club, just as they socialized with merchants of American and foreign backgrounds in chambers of commerce, merchants' reading rooms, stock exchanges, and corporate boardrooms. Still, non-Hanseatic elite Germans whom Hanseats encountered in the United States had not much more in common with them than the shared written language. The same peculiarities that set Hanseats apart from American merchants also distinguished them from other German merchants.[20]

Hanseats had even less in common with the mass of German immigrants than they had with elite Germans in the United States. While they were bringing increasing numbers of them to the country, Hanseats did not see themselves as part of the German immigrant community in America. As the common folk of German extraction discovered their shared ethnicity in the emigration,[21] Bremen's

---

[18] Engelsing, "England und die USA," 55.

[19] Blumin, Stuart M., *The Emergence of the Middle Class: Social Experience in the American City, 1760–1900*, Cambridge and New York, 1989; Kocka, Jürgen and Allen Mitchell, eds., *Bourgeois Society in Nineteenth-Century Europe*, Oxford and Providence, RI, 1993.

[20] The spoken languages among many Hanseats seem to have been English and Lower German, while merchants from the Rhineland or Southern Germany would have spoken in different dialects of German. Although educated Germans would have been able to communicate in High German, modulations owed to the habits of speaking dialect, or, as in the case of Lower German, a different language altogether, can render smooth conversation among Germans of different regional backgrounds hard to achieve, even today. See Engelsing, Rolf, "Bremisches Unternehmertum. Sozialgeschichte 1780/1870," in *Jahrbuch der Wittheit zu Bremen* 2 (1958), 7–112; idem, "England und die USA," for the social distance between Bremen's merchants and German hinterland elites.

[21] See, e.g., Echternkamp, "Emerging Ethnicity."

merchants behaved as the members of a privileged estate, not of a *Volk*. Political refugees from the liberal German middle class became ethnic politicians in the United States. Here, they could build the democratic polity they had striven in vain to create in Germany.[22] Hanseats, by contrast, maintained an attitude toward the many that demanded deference toward one's social betters. As they did in Bremen, Hanseats in the United States related to the mass of Germans through charity, maintaining the same stance of "patronage and protection" that they assumed in the old country.[23]

In reconstructing the world the Hanseats made, we can recover the quintessentially transnational character of the United States during a time in its history that on the surface appears as one of its most inward-looking periods. Consider Emanuel Leutze's monumental history painting, *Washington Crossing the Delaware* (1851). An icon of American national identity, the original of this work hung in Bremen's Art Museum (*Kunsthalle*), after it had been bought in 1863 with donations from Bremen's mercantile elite. Here, it served as a reminder of Bremen's cordial relations with the United States.[24]

This affinity for the United States was not politically neutral, however. Hanseats discovered early on that they shared much more with Whigs than with Democrats. Regarded from a Hanseatic vantage point, Whigs show themselves as promoters of international exchange, not just builders of a national, industrial market society, and Democrats show themselves as economic isolationists, in spite of their desire to export the American Revolution. Where politicians from these parties engaged with Bremen merchants, they applied their basic convictions, founded in the fundamental conflicts of the Second Party System, to international politics. In doing so, they betrayed the indebtedness of these convictions to broader, transnational intellectual currents. The protracted struggle between Jeffersonians and Hamiltonians was not exceptional to the United States, it merely was the specifically American manifestation of a conflict common to all industrializing countries, pitting liberal against conservative bourgeois politics. Hanseats recognized themselves in this political landscape and took sides accordingly.

[22] Nadel, Stanley, *Little Germany: Ethnicity, Religion, and Class in New York City, 1845–80*, Urbana, IL, 1990; Wittke, Carl F., *Refugees of Revolution: The German Forty-Eighters in America*, Philadelphia, 1952; Levine, Bruce, *The Spirit of 1848: German Immigrants, Labor Conflict, and the Coming of the Civil War*, Urbana, IL, 1992; Trefousse, *Carl Schurz*.

[23] Schulz, Andreas, *Vormundschaft und Protektion: Eliten und Bürger in Bremen, 1750–1880* (Gall, Lothar, ed., Stadt und Bürgertum, vol. 13), Munich, 2002 (Habilitationsschrift, Universität Frankfurt [Main], 2000).

[24] Andree, Rolf, and Ute Rickel-Immel, *The Hudson and the Rhine: Die amerikanische Malerkolonie in Düsseldorf im 19. Jahrhundert*, Kat. Ausst. [Exhibition Catalog], Düsseldorf, Kunstmuseum, 1976; Groseclose, Barbara S., *Emmanuel Leutze, 1816–1868: Freedom Is the Only King*, Exhibition Catalog, National Collection of Fine Art, Smithsonian Institution, 1976, Washington, DC, 1976; Howat, John K., "Washington Crossing the Delaware," *Metropolitan Museum of Art Bulletin* 26, no. 7 (March 1968), 289–99; Hutton, Ann Hawkes, *Portrait of Patriotism: "Washington Crossing the Delaware*," Philadelphia and New York, 1959. The latter offers insight into Leutze's political views based on primary documents. Although painted in Germany, and popular there as a comment on the aspirations of the revolution of 1848, Leutze's intent in his travels had been to perfect his art for his program of expressing the essence of America on the canvas. In that spirit, he had relied exclusively on American travelers who passed through Düsseldorf, where he was a student at the academy, to sit for the figures in the Washington painting.

Even in the 1860s, when the fight over slavery and free labor seemed to set apart the United States from European countries – which, after all, had abolished their colonial slave regimes and had never seen plantation slavery on their own soil – the terms of the debates between opponents and defenders of guilds in Germany, and between abolitionists and slaveholders in the United States, suggest a frame of reference of political ideas shared between actors in both countries (see Chapter 4).

In that decade, the conservative bourgeois currents in Germany and the United States that previously had supported capitalist modernization contained by a policy of social control and moral improvement were revising their vision of social development to include an embrace of free labor and contractual relations freed from the restraints of legislation limiting mobility and prescribing moral codes. German bourgeois conservatives condemned guilds on the same grounds that their American counterparts criticized slavery. Both labor systems appeared detrimental to the moral and material improvement of individuals by virtue of denying them the exercise of their right to "free labor," that is their participation in an unrestrained labor market.[25]

Realizing the competitive benefits in an industrial world market conferred on a national economy by free labor, bourgeois conservatives literally made a virtue of the necessity of wage labor by morally overdetermining contractual relations. Recent U.S. scholarship has demonstrated that ideas of free labor and contracts originated in conservative notions of social control and a good moral-political order. In the arguments of Amy Dru Stanley, Heather Cox Richardson, and Sven Beckert, the Civil War became a catalyst for this ideological transformation that entailed a departure from earlier, organicist ideals.[26]

Linking the ideas inspiring German elites to a project of modernization similar to that pursued by their American counterparts, a transnational perspective offers a transformation of our understanding of this ideological shift as reflecting an experience shared across the Atlantic and giving rise to a discourse of free labor that was transnational in its extent.

Thanks to the work of Daniel Rodgers, in present U.S. historiography, transnationality almost has a default association with progressivism in its broadest sense.[27] From the point of view of postwar historiography in Germany and the United States, likewise, an "Atlantic orientation" is coterminous with democratic politics, and opposition to monarchical reaction in the nineteenth or to Fascism in the twentieth century.[28] In

---

[25] Ashworth, John, *Slavery, Capitalism, and Politics in the Antebellum Republic*, 2 vols., vol. 1: *Commerce and Compromise, 1820–1850*, Cambridge, 1995; Oberg, Jan, "Strange Sailors: Maritime Culture in Nineteenth-Century Bremen," in *Bridging Troubled Waters: Conflict and Co-operation in the North Sea Region since 1550*, ed. David J. Starkey and Morten Hahn-Pedersen (7th North Sea History Conference, Dunkirk 2002) (Fiskeri- og Søfartsmuseets Studieserie, vol.17), Esbjerg, Denmark, 2005, 113–33.

[26] Beckert, *Monied Metropolis*; Richardson, Heather Cox, *The Death of Reconstruction: Race, Labor, and Politics in the Post–Civil War North, 1865–1901*, Cambridge, MA, and London, 2001; Stanley, Amy Dru, *From Bondage to Contract: Wage Labor, Marriage, and the Market in the Age of Slave Emancipation*, New York, 1998.

[27] Rodgers, Daniel, *Atlantic Crossings: Social Politics in a Progressive Age*, Cambridge, MA, and London 1998.

[28] Dippel, Horst, *Die amerikanische Verfassung in Deutschland im 19. Jahrhundert. Das Dilemma von Politik und Staatsrecht*, Goldbach, Germany, 1994; Engelsing, Rolf, "England und die USA in der

Hanseats, however, we see the emergence of a transnational, modern conservatism that is the specific product of a German–American exchange. In the light of this exchange, Whigs begin to look like members of a Conservative International who joined forces with like-minded foreigners in a transnational struggle against the threat of democracy and mob rule and for an "improvement" of a fundamentally good social order.

Shared by Hanseats and Whigs, the politics of notables who strove to modernize society while shoring up morality and deference to dampen the disruptive effects of change was a transnational phenomenon. Processing German and American intellectual influences, Hanseats formed an important link within this transatlantic current of conservative modernizers who advocated international improvement. On this solid foundation of a fundamental agreement on politics and values, Whigs and Hanseats were able to find common ground even when their immediate interests conflicted. Thus Whigs' advocacy of a high tariff and the enmity toward immigrants among some party members did little to alienate Hanseats from their American allies (see Chapter 5).

By knowing the people who mattered, Hanseats may have had a more enduring influence on American politics than ethnic politicians could ever have hoped for. In Baltimore and New York, Hanseats played leading roles in the local chambers of commerce, which, in turn, helped shape local and national politics. Chief Justice Roger B. Taney lived next door to Bremish consul Albert Schumacher in Baltimore's upscale Mount Vernon neighborhood.[29] Abraham Lincoln's only visit to a diplomat's residence took place on the eve of his inauguration, when Rudolf Schleiden, Bremen's minister-resident in Washington, hosted a small dinner party for the president-elect.[30] And Bremen's leading newspaper, the *Weserzeitung*, served as the official organ for notifications by the U.S. federal government in Germany.[31]

On the local and state levels, Hanseats' influence followed the same pattern of gentlemanly lobbying. It depended on a mode of politics that we associate with a predemocratic era. But even in an age of popular suffrage, when the masses no longer deferred to their social betters in political matters, deals among men of standing did not cease to be important. In some jurisdictions, decision-making

---

bremischen Sicht des 19. Jahrhunderts," *Jahrbuch der Wittheit zu Bremen* 1 (1957), 33–65; Moltmann, Günter, *Atlantische Blockpolitik im 19. Jahrhundert. Die Vereinigten Staaten und der deutsche Liberalismus während der Revolution von 1848/49*, Düsseldorf, 1973; Mustafa, Sam A., *Merchants and Migrations: Germans and Americans in Connection, 1776–1835* (Aldcroft, Derek H., ed., Modern Economic and Social History Series, unnumbered vol.), Aldershot, UK, 2001; Nadel, Stanley, *Little Germany: Ethnicity, Religion, and Class in New York City, 1845–80*, Urbana, IL, 1990; Levine, Bruce, *The Spirit of 1848: German Immigrants, Labor Conflict, and the Coming of the Civil War*, Urbana, IL, 1992; Struve, Walter, *Germans & Texans: Commerce, Migration and Culture in the Days of the Lone Star Republic*, Austin, TX, 1996; Trefousse, *Carl Schurz*; Wittke, Carl F., *Refugees of Revolution: The German Forty-Eighters in America*, Philadelphia, 1952.

[29] Justice John A. Campbell, later Confederate States of America assistant secretary of war, in his concurring opinion to Taney's majority opinion in the Dred Scott case, pointed specifically to Bremen in stressing the contrast between German Law that confers freedom to a person by virtue of his presence in a specific territory and the American legal situation. See *Dred Scott v. Sandford*, U.S. Supreme Court, Mr. Justice Campbell concurring, http://www.tourolaw.edu/patch/Scott/Campbell.asp (accessed October 1, 2005) (Touro College Law Center, Project P.A.T.C.H.).

[30] See Chapter 8.

[31] Engelsing, "England und die USA," 53.

power was delegated outright to notables. For example, New York gave a private club dominated by Hanseats, the German Society, some power over immigration policies.[32]

Until the late 1850s, Hanseats never became ethnic politicians who rallied their compatriots to gain office. Even then, few chose that career path. Mostly, they remained notables who expected their voice to be weighed, not counted. This was the way of doing politics and business they were used to at home, and they were not ready to abandon their ways simply because they lived in a different country – especially because these traditions served them so well.

Elite politics, although relegated to the back of our historical consciousness by three decades of social and cultural history, was not dead in the nineteenth-century United States. In recent years, historians like John Ashworth, Sven Beckert, and Eugene Genovese have shown that antidemocratic sentiment in upper-class circles survived the challenges of Jacksonian Democracy and the Civil War surprisingly intact. If anything, decades of popular participation in politics strengthened conservatives' disdain for the aspirations of the masses. Unlike Genovese, who idealizes slaveholders as anticapitalist intellectuals, Beckert and Ashworth have shown that bourgeois Americans were capable of embracing capitalist development, while seeking to limit the subversion of the republic by democratic influence.[33]

Hanseats listened to their conservative American counterparts and engaged their ideas in their American homes and in their old home, Bremen. As citizens of a republic, the reactionary politics of Old Regime, legitimist conservatism were distasteful to Hanseats. As notables who ruled Bremen in a constitutional frame-work designed to guarantee mercantile dominance, they were just as unwilling to embrace democracy. As global merchants whose capital depended on ever-accelerated circulation, they were eager to embrace technological advances and a legal order that removed just enough of the traditional fetters of privilege to create a free market for commodities and wage labor, while leaving in place their own privileges. In American conservatism, they found an ideology ideally suited to these specific interests. Thus political ideas flowed both ways across the Atlantic, and Hanseats served as an important conduit.

Hanseats were centrally involved in creating and maintaining the arteries and veins of the rise of American industrial capitalism. While the transnational exchange of ideas and the proliferation of institutions and practices are the stuff of transnational history, Hanseats remind us that transnationality had concrete sociological conditions. Hanseats' success as a group of merchants active on both shores of the Atlantic depended on an interplay of cultural, economic, and political factors that sustained their cosmopolitan-conservative outlook.

---

[32] Ibid., 45; Beckert, *Monied Metropolis*, 65; Wätjen, Hermann, *Aus der Frühzeit des Nordatlantikverkehrs. Studien zur Geschichte der deutschen Schiffahrt und deutschen Auswanderung nach den Vereinigten Staaten bis zum Ende des amerikanischen Bürgerkrieges*, Leipzig, 1932, 180–1.

[33] Sellers, Charles, *The Market Revolution: Jacksonian America, 1815–1846*, New York and Oxford, 1991; Ashworth, John, *"Agrarians" and "Aristocrats": Party Political Ideology in the United States, 1837–1846*, London and Atlantic Highlands, NJ, 1983; idem, *Slavery, Capitalism, and Politics in the Antebellum Republic*, 2 vols., vol. 1: *Commerce and Compromise, 1820–1850*; Genovese, Eugene, *The World the Slaveholders Made*, New York, 1969; Beckert, *Metropolis*.

TRANSNATIONAL SOCIAL HISTORY

The standard tools of social history may need some recalibration if they are to be applied to the task of grasping the essence of Hanseats as a group of historical actors. Today, most works of social history frame their accounts of nineteenth-century life in cultural terms. Social classes appear as entities that owe their emergence to shared beliefs and shared practices that spring from those beliefs at the same time as they serve to reinforce them. A group forms its identity, or class consciousness, in relation to others, as well as in interactions between the genders within one's own group. This approach is informed by a wish to avoid two pitfalls associated with an older, Marxist school of social history. This school presumably was guilty, first, of essentializing classes as groups primarily bounded by static economic factors and, second, of holding up such classes to the normative standard of a class consciousness that conformed to Marx's scheme. Rather than asking when and how a class that was a "class in itself" became a "class for itself," current social history wants to restore to historical actors an active part in the making of their social group.[34]

This cultural approach has two major shortcomings. First, it tends to under-emphasize the importance of economic activities and the concrete ways in which historical actors made their living. This is a particular problem for the study of elites: to lead a lifestyle that culturally signals distinction, one has to be able to afford it. Second, it is almost entirely local in scope, because it depends for its main categories on face-to-face contacts between members of different groups.

Recently, Andreas Schulz has added to our understanding of the world of Hanseats in his seminal work, *Vormundschaft und Protektion*.[35] His study is mainly driven by a relational view on class formation on the local level. Schulz explains the political and social behavior of different local groups as a function of the relations between these groups. Bremen's mercantile elite strove for hegemony over other social groups in the city of Bremen. For Schulz, merchants made their political and social identity through the resulting confrontation with the urban lower middle class, artisans, and the emerging proletariat in Bremen.

Although a definitive social history of Bremen, Schulz's work cannot claim to be a complete account of the history of the city's mercantile elite during the nineteenth century. He acknowledges that young men and women from the Hanseatic elite went abroad on business, yet these actors drop off his analytical map at the point of their departure. Arguably, however, Hanseats' ties with their peers abroad were at least as important as their relations with other, local social groups in shaping their worldview. Moreover, Hanseats related to New York artisans and merchants, London bankers, Southern planters, and Indian princes just as much as they did to Bremish shopkeepers and stevedores. To understand Bremish history, we have to

---

[34] Bushman, Richard, *The Refinement of America: Persons, Houses, Cities*, New York, 1992; Grier, Katherine C., *Culture and Comfort: Parlor Making and Middle-Class Identity, 1850–1930*, Washington, DC, 1997; Nelson, Elizabeth White, *Market Sentiments: Middle-Class Market Culture in Nineteenth-Century America*, Washington, DC, 2004; Rosenbaum, Julia B., and Sven Beckert, eds., *The American Bourgeoisie: Distinction and Identity in the Nineteenth Century* (Palgrave Studies in Cultural and Intellectual History, unnumbered vol.), New York, 2010.

[35] Schulz, *Vormundschaft und Protektion*. The title translates as "paternalism and protection."

follow its mercantile elite as it journeys from Bremen for American shores. Through their eyes, we will likewise gain a clearer perspective on American history.

Any translocal social category, such as that of a "national bourgeoisie" or even an "American middle class," is difficult to theorize in a work of social history that rests on a local case study. Sven Beckert, in his *The Monied Metropolis*, offers a solution to this problem.[36] He tells the story of the "consolidation of the American bourgeoisie" by declaring his findings on New York to be universally applicable. The plausible basis for this claim is New York's dominance over all lesser communities, as *the* center of culture, fashion, manufacturing, and finance in the United States.

In the political realm, Beckert argues that the nation-state formed a common frame of reference for local elites. It is to that nation-state that they turned to implement policies that benefited them as a class. Thus New York's elites exerted political influence to move state governments and the federal government not to pay for public works or relief for the unemployed, to discourage strikes, to uphold the sanctity of contracts, and to maintain monetary and foreign trade policies beneficial to their business interests. These policies bound them to their lesser counterparts in the provinces, who shared these political goals and economic interests. The sensibilities acquired by the middle class on the local level guided their approach to national policies. It was the same defense of their business interests, often mixed with a moral vision for the masses, that manifested itself in the program of national middle-class politics. Class as an economic category thus becomes a foundation for explaining the dissemination of middle-class values and politics, without reducing the latter to a mere reflex to economic structure.

What baffles the Hanseatic historian who reads Beckert's work is the conspicuous absence of Bremish merchants from this account. Beckert found that in 1855, 6 percent of New York's elite were German-born, a share that rose to 23 percent by 1870.[37] One Hanseat – Gustav F. Schwab – makes a few token appearances, but Beckert does not point out Schwab's specific background. If New York's local elite had a disproportionate impact on the making of an American bourgeoisie, Hanseatic influence among that group suggests a role of Bremen merchants in shaping America that goes far beyond their small number.

Beckert is no doubt correct in characterizing the story of New York's elite in the decades following the Civil War as that of the homogenization of a ruling class formerly divided into merchants and manufacturers who did not mingle. Likewise, his interpretation that the nation-state, national politics, and national economic interdependence played central roles in effecting that homogenization is convincing. For the 1850s and even the 1860s, however, he misses a major part of the story by excluding transnational connections from his account. Where, if not from the Hanseatic cities, did Mayor Fernando Wood get the idea to break New York City away from the Union to make it into an independent city-republic?[38] To understand the history of the United States, we have to follow the traces that link it to foreign shores.

[36] Beckert, *Metropolis*.

[37] Ibid., 31, 147.

[38] Anbinder, Tyler G., "Fernando Wood and New York City's Secession from the Union: A Political Reappraisal," *New York History* 68 (January, 1987), 67–92, explains the secession plan as a response to a long history of attempts by New York State politicians to gain control over crucial municipal

While politics and economic interest drove local elites to make themselves into national bourgeoisies, contemporaries and historians alike have perceived the nineteenth century as the heyday of a Western and bourgeois culture of virtually global reach. Learning, political rights, and technology were supposed to liberate all of mankind from the narrowness of an earlier age. World exhibitions celebrated progress as a universal phenomenon. Revolutionaries and nationalists hailed their counterparts in foreign countries as participants in the same worldwide struggle. Literature and music – classical and modern – helped shape a shared sense of aesthetics across national boundaries and language barriers, and galvanized a sense of national identity in different countries. Thus a local elite can be conceived with as much justification as part of a national bourgeoisie as it can be considered as part of a class-specific, Victorian culture that had an international, if not global, character. Hanseats, like many of their contemporaries, partook of this culture.[39]

If culture was an essential ingredient in the making of classes and was an essentially global phenomenon then any social history would have to look beyond national boundaries to explain the beliefs and actions of its subjects. Moreover, Victorian culture was consumer culture, in which the tastes of consumers were inextricably intertwined with the commodities that entered the household and the clothes that marked the respectable. Belgian bonnets, German linens, and Steinway pianos from New York were not just signifiers of the lifestyle of a better sort, but they were also materializations of value and objects set in motion by capital in search of valorization. As such, they were the artifacts of global capital circulation and capitalist production that were visible to a larger public, but that required for their availability infinitely larger amounts of capital invested in raw materials, ships, and factories; put in circulation as credit or transferred as bills of exchange; and transformed by wage labor into commodities. The objects of consumer culture are the tip of the iceberg of the world market. Thus to take culture seriously as a decisive element in the making of social groups would mean to take equally seriously its global dimensions, including those of political economy.

COMMUNITY, SOCIETY, AND COMMERCE

To do full justice to Hanseats, we have to turn to theorists who derived their concepts from a world that preceded a liberal market society. The German sociologist Ferdinand Tönnies was just such a theorist. We find that his work expresses the same notion of an organic unity of different moments of social life that was held by the Hanseats.[40]

The tenacity of Hanseats' attitudes and way of life rested on the intertwining of the principles that governed their economic, domestic, and political existence. For Ferdinand Tönnies, the essence of *community* (*Gemeinschaft*) – as opposed to *society* (*Gesellschaft*) – was the organic unity of all spheres of life. Work, authority, and love were not relegated to separate spheres, each with a different set of rules, but formed

---

institutions. Still, if Wood contemplated in earnest the founding of a new city-republic, he would not have found many modern examples besides the Hanseatic cities.

[39] Cf. Hobsbawm, Eric, *The Age of Capital, 1848–1875*, London, 1975, 230–48, 277–302, 317.

[40] Tönnies, Ferdinand, *Community and Civil Society*, trans. José Harris and Margaret Hollis (Cambridge Texts in the History of Political Thought, unnumbered vol.), Cambridge, 2001 (1887).

aspects of the same substance, a life based on "reciprocal sentiments of affection and reverence" shaped in the family. Although Tönnies believed that the most stable community depended on its roots in a particular place, he granted that those "knowing one another like members of a craft or professional group, will feel themselves united everywhere," not unlike "comrades in faith." Bremen constituted such a particular place, and the merchants who had grown up there remained connected to it in manifold ways even when they went abroad. They continued to correspond with and visit each other across the ocean. Hence, even absent face-to-face interaction, Hanseats continued to "feel themselves united everywhere."[41]

Past and present antimodernists and others who bemoan the loss of community and its "feudal, patriarchal, idyllic relations" might find Hanseats to be kindred spirits whose lives represented the ideal of an organic whole.[42] Inconveniently, however, Hanseats were also merchants, and their community was cosmopolitan in its geographical extent and prevalent ideology. Thus Wilhelm Kiesselbach, an organic intellectual of Bremen's elite, gave voice to a corporatist vision of social order while promoting capitalist exchange relations (see Chapter 3). A moral economy based on reciprocity and exchange relations embedded in a Calvinist ethos supported by mutual social control characterized the *internal* life of the Hanseatic community, but less and less of its *external* interactions.

Modern political theory has interpreted commerce as an agent of the dissolution of traditional communities. Ferdinand Tönnies's ideal-type of *Gemeinschaft* – a community characterized by the inseparable unity of kinship, economy, religion, and government under benevolent patriarchal authority – finds its highest embodiment in the objects of reverence that form the geographical and spiritual center of life in an urban community.[43] In Bremen, that center is the Roland, an eighteen-foot stone statue of a knight carrying a sword and a shield with the coat of arms of the city. Standing in the market square, the Roland statue is a symbol of commerce and of the power of the group that made Bremen a center of world trade. For Bremen's merchants, the Roland statue was a spiritual center of their transnational community. In Bremen, commerce was not an agent of the dissolution of tradition. It was the central content, the very essence, of tradition. Hence, Hanseats could understand their economic and political activities as an outgrowth of tradition, no matter how much innovation they actually entailed.[44]

Tönnies's sociology finds an echo in current scholarship. In a narrative of modernization or globalization shared among scholars critical or supportive of liberal capitalism, our modern age is characterized by a supplantation of place by space.[45]

---

[41] Ibid., esp. pp. 17–91, quotes on pp. 27, 29.

[42] Marx and Engels, "Manifesto," 475.

[43] Tönnies, *Community*.

[44] Ibid.; Loose, Hans-Dieter, "Nutzbares Erbe oder belastende Relikte einer glorreichen Vergangenheit? Der hanseatische Umgang mit dem Londoner Stahlhof und dem Antwerpener Haus der Osterlinge in der ersten Hälfte des 19. Jahrhunderts," in *Ausklang und Nachklang der Hanse im 19. und 20. Jahrhundert*, ed. Antjekathrin Graßmann (Hansischer Geschichtsverein, ed., Hansische Studien, vol. 12), Trier, Germany, 2001, 31–42. See also 140–1.

[45] Fremdling, Rainer, and Richard H. Tilly, eds., *Industrialisierung und Raum. Studien zur regionalen Differenzierung in Deutschland des 19. Jahrhunderts*, Stuttgart, 1979; Friedman, Thomas L., *The World Is Flat: A Brief History of the Twenty-First Century*, New York, 2005.

People in traditional communities are emotionally and practically committed to a particular place. In modern societies, places are linked in manifold ways by exchange, communication, and governance. Commodity exchange reduces incommensurable objects to a common denominator and subjects local production to international market forces; every new medium, from print through television to the Internet, sacrifices local idiosyncrasies to idioms shared across a larger space. The individual as the citizen of a large territorial state can no longer know his peers in the way a small-town burgher could. Equality comes at the price of anonymity and the loss of particularity.

In these processes, geography is reduced to an abstract space, just as the particularity of places is leveled and eventually lost to the abstractions that tie them into these larger systems. The small town can be a home, but a shopping mall cannot. Although perhaps useful as a model, or as a critical tool, the dichotomy of space and place fails accurately to describe Bremen. Here, space and place were dialectically dependent on each other, with hometown traditions driving the elite to conquer an Atlantic space.[46]

Hanseats were pioneers of changes in exchange and communication. The core of their mercantile interest was the extension of commodity exchange. As a consequence of their mercantile activities, they developed an interest in improving the means of communication, including steamships, railroads, and the telegraph – all of which accelerated the pace of information across the globe.[47] In exchange and communication, Hanseats were at the cutting edge of a movement that transformed the world into a leveled, uniform space from which frictions that hindered the circulation of commodities or capital were increasingly removed.

Even so, Hanseats' ability to engage in these activities was to a great extent dependent on the coherence lent to their international network of families and firms by the political support of and by the state of Bremen. The social and political order within that state continued to embody a wish to uphold the customs and traditions of the mercantile estate. This wish was alive and vigorous even in the 1860s, as Wilhelm Kiesselbach's works demonstrate.[48]

Kiesselbach's ideal of a "social-economic state" may best be characterized as corporatist, or, rather, etatist. Unlike other conservative proponents of a corporatist, "organic" social order, however, Kiesselbach was not an enemy of capitalism by any means. This set him apart from both German reactionaries and the Southern conservative tradition in the United States.[49] At the same time, Kiesselbach shared with these latter contemporaries the view that the person is more than a bearer of

---

[46] Marx and Engels, "Manifesto," 473–500; Barber, Benjamin, *Jihad vs. McWorld: How Globalism and Tribalism Are Reshaping the World*, New York, 1995; Harvey, David, *The Condition of Postmodernity: An Inquiry into the Origins of Cultural Change*, Cambridge, MA, and Oxford, 1990, esp. pp. 201–323.

[47] See also Chapter 5.

[48] See Chapter 3.

[49] Riehl, Wilhelm Heinrich, *Die bürgerliche Gesellschaft*, Stuttgart, 1861, e.g., pp. 174–5; Genovese, Eugene D., *The World the Slaveholders Made: Two Essays in Interpretation*, New York, 1969, esp. part II on George Fitzhugh, whose thought has a strong resemblance to both Riehl's and Kiesselbach's; idem, *The Slaveholders' Dilemma: Freedom and Progress in Southern Conservative Thought, 1820–1860*, Columbia, SC, 1992; Gentz, Friedrich von, *The French and American Revolutions Compared*, translated by John Quincy Adams (1800), in *Three Revolutions*, ed. Stefan T. Possony, Chicago, 1959.

abstract rights.[50] Overall, his views most closely resembled those one might find among Whigs in the United States.[51] Within Germany, he remained a unique figure, reflecting the peculiar position of Hanseats in the society of the German states (see Chapter 3).

Unlike Kiesselbach and other theorists of organicism, Tönnies was aware that trade and industry, while evolving from within traditional community, carry with them the seeds of its dissolution, or its evolution into a liberal *Gesellschaft*. Throughout this study, we will therefore trace the elements of Hanseatic community life that represented such seeds of dissolution. Most importantly, global commerce came with an imperative of competitiveness, eventually forcing Hanseats to adapt their business practices, their values, and the social and political order of their hometown, thus undermining the foundations of community life. Although these seeds of dissolution were sown, they did not begin to reduce the Hanseats' ability to practice their accustomed ways of a cosmopolitan community engaged in transatlantic commerce until the 1860s. Until then, they were able to use their very rootedness in a stable network as a resource for furthering their political and social interests.

HISTORICAL ANTECEDENTS

In writing a social and economic history of an elite with ties to multiple distinct societies and polities, this study is indebted to a great many scholars whose works this author has consulted. Maritime history; business history; the histories of art, religion, and literature; diplomatic history; military history; and other fields too numerous to mention passed through the untrained hands of this author, as he realized the need to cast his nets widely if he was to have any chance of catching the elusive Hanseat in all his multifaceted glory. This study cannot pretend to weigh and appreciate adequately the debates and methodological concerns of all these fields of historical scholarship.

It is therefore in the hope that those whose efforts this study is built upon will excuse errors of judgment this author has committed in weighing their contributions, and that he offers his apologies for any such blunders, as well as his sincere gratitude for the wealth of historical expertise he was able to draw upon. Rather than overburden this introduction with a series of historiographical essays, the reader may turn directly to the subsequent chapters in finding mention of, and brief introductions to, those fields of scholarship that are pertinent to the matter at hand in each section of this study.

SECTIONS, CHAPTERS, AND SOURCES

In its first section, this study reconstructs the world Hanseats had made, as a transnational community of merchants. Chapters 1 through 3 highlight different aspects of this world: its economic, cultural, and political dimensions, respectively. In all three

---

[50] For the roots of this position in German Enlightenment and Romantic thought, see Harada, Tetsushi, *Politische Ökonomie des Idealismus und der Romantik. Korporatismus von Fichte, Müller und Hegel* (Volkswirtschaftliche Schriften, vol. 386), West Berlin, 1989. A shared ancestor of English, German, and American proponents of this view was Burke, Edmund, *Reflections on the Revolution in France*, London, 1986 (1790).

[51] See Ashworth, John, "Agrarians" and "Aristocrats"; Howe, Daniel Walker, *The Political Culture of the American Whigs*, Chicago and London, 1979.

spheres, Hanseats were guided by the same principles. A conservative spirit that emphasized prudence in business, Christian ethics in family life, and a hierarchical social order in politics permeated all aspects of Hanseats' social existence. In Hanseats' minds – and in practice – business, family, and the state were mutually dependent on each other: each relying on the other two for upholding the moral economy of the whole, and all contributing to the welfare of the estate. Although, following Tönnies, we might think of such a communal, moral economy as essentially rooted in a particular place, Hanseats managed to maintain a tightly knit network across the space of the Atlantic, uniting merchants in Bremen, Baltimore, and New York in the same community.

The second section explores Hanseatic engagement with a changing world. International competition and a wish to "improve" upon a fundamentally good, hierarchical social order combined in motivating Hanseats to transform social relations in Bremen (Chapter 4) and to cooperate with American Whigs in modernizing international shipping and communication (Chapter 5). Hanseats and Whigs hoped to preserve social hierarchy and firm Christian values in the face of the dangers of democracy and unfettered market relations. Ironically, the result of their efforts was to hasten along social processes that furthered both of the latter. Chapter 6 explores the tension in Hanseats' ideas and politics between, on the one hand, a cosmopolitan elitism, and, on the other hand, nationalism and racism. This chapter places them in the context of an Atlantic World dominated by the British Empire in which they encountered "others" in various exchanges on their journeys. When they did, status often trumped race and nationality.

The third and final section of this study examines the consequences for Hanseats of the dual processes of nation making and the transformation of Germany and America into industrial-capitalist societies. To compete successfully in a world market based on industrial production, Bremen's merchant elite was compelled to depart from its customary ways of doing business (Chapter 7). The rise of consolidated German and American nation-states in the wars of the 1860s diminished the Hanseats' ability to influence the political conditions under which they lived. This decline of Hanseatic political power culminated in the loss of Bremen's independence to the Prussian-led Northern German Union in 1867. In responding to the challenge of the rising nation-states, Bremen's merchants politically divided, further undermining their effectiveness in influencing the events of the day (Chapter 8). Once the nexus of business, family, and politics that had held together Hanseats as a transnational community had been destroyed, the family networks that had defined the Bremish elite throughout the first two-thirds of the nineteenth century began to fray. By 1900, this past transnational world was but a memory for the descendants of the mid-century merchants who had lived in it. Even as individuals who had grown up within this network went on to have impressive careers in business and politics, in both Germany and America, they had come to identify themselves with the emerging national bourgeoisie of their home country (Chapter 9).

This study draws on a wide range of sources, from the private and business correspondence of merchants to published records, such as parliamentary debates and printed recollections. The most important and extensive archival collection used in the writing of this study is the John Christopher Schwab Family Papers, held by

Yale University and previously untapped by historians. The interpretations brought forth in Chapters 2 and 6 rely especially heavily on this body of material that offers a richly textured impression of the mentality of one Hanseatic merchant, Gustav Friedrich Schwab (1822–88). Born in Stuttgart, the capital of the Kingdom of Württemberg, but socialized from an early age into the Hanseatic network, he rose by 1860 to become the best-known and most successful Hanseat in New York.[52]

The son of a poet and minister, Gustav Benjamin Schwab, Gustav Friedrich Schwab had learned to express his views in writing, perhaps beyond the extent of what was usual in Bremish circles. His family ties to the larger world of the German educated bourgeoisie (*Bildungsbürgertum*) did not make him an exceptional case for a Hanseat, as all Bremish merchants shared the spirit of this world in their education. Rather, his background enabled Schwab to express more eloquently what others in Bremen's mercantile estate likewise believed. This role as a worthy representative for the Hanseatic city received recognition in 1861, when Schwab became the last consul of an independent Bremen in New York.[53]

[52] Vagts, Alfred, "Gustav Schwab 1822–1880. Ein deutschamerikanischer Unternehmer," in *1000 Jahre Bremer Kaufmann. Aufsätze zur Geschichte bremischen Kaufmannstums, des Bremer Handels und der Bremer Schiffahrt aus Anlaß des tausendjährigen Gedenkens der Marktgründung durch Bischof Adaldag 965* (Bremisches Jahrbuch, vol. 50), Bremen, 1965, 337–60.

[53] Heinrich Smidt to Rudolf Schleiden (in Washington, DC), Bremen November 6, 1861, manuscript copy, Staatsarchiv Bremen (hereafter referred to as StAHB) 2,B.13.b.3, *Hanseatica. Verhältnisse der Hansestädte mit den Vereinigten Staaten von Nordamerika. Hanseatische diplomatische Agenten, Konsuln usw. bei den Vereinigten Staaten von Nordamerika und Korrespondenz mit denselben.* In New York, 1815–1868, file no. 10, "Acta betr. die Resignation des Consuls Keutgen zu Newyork und Ernennung des Kaufmanns Gustav Schwab daselbst zu seinem Nachfolger, 1861 Mai 27.–Decbr. 18," 59.

PART I

Moorings of the Hanseatic Network

I

Prudent Pioneers

Hanseats in Transatlantic Trade, 1798–1860

BREMEN'S MERCHANT CAPITALISTS IN AMERICA

Hanseats were classical merchant capitalists: they bought cheap to sell dear. Mid-nineteenth-century economists agreed that the way Hanseats did business was closer to early-modern times than to the new era of an industrial world economy that dawned after the Napoleonic Wars. Karl Marx saw cities like Bremen as an anachronism. In *Capital*, he wrote that "where merchant capital dominates, anachronistic conditions dominate. This is even true within a country, where, for example, the purely mercantile cities form quite different analogies with past conditions than the factory towns."[1] Marx specifically had Bremen in mind when he wrote this. He and Engels were intimately familiar with the Hanseatic city. Engels had received his mercantile education in Bremen and had made fun of its antiquated ways in a series of newspaper articles in the 1840s.[2]

Thus, it was not by accident that when Marx sought to illustrate his point that the "purely mercantile cities" live in their glorious past and utterly lack all comprehension of modern capitalist times, he cited a work by Wilhelm Kiesselbach, a historian and economist from an old Bremish mercantile family.[3] Kiesselbach was a prominent protagonist in the debates over Germany's economic development, and particularly the tariff policy of the *Zollverein* (Customs Union). The liberal public considered his positions as an expression of the point of view of Bremen's merchant capital.[4] Unlike Marx, Kiesselbach credited merchant capital with a civilizing mission and attributed much of the social and political progress of the past few centuries to its beneficial influence. For Kiesselbach, Hanseats' commitment to tradition was a strength. No class was in a better position to drive forward the material and moral improvement

---

[1] Marx, Karl, *Capital*, 3 vols. (Karl Marx and Friedrich Engels, *Werke* [from here on abbreviated as MEW], vols. 23–5), vol. 3, Berlin 1979 [1894], 339. The translation provided here is my own. All other translations from German, unless otherwise noted, are also mine.

[2] Engels, Friedrich, [Reports from Bremen], in *Morgenblatt für gebildete Leser*, nos. 181–2, July 30–1, 1840, and nos. 196–200, August 17–21, 1841.

[3] Wilhelm Kiesselbach, *Der Gang des Welthandels im Mittelalter*, Bremen, 1860, cited by Marx in *Capital*, vol. 3, 327, 339.

[4] Etges, Andreas, *Wirtschaftsnationalismus. USA und Deutschland im Vergleich (1815–1914)*, Frankfurt and New York, 1999, 125, including note 139. Wherever I write about "merchants" or "merchant capital" in the context of Bremen, I refer to "overseas wholesale merchants," unless otherwise stated.

of the world, while stemming the tide of the "corrosive," modern political ideologies such as democracy, atheism, and nationalism.[5]

The historical record offers support for both Marx's and Kiesselbach's takes on Hanseats. While stubbornly wedded to tradition in business as well as politics, Bremen's merchants managed to extend the reach and density of transatlantic trade. In doing so, they helped create the modern world market for industrial goods and raw materials that was one of the conditions for the takeoff of industrialization across Europe and America. Still, while capital poured into industrial production, Hanseats kept theirs mostly in commodity circulation. Within that fairly narrow segment of the world economy, however, Hanseats enjoyed success far beyond what one might expect from a comparatively small city in an unfavorable geographical location in Northern Germany. One foundation of that success was their peculiar combination of tradition and innovation in their economic activities. The strongest asset for this success was the closely knit character of their group, which tied families and firms on both sides of the Atlantic into one network, infused with a shared commitment to customary ways of doing business.[6]

Bremen's merchants played a pioneering role in opening the United States to direct trade with the continent of Europe. Before American independence had broken the United States out of the cage of the Navigation Act, Bremen's rival sister city, Hamburg, had largely dominated the trade links between Germany and the Atlantic. Hamburg's Hanseats specialized in trade with England, and continued to do so after the turn of the nineteenth century. Bremen, by contrast, had discovered that direct trade with America was a profitable business.[7]

---

[5] Cf. Chapter 3.

[6] There exists an extensive body of literature on Hanseatic merchants and their business endeavors in the nineteenth century: Engelsing, Rolf, *Bremen als Auswandererhafen, 1683–1880* (Karl H. Schwebel, ed., Veröffentlichungen aus dem Staatsarchiv der Freien Hansestadt Bremen, vol. 29), Bremen, 1961; Hardegen, Friedrich and Käthi Smidt, *H. H. Meier, der Gründer des Norddeutschen Lloyd. Lebensbild eines Bremer Kaufmanns 1809–1898*, Berlin and Leipzig, 1920; Scholl, Lars U., *Bremen und Amerika. Die Verbindung der Hansestadt mit den Vereinigten Staaten* (Jahrbuch der Wittheit zu Bremen, 2008/2009), Bremen, 2009; Schramm, Percy E., "Hamburg – Brasilien: Die Forderung einer Dampferverbindung, 1854 verwirklicht," *Vierteljahrschrift für Sozial- und Wirtschaftsgeschichte* **52**, no. 1 (1965), 86–90; Schulz, Andreas, "Weltbürger und Geldaristokraten. Hanseatisches Bürgertum im 19. Jahrhundert," *Historische Zeitschrift* **259** (1994), 637–70; Schwebel, Karl H., *Bremer Kaufleute in den Freihäfen der Karibik. Von den Anfängen des Bremer Überseehandels bis 1815* (Adolf E. Hofmeister [Hg.], Veröffentlichungen aus dem Staatsarchiv der Freien Hansestadt Bremen, Bd. 59), Bremen, 1995; Schwebel, Karl H., "Bremen Merchants Throughout the World," in *Bremen – Bremerhaven. Häfen am Strom – River Weser Ports*, ed. Gesellschaft für Wirtschaftsförderung Bremen, Bremen, 1966, 229–51; Struve, Walter, *Germans & Texans: Commerce, Migration and Culture in the Days of the Lone Star Republic*, Austin, TX, 1996; Wätjen, Hermann, *Aus der Frühzeit des Nordatlantikverkehrs. Studien zur Geschichte der deutschen Schiffahrt und deutschen Auswanderung nach den Vereinigten Staaten bis zum Ende des amerikanischen Bürgerkrieges*, Leipzig, 1932.

[7] Beutin, Ludwig, *Von 3 Ballen zum Weltmarkt. Kleine Bremer Baumwollchronik 1788 bis 1872*, Bremen, 1934; Pitsch, Franz Josef, *Die wirtschaftlichen Beziehungen Bremens zu den Vereinigten Staaten von Amerika bis zur Mitte des 19. Jahrhunderts* (Karl H. Schwebel, ed., Veröffentlichungen aus dem Staatsarchiv der Freien Hansestadt Bremen, vol. 42), Bremen, 1974; Mustafa, Sam A., *Merchants and Migrations: Germans and Americans in Connection, 1776–1835*, Aldershot, UK, 2001. The latter provides an account of the beginnings of Hanseatic trade with the United States.

Graph 1. Ports of Embarkation of German Immigrants Arriving in New York, 1844–1864.

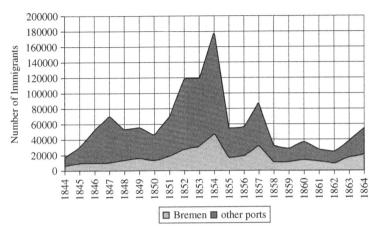

Source: Wätjen, Hermann, *Aus der Frühzeit des Nordatlantikverkehrs. Studien zur Geschichte der deutschen Schiffahrt und deutschen Auswanderung nach den Vereinigten Staaten bis zum Ende des amerikanischen Bürgerkrieges*, Leipzig, 1932, 87, 190–3. There are no data on the number of vessels that arrived in New York in 1848 and 1849.

As Hamburg remained a larger city and market throughout the 1800s, Bremen thrived by aggressively cultivating its niche. The Napoleonic Wars had brought the liberation of formerly bound peasants from their feudal ties, opening the gates for a steadily increasing stream of migrants to North America. By attracting a growing share of German emigrants (Graphs 1 and 2), Bremen's merchants were able to offer highly competitive cargo rates on American exports. Bremish historian Ludwig Beutin estimates that the cost of a new sailing vessel could be recouped in four to five years by the revenue from passages alone. In 1820, only ten of fifty-four vessels (19 percent) arriving in Bremen from the United States had belonged to Bremish firms. By 1830, Bremen's share of such vessels had risen to 36 percent (32 of 92 vessels). By 1839, Bremen merchants had come to dominate this route, with 81 percent of vessels (72 of 89) arriving in the Hanseatic city from the United States flying the bacon flag.[8]

From a comparison of Graphs 1 through 4 (Graph 5), a general pattern emerges. The ebb and flow of Bremish commerce went with the tides of German emigration. During the 1850s, Hanseats adjusted capacity to meet demand, while slowly increasing their share of the overall emigrant traffic. Between 1850 and 1852, Bremen lost some market share in an expanding market, but quickly caught up in 1853 and 1854, when its share rose while absolute demand continued to grow. In 1857, Bremish carrying capacity more than sufficed to meet demand, allowing

---

[8] Engelsing, *Auswandererhafen*, 64, 71–3; Pitsch, *Beziehungen*, 100–1, 192, 196; Beutin, Ludwig, *Bremen und Amerika. Zur Geschichte der Weltwirtschaft und der Beziehungen Deutschlands zu den Vereinigten Staaten*, Bremen, 1953, 47. Bremen's flag shows a checkerboard panel of red and white squares in its left fifth, and alternating red and white horizontal bars in the remaining space. This resemblance with strips of bacon has led to its popular moniker.

Graph 2. Share of German Immigrants Arriving in New York via Bremen, 1844–1864.

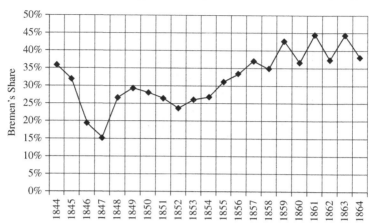

Source: Wätjen, Hermann, *Aus der Frühzeit des Nordatlantikverkehrs. Studien zur Geschichte der deutschen Schiffahrt und deutschen Auswanderung nach den Vereinigten Staaten bis zum Ende des amerikanischen Bürgerkrieges*, Leipzig, 1932, 87, 190–3. There are no data on the number of vessels that arrived in New York in 1848 and 1849.

Graph 3. Bremish Sailing Vessels Arriving in New York, 1845–1865.

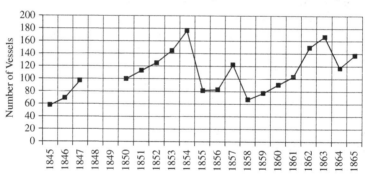

Source: Wätjen, Hermann, *Aus der Frühzeit des Nordatlantikverkehrs. Studien zur Geschichte der deutschen Schiffahrt und deutschen Auswanderung nach den Vereinigten Staaten bis zum Ende des amerikanischen Bürgerkrieges*, Leipzig, 1932, 87, 190–3. There are no data on the number of vessels that arrived in New York in 1848 and 1849.

Hanseats to increase their market share even as immigrant numbers peaked once more.

By the end of the decade, as steamers (not included in Graphs 3 and 4) were making inroads into the emigrant business, the number of passengers on sailing vessels shrank. Nonetheless, after a low in 1858, Bremen's merchants began once more to increase the number of vessels sailing to the United States. In 1861 and 1862, the number of vessels sailing to New York grew in spite of shrinking numbers of emigrants. For better or worse, emigrants were no longer the main inducement

Graph 4. Average Number of Immigrants on Bremish Sailing Vessels Arriving in New York, 1845–1865.

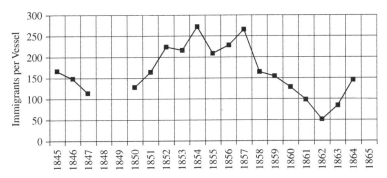

Source: Wätjen, Hermann, *Aus der Frühzeit des Nordatlantikverkehrs. Studien zur Geschichte der deutschen Schiffahrt und deutschen Auswanderung nach den Vereinigten Staaten bis zum Ende des amerikanischen Bürgerkrieges*, Leipzig, 1932, 87, 190–3. There are no data on the number of vessels that arrived in New York in 1848 and 1849.

Graph 5. Patterns of Bremish-American Trade, 1844–1864.

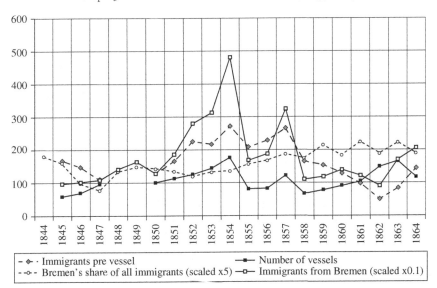

- ◆ · Immigrants pre vessel   —■— Number of vessels
- -○- Bremen's share of all immigrants (scaled x5) —□— Immigrants from Bremen (scaled x0.1)

Source: Based on Graphs 1–4.

for Bremish ventures to the United States. The growing Hanseatic share of American commodity exports merited regular voyages, even if fewer emigrants were aboard on the westbound journey.

Although British houses remained the dominant force in Euro-American trade, Hanseats made significant inroads in the markets for cotton and tobacco. By 1860, Bremen's merchants had cut Liverpool out of the direct American-German cotton trade and came in a close second to Britain in the American export market for

TABLE 1. *U.S. Tobacco Exports, 1855–1860*

Country	Value of Exports	Percentage
Britain	$24,797,516	24%
Bremen	**$19,199,320**	**19%**
France (both coasts)	$13,607,603	13%
Holland	$9,804,766	10%
Other	$34,970,309	34%
All	$102,379,514	100%

Source: Computed from the Annual Report of the Secretary of the Treasury, Transmitting a Report from the Register of the Treasury, of the Commerce and Navigation of the United States for the Year Ending June 30, [1856–60], Washington, D.C. [1856–60], Congressional Serial Sets 886 [1856], 931 [1857], 989 [1858], 1034 [1859] and 1087 [1860].

TABLE 2. *U.S. Cotton Exports, 1855–1860*

Country	Value of Exports	Percentage
Britain	$615,559,369	66%
France, Atlantic Coast (Le Havre)	$149,678,595	16%
Spain, Mediterranean Coast	$32,354,702	3%
Bremen	**$30,079,116**	**3%**
Russia, Baltic and North Sea	$19,111,680	2%
Hamburg	$7,458,878	1%
Other	$82,150,564	9%
All	$936,392,904	100%

Source: Computed from the Annual Report of the Secretary of the Treasury, Transmitting a Report from the Register of the Treasury, of the Commerce and Navigation of the United States for the Year Ending June 30, [1856–60], Washington, D.C. [1856–60], Congressional Serial Sets 886 [1856], 931 [1857], 989 [1858], 1034 [1859] and 1087 [1860].

tobacco.[9] In 1860, Bremen's share of all traffic in passengers, commodities, and migrants between Germany and North America left the main competitors – Hamburg, Antwerp, and Le Havre – behind (see Tables 1–3 and Graph 6).

Bremish trade mediated the relations between disparate, peripheral regions and the world market. Hanseats fed the staples of the American slave states to the emerging industrial districts of Germany, thus contributing to the ever-intensifying exploitation of slave labor. Hence, it was not too much of a flight of fancy if A. Dudley Mann, a diplomat and steamship promoter from the American South who had served as American consul to Bremen from 1842 to 1845, looked to the

---

[9] Pitsch, *Beziehungen*, 148–64, 237–53.

TABLE 3. *Major Foreign Ports Mentioned in the* New York Times, *1851–1869, by Decade*

Port/Instances	1850s[a]	Average per Day	1860s	Average per Day
Liverpool	13,602	4.49	18,220	4.99
Cork	1,502	0.50	5,971	1.64
Bremen	3,391	1.12	5,562	1.52
Le Havre	4,060	1.34	4,434	1.21
Southampton	2,650	0.87	3,263	0.89
Hamburg	1,620	0.53	3,156	0.86
Antwerp	1,729	0.57	3,000	0.82
Rotterdam	771	0.25	1,339	0.37
Marseille	1,680	0.55	690	0.19

[a] Beginning with the first issue, September 1, 1851.
Source: *New York Times* archive, online search engine at http://pqasb.pqarchiver.com/nytimes/
advancedsearch.html (accessed July 18, 2005), using the option "Search Articles, Advertisements
and Listings" and using the city name as the search term in year-by-year searches.

Graph 6. Major Foreign Ports Mentioned in the *New York Times*, 1851–1870, by Year.

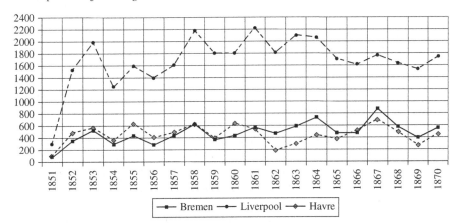

Source: *New York Times* archive, online search engine at http://pqasb
.pqarchiver.com/nytimes/advancedsearch.html (accessed July 18, 2005), using the
option "Search Articles, Advertisements and Listings" and using the city name as
the search term in year-by-year searches. The year 1851 begins with the
first issue, September 1.

city as an ally for his plans to make the trade of the slaveholding states independent
of Britain and the American North.[10]

At the same time, however, Hanseats supplied free labor for the industrial and
territorial expansion of the free American states by shipping to the west a German

---

[10] Beutin, *Bremen*, 277 (note to p. 33), 284 (note to p. 57), and 290 (note to p. 81). Mann (1801–89) was
made an honorary Bremish citizen in 1847.

population displaced by an as yet incomplete transition from feudal to capitalist social relations that left idle thousands of people no longer bound to their craft or soil, but not yet absorbed into the wage-labor force.

Unlike Britain, the center of the world economy, Germany and America had not yet been turned into fully capitalist, commodity-producing societies. Industrial commodity production and wage-labor relations had not yet become the dominant source of income for the populations of Germany and America. Hence, Hanseats made their fortunes in the traditional manner of merchant capital, by linking qualitatively different modes of production to each other, exploiting the possibility for arbitrage profits that arise from that difference, and making them commensurable through establishing commodity prices.[11]

In so doing, Bremen's merchants helped create an industrial world market and turn the societies they linked into modern capitalist societies. Up to around 1860, Hanseatic trade, however, was not entirely a modern capitalist endeavor. Trade between and within countries that have fully embraced capitalist commodity production becomes "a particular moment of capital investment in general." By contrast, Bremish merchant capital retained its independence, based on an early-modern way of doing business distinct from the practices and institutions of modern industrial, financial, and commodity-trading capital.[12]

BREMEN AS A LIBERAL, FREE-TRADING PORT

What was the secret of success that propelled Bremen to such prominence in the commercial centers of the United States? The economy of the Hanseatic cities of Bremen, Lübeck, and Hamburg was based on long-distance, wholesale trade. The three cities each specialized in trade with different areas. Bremen held a virtual monopoly on the North American trade, Hamburg's ships sailed to England and South America, and Lübeck's merchants operated in the traditional core area of the medieval Hanse, the Baltic Sea. For Bremen, the *entrepôt* trade had special significance. Up to one-third of the volume of imports was reexported to Scandinavia and Russia. In spite of this specialization, the three cities had more in common with each other than with the rest of Germany.[13]

In an age when the German economy was still largely agricultural and indus-trial manufacturing was slow to start, Hanseats provided the hinterland with some commercial services. Hamburg relied mostly on the import of English manufactured goods into Germany and the export of East Elbian wheat to Britain. Bremen merchants sold cotton to textile factories in Saxony and tobacco to manufacturers in Westphalia. Far fewer goods were exported, mostly fine textiles and other luxury craft products such as Solingen metalwares, making the

---

[11] Marx, *Capital*, vol. 3, 342.

[12] Ibid., 339.

[13] Böhmert, Victor, "Die Stellung der Hansestädte zu Deutschland in den letzten 3 Jahrzehnten," *Vierteljahrsschrift für Volkswirthschaft und Cultur* 1 (1863), 73–115; Duckwitz, Arnold, *Denkwürdigkeiten aus meinem öffentlichen Leben von 1841–1866. Ein Beitrag zur bremischen und deutschen Geschichte*, Bremen, 1877.

search for a profitable westbound cargo imperative. Lübeck's merchants served a local market and mainly relied on coastal trade for their livelihood.[14]

Before railroads, the availability of river transportation defined the "natural" hinterland for Bremen and Hamburg. Hamburg's Elbe River connected the city to Anhalt, Brandenburg, and Saxony. Bremen's Weser River ran north from Hesse, through Prussian Westphalia, Schaumburg-Lippe, and Hannover, before it reached the city. Southern Germany, where most emigrants came from, and the Rhineland with its growing textile industry had more easy access to Belgian and Dutch ports via the Rhine, than to Bremen or Hamburg by land.[15]

Only after the coming of the railroad in the late 1840s was Bremen able to draw more of the business from western and southern Germany into its port. A "national" rhetoric by Bremen merchants, who advertised the city as "the *German* port," was directed against prevalent dislike for the Hanseats in these areas of the German Confederation. The popular economist, Friedrich List, considered one of the intellectual fathers of the customs union, contributed strongly to the spread of an argument that blamed the Hanseatic cities for destroying southern German manufacturers by importing cheap British goods after 1815.[16] Bremen's publicists were able to deflect much of this anticommercialism onto its rival, Hamburg. Hamburg's government played into the hands of Bremish merchants when it discouraged emigrants from using the city's port, because it was afraid that paupers unable to pay their passage would remain in town. Only in the 1850s, in the light of Bremen's success in the emigrant trade and in the American export market, did Hamburg change its policy.[17]

In 1863, the economist Victor Böhmert, an official (*2. Syndicus*) of the Bremish *Handelskammer*, offered an explanation for Bremen's steep rise from a provincial center to a world city, in which he stressed a successful combination of dynamism and solid experience:

Transatlantic trade requires large amounts of capital, years of experience, tried and true trade connections abroad, branch locations in the most important transatlantic places, significant ship-ownership; further, it requires that the place where a transatlantic trade is to be conducted be a great commodity market, where many buyers and sellers, and the intermediaries of trade, converge; where extensive shipments find a ready market, where supply and demand in transatlantic products is plentiful and regular, and where a number of mercantile auxiliary services,

---

[14] Two works treating the economic development of the German states in the 19th century in terms of "integration" and "uneven development" are Abelshauser, Werner et al., *Wirtschaftliche Integration und Wandel von Raumstrukturen im 19. und 20. Jahrhundert* (Josef Wysocki, ed., Schriften des Vereins für Socialpolitik, Gesellschaft für Wirtschafts- und Sozialwissenschaften; N.F., vol. 232), Berlin, 1994; and Fremdling, Rainer, and Richard H. Tilly, eds., *Industrialisierung und Raum. Studien zur regionalen Differenzierung in Deutschland des 19. Jahrhunderts*, Stuttgart, 1979. Unfortunately, both works are characterized by the Borusso-centric focus still common in the historical social sciences in Germany, and are thus of little value for the study of a Hanseatic city.

[15] Ludwig, *Bremen*, 34–68.

[16] Apelt, Hermann, "Friedrich List und die Hanseaten," *Der Schlüssel, Bremer Beiträge zur Deutschen Kultur und Wirtschaft* **6**, no. 8 (1941), 133–43.

[17] Engelsing, Rolf, *Bremen als Auswandererhafen, 1683–1880* (Karl H. Schwebel, ed., Veröffentlichungen aus dem Staatsarchiv der Freien Hansestadt Bremen, vol. 29), Bremen, 1961; Wätjen, *Frühzeit*.

institutions, and usages all serve to promote and facilitate the one great gainful pursuit – trade. These essential elements of flourishing commerce can be found nowhere in Germany in as extensive a degree, and in as fruitful a collaboration, as in Hamburg and Bremen.[18]

A reliance on serving the German hinterland, alone, could not have created the critical mass of supply and demand to sustain a market of this scope and scale in Bremen. Bremen's Weser River has a much smaller drainage area than the Rhine or Hamburg's Elbe River. After 1848, railroads somewhat alleviated this natural disadvantage, but Bremen's rise had begun before the first railroad had been opened in Germany. What made the difference was the strong reexport trade from Bremen to other European countries. Böhmert knew that because the city was "a commodity market and a trade emporium for all of Northern Europe; [and hence] a center of world trade, [Bremen] is capable of standing its ground in competition with the most powerful commercial peoples in neutral markets." To illustrate his point, he cited the 1861 statistics for tobacco. Bremen imported 86,556,474 pounds of tobacco and exported 67,612,579 pounds. More than half of that export did not go to countries of the German *Zollverein*, but went to European countries stretching from Spain to Russia and from Switzerland to Sweden. Even South America and Africa were supplied with Bremish tobacco. Based on the mass and variety of the commodities the city traded, Bremen had managed to dominate the transatlantic trade of many northeastern European countries. Russia, for example, received its tobacco largely through Bremen.[19]

Böhmert argued that political liberty was an essential ingredient of success in the world market. The illiberal political climate of the interior states stifled the free flow of people, ideas, and commodities. Bremen did not discourage its young men from going abroad for their mercantile pursuits, while most German states kept their male subjects under close supervision to prevent them from evading the draft. The liberal spirit of the Hanseatic cities also directly invigorated markets. Free trade meant that "the flags of the most diverse nations ... fly in a joyful competition" in the Bremish ports. In this climate, the "private efforts of diligent merchants" produced prosperity and progress. Subjecting these same merchants to too much of the "solicitude of the state," as the interior German states were prone to do, was the safest way of squashing competition and stifling profitable exchange.[20]

As a foreigner hired by Hanseats as an ideologist, or spokesman, Böhmert expressed a somewhat one-sided view of Bremish trade. While the truisms of political economy he cited may well have been applicable to the Bremish market, the free utilization of capital, labor, and nature was not all that there was to the Hanseats' success. There is overwhelming evidence that the Hanseats did best where they did not act as purely self-interested individuals who came to market with a single-minded attitude of profit maximization, but where instead they acted in concert.

---

[18] Böhmert, Victor, "Die Stellung der Hansestädte zu Deutschland in den letzten drei Jahrzehnten," *Vierteljahrschrift für Volkswirtschaft, Politik und Kulturgeschichte* 1 (1863), 73–115, here: pp. 109–10.
[19] Ibid., 88–9, 108; quote on p. 88.
[20] Ibid., 107, 109–10, 113; quote on p. 110.

One payoff of close cooperation among Hanseats was an informational advantage over other, competing merchants. In what can only be understood as a kind of mysticism that evokes Marx's commodity fetish, Hanseats believed in their ability to intuit market developments. But like the figure of thought described in Marx's concept, this belief had a rational core: Böhmert pointed out that the regular exchange with foreign countries increased the knowledge available to Hanseats. Being well informed about the political situation abroad, being able to discern qualities of commodities, and knowing the markets for imports and exports in foreign ports were essential for success in a volatile business in which "often the price of an imported commodity can have fallen by 20, 30 or more per cent by the time it arrives at its destination." In a large marketplace that bundled streams of communication and commodities, an experienced merchant could hedge his bets by cultivating a sense for "that intangible something, which plays such a great role in commerce – *the opinion*."[21] The combined decades of experience assembled in Bremen's countinghouses formed the substance of this "opinion."

The depth and range of the collective experience on which Hanseats could draw to gauge market developments, and that gave them a competitive edge over others, was a function of the extent and stability of their network, not of a special gift of divination. It was not a matter of individual knowledge and skill, but of the cooperation between the members of this elite that rested on a shared approach to business that had fairly little to do with that of the self-interested, profit-maximizing individual of classical political economy.

HANSEATS AS ECONOMIC CONSERVATIVES

According to Ludwig Beutin, an economic historian who, in the 1950s, wrote what is still the most extensive survey of Bremen's trade in the nineteenth century, a distinctive characteristic of the way Hanseats did business up to 1860 was their economic conservatism. For example, the city's merchants owned the commodities they traded and the vessels on which the commodities were transported. Shipownership made sense for Hanseats, considering that their competitiveness as traders depended on the income from westbound emigrants. With most of their capital tied up in goods and infrastructure, Hanseats derived a comparatively low share of their profits from commissions on the shipping of commodities owned by wholesalers, forwarders, or producers. Instead, like the factors of the American South, Hanseats bought directly from producers, often extending long-term credit to them. Until the tobacco or cotton was sold from their storehouses in Bremen to merchants specializing in inland trade or to manufacturers, the commodities remained the property of the transatlantic merchant.[22]

---

[21] Ibid., 111–12; quote on p. 112.

[22] Beutin, *Bremen*, 48, 71–2, 110–11. Beutin's account is problematic in that he never tells us how he knows how individual Hanseats made their money. Few actual business records survive today, though Beutin conducted most of his research before World War II, and might have had access to family collections. His reluctance to divulge detailed knowledge of balance sheets might hence be a

As William Cronon has shown in his study of the rise of Chicago as the center of trade for the Great Plains, mercantile activity from the mid-nineteenth century on was characterized by a growing detachment of capital from commodity ownership. Increasingly, merchants became money-trading and commodity-trading capitalists dealing in futures and giving circulation credit, rather than acquiring commodities on their own account.[23] Marx saw this movement away from "buying cheap to sell dear" as part of the transformation by which merchant capital was "reduced from its formerly independent existence to a particular moment of capital investment in general." The result of this transformation was the "subsumption of merchant capital under industrial capital." On a world-historical scale, Marx considered this subsumption completed by "the fall of Holland as the dominant mercantile nation."[24] The case of Bremen's merchants suggests that the point in time when this subsumption was completed differed in individual countries. In the German states, with their relatively underdeveloped economies, merchant capital continued to play an independent role well into the nineteenth century.[25]

In a developed capitalist world market, equivalents are exchanged, and the possibilities for individual capitalists to manipulate prices are minimized. Hanseats, however, enjoyed at least three possible sources of nonequivalent exchange: first, they were able to undersell their competitors on cargo rates, due to their profits from transporting emigrants; second, they enjoyed an informational advantage by virtue of the network character of their group, at a time when slow venues of

function of Hanseatic discreteness. Hermann Wätjen, however, a historian from an old Hanseatic family, already complained in 1933 that too few business records are extant to write an economic history of individual firms (see his *Aus der Frühzeit des Nordatlantikverkehrs*, Introduction). Most likely, therefore, Beutin's interpretation that "Hanseats did not engage in speculation" is based on three sources: 1) aggregate data, which do suggest that Hanseats' business practices were fairly conservative; 2) qualitative sources, such as statements by nineteenth-century merchants who state their conservative approach to business; and 3) a commitment to a specific anticapitalist tradition. Ad 1), the sources cited by Beutin confirm that Hanseats were reluctant to embrace a modern capitalist business ethic. My own research supports the same interpretation, although not Beutin's assertion that Hanseats completely eschewed all modern financial instruments or business practices. Hanseats did "speculate" and they did trade on commission, but they might have done so to a lesser extent than others. The ease with which Bremen survived the crisis of 1857 remains the strongest indicator of the solidity of their enterprises. Ad 2), these firsthand accounts might have to be taken *cum grano salis*. Nineteenth-century Hanseats had a stake in demonstrating to their anticommercialist critics that they were not "handmaidens of English manufacturers." Ad 3.), Beutin wrote an essay in 1937 (Beutin, Ludwig, *Bremisches Bank- und Börsenwesen seit dem 17. Jahrhundert. Von der Wirtschaftsgesinnung einer Hansestadt* [Abhandlungen und Vorträge herausgegeben von der Bremer Wissenschaftlichen Gesellschaft, vol. 10, no. 4, December 1937], Bremen, 1937) in which he argued that nineteenth-century Hanseats conformed to National Socialist business ethics. The Nazis associated speculation with Jewish capital and commodity production with Aryan capital, where only the former was guilty of exploitation. In his 1937 essay, Beutin points to the exclusion of Jews from Bremen, and to the strained ties between Bremish businesses and Jewish banks, as evidence of the truly "German" character of Bremen's merchants. The same arguments reappear in his 1953 book (*Bremen und Amerika*, see note 8), although purged from any direct reference to the Jewish character of financial capital and speculation. In summary, therefore, Beutin's interpretations have to be treated with caution.

[23] Cronon, William, *Nature's Metropolis: Chicago and the Great West*, New York and London, 1991, esp. pp. 97–147.

[24] Marx, *Capital*, vol. **3** (MEW, vol. 25), 339, 346.

[25] Ibid., 340.

communication meant that market reports were not yet universally available in "real time"; third, they indirectly benefited from slave labor, which involves a nonequivalent exchange in procuring labor power.[26]

Hanseatic business practices matched the early-modern nature of their role in the world market. Bremen's capital, for the most part, appears to have been invested in tangible assets, such as ships, warehouses, wharfs, and commodities. Compared to the novel ways of facilitating trade described by Marx and Cronon, Hanseatic capital was at a disadvantage because of its much slower turnover. At the same time, it was less subject to volatility in times of crisis. Whether Hanseats' reliance on tangible assets stemmed directly from distrust in "speculation," as Beutin claims – whether it represented a certain inertia resulting from an ethos that stressed prudence and tradition or whether it was a result of path dependency, in that capital committed to long-term investments cannot easily be liquidated – it appears that Hanseats stuck to their conservative business practices up to 1860.[27]

Beutin's interpretation of Hanseats as conservative businessmen is supported by Hanseats' initial skepticism about stocks. In the Netherlands and in England, joint-stock companies had been in use as a form for long-distance trading concerns since the eighteenth century. Only in the mid-1850s were the first large-scale joint-stock companies founded in Bremen, a bank and a steamship company, the North German Lloyd. Both these concerns were immediately tied to the trading interests of the city and were led by the same, well-established Bremish merchant, Hermann Henrich (H. H.) Meier.[28] Meier had initially wanted to prevent the Lloyd's shares from being traded publicly, in order to discourage speculation. This proved impractical, because the scale of the enterprises required involving the financial markets beyond the city. Bremen's mercantile estate remained strongly represented among the stockholders of both firms, but was not able to keep all stock, as it were, in the family. Initially, about half the Lloyd's shares were held by German investment banks in the hinterland.[29]

[26] With an econometric approach, O'Rourke, Kevin H., and Jeffrey G. Williamson, *Globalization and History: The Evolution of a Nineteenth-Century Atlantic Economy*, Cambridge, MA, and London, 1999, show that price differentials shrink, where tariffs and transportation costs sink. Their research confirms Marx's assertion that the possibility for arbitrage profits is largely removed by the creation of a world market for industrial commodities and resources. See his *Capital*, vol. 3, 341. See also Beckert, Sven, *The Monied Metropolis: New York City and the Consolidation of the American Bourgeoisie, 1850–1896*, Cambridge, MA, 2001, 151 and notes.

[27] Beutin, *Bremen*, 71–2.

[28] Meier's Bremish acquaintances pronounced his nickname-initials in English, rather than German, reflecting the strong ties between the Hanseatic city and the United States. Engelsing, Rolf, "Bremisches Unternehmertum. Sozialgeschichte 1780/1870," *Jahrbuch der Wittheit zu Bremen* **2** (1958), 7–112.

[29] The response the Lloyd's board of directors gave investors who complained about low dividends in 1873, quoted by Beutin, illuminates the persistence of an attitude that abhorred "speculation": "In the interest of the public, which is served by this great enterprise, it is evident that its stock should stay in such hands as are not interested in a one-time payment of high dividends, or a temporary, high share price." Beutin, *Bremen*, 82. Of the total capitalization of the Lloyd (4,000,000 Thaler Gold), Bremish merchants owned 32.5% (1.3 Mio) through previous stockownership in four river-steamboat companies that had been merged into the Lloyd. Another 37.5% (1.5 Mio) were held by the *Dessauer Creditanstalt für Industrie und Handel*, located in Anhalt. Of the remaining 30% (1.2 Mio), some stock was held by Bremish merchants, but a large packet of this stock was held by another

Furthermore, Hanseats displayed a reluctance to invest in industry. Cigar manufacturing made an exception, with Bremen cigars becoming a coveted article of importation in the United States. It reached its high point in the early 1850s, when almost ten thousand out of an estimated sixty thousand inhabitants of the city were involved in cigar manufacturing. Cigar making was an industry of low capital intensity, because it did not use machines. The merchant supplied the material to and bought the finished product from the owners of small workshops. This industry, however, was not financed by the long-distance merchants, but by merchants specializing in the hinterland trade. When Hannover and Oldenburg, which surrounded Bremen, joined the *Zollverein* in 1854, tobacco manufacturing in Bremen collapsed. Instead of paying high import dues on cigars, upland merchants now shipped raw tobacco to workshops outside of Bremen, mainly in Westphalia, where it was made into cigars for *Zollvereinland* consumption. For decades, Bremen remained a city with few industrial enterprises.[30]

Thus Hanseats displayed a thorough economic conservatism. They stayed clear of the business practices that define modern industrial and financial capitalism. Beutin argues that this conservatism explains why Bremen's merchants on both sides of the Atlantic were left largely unscathed by the Panic of 1857. Those regions and individuals most involved in the world financial markets were the ones most affected by this first worldwide crisis of modern capitalism. The Hanseats' ability to emerge from the Panic of 1857 with few losses was a function of Bremen's comparative backwardness.[31]

The root of this backwardness, as well as the source of the Hanseats' success, was their reliance on tight cooperation between the individual firms that made up their network. This cooperation, in turn, rested on the close personal ties between the men who ran Hanseatic countinghouses and on the families that backed their business ventures morally and financially. This network was densest between Bremen and the main American ports.

SMALL FIRMS, BIG BUSINESS

The shared economic conservatism among Hanseats rested upon the close ties of familiarity and trust that extended across the Atlantic among the members of the network. When Hanseatic merchants arrived in America, they were not cast into an atomized marketplace where they had to succeed as individuals. They remained part of a group that cooperated locally and transatlantically. Bremen remained the anchor point in these transnational relationships. Commonly, those who went abroad were the younger sons or clerks of older merchants who remained in Bremen. Once in the New World, they conducted trade with the firms of their fathers or former employers. When they formed business partnerships in foreign

investment bank from the hinterland, the *Darmstädter Bank*. Before the Lloyd bought back the *Darmstädter Bank*'s shares in 1859, Hanseats had held just about half of the Lloyd's stock. See [North German Lloyd Steamship Company, Bremen], *70 Years North German Lloyd Bremen, 1857–1927*, Berlin, 1927, 25–32.

[30] Beutin, *Bremen*, 53–4, 126–7.

[31] Ibid., 112–14.

ports, they mostly chose their associates from the community of Hanseats. In the course of the nineteenth century, some of the older Hanseatic firms in the United States passed into the hands of the American-born descendants of their founders. Still, the second and third generations of Hanseatic Americans remained tied into this same network. American Hanseats sent their foreign-born sons to Bremen for apprenticeships in the many merchant firms of that town – often in the counting-house of a relative.[32]

The extent of the capital brought into the firm by the associates limited the scale of a company's activities. When H. H. Meier, as a junior agent in the 1830s, proposed expanding the business of his late father's firm by trading on commission with South America, the head of the merchant house, Johann H. Adami, told him not to: "We have enough business to feed everyone, there is no need for such an extension."[33] In a capitalist business, profits are largely reinvested in a quest for even more profits. Hanseats followed a different path. For them, the welfare of the family remained a fundamental source of legitimacy for profit, just as the family fortune laid the foundation of their business ventures.

For the first quarter of the nineteenth century, most Hanseats preferred to invest their trading profits in real estate. For its long-term prospects, they preferred the steady income from a manor to the dangers of capital circulation in trade. The crisis of agriculture after the Napoleonic Wars increasingly rendered agriculture less profitable than trade. Hanseats still bought rural estates, but began using them as country homes rather than working farms. Until about 1850, these estates still functioned as safe, long-term investments. Only in the second half of the century did country estates begin to become objects of a conspicuous enjoyment of wealth.[34]

As opportunities for trade increased in the second quarter of the century, Hanseats began reinvesting their profits in trade, keeping their growing capital stock permanently in circulation. Official statistics reflect this expansion of Bremish trade: The number of ships owned by the city's merchants grew from 95 in 1826 to 225 in 1846.[35] Between 1840 and 1856, the value of Bremen's imports from the United States quadrupled and the value of Bremen's exports to the United States quintupled. Of all overseas imports to reach Bremen in 1856, 39 percent came from the United States. In the same year, the share of Bremen's overseas exports destined for the

---

[32] Fundamental for establishing the degree of intermarriage among Hanseats: Brandes, Erika, "Der Bremer Überseekaufmann in seiner gesellschaftsgeschichtlichen Bedeutung im 'geschlossenen Heiratskreis,'" *Genealogisches Jahrbuch* 3 (1963), 25–48. See also Engelsing, Rolf, "England und die USA in der bremischen Sicht des 19. Jahrhunderts," *Jahrbuch der Wittheit zu Bremen* 1 (1957):, 33–65, esp. p. 49.

[33] Hardegen and Smidt, *H. H. Meier*, 22.

[34] Engelsing, Rolf, "Bremisches Unternehmertum. Sozialgeschichte 1780/1870," *Jahrbuch der Wittheit zu Bremen* 2 (1958), 7–112. See, e.g., Hardegen and Smidt, *H. H. Meier*, 151–2 (Meier's estate of Radau, bought 1860, sold 1891); Schleiden, Rudolph, *Jugenderinnerungen eines Schleswig-Holsteiners*, Wiesbaden, 1886, 52, 123 (Ascheberg manor, bought by Schleiden's father in 1811, sold in 1825). See also Chapter 2.

[35] Beutin, *Bremen*, 21, 23. Total tonnage increased from 14,500 Register-Tons in 1826 to 50,000 in 1846. The tonnage of the average Bremish ship would hence have increased from 153 to 222 Register-Tons.

United States was 67 percent.[36] The wealth of the city's elite – full citizens who owed taxes on more than 3,000 Thaler – more than tripled between 1813 and 1848.[37]

Bremen's rising prominence in transatlantic trade was evident in New York, the most important commercial center in North America. Americans took notice of the small German city. A survey of the *New York Times* for the years 1851 to 1869 shows a slow but steady increase in the number of times Bremen was mentioned on the pages of the paper. At least three-quarters of the instances when a reader would have found the city's name on the pages of the daily would have been in the context of market reports or private advertisements for commodities or shipping. Although admittedly more anecdotal than a thorough analysis of trade flows, this method nonetheless allows for conclusions on the relative commercial importance of certain foreign ports for New York business (Table 3 and Graph 6).

In the 1850s, Bremen held a steady third rank immediately behind Le Havre, and, unsurprisingly, far behind Liverpool, but ahead of Cork and Southampton. In the 1860s, Bremen moved ahead of Le Havre, with the exception of 1860 and 1866. The Hanseatic city also closed up on Liverpool. While Cork assumed the second rank during this decade, the Irish city was linked to many general news reports in the *Times* received "via the city of Cork," the last major port before ships entered the Atlantic. Hence, the frequency with which Cork was mentioned is not an indicator of its commercial importance. It appears that, in the 1860s, Hanseatic trade with the United States kept growing, if perhaps at a slower pace (Table 3 and Graph 3).

This expansion of trade, however, did not lead to a corresponding expansion of the scale of the activities of individual firms. In 1846, at a time when Hanseats had been keeping their capital permanently in circulation for two decades, the average German-American firm still only had 1.5 associates and 1.6 clerks (Table 4). Associates conducted much of the business in person, and the firm, overall, continued to avoid taking on more business than the low numbers of men who worked in the countinghouse could handle.

Although the statistic does not allow us to say precisely how the numbers of clerks and associates differed between Hanseatic and non-Hanseatic firms, it does indicate that the number of clerks per associate was higher where Hanseatic firms dominated and was highest in the commercial seaports most important to the export of tobacco and cotton. Even in New York, however, each associate made do with an average of just two clerks. These numbers support the conclusion that the attitude of Johann H. Adami of limiting business to what was needed for the livelihood of the associates and their families prevailed throughout Hanseatic circles even at this time. Although statistics of this kind are unavailable for the 1850s, an

[36] Borries, Bodo von, *Deutschlands Außenhandel 1836 bis 1856. Eine statistische Untersuchung zur Frühindustrialisierung* (Knut Borchardt et al., eds., *Forschungen zur Sozial- und Wirtschaftsgeschichte*, vol. 13), Stuttgart 1970, 134–5. Bremen's oversea imports in 1856 were valued at 36 Mio. Thaler Gold; overseas exports, 22.7 Mio. Thaler Gold. The "Thaler Gold" was the currency unit of Bremen. According to Hermann Wätjen, *Aus der Frühzeit des Nordatlantikverkehrs. Studien zur Geschichte der deutschen Schiffahrt und deutschen Auswanderung nach den Vereinigten Staaten bis zum Ende des amerikanischen Bürgerkrieges*, Leipzig 1932, 35, 1 Thaler Gold = 1.44; US\$ = 0.288 £.

[37] The wealth of this group grew from 17.2 Mio Thaler Gold in 1813 to 60.2 in 1848. The number of people in this category increased from 1,084 to 2,700 during that time, which means that each individual owned an average of 15,867 Thaler Gold in 1813, and 22,296 in 1848. Beutin, *Bremen*, 72.

TABLE 4. *German Long-Distance Merchant Firms in the United States, 1846*

Place	Hanseatic Firms	Non-Hanseatic Firms	Associates	Clerks	Associates per Firm	Clerks per Firm	Clerks per Associate
New York	35	27	64	132	1.03	2.13	2.06
Baltimore	14	9	28	42	1.22	1.83	1.50
Philadelphia	7	2	17	16	1.89	1.78	0.94
New Orleans	7	2	17	25	1.89	2.78	1.47
St. Louis	5	11	20	16	1.25	1.00	0.80
Cincinnati	3	2	7	5	1.40	1.00	0.71
Louisville	2	8	15	6	1.50	0.60	0.40
Others	27	14	N/A	N/A			
TOTAL	100	75	168	242	1.45	1.59	1.13

Source: *Weser Zeitung*, 1846/02/10, quoted in Beutin, *Bremen und Amerika*, 287. Apprentices are not counted here, but would roughly have matched the number of clerks.

extensive survey of mercantile correspondence and biographies suggest that this pattern continued well into the 1860s.[38]

Instead of keeping their profits in their own firms, Hanseats largely made them available to their descendants or in-laws for the establishment of new companies. In this way, the Bremish network expanded by spawning an ever-increasing number of mercantile houses, giving a livelihood to Hanseats' sons and daughters and their spouses. Through childhood friendships, intermarriage, and business partnerships, the resulting multitude of companies were connected to each other, creating the trust and stability that supported Hanseats' conservative attitude to business and their success in expanding the scale of their economic activities as a group.

A closer look at the situation in Baltimore during the 1850s illuminates the extent, density, and stability of the Hanseatic network. Bremish merchants in this city were a closely knit group. Moreover, these mercantile houses were linked to those of their peers in other centers of Hanseatic activity on both sides of the Atlantic. In Baltimore, Hanseats as a group were highly successful in drawing more and more business to Bremen. Overall, the number of Hanseatic firms grew at a pace that suggests that Bremish merchants in this city followed the conservative pattern of limiting the business of individual firms, while extending the network by forming new firms. This practice might explain the stability of Hanseatic firms, while the reach of Hanseats' ties to other centers of trade might have been responsible for their overall success as a group.

Hanseatic merchants in Baltimore numbered approximately 150 men in 1860.[39] German firms were among the most stable merchant houses in the city. In 1849,

---

[38] I base this conclusion on the entirety of sources examined for this thesis. The subsequent chapters will support this point. For Adami, see note 33.

[39] Browne, Gary Larson, *Baltimore in the Nation, 1789–1861*, Chapel Hill, NC, 1980, 179, counts 1,544 merchants in Baltimore in 1850, 10% of whom were German. In 1846, the Weser Zeitung had

four among a total of ten commission and shipping merchant firms listed in the city directory had German owners. In 1859, six of fifty commission and shipping merchants were persons with German names. Three of these six had already been active in 1849. These were Brothers Boninger, Oelrichs & Lurman, and A. Schumacher & Co.[40] The first was a house connected to an importer in the Rhineland, Boninger & Co. of Duisburg, but the latter two were Hanseatic firms. The Baltimore Boningers had two vessels sailing under their name to Bremen, which suggests that they relied for their trade on the Hanseatic network, as well.[41]

An analysis of the record of vessels entered and cleared at the port of Baltimore, kept at the Merchants' Exchange reading room, paints a similar picture of continuity. In the spring of 1851, eight German firms had regularly consigned cargo to vessels leaving Baltimore. By 1860, the number of such firms had grown to thirteen. Six of these thirteen had been part of the original eight firms in 1851.[42] In spite of the Panic

counted 23 German-owned firms in Baltimore. These 23 firms were run by 28 owners and 42 clerks. Retail firms were explicitly excluded from this tally (Table 4). Browne notes that the designation "merchant" was "inflated" by 1850. Hence, although the number of firms may have been 150, not all of them will have engaged in foreign, wholesale trade. By contrast, the clerks of Baltimore's German-owned merchant firms that had trading ties to Bremen, and would thus have shown up in the Weser Zeitung's survey, may be included in the social group under discussion here. They often identified with their employers, and were often likely to become independent merchants. Many of them would have been relatives of the firms' associates. My own estimate for 1860 is based on Ferslew, Eugene, *Baltimore City Directory, for 1859–60*, Baltimore, 1859, as well as on membership numbers in the Germania Club, see following.

[40] *Mitchett's Baltimore City Director* [sic] *for 1849–50*, Baltimore, 1849; and *Mitchett's Baltimore City Director* [sic] *for 1855–56*, Baltimore, 1855; Ferslew, *Baltimore City Directory, for 1859–60*. Rather than signaling a relative decline of the importance of Hanseats for Baltimore's mercantile community, the lower share of German firms in 1859 (12% of all Commission and Shipping Merchants, after 40% in 1849) may well be a function of the inflated use of the term *Commission and Shipping Merchant*, as suggested by Browne (see previous note). The Lürmans – including those born in the United States – consistently spelled their name with the umlaut in private and business correspondence, while often using the letter "u" in the name of the firm. Their English-speaking correspondents did not use the umlaut. The Maryland Historical Society followed the anglicized spelling in titling the collection of Lürman's papers (see note 46). In this study, I follow the original appearance of the name in the sources, unless when quoting the titles of documents or manuscript collections. Unfortunately, staying true to the sources will come at the expense of consistency in the spelling of this name.

[41] For the Boningers' ties to Duisburg: New York Public Library, Research Library, Special Collections Department, Garrit F. Watson (attorney for Brothers Boninger) to U.S. Army, Army of the James, Quartermaster's Department, Richmond, June 9, 1865, and F. W. Hanewinckel (Bremish Consul) to idem, Richmond, June 9, 1865, in: U.S. Army – Quartermaster's Department – Copy Book – Virginia Merchants – Tobacco Claims – 1865 May–June, 44–5. See 42–8 of this copy book for the Boningers' request to restitute more than 700 hogsheads of tobacco bought in 1861. For the Boningers' vessels, see the record books cited in the following note.

[42] The six firms in question were Boninger Bros., F. L. Brauns & Co., F.W. Brune & Sons., von Kapff & Arens, Schaer & Kohler, and A. Schumacher & Co. All but Boninger Bros. can be identified as Hanseatic firms. Baltimore. Merchants' Exchange Reading Room, record books, 1832–1899, 72 vols., Manuscripts Department, Maryland Historical Society Library (from here on abbreviated as MdHS), MS.610, boxes 41 and 44. We know that Oelrichs & Lurman owned their own vessels, as well as a half share in a wharf in Fells Point. Their absence from port records might indicate simply that they did not sail during the period covered by the sample, or, more likely, that vessels loaded in Fells Point do not show up in the Baltimore records. For Schaer & Kohler [Köhler], see Heinrich to Julius Wilkens (in Bremen), Baltimore, June 9, 1865 Wilkens, Julius, 1838?–1898, Papers, 1849–83, MdHS MS.439.

of 1857, most firms existing at the beginning of the decade were still around at its end and had been joined by roughly one new firm for each surviving old firm. This picture of stability is supported most strongly by the firm of Gieske & Niemann. Recruited from rural Oldenburg towns into the Hanseatic network, its owners started their business in the 1850s. Owing to their connections to Bremen, their business thrived. By 1865, in the middle of the slow tobacco trade in the summer of that year, they sold 250 hogsheads of tobacco. This firm proved the longest-lived of those active in the 1850s. The last owner, Edward Gieske, sold it in 1993. Quite possibly, it had been the last independently owned tobacco-merchant house in Maryland.[43]

Baltimore Hanseats engaged in a highly successful endeavor: while German firms freighted a share of only 4 percent of all vessels leaving this port, they consigned cargo to about half of those going to Europe. This high share, remarkable for a time when the United States conducted most of their transatlantic trade with Britain, can be explained by the high share of the tobacco trade that Bremen had drawn into its port. From 1851 to 1860, the German share of Baltimore's foreign trade grew from 12 percent to 18 percent and the German share of the European trade grew from 45 percent to 50 percent. During the 1850s, traffic to Bremen increased at a higher rate than that to any other destination, in spite of a decline in the overall share of ships that sailed from Baltimore to engage in foreign trade (Tables 5–7).

Comparing the increase in the number of vessels freighted by Germans with the increase in the number of German firms that consigned cargo to ships leaving Baltimore, we find that the overall volume of trade handled by all German firms grew 2.5 times as much as the volume of trade handled on average by each individual German firm. Although the total amount of cargo shipped by Germans increased by 182 percent, the average amount of cargo shipped by each individual firm grew by 73.5 percent. Much of the growth in the volume of trade between Baltimore and Bremen was picked up by new companies. The number of German firms grew by 62.6 percent (Table 8).

In Table 8, the volume of trade is measured by weight, rather than value. Still, these numbers lend strong support to the conclusion that the Hanseatic network grew faster extensively than it did intensively. It expanded by spawning new firms, thus increasing the capital turned over by each individual firm at a pace much slower than that of the growth of the business handled by the group overall.[44] The pattern of a network growing by spinning off new firms becomes even more clearly visible when we consider the histories of individual merchants, their families, and the firms they founded.

---

[43] Heinrich to Julius Wilkens, May 20, 1865, Wilkens, Julius, 1838?–1898, Papers, 1849–83, MdHS MS.439; Gieske, Edward, in interview with the author of this thesis, February 23, 2001.

[44] This pattern is further supported by Beutin's evidence cited in note 37. The total wealth of Bremen's wealthiest taxpayers grew by 250% between 1813 and 1848, while the wealth of the average individual in this group grew by 41%. Consider for comparison Table 8, which shows that the volume of trade handled by German merchants in Baltimore (most of whom were Hanseats), overall, grew by 182% over the course of the 1850s, while the volume of trade handled by the average individual German firm in Baltimore grew by 78% over the same time period. This comparison might suggest that the pace at which individual firms or families accumulated wealth increased considerably, but still lagged behind the rate at which the group, overall, accumulated wealth.

TABLE 5. *Vessels Cleared at Baltimore Port, March through July 1851*

Destination	Total	Destination Share of Total (percent)	U.S. Consigners	U.S. Consigners' Share to This Destination (percent)	German Consigners	German Consigners' Share to This Destination (percent)
Domestic	451	69	449	100	2	0
Non-U.S. America	166	26	156	94	10	6
Bremen	**8**	**1**	**0**	**0**	**8**	**100**
Non-Bremen Europe[a]	21	3	16	76	5	24
Other	3	0	3	100	0	0
Total	**649**	**100**	**624**	**96**	**25**	**4**
All Europe	29	4	16	55	13	45
All Foreign	198	31	175	88	22	12

[a] Includes Britain and one departure to Hamburg.
Source: Baltimore. *Merchants' Exchange Reading Room, record books, 1832–1899*, 72 vols., MS 610, Manuscripts Department, Maryland Historical Society Library, box 41 (1851) and 44 (1860). Small vessels serving the Chesapeake Bay were not included in these records. The nearest domestic ports listed are Georgetown, D.C., and Philadelphia, PA. The time span from March to July was chosen because traffic increased with the end of winter.

OLD BOYS' NETWORKS

The strong ties among Hanseats in Baltimore, as well as between Hanseats in Baltimore and those in Bremen and New York, were the foundation of the economic stability and success of their business ventures. The Baltimore Hanseatic merchant community of the 1850s encompassed three cohorts. Some firms had been established around 1800, and these were led by merchants born in the United States. The firm of F.W. Brune & Sons was one such enterprise.[45] Another generation of merchants had come to the United States in the 1820s and 1830s. Among them were Heinrich Hermann Graue, Gustav Lürman, and Albert Schumacher. By the 1850s, their firms were well established.[46] A third generation of merchants had come in the 1850s. The numerous brothers Wilkens, the Gieskes, Geyers, and Niemanns were part of that last cohort.[47]

In every case, the reason for these men to move to the United States was their activities as part of the merchant community of Bremen. Once in the United States,

[45] Mustafa, "Hanseatic Cities"; Brune, Frederick W., 1776–1860, Brune Family Papers, 1831–97, MdHS MS.1921.1; Brune, Emily Barton, 1826–1908, Papers, 1782–1972, MdHS MS.2004.
[46] Graue, Heinrich H., fl. 1834–1871, Papers, 1834–1871, MdHS MS.2826; Lurman, Gustavus W., 1809–66, Papers and genealogy, 1833–1945, MdHS MS.541; Lurman, John S., Genealogy of the Lurman and Allied Families, Baltimore, 1904.
[47] Wilkens Papers, MdHS MS.439.

TABLE 6. *Vessels Cleared at Baltimore Port, March through July 1860*

Destination	Total	Destination Share of Total (percent)	U.S. Consigners	U.S. Consigners' Share to This Destination (percent)	German Consigners	German Consigners' Share to This Destination (percent)
Domestic	908	79	906	100	2	0
Non-U.S. America	189	16	171	90	18	10
Bremen	**17**	**1**	**0**	**0**	**17**	**100**
Non-Bremen Europe[a]	37	3	27[b]	73	10	27
Other	5	0	5	100	0	0
Total	**1156**	**100**	**1109**	**96**	**47**	**4**
All Europe	54	4	27	50	27	**50**
All Foreign	248	21	203	82	45	**18**

[a] Includes Britain.
[b] Includes at least two vessels under the flag of Bremen.
Source: Baltimore. *Merchants' Exchange Reading Room, record books, 1832–1899*, 72 vols., MS 610, Manuscripts Department, Maryland Historical Society Library, box 41 (1851) and 44 (1860). Small vessels serving the Chesapeake Bay were not included in these records. The nearest domestic ports listed are Georgetown, D.C., and Philadelphia, PA. The time span from March to July was chosen because traffic increased with the end of winter.

TABLE 7. *Destination of Vessels Cleared at Baltimore Port, 1851 and 1860*

Destination	Absolute Change	Percent Increase of Absolute Numbers
Domestic	+457	+101
Non-U.S. America	+23	+14
Bremen	**+9**	**+113**
Non-Bremen Europe[a]	+16	+76
Other	+2	+66
Total	**+507**	**+78**
All Europe	+25	+86
All Foreign	+50	+25

[a] Includes Britain.
Source: See Tables 5 and 6.

they did not cease to be part of that community. Hanseatic merchants arrived in Baltimore as young men who had just finished their apprenticeship, or had gathered a few years of experience in the merchant firms of their fathers or uncles. In Hanseatic merchant families, the practice of sending young men to America to found their own firms, join partnerships with relatives or acquaintances, or set up a

TABLE 8. *Growth of Hanseatic Business in Baltimore over the Course of the 1850s*

	1851	1860	Increase (percent)
German merchants assigning cargo[a]	8	13	62.6
Vessels sailed, freighted by Germans[a]	25	47	88
Vessels sailed, freighted by Germans, weighted to account for increased size of vessels[b]	25	70.5	182
Vessels (weighted for increased size[b]) freighted by Germans per German firm	3.13	5.42	73.5

[a] In March–July 1851 and March–July 1860, respectively.
[b] Vessel size: 1851 = 100, 1860 = 150. Estimate based on Pitsch, Franz Josef, *Die wirtschaftlichen Beziehungen Bremens zu den Vereinigten Staaten von Amerika bis zur Mitte des 19. Jahrhunderts* (Karl H. Schwebel, ed., Veröffentlichungen aus dem Staatsarchiv der Freien Hansestadt Bremen, vol. 42), Bremen, 1974, 92, who finds that the average Bremish vessel measured 142 *Last* in 1842, and 205 *Last* in 1851; and Handelskammer Bremen, *Berichte der Handelskammer in Bremen für die Jahre 1870–1873, erstattet an den Kaufmanns-Konvent*, Bremen, 1874, 71, according to which the average Bremish sailing vessel measured 369 *Last* in 1872, and 404 *Last* in 1873.
Sources: See notes 40 and 42 and Tables 5 and 6.

branch location for their parent firm dated back to the 1790s, and continues to this day. Older and younger merchants had shared this experience, only at different times.[48]

Much like the merchant class of Bremen, those from their ranks who settled abroad maintained close ties with each other. In Baltimore, the institutional embodiment of group cohesion was the exclusive Germania Club, founded by thirteen men in 1840. By 1844 membership had risen to 105, and growth continued at a slower pace from then on, to reach 156 members by 1860. The four-story clubhouse on Lombard Street housed a bar and restaurant; a library holding the newest German literature and periodicals; a pool table; a lounge; and meeting rooms.[49]

In the letters and papers of Baltimore Hanseats, we find frequent reference to the Germania Club. Among the few items other than the letters that Julius Wilkens kept is a dance card for the German Ball in 1862 and a handwritten invitation for a game of whist by Eduard Schumacher, a fellow mercantile clerk. "Niemann is in for it & I think Bolenius will take a hand," Schumacher had scribbled down. "We might meet at '*Germania*' between 7 ½ –8 p.m."[50] Edward Niemann was one of the

[48] Bohner, Theodor, *Der deutsche Kaufmann über See*, Hamburg, 1956; Müller, Karin, *Die Freie Hansestadt Bremen – Zentrum des Baumwollhandels in Mitteleuropa*, Nürnberg, 1985 (Diplomarbeit, Friedrich-Alexander-Universität Erlangen-Nürnberg, Fachbrereich Betriebswirtschaftslehre), esp. p. 37; Schwebel, "Bremen Merchants"; Schramm, Percy Ernst, *Hamburg, Deutschland und die Welt. Leistung und Grenzen hanseatischen Bürgertums in der Zeit zwischen Napoleon I. und Bismarck. Ein Kapitel deutscher Geschichte*, Munich, 1943.
[49] Cunz, Dieter, *A History of the Germania Club of Baltimore City, Maryland, 1840–1940*, Baltimore, 1940, 7, 10–11, 13.
[50] Dance card, New Assembly Room, February 21, 1862; Eduard Schumacher to Julius Wilkens, September 27, 1861, MdHS MS.439, English in the original. All quotes from German sources were

partners in the firm of Gieske & Niemann, and George Henry Bolenius was an agent at Geyer & Wilkens. Although there was a clear status distinction between associates, agents, clerks, and apprentices, these groups could mingle socially. After all, every associate had started out in a dependent position and knew that those in the lower ranks were possible future partners, friends, or even in-laws.

Club life brought merchants together across the generations. Albert Schumacher was the most prominent member of the Hanseatic merchant community in Baltimore. His ascent to wealth and moderate fame was probably the steepest among his peers. In the 1850s, he moved into a new house, located on fashionable Mt. Vernon Square.[51] In the 1860s, thirty years after his arrival in America, he was still active in the life of the Germania Club. In 1863, Schumacher became its president. Younger men regularly frequented the club to drink, talk, or play billiards. One might imagine that they sought Schumacher's company in the exclusive halls of the clubhouse in order to lay the groundwork for possible future patronage or credit.[52]

Schumacher also contributed financially to the German Society, a benevolent organization to aid needy German immigrants, founded in the 1760s. This philanthropic institution, led by the brothers Cohen from 1825 to 1875, followed a pattern of mercantile welfare activities that was well established in Bremen as well as Hamburg. It differed in one important respect, and that was the cooperation between Jews and gentiles, inconceivable in Bremen. While the funds of the society helped immigrants abroad, the activities of this society reaffirmed patterns of social activity familiar from home. Giving to those in need was considered a duty of a successful merchant. Charity to insolvent German immigrants was also a wise investment. It helped maintain the respectable image of the population on whose continued transportation to America Hanseatic success was founded.[53]

Economically and politically, Hanseats' ties extended beyond their core network. In addition to their mercantile activities, the owners of the older and larger Hanseatic houses often held consulships for German states and directorships of banks. The latter activity attests to their social connections with native members of the Baltimore elite, while the former indicates strong connections home. Albert

---

translated by the author of this paper. If a German author used English in the source, the original language will be identified as such.

[51] Chalfant, Randolp W., "Calvert Station: Its Structure and Significance," *MdHM* 74, no. 1 (March 1979), 11–22, for Schumacher's house, 14; Mayer, Brantz, *Baltimore, As It Was and As It Is: A Historical Sketch of the Ancient Town and Modern City from the Foundation, in 1729, to 1870*, Baltimore, 1871, 449–52; for Schumacher and Heineken as neighbors: Stein, Rudolf, *Klassizismus und Romantik in der Baukunst Bremens*, 2 vols. (Senator für das Bildungswesen, ed., Forschungen zur Geschichte der Bau- und Kunstdenkmäler in Bremen, vols. 4 and 5), Bremen 1964/1965, vol. 2 (1965), *Die Vorstädte und die Stadt-Landgüter Vegesack und Bremerhaven*, 265–9.

[52] Cunz, "Maryland Germans in the Civil War," *Maryland Historical Magazine* 36, no. 4 (December 1941), 415.

[53] Fein, Isaac M., "Baltimore Jews during the Civil War," *American Jewish History Quarterly* 51, no. 2 (1961/62), 67–96; Hennighausen, Louis P., *History of the German Society of Maryland*, Baltimore, 1909, 35–39 on date of foundation, and p. 174 passim for lists of members and officers; Schwarzwälder, *Geschichte*, vol. 2, 244–9; Schulz, Andreas, *Vormundschaft und Protektion. Eliten und Bürger in Bremen 1750–1880* (Stadt und Bürgertum, vol. 13), Munich, 2002 (also Habilitationsschrift, University Frankfurt [Main], 2000), 323–43.

Schumacher was a director of two banks, the Commercial and Farmers' Bank and the Savings Bank of Baltimore. He also served as the consul for Hamburg and Bremen. Henry Oelrichs likewise held a post as a consul, representing the Grand Duchy of Oldenburg, just across the Weser River from Bremen. Oelrichs's partner, Gustav W. Lürman, was a director of the Merchants' Bank, and in this function, he was a colleague of Johns Hopkins. Another person of Hanseatic descent on the board of the Merchants' Bank was John C. Brune. He had joined his father's firm in the 1840s and managed the business on his own after his father's death in 1854. John C. Brune's brother, Frederick William Brune II, a lawyer and brother-in-law of George William Brown, who became mayor of Baltimore in 1860, joined Albert Schumacher for the board meetings of the Savings Bank of Baltimore.[54]

FAMILY NETWORKS

The "old boys' networks" of clubs and countinghouses were not the only ties that bound Bremen's merchants together. The bonds between Hanseatic men rested on family connections, often through multiple intermarriages, and sometimes dating back generations. Intermarriage provided the emotional bonds that invested business relations – even if founded on long personal acquaintance or even friendship – with a necessary element of higher purpose. Family ties also were an essential basis for the cooperation between firms and a major source of capital.

The Lürman Family

Gustav Wilhelm Lürman's vita was exemplary for a Hanseat in the second third of the nineteenth century. He arrived in Baltimore in late 1830 at twenty-one years of age. He had a classically Hanseatic array of merchants, aldermen, and Reformed ministers among his ancestors, and had learned his profession in a Bremish countinghouse before embarking for the New World. En route to Baltimore through Britain, he had arranged to form a business partnership with a distant cousin, E. G. Oelrichs, who lived in London. As their two references, the new firm could cite Nicholas Biddle, president of the Bank of the United States, and the brothers Baring, the British merchant bankers. Oelrichs & Lurman served as exchange agents for the latter and frequently commissioned goods to them.[55]

---

[54] Browne, *Baltimore*, 214; *Mitchett's Baltimore City Director* [sic] *for 1849–50*; Ferslew, *Baltimore City Directory, for 1859–60*.

[55] Lurman, John S., Genealogy; Letter from Gustav Wilhelm Lurman to Col. Hesse, Manchester, August 12, 1830, folder "1817–1865; n.d. Gustav[us] [W.] Lürman – Correspondence," box 1, MdHS MS.541; "Notice of partnership" (November 1, 1830) and handwritten account of the history of his firm by Gustav W. Lürman (1866), folder "1830–1867 E.G. Oelrichs and Lurman Company," box 2, MdHS MS.541. Hidy, Ralph W., *The House of Baring in American Trade: English Merchant Bankers at Work, 1763–1861* (Harvard Studies in Business History, vol. 14), Cambridge, MA, 1949, contains frequent references to the business relation between Baring Bros. and the firm of Oelrichs & Lurman. Lürman's activities clearly contradict Beutin's generalization that Hanseats stayed completely clear of speculation: Lürman was a banker and active commission merchant. Still, Table 12 (Chapter 7) shows that as late as 1860, Lürman derived nearly half his profit from trade carried on his own vessels.

In 1835, Lürman married Frances Donnell, the daughter of a prominent Baltimore merchant of Scottish birth, John Donnell. The previous year, Donnell & Son had failed to meet their obligations toward Baring Bros. It is likely that Oelrichs & Lurman were involved in the settlement that saved the Donnells. Furthermore, a shared Calvinist faith may have facilitated this union. Lürman had attended boarding school in Bückeburg, in the Principality of Schaumburg-Lippe, a hotbed of orthodoxy. The Oelrichs, too, were Reformed Protestants. An eighteenth-century ancestor had been the first Reformed minister in the city of Hannover.[56]

Lürman's ties to Bremen remained strong. Alderman Theodor Gerhard Lürman in Bremen was Gustav W. Lürman's half-brother. This man's sons grew up to become *Senatoren* and judges in Bremen.[57] Through this side of his family, Gustav W. Lürman stayed connected to Bremish decision makers. His mother's family, the Oelrichs, likewise was a presence in all ports where Hanseats did business. Many of them would have recognized Lürman as part of their family network. In 1838, Henry Oelrichs, a brother of E.G. Oelrichs, came to Baltimore to join the firm of E. G. Oelrichs & Lurman as an associate. When the older Oelrichs left Baltimore in 1842, Henry Oelrichs and Gustav W. Lürman founded a new firm, named Oelrichs & Lurman.[58]

The further development of the firm of Oelrichs & Lurman continued to follow a pattern of extended family business. In the mid-1850s, Lürman's son John Stephen, and the firm's clerk, J. Emil Hirschfeld, joined the firm. Hirschfeld, too, was family: the grandson of a daughter from Lürman's father's first marriage.[59] Henry Oelrichs relocated to New York in 1860, and thus left the firm on January 1,

---

[56] Hidy, *House of Baring*, 180; Homepage of the Evangelische Landeskirche Schaumburg-Lippe, http://www.ekd.de/schaumburg/ (accessed April 17, 2001); Lurman, John, *Genealogy*. There is some indication that the connection between the Lürmans and Donnells might date back to 1823. When Louise Kalisky traveled in the United States in that year, she wrote in her diary that "in Baltimore, [on the night of December 11th, 1823,] a very beautiful Mrs. O'Donnell came over for tea, and showered me with kind invitations." Half a year later, Kalisky married Hermann Friedrich von Lengerke, whom she had met in Philadelphia. There, von Lengerke, who had received his mercantile education in Bremen and in a Hanseatic firm in Bordeaux, was an associate in the merchant house of Vezin & Co. Their daughter, Johanne Juliane von Lengerke, was to marry Stephan August Lürman, Gustav W. Lürman's cousin, in 1860. If the von Lengerkes and the Lürmans had been acquainted in the 1820s, which is likely, considering their shared ties to Bremish trade, Gustav W. Lürman may well have come to Baltimore with a recommendation to the Donnells from von Lengerke or his wife. See Louise Kalisky, "Tagbuchauszug der Louise Kalisky (später verh. von Lengerke) *1806, von einem Aufenthalt in den USA, 1.9.1819–1824," folder "Briefe, Tagebuchaufzeichnungen und Dokumente der Familie Lürman in Bremen" (typescript), 17–57, entry of December 11, 1823, 38–41, Staatsarchiv Bremen (from here on abbreviated as StAHB) 7,128, Lürman [family papers], box 1; Julie [Johanne Juliane] Lürman, née von Lengerke, "Etwas aus dem Leben meines lieben Vaters F. v. Lengerke," ibid., 58–9; Hirschfeld, George W., genealogical overview to "Stephan Lürman, Brief an meine Kinder aus 2. Ehe (1813)," typescript 1977, unmarked, orange binder, StAHB 7,128, Lürman [family papers], box 3.

[57] The *Senat* was Bremen's executive body. To avoid confusion with the U.S. legislative body of the same name, the word will be italicized when referring to Bremen.

[58] Lürman, Gustav W., handwritten account, see note 55. Hidy, *House of Baring*, 292.

[59] Hirschfeld, George W., genealogical overview to "Stephan Lürman, Brief an meine Kinder aus 2. Ehe (1813)," typescript 1977, unmarked, orange binder, StAHB 7,128, Lürman [family papers], box 3. Gustav W. Lürman was a son from his father's third and final marriage.

1861.[60] J. E. Hirschfeld left the firm, now called Lurman & Co., by the end of 1865, whereafter father and son ran the business jointly.[61]

When it came to settling Lürman's account after his death in 1866, there were open bills of $169,759.44 to pay. But after settling the estate, enough of Lürman's assets were left to enable his son, John Stephen, to continue the business throughout the rest of the century.[62] Lürman's is a story of success. Few people in 1860s Baltimore would have been able to pay a bill of $170,000. For the sake of comparison, the two men who were by far the richest members of the Maryland legislature in 1861, bank president J. Hanson Thomas and civil engineer Ross Winans owned property (real and personal combined) worth $400,000 and $251,700, respectively. Only two other members of the legislature owned more than $100,000 worth of property.[63]

The Meier Family

The most important Hanseatic firm in New York, likewise, was a tightly knit family concern. Caspar Meier and his brother, Herman Henrich,[64] together with their descendants, had established this most important dynasty of German-American traders of the nineteenth century, based in Bremen and New York. Caspar Meier established his firm in New York in 1798, while Herman Henrich ran the Bremen house. The brothers formed a contract between their houses that established the New York and Bremen firms as branches of the same company:

Any business done by either party for his own account between Europe and America shall be considered as for joint account.... It is therefore agreed that, as an unlimited confidence is to take place, each of the parties shall consent to any shipment made by the other party for the joint account between this place [New York] and Bremen, unless they are of a hazardous nature, it being expected and understood that neither of them would enter into any business which would, reasonably expected, not meet the approbation of the other party.[65]

This contract, which essentially laid the groundwork for a "multinational" enterprise, was repeatedly renewed, even between the successors of the two founding brothers. It was only allowed to expire at the end of 1864.[66]

---

[60] Because Gustav Lürman was a strong supporter of the Confederacy (see Chapter 6), the dissolution of the firm, and Oelrichs' move to New York, might have had to do with political disagreement among the business partners.

[61] Maynard Sons & Co, London, to G. W. Lurman, February 6, 1865; Lurman & Co., notice of change in partnership, January 1, 1861, folder "1830–1867 E.G. Oelrichs and Lurman Company"; Lurman & Co., circular, July 16, 1866, folder "1866, Lurman & Co.," box 2, MdHS MS.541.

[62] Folder "Frances Lurman Donnell – Ledger," folder "Agreements and Covenants," and folder "1866–1867, Gustavus Wilhelm Lurman – Estate Papers," box 1, MdHS MS.541; Bevan, Edith Rossiter, "Willow Brook, Country Seat of John Donnell," *MdHM* 44, no. 1 (March 1949), 33–41, esp. p. 37.

[63] Lurman, John, Genealogy, Wooster, Ralph A., "Sidelights – The Membership of the Maryland Legislature of 1861," *MdHM* 56, no. 1 (March 1961), 94–102, Appendix 1.

[64] Herman Henrich Meier, I. (17**–1821), father of Herman Henrich Meier, II. (1809–98). Unless indicated, reference to Herman Henrich, or H. H., Meier throughout this thesis will mean the younger Meier, the politician and founder of the Lloyd and the Bremer Bank.

[65] Oelrichs & Co., *Caspar Meier and His Successors*, New York, 1898, 19–20.

[66] Ibid., 20.

Meier & Co. of Bremen and New York were not just an example of a multinational family firm; they were also emblematic for the close ties between different families within the Hanseatic network. The Meiers' interests connected seamlessly with those of other Hanseats. In Bremen, Stefan Lürman, father of Gustav Lürman, was a regular correspondent of Caspar Meier's before H. H. Meier & Co. assumed the role of prime business contact for that port. In Baltimore, C. A. Heineken & Co. was the Meiers' main trading partner. This firm came to be known as Albert Schumacher & Co., once its new namesake – a former apprentice in the firm of H. H. Meier & Co. in Bremen – took over as senior associate.[67] The Oelrichs formed an additional link between the Meier and Lürman families. As shown previously, members of the Oelrichs family in Baltimore set up shop with Lürman, while those in New York entered into a partnership with Meier. Meier & Co. of New York changed its name to Oelrichs & Co. in 1852, when Edwin A. Oelrichs became the senior member of the firm.[68]

In linking his firm to additional, well-established Hanseatic families, Caspar Meier strengthened its ties to the overall Bremish network. On a trip to Bremen in 1822, Meier met Lawrence Henry von Post, a clerk in the firm of Meier's brother. He recruited the twenty year old on the spot and took him back to New York, where he made him a partner in his firm in 1826. A year later, von Post was wedded to Meier's eldest daughter, Eliza. Like Meier, von Post had a distinguished lineage of merchants and *Senatoren* on both sides of his family, making him a good choice for a son-in-law.[69] As a junior partner in the firm of Caspar Meier & Co., L. H. von Post followed in his mentor's footsteps, when he went to Bremen in 1833 and picked another of H. H. Meier's clerks, Hermann Oelrichs, as an additional business partner for the New York firm. Oelrichs, then twenty-four years old, gladly accepted the opportunity. He might have had a chance to join his brother, Henry, in Baltimore, but probably found doing business in New York more promising.[70] Another brother of Hermann Oelrichs, Edwin Adalbert, joined the firm as an associate in 1844. In 1852, Caspar Meier's grandson, Herman Caspar von Post, rose from clerk to associate in the countinghouse and stayed with the firm for the rest of the century.[71]

Like von Post, H. H. Meier might have married an American during his stay in Boston as an agent for Meier & Co. in the 1830s. In his own recollection, he had been popular among young Brahmins, who admired his horsemanship, poetry, and rowing. The parents of his prospective bride objected to their marriage, however, and Meier married a fellow Hanseat not long after his return to Bremen. Indicating the degree to which Hanseats could swim in the mainstream of American elite life, Miss Frances E. Appleton later married Henry Wadsworth Longfellow, the poet.[72]

---

[67] Ibid., 27.
[68] Ibid., 32.
[69] Ibid., 22–3.
[70] Ibid., 23.
[71] Ibid., 30–2.
[72] "Longfellow, Henry Wadsworth," *Dictionary of American Biography* 6, New York 1933, 239–40; Hardegen and Smidt, *H. H. Meier*, 30.

CONCLUSION

The way in which Hanseats organized their business partnerships was not exceptional. Business in the antebellum period, especially commerce, was still mostly a
matter of small firms. Two or three owners, actually present in the office, and with
intricate knowledge of the commodities the firm dealt in, usually ran a business.[73]
Yet continuity and stability were not major features of mercantile operations in the
nineteenth century. In this regard, the stories of these Hanseatic families are
remarkable exceptions. What allowed them to keep their firms in the hands of
the family over multiple generations was the closely knit character of their transatlantic community. Across generations and families, Hanseats continued to socialize in clubs and countinghouses, assuring through familiarity the reproduction of
basic, shared attitudes toward business and the stability of the network in times of
crisis.

On the basis of this family network reminiscent of eighteenth-century traders,
Hanseats were able to direct a significant branch of the swelling stream of trans-
atlantic trade to their city.[74] The quick pace of the expansion of Hanseats' share of
American foreign trade was matched by that of the extension of their network.
They founded new firms by giving credit to younger men who had been socialized
into the mercantile estate during long apprenticeships, while expanding the capital
handled by existing firms at a pace that lagged behind the overall growth of business.
More often than not, capital was transferred to new firms or to junior associates in
an existing firm, as a long-term credit or as a dowry.

The way Hanseats did business confirms Marx's assertion that the mercantile
cities looked toward the past. The "livelihood" of the family and its offspring drove
the expansion of the Hanseatic network just as much as did a desire to accumulate
capital. Nevertheless, their traditionalism served Bremen's merchants well. As long
as the linkage between emigration and importation allowed them to offer cheap
freight rates, their business of buying commodities cheaply, while selling them at a
higher price to industrial consumers in Europe, remained profitable. With only a
limited use of modern financial instruments, Hanseats became one of the major
trading partners of the United States in the decades leading up to the Civil War. To
be sure, once Hanseats put their funds into circulation, they were subject to the
exigencies of political economy. On the world market, capital, expertise, prudence,
and reliable business contacts were indispensable ingredients of success. The
Hanseats' transatlantic network amply supplied them with these very ingredients.

In one essential respect, the image of traditionalism does not hold up. As far as
wholesale trade was concerned, Hanseats were uncompromising, radical liberals;
their most prominent employee, the *Handelskammer*'s *Syndikus* Victor Böhmert,
gave voice to this position. As owners of emigrant ships, Hanseats promoted the free

---

[73] Perkins, Edwin J., *Financing Anglo-American Trade: The House of Brown, 1800–1880*, Cambridge, MA,
1975; Pitsch, *Beziehungen*, 197–207; Porter, P. Glenn, and Harold C. Livesay, *Merchants and
Manufacturers. Studies in the Changing Structure of Nineteenth-Century Marketing*, Baltimore, 1971,
esp. pp. 17–22.

[74] Hancock, David, *Citizens of the World: London Merchants and the Integration of the British Atlantic
Community, 1735–1785*, Cambridge and New York, 1995.

flow of people along with that of commodities and money. A closer look at the content of their social and political value systems in the two following chapters, however, will show that we have to recognize the limits of the Hanseats' willingness to embrace the liberal creed, beyond the freedom of trade and circulation. The history of the Hanseats' transatlantic network after 1860, likewise, will illuminate the limits of their peculiar way of doing business, no longer sustainable in a developed, industrial world economy. In the decades between the Napoleonic Wars and the year 1860, however, Bremen's merchants could live in a world that allowed them to stick to their traditions, while contributing to a revolution of this world economy. On the world market, however, Hanseats did not simply rely on "private enterprise," but on their membership in a tightly knit, exclusive group that provided them with indispensable financial, moral, and emotional resources.

2

The Hanseatic Household

Families, Firms, and Faith, 1815–1864

THE SPIRIT OF THE HANSEATIC HOUSEHOLD

We cannot understand Hanseats' performance on the emerging global marketplace without understanding their private lives. We have seen that the family, not the enterprising individual, was the primary unit of Hanseatic business activities. Family life took place in the household, in its broadest sense. The household provided merchants with the emotional, ideological, and financial resources that ensured their success. For analytical purposes, and for the sake of clarity, it makes sense to consider the household separately from Hanseats' political and economic lives. We should, however, keep in mind that for Hanseats, these spheres were not sharply separated. Business ventures, a mercantile ethos, and the political privilege they enjoyed as members of an estate formed the interdependent moments of Hanseat life as a cosmopolitan community.[1]

To Hanseats, family, firm, and faith were equally important in defining who they were. Marriage was not simply a source of capital and business connections. It was a sacred bond between husband and wife, based on a shared commitment to Calvinism. Within the parameters set by this creed, women enjoyed significant independence, financially, politically, and socially. Men and women were held to similar standards of respectability that rested on sound Christian convictions. Together, they actively reproduced an ideology that sanctioned commercial activities. Because Hanseatic men and women considered the welfare of the family as the ultimate end of mercantile enterprise, they were equally committed to upholding the gender arrangements that had proven essential for their success as a group.

The moral economy reproduced within the Hanseatic household served to cement the ties within this transnational community. It imbued its members with the sense of a higher calling. Doing God's work by linking distant lands in commerce was a self-consciously collective effort. At the same time as their beliefs kept Hanseats together, they also linked them to a larger world of Calvinism outside of their immediate

[1] See Beckert, Sven, *The Monied Metropolis: New York City and the Consolidation of the American Bourgeoisie, 1850–1896*, Cambridge, MA, 2001, 17–45, for the role of family ties for the broader merchant class of New York; and Evans, Richard J., "Family and Class in the Hamburg Grand Bourgeoisie 1815–1914," in *The German Bourgeoisie: Essays on the Social History of the German Middle Class from the Late Eighteenth to the Early Twentieth Century*, ed. David Blackbourne and Richard J. Evans, London and New York, 1991, 115–39.

network. Bremen was a point on the Calvinist Axis stretching from Switzerland to New England. These religious ties reinforced those woven by commerce.

Hanseatic children were brought up to perpetuate this cosmopolitan community, by mastering both the rigid demands of traditional, Calvinist morality and the skills required for doing well in a rapidly changing world of markets and machines. In educating their successors, Hanseats relied on the household in its widest sense, encompassing the far-flung family network as well as domestic employees. Thus, in bringing up their children, Hanseats confirmed the mutual dependence of the household and the network of families.

While the ethos that permeated the Hanseatic household united Bremen's merchants with one another and with the larger world of Protestantism, it also established a boundary that separated Hanseats' from other social groups. In interactions with the "lesser sort," Hanseats felt assured of their superior morality. In their minds, diligence, prudence, sobriety, and modesty had not only contributed to their economic success, but also made them models of behavior for those who were not as fortunate. The family home, and the domestic life that filled it, embodied these social distinctions.

Family, firm, and faith were initially united under one roof, that of the counting-house. When Hanseats began to move their residences to the countryside in the second half of the century, they nevertheless insisted on the unbroken continuation of the harmony between the domestic sphere and the marketplace. Still, Hanseatic family homes were increasingly ostentatious, requiring a heightened ideological effort for maintaining the idea of undivided spheres of life governed by the same ethical principles. Up until the 1860s, however, Hanseats clung to the traditional ways that posited their commercial activities as an outgrowth of their communal ethos whose wellspring was the household.

CHRISTIAN SEAFARING

In the winter of 1839, the ship *Pauline*, built for Meier & Co., was ready to leave the slipway. Lucy Meier had asked Gustav B. Schwab to contribute a poem for the ship's christening ceremony. His words provide a synthesis of morality and exchange in "Christian seafaring":

Der, welcher ins Verborg'ne	He who occludes
Des Wassers Tiefen legt,	The waters' depths
Ist's, der auf seiner Rechten	Is who almightily in his right hand
Dies Haus allmächtig trägt.	Carries this house.
Er heftet ihm wie Flügel	Like wings he pins
Gefüllte Segel an;	filled sails to it
In seinem Botendienste	As his messenger
Furcht es den Ozean	It plows the ocean
Und so durch Wellenbrausen,	Thus through the waves' raging
Und so durch Wellenruh	Thus through the waves' calm
Führt es im Tausch die Schätze	It carries treasures in exchange
Getrennten Ländern zu.	Between separate lands.

Zu unsres Bremens Ehre,	To our Bremen's honor,
Zu Deiner Herren Glück,	To your masters' gain,
Mit schwerer Ladung scheide	Leave with a heavy load,
Mit schwerer komm zurück!	And return with one again.[2]

The ship is God's messenger. Her errants have his blessing. He helps her weather the elements, his creation. Exchange between lands separated by oceans is a work worthy of divine support. It is, therefore, a Christian deed to facilitate this exchange. The glory obtained in accomplishing this deed reflects back on the community as honor, and only secondarily on the ship's masters as gain. The commercial success of individual merchants and the honor of their state – the success of the political collective of Hanseatic merchants – reflect God's blessing, earned for doing his work.

Schwab's poem expresses the self-image of Hanseatic merchants. In their minds, their commercial activities answered a higher calling, and the community of Bremish merchants was the basis for their success and their beliefs. It may not be surprising to find merchants convinced that they are following a higher calling in going about their business. It takes some faith to commit one's fortune to an uncertain fate aboard a sailing vessel, and in the market. At first sight, it may be more surprising to see Gustav B. Schwab, the parson of the village of Gomaringen, located in the Kingdom of Württemberg, the hotbed of southwest German anti-commercialism, endorse this Hanseatic view.[3]

Gustav B. Schwab was a family friend of the Meiers, whose acquaintance he had made in 1815 while visiting his old university friend, Pastor Treviranus, in Bremen. In 1823, the recently widowed Lucy Meier had decided to send her youngest son, Herman Henrich, and her daughter, Betty, to be educated in the Stuttgart academy, where Gustav B. Schwab was a teacher at that time. In 1838, in turn, Gustav and Sophie Schwab sent their son, seventeen-year-old Gustav F. Schwab, to be apprenticed as a merchant in the Meiers' countinghouse, where the younger Herman Henrich Meier was about to become an associate. In the 1850s, young Schwab was to become head of the New York branch of Meier's merchant firm. Hence, the christening ceremony of the *Pauline* would have been like a family reunion, bringing together two generations of Meiers and Schwabs.[4]

---

[2] Cited in Hardegen, Friedrich, and Käthi Smidt, geb. Meier, *H. H. Meier, der Gründer des Norddeutschen Lloyd. Lebensbild eines Bremer Kaufmanns, 1809–1898*, Berlin and Leipzig, 1920, 111.

[3] Friedrich List, the father of national economy (as opposed to Adam Smith's "cosmopolitan economy"), was from Württemberg. In his attacks against the Hanseatic cities, contemporaries saw him as a spokesman for Southwestern manufacturers. See List, Friedrich, *The National System of Political Economy*, trans. Sampson S. Lloyd, London, 1928 (1841); Etges, Andreas, *Wirtschaftsnationalismus. USA und Deutschland im Vergleich (1815–1914)*, Frankfurt and New York, 1999.

[4] Klüpfel, Karl [and Sophie], *Gustav Schwab: Sein Leben und Wirken*, Leipzig, 1858, 32–7, 77, 125–6, 321–2; Hardegen/Smidt, H. H. Meier, 6–7, 16. Klüpfel, Gustav Schwab, is a biography of Gustav Benjamin Schwab from the pen of his daughter and son-in-law. For additional detail on the relationship between the Schwab and Meier families, please refer to the original manuscript of the dissertation by the author of this study: Maischak, Lars, "A Cosmopolitan Community: Hanseatic Merchants in the German-American Atlantic of the Nineteenth Century" (Johns Hopkins University, 2005).

Still, Gustav B. Schwab's presence in Bremen in 1839 was not just a matter of accidental family connections. His poetic praise for Hanseatic commerce was not merely a service for old friendship's sake. Between Württemberg and Bremen, there existed a broader connection, resting on, yet going beyond, a shared faith. While technically Lutheran, the State Church of Württemberg had had a distinct Zwinglian influence from the 1530s. Since the 1680s, Pietism, a close relative of Evangelical Protestantism, had gained a strong presence there. This general influence was amplified in the Schwab family. Gustav B. Schwab, the poet, was the son of Johann Christoph Schwab, a philosopher who had spent his formative years in Geneva. Both Gustav and Sophie Schwab had been deeply affected by the revival movement that struck Württemberg after the end of the Napoleonic Wars.[5]

In his evening job as a poet, Schwab had by the time of the *Pauline*'s christening made a name for himself as one of the main exponents of the Swabian School of Poetry. His subjects were the landscape and culture of his native Swabia, the heart of Württemberg. Although his piety alienated him from the radical liberals in the German literary world, Schwab was too much of a rationalist to be subsumed easily under the Romantic label either. His translations of classical Greek mythology into German, and from there into numerous other languages, remain standard versions of these texts to this day. His deep appreciation for the sophistication of these ancients, combined with the rigorously methodical theological training he had received in the seminary of Tübingen University – Hegel's *alma mater* – imbued his faith with a reflexivity that was inimical to the Pietist reliance on the heart alone. In this, Schwab's version of the Protestant creed harmonized with the variety one might find among Bremen's elite.[6]

The friendship between the Schwabs and the Meiers shows that Bremen's elite was a part of a specific, Calvinist segment of the larger world of the German educated bourgeoisie (*Bildungsbürgertum*). This Calvinist current, however, was not limited to Germany, but linked its members to fellow believers across the world.

THE CALVINIST AXIS

Bremen and Württemberg were located on what one might call a Calvinist Axis that connected the scattered strongholds of this creed, and which included Bremen, the Principality of Schaumburg, parts of Württemberg and of Northern Baden, the area around Heidelberg, and much of Switzerland. Connections between Bremen and Württemberg were not exclusively based on this shared faith, but the shared faith facilitated a dense web of business, family, and educational ties. Württemberg was a major source of wine and emigrants, both essential items in Bremen's shipping business. Hanseats who traveled to the southwest might seek an education at Tübingen University, with its renowned faculties of theology and law. They

---

[5] Evangelische Landeskirche in Württemberg, Die Geschichte der Evangelischen Landeskirche in Württemberg, http://www.elk-wue.de/landeskirche/zahlen-und-fakten/geschichte-der-landeskirche/ (accessed November 16, 2005); Fischer, Hermann, "Schwab, Gustav [Benjamin]," *Allgemeine Deutsche Biographie* 33, 153–5; Gatter, Nikolaus, "Schwab, Gustav Benjamin," *Neue Deutsche Biographie* 23, Berlin, 2007, 772–4; Klüpfel, *Gustav Schwab*, 37, 84–5.

[6] Klüpfel, *Gustav Schwab*, 84–5.

might look for recreation in the Black Forest, on the highland of the Swabian Alb, or on the shores of Lake Constance. Bonds forged in commerce or education would last over generations, with families sending their children to Württemberg for their primary or academic education, or to Bremen for a mercantile apprenticeship. Württembergers who vacationed on the seashore might stop over in Bremen on their way.

Senator John Meier and his daughters were frequent visitors to Württemberg. Conversely, whenever the Schwabs went to Bremen, visits with the various Meiers in town were always part of the program.[7] Judge C. W. Pauli of Lübeck had been friends with Gustav B. Schwab since their days in the Tübingen seminary in the 1810s. Pauli had known Sophie Schwab since before her marriage to Gustav B. Schwab in 1818, and remained friends with the family throughout his life. On several occasions in the 1850s, he visited Sophie Schwab, now widowed, and kept up an exchange of letters with her, sometimes sending her presents. Among those presents, the biography of Pauli's pious cousin, the Protestant reformer Amalie Sieveking, was Sophie Schwab's favorite.[8]

In other places along the Calvinist Axis, merchants' biographies intersected as well. During the Napoleonic Wars, C. W. Pauli's family had lived in Bückeburg, the seat of government of Schaumburg. In the same town, young Gustav W. Lürman was a student in a boarding school in 1817. Decades later, Herman Henrich Meier (II) was to represent the principality in the German *Reichstag*.[9] Neighboring Lippe-Detmold, with its fashionable spa of Pyrmont and its natural wonders was a meeting place of German nobility and mercantile aristocracy during the summers.[10]

Personal friendships along the Calvinist Axis were not limited to the Schwabs and Meiers, but extended to other important Hanseatic families. The Vietor family in Bremen maintained close ties to the New York and Stuttgart Schwabs. Vietor & Co. was the main business partner of Schwab & Recknagel in New York, and frequently conveyed items sent as presents between the branches of the family as part of their regular shipments to and from the United States, which included emigrants from Württemberg.[11] When the Vietors traveled to Stuttgart in 1857,

[7] Sophie Schwab to Gustav F. Schwab, Stuttgart August 2 (b), 1857, MSS 434, John Christopher Schwab Family Papers. Manuscripts and Archives, Yale University Library, series I, box 2, folder 34; and Stuttgart, November 11, 1860, MSS 434, Schwab Papers, series I, box 2, folder 36. Sophie Schwab and Christoph Th. Schwab to Gustav F. Schwab, Stuttgart, April 9, 1861, MSS 434, Schwab Papers, series I, box 2, folder 37. Christoph Th. Schwab to Gustav F. Schwab, Stuttgart, September 28, 1859, MSS 434, Schwab Papers, series I, box 2, folder 35.

[8] Klüpfel, *Gustav Schwab*, 31–7, 77, 301; Sophie Schwab to Gustav F. Schwab, Stuttgart, August 2 (b), 1857 and August 28, 1857, MSS 434, Schwab Papers, series I, box 2, folder 34; Stuttgart, April 1, 1860, MSS 434, Schwab Papers, series I, box 2, folder 36.

[9] Klüpfel, *Gustav Schwab*, 31, 37; Gustav Wilhelm Lürman to Charlotte Lürman, n.d. [1817], folder "1817–1865, n.d.; Gustav[us] [W.] Lürman – Correspondence," box 1, MdHS MS.541; Hardegen/Smidt, H. H. Meier, 224.

[10] Möller, Kurt Detlev, "Zur Politik der Hansestädte im Jahre 1806," *Zeitschrift des Vereins für Hamburgische Geschichte* 41 (1951) (Festschrift für H. Reincke), 330–52; Lippe, Pauline, Fürstin zur, *Eine Fürstin unterwegs. Reisetagebücher der Fürstin Pauline zur Lippe, 1799–1818*, ed. Hermann Niebuhr (Lippische Geschichtsquellen, vol. 19), Detmold, Germany, 1990.

[11] Sophie Schwab to Gustav F. Schwab, Stuttgart, August 28, 1857, MSS 434, Schwab Papers, series I, box 2, folder 34; Stuttgart, April 3, 1858, MSS 434, Schwab Papers, series I, box 2, folder 35.

they attend the German Protestant Convention (*Kirchentag*) in that city, a gathering bringing together the pious of all regional Protestant churches.[12] The house of Noltenius in Bremen, likewise, was involved in varied exchanges along the Calvinist Axis. Like the Vietors, they facilitated transactions between New York and Stuttgart, and went to both places for vacation, education, and business. When Sophie Klüpfel, Sophie Schwab's daughter, traveled to the North Sea to reconvalesce after a lengthy illness, she availed herself of this established network, paying a visit to the Noltenius in Bremen, before journeying on to the island of Norderney, where she stayed in a guesthouse recommended by one of the Vietor's daughters and run by a pastor's widow.[13]

But Calvinism was not limited to Germany. Abroad, Hanseats found fellow believers across the Atlantic World. Like their pious eighteenth-century predecessors, Hanseats considered this ocean as "the great Sea of Protestant Industry," where Bremen's ships were on the same mission as their Scottish, Dutch, and New England sisters.[14] Thus Hanseats' beliefs connected them to a transatlantic space just as much as it made them a part of the German educated bourgeoisie. Like their vessels, which the Lord carried in his right hand, so the network of Hanseatic families relied on a religious basis to give meaning and strength to their personal and public endeavors. They found this basis in Calvinism, whose global extent conveniently matched that of their business interests. Families and firms were intertwined through numerous connections between different kinship networks, and ships connecting ports on two continents carried the cargo that built the economic foundation of these networks. Hanseats infused the entirety of these personal and public links with religious meaning.

Family ties played a particularly central role in the world that Hanseats made. Marriage was expressly charged with religious significance, intermarriage was a major tool of pooling capital resources, and family life was the location in which a comprehensive ideology linking families, firms, and faith was constantly recreated in the negotiations between the genders over the allocation of emotional and financial resources.

MOTHERS, SISTERS, AND WIVES

Kinship, friendship, and business interest overlapped to provide multiple connections between Hanseats in Bremen, Baltimore, and New York. Memories of a childhood or an apprenticeship shared in Bremen, refreshed by correspondence, trade, or joint summer vacations, formed a strong bond among the male heads of Hanseatic firms. Nevertheless, women played a central role in establishing and maintaining the ties between Hanseatic families − unmarried Albert Schumacher,

---

[12] Sophie Schwab to Gustav F. Schwab, Stuttgart, October 17–19, 1857, MSS 434, Schwab Papers, series I, box 2, folder 34.

[13] For this and further examples, see Sophie Schwab to Gustav F. Schwab, Stuttgart, February 26, 1860, April 1, 1860, and June 29–30, 1860; Niedernau, June 22, 1860 (folder 36); Sophie Schwab to Gustav F. Schwab, Stuttgart, April 9, 1861 and May 9, 1861 (folder 37), MSS 434, Schwab Papers, series I, box 2, folder as indicated.

[14] Kiesselbach, Wilhelm, *Der Gang des Welthandels im Mittelalter*, Bremen, 1860.

the Bremish consul in Baltimore, tended to drop off the social map for prolonged periods of time.[15]

Marriage helped to cement and rejuvenate Hanseatic family networks. Men apparently could more easily marry outside of Hanseatic society, especially if the connections they established brought with them added opportunities for trade. Hanseatic women seemed more likely to marry a young man already recruited into the network as an apprentice or associate. Whether his background had originally been a Hanseatic one seemed secondary. The five or more years spent in the countinghouse during a formative time of any man's life would have given him a sufficiently Hanseatic socialization. It would be misguided, however, to conclude that women played a subordinate role in Hanseatic family life. As guardians of existing family ties, and as those who established new ones, women had a centrally important role to fill.

An astonishing number of Hanseats lost their fathers at an early age. Hermann Henrich Meier's father died in 1821, when his son was eleven years old.[16] Gustav Lürman lost his father in 1816, at the tender age of seven.[17] Rudolf Schleiden could almost count himself lucky to have grown to age eighteen by the time his father died in distant Mexico in 1833, though, at that point, father and son had not seen each other in more than two years.[18] Eleven-year-old Laurence Henry von Post was orphaned in 1839. He and his four sisters were left to the care of their grandmother.[19] As men worked themselves to an early death in mercantile professions, the importance of mothers grew beyond the task of bringing up sons and daughters to include the burden of keeping together a family and its fortune. This burden included maintaining ties with other families and assuring a smooth succession at the head of the family firm.[20]

Even when their husbands were still alive, relations between mothers linked different families with each other, cementing connections among Hanseatic merchants in Bremen, Baltimore, and New York. For example, the mother and sister of Julius Wilkens were friends with the mother of Johann Stellmann, co-owner of the house of Stellmann & Hinrichs in Baltimore. Eleonore Wilkens wrote to her brother: "I visited Madame Stellmann. They have a nice house on

---

[15] On one occasion, Rudolf Schleiden, who complained about Schumacher's elusiveness, expressed worry to Gustav F. Schwab because he had not heard from Schumacher in a while: Rudolf Schleiden to Gustav F. Schwab, Brattleboro, August 29, 1860 and August 31, 1860; and Newport, September 19, 1860, MSS 434, John Christopher Schwab Family Papers. Manuscripts and Archives, Yale University Library, series I, box 2, folder 38.

[16] Hardegen and Smidt, *H. H. Meier*, 10.

[17] Hirschfeld, George W., genealogical overview to "Stephan Lürman, Brief an meine Kinder aus 2. Ehe (1813)," typescript 1977, unmarked, orange binder, StAHB 7,128, Lürman [family papers], box 3.

[18] Schleiden, Rudolph, *Jugenderinnerungen eines Schleswig-Holsteiners*, Wiesbaden, 1886, 84–5, 146, 171–3. It took three months for the news of his father's death to reach Schleiden. Apparently, he only had a chance to visit the grave in 1853.

[19] Oelrichs & Co., *Caspar Meier and His Successors*, New York, 1898, 32.

[20] The prevalence of financially independent widows in the larger circles of the German bourgeoisie is suggested by the story of Rosa Sutro, mother of Otto and Emma Sutro. After the death of her husband, a textile manufacturer in Aachen, in the Prussian Rhineland, Rosa Sutro took the children to Baltimore, where she apparently ran a business as a textile importer. Scharf, J. Thomas, *History of Baltimore City & County*, 2 vols., Philadelphia, 1881, vol. 2, 673–4.

Kohlhökerstraße."[21] Madame Stellmann was apparently part of a larger circle of women. Johann Georg Graue wrote to his brother, Heinrich Hermann, in 1856 that their mother, Mrs. Stellmann, and Mrs. Hinrichs planned to travel to Baltimore together to visit their sons and their families. This circle of matriarchs in Bremen thus established a link between at least four of the Hanseatic firms in Baltimore.[22]

Considering their importance for keeping the family together, whether or not their husbands were still alive, the presence of strong and independent women in Bremish circles was not surprising. Widowed in 1821, Lucy Meier was typical for a Hanseatic lady of her house. She had entered her marriage to Herman Henrich Meier (I) with a substantial endowment that contributed to the initial capital stock of H. H. Meier & Co. As was customary, the spouses' stakes in the business were kept separate by a prenuptial agreement. The older H. H. Meier was in charge of day-to-day business decisions, but we can assume that he would have considered his wife's opinion before making major investments.[23]

After her husband's death, full control over her capital reverted back to Lucy Meier. Other merchants' widows before her had been known to run a counting-house while the sons were not yet of age. In the Meiers' case, the oldest son, Hermann Henrich, was years from reaching his twenty-first birthday. Lucy Meier kept her late husband's associate, Johann Helfrich Adami, in charge of the firm.[24]

While leaving countinghouse operations to Adami, Lucy Meier stayed in control of hiring policies for H. H. Meier & Co. To decide who became an apprentice meant to control who would become an associate. By keeping these choices to herself, Lucy Meier made sure not to yield influence over the future direction of the firm to Adami, whose own sons might otherwise have risen within its ranks. One way of keeping her sway over the firm was to pick an apprentice from a family with no prior mercantile interests of its own, but with a background that guaranteed the young man's sound morality. In 1829, when visiting the Schwabs in Stuttgart, Lucy Meier offered that if they picked one of their sons for a mercantile career, she would ensure that he would be trained alongside her own sons in Adami's countinghouse. The choice fell on six-year-old Gustav F. Schwab.[25] Almost three decades later, when Gustav F. Schwab was made a partner in the firm of Oelrichs & Co. in New York, his mother, Sophie Schwab, wrote that "this would have been to the wishes of Madame Meier, and she may already have foreseen this, when she called you to Bremen."[26]

---

[21] Eleonore to Julius Wilkens, Bremen, December 19, 1862, MdHS MS.439. Cunz, *Germania Club*, 7. Kohlhökerstraße was one of the first addresses in the new suburbs. See the discussion on 3–3, in the following text, and Map 1.

[22] Johann Georg to Heinrich Hermann Graue, May 14, 1856, Graue, Heinrich H., fl. 1834–1871, Papers, 1834–1871, MdHS MS.2826, box 4. These firms were Stellmann & Hinrichs, Wilkens & Geyer, Graue & Co., and Wilkens & Niemann, and possibly further ventures by other relatives. On Stellmann, see Scharf, *History of Baltimore City & County*, vol. 1, 417–18.

[23] Hardegen and Smidt, *H. H. Meier*, 10.

[24] The firm of "Johann Lange's Son's Widow & Co." (Joh. Lange Sohns Wittwe & Co.) is a case in point. Oelrichs & Co., *Caspar Meier and His Successors*, 35.

[25] Klüpfel, Karl, *Gustav Schwab*, 126.

[26] Sophie Schwab to Gustav F. Schwab, Tübingen, October 22, 1858, MSS 434, Schwab Papers, series I, box 2, folder 35.

In 1836, when Lucy Meier's own son, Hermann Henrich, then an employee of the firm, wanted to be transferred from Boston to New York, he lobbied his mother, rather than Adami. Meier and Adami, however, agreed that the young man – then twenty-seven years old – was not yet ready for the big city. He had recently lost significant amounts speculating in land in the American West, and his mother had used her own funds to cover these losses. Although designated as the future head of the firm, H. H. Meier had yet to arrive at a point where he was deemed experienced enough to be put in charge of business at the most important American port. Lucy Meier wanted to be certain that her heir would be a conscientious caretaker of the family business. Perhaps the choice of young Gustav F. Schwab, son of her closest friend, was meant as insurance for the case that her own Herman Henrich did not turn out as desired and failed to shed his proclivity for haughtiness and recklessness.[27]

HANSEATIC WOMEN AND THE FAMILY FORTUNE

In Germany and in the United States, where women had gained more rights to financial independence in marriage, Hanseatic marriages were usually accompanied by prenuptial agreements.[28] Even absent such agreements, families made sure that their daughters would retain some financial independence in marriage. For example, Frances Donnell Lürman, Gustav Lürman's wife, kept her estate separate from his in their marriage.[29] For his daughters, Gustav F. Schwab prescribed "that the portion of my property and estate which may go under this will to any female is to be for her own sole and separate use, free from control of any husband," following the standard usage of Hanseats.[30] And when H. H. Meier's brother, Judge Diedrich Meier, died, another brother of theirs, *Senator* John Meier, married the widow, Meta – a move that helped to consolidate the family fortune and that was approved by the family and its friends.[31]

These gender arrangements were rarely discussed in public as long as they could be taken for granted. Hanseats simply seemed to assume that their wives would be financially independent and created the legal conditions to this end. Germanic (common) law, which assumed coverture and joint property (*Gütergemeinschaft*) under the control of the husband, did not recognize prenuptial agreements that

---

[27] Hardegen and Smidt, *H. H. Meier*, 30.

[28] Chused, Richard H., "Married Women's Property Law, 1800–1850," *Georgetown Law Journal* 71, no. 5 (June 1983), 1359–1426. See also Hartog, Hendrik, *Man and Wife in America: A History*, Cambridge, MA, 2000.

[29] Folder "Frances Lurman Donnell – Ledger," folder "Agreements and Covenants," and folder "1866–1867, Gustavus Wilhelm Lurman – Estate Papers," box 1, MdHS MS.541, Lurman, Gustavus W., 1809–66, Papers and genealogy, 1833–1945; Bevan, Edith Rossiter, "Willow Brook, Country Seat of John Donnell," *MdHM* 44, no. 1 (March 1949), 33–41, esp. p. 37; Lürman, Gustav W., manuscript account of the history of his firm (1866), folder "1830–1867 E.G. Oelrichs and Lurman Company," box 2, MdHS MS.541; Lurman, John, *Genealogy*; Wooster, Ralph A., "Sidelights – The Membership of the Maryland Legislature of 1861," *MdHM* 56, no. 1 (March 1961), 94–102, Appendix 1.

[30] Gustav F. Schwab, Will, New York, April 18, 1877, MSS 434, Schwab Papers, series I, box 2, folder 61.

[31] Sophie Schwab to Gustav F. Schwab, Stuttgart, August 1, 1858, MSS 434, Schwab Papers, series I, box 2, folder 35.

established separate estates. Yet, in Bremen, they were legalized under provisions borrowed from Roman law.[32] Although prenuptial agreements remained heavily regulated and had even been officially discouraged by Bremish law since 1754, in practice they were the norm in mercantile marriages.[33]

Hanseats valued the independence of the women of their estate as a part of their traditional practices. The basis of their economic activities was the household, encompassing the countinghouse and country home in an arrangement between the genders that did not yet draw a clear line between a male (public) and a female (private) sphere. In this world of intertwined families and firms, women had more power than under a modern regime of legal codes based on the person as a subject of rights, which limited women's claims to personal rights.

The modernization of law implemented by German legal reformers in the mid-nineteenth century tended to grant equal rights to males, while abolishing the ancient privileges that had benefited elite women. In early 1863, a bill to make the new German Commercial Code (*Allgemeines Deutsches Handelsgesetzbuch*) part of Bremish law was before the *Bürgerschaft* (legislature).[34] The *Handelskammer* – the official organ of the mercantile estate – initially embraced the new legal foundation for business transactions, because it would standardize procedures across the different German states, facilitating trade with the hinterland.[35] When Hanseats realized that the new code threatened existing gender arrangements, however, they adamantly defended the financial independence of the female members of their estate, framing their position as an appeal to the protection of orphans and widows.

One of the key innovations inscribed throughout the proposed Commercial Code was the idea of the corporation as a natural person. In Bremish law, as in all countries under simple Roman law or common Germanic law, only individuals could own property. Under the old laws, the capital a merchant invested in his firm

---

[32] Schnelle, Albert, *Bremen und die Entstehung des allgemeinen deutschen Handelsgesetzbuches (1856–1864)* (Wilhelm Lührs, ed., Veröffentlichungen aus dem Staatsarchiv der Freien Hansestadt Bremen, vol. 57), Bremen, 1992, 112–14, and notes 234, 237, and 238 to these pages.

[33] Ibid., 112–14, and notes 234, 237, and 238 to these pages. In many instances, local law under the old Holy Roman Empire of the German Nation was drafted officially to comply with Reich standards, while local jurisdiction would continue to follow traditional practice, creating a wide divergence between the text and the reality of the law. A well-known example is the Reichshandwerksordnung of 1734, which was intended to curb the power of guilds, and was frequently sabotaged by local courts and authorities. The same might have applied to Bremish marital law, considering that the 1754 law followed a Reich mandate to curb female financial independence. See Stürmer, Michael, ed., *Herbst des Alten Handwerks. Meister, Gesellen, und Obrigkeit im 18. Jahrhundert*, Munich, 1986; Grießinger, Andreas, and Reinhold Reith, "Obrigkeitliche Ordnungskonzeptionen und handwerkliches Konfliktverhalten im 18. Jahrhundert. Nürnberg und Würzburg im Vergleich," in *Deutsches Handwerk in Spätmittelalter und Früher Neuzeit*, ed. Rainer S. Elkar (Göttinger Beiträge zur Wirtschafts- und Sozialgeschichte, vol. 9), Göttingen, 1983, 117–80.

[34] Schnelle, *Handelsgesetzbuch*, for the history of this work of law. Drafted by a committee convened by the German Confederation, this law, like all laws emanating from this loose political framework, had to be made into law by the states, and would not automatically take effect in any state that did not adapt it.

[35] Although *Handelskammer* technically translates as *chamber of commerce*, the German original seems more appropriate to be used, because the English term, especially in its American context, fails to convey the corporatist connotation and medieval origins of the Bremish body. For a detailed discussion of the institutions of Bremen's government and their respective roles, see Chapter 3.

remained indistinguishable from his private funds.[36] As a consequence, a widow or an orphan would inherit the entirety of a deceased husband's or father's property, including any part invested in a mercantile business. Moreover, funds that had been brought into a marriage by a wife, and kept separate from her husband's fortune in a prenuptial agreement, would revert to her in the case of her husband's death, even if her capital had been invested in his firm.[37]

The modern legal construct of the corporation called into question existing arrangements between the genders. Under the new commercial code, capital invested in a business became the property of that abstract entity, the corporation-as-natural-person, and was no longer at the unconditional disposal of the original investor, an actual person. Creditors could directly hold the corporation accountable for its debts and did not have to rely on the solvency of any of its owners. More importantly, according to the new law, creditors' claims preceded heirs' claims to corporate funds. If a deceased merchant had left behind a failed company, his widow would have no way of rescuing her funds from the remaining assets of the company. Instead, any proceeds from assets would first have to be employed to pay off creditors.[38]

The *Senat*, which had at first wholeheartedly supported the new Commercial Code, reversed its position once its members realized the full implications of the new idea of the corporation. In its ultimate statement against an unaltered implementation of the code, the *Senat* based its case on an argument in favor of traditional marriage arrangements:

In considering our peculiar social circumstances and legal institutions, the *Senat* cannot consider the introduction of that principle, which holds that a commercial association owns its particular funds as a corporation; nor that of the consequences that follow from this principle, as well-advised. If this principle is introduced, it will impair the inner conditions and the well-being of families and their fortunes.... It will annul rights whose abolition may, in the case of bankruptcies, cause the loss of entire fortunes. This principle, therefore, has to be removed [from the Code].[39]

By the early 1860s, many leading Hanseats had become convinced that a modernization of Bremen's legal system was a necessity. Creating compatible standards throughout the area in which they did business was a matter of staying competitive. The new model of the corporation promised to ease the recovery of outstanding debt from a failed company, adding a measure of accountability beyond the trust in a person's good name. These considerations had driven the initial approval among mercantile representatives in the *Handelskammer* and the *Senat*. It was for the same reasons that H. H. Meier favored the principle of the corporation-as-natural-person in his speeches in the *Bürgerschaft*, and that a majority of that body was willing to follow his lead.[40]

---

[36] Schnelle, *Handelsgesetzbuch*, 90–122, esp. pp. 91–2.

[37] Ibid., 209–16.

[38] Ibid., 112–15.

[39] Cited from Schnelle, *Handelsgesetzbuch*, 208–9.

[40] Ibid., 195–213.

In spite of a widely held conviction among Hanseats that the international standardization of laws was good for business, many merchants were willing to put family fortunes first. The *Senat*'s veto against the *Bürgerschaft*'s endorsement of the new Commercial Code gave voice to these reservations. It took another year of negotiations between the two organs, until the spring of 1864, before a compromise was reached that made it possible to accommodate the Hanseats' conflicting desires.[41]

The resulting law introduced the new idea of the corporation into Bremish law, in principle, while allowing for a continuation of the customary gender arrangements, in particular. Paragraphs 16 and 52 of the law that implemented the Commercial Code in Bremen created two groups of private debtors who were defined as privileged claimants on corporate funds: children and wives. The capital that had been brought into a corporation by a man who did not own this capital, but merely held it in trust for a wife or child, was to be identified in the books and to be treated as separate from the total funds of the corporation for purposes of inheritance.[42]

This compromise established the corporation-as-natural-person in Bremish law. The one item it salvaged from the old legal tradition was the peculiar gender arrangement that ensured the independent role of merchants' wives. If those merchants who had initially supported the unaltered introduction of the new Commercial Code had been categorically opposed to a continuation of the traditional gender arrangements, this compromise would not have been possible. The outcome of the legislative process thus suggests that, even as many Hanseats began to advocate a departure from the accustomed ways of their estate, a majority was so committed to the traditional gender arrangements that they were willing to incur a competitive disadvantage by blocking a standardization of German law, if this was necessary to save women's financial independence.

Twentieth-century commentators and scholars of German law have denounced this compromise as contradictory and exceptional, because it failed to carry through the principle of the modern corporation. Albert Schnelle, on whose work this account of the legal tradition of Bremish commercial law and the principles of the new German Commercial Code rests, faults the *Senat* for "entirely ignoring economic considerations, which would have had to favor a separation of [private and company] funds." Somewhat puzzled by his discovery, Schnelle found that what he regarded as an *extraeconomic* consideration was paramount in the eyes of many Hanseats: the family fortune and especially the welfare of widows and orphans.[43]

Counter to this somewhat teleological account of legal modernization, which perceives the introduction of the corporation-as-natural-person as a logical and

---

[41] Ibid., 212–17.
[42] Ibid., 214–15.
[43] Schnelle, *Handelsgesetzbuch*, 209. On p. 114, note 237, Schnelle acknowledges that marriage was an economic act, yet fails to apply this insight in the main body of his text, and contradicts it throughout the remainder of his discussion of the merits of traditionalists' opposition to the new legal principle of the corporation-as-natural person.

necessary step to a rational economic order, and thus as an innovation that merchants ought to have viewed as serving their best interest, Hanseats' experience led them to attribute central importance to the family as a key institution for their economic success. Their ardent defense of the specific legal arrangements that defined the traditional relations between husbands and wives in their domestic life – most of all, prenuptial agreements – was thus not driven by extraeconomic considerations. Rather, it reflected a different definition of *the economy* – one that operated from the basis of the household, not from the logic of a purely profit-maximizing individual.

In the larger picture of international legal development, Hanseats' defense of their peculiar family arrangements was a battle of retreat. But it was nevertheless a battle tradition-minded Hanseats wished to pick. Considering the ubiquity of the practice of prenuptial agreements, the contribution of women to their husband's firm, and the ties between families established by the transfer of capital into newly formed marriages, we can conclude that the specific arrangement between the genders in Hanseatic families was somewhere very near the core of their social identity. After all, marriage was what connected families and firms. The nexus of family and fortune, moreover, invested business with a certain moral quality arguably lacking from the depersonalized corporation that legally personifies capital in the abstract. Hanseats did not think of themselves as mere agents of the "automatic subject," capital, but as providers of a public good. Families not only bundled and focused capital streams, but did the same for the reproduction of this ideology.

HUSBAND AND WIFE IN THE CHRISTIAN FAMILY

Family ties played a crucial economic role for Hanseats, and women played a central part in perpetuating the household as an economic unit. At the same time, marriage, and the gender arrangements within the family, established an indispensable moral household. In Hanseats' minds, the respectability and independence of husbands and wives – their moral and economic existence alike – rested on a shared faith and on the sanctity of the bonds of marriage which it tied. For Hanseats, the family as an economic unit and the family as a bulwark of faith were one and the same.

The idea of marriage as a sacred compact against original sin, which they shared with fellow Reformed Protestants, was one of the cornerstones of Hanseats' morality. Gustav B. Schwab, the poet, summed up the function of marriage in a letter to his future wife, Sophie, in 1817:

> My temperament will certainly never leave me alone; I think, however, that when one is united in an honest striving towards heaven – when one reads together in the Holy Scripture, when one prays together daily – that then, one might be too ashamed, on the very same day that one solemnly practiced those holy acts together, to submit oneself to sin, to anger, to fervor, or to other passions.[44]

Gustav F. Schwab shared his father's take on marriage. His letters to his wife, Eliza, breathe the spirit of the poet's words. They bespeak a constant, conscious struggle

---

[44] Gustav B. Schwab to Sophie Gmelin, n.p. 1817, quoted in Klüpfel, *Gustav Schwab*, 89–90.

with temptations – a struggle fought and won in each instance in the name of the spouses' joint commitment to Christian morality.

After a few months of business travel through Italy, where he had often felt strangely enchanted by the pagan art of classical cultures, Schwab turned his steps back north. As he was returning within the orbit of Protestantism, he reassured himself and his wife of the firmness of his Christian convictions:

> Today, I took part in the Lord's Supper in the Lutheran church here [in Venice]. I much regretted that once again you and I could not enjoy the Holy Communion on this Holiday [Easter], together.... After so much diversion it is edifying to collect one's mind; and before this spiritual nourishment, all the enjoyment of the arts pales as a weak likeness of eternal beauty and truth. I am glad that you, too, will take communion tomorrow, and I hope it will be a blessing for both of us, and that next time we can celebrate it together all the more joyfully.[45]

Like his father, Gustav F. Schwab considered Christianity a bond between husband and wife, and marriage a bond between man and his God. These bonds were all the more necessary, since mankind, and the educated bourgeoisie in particular, had enjoyed the apple of ancient art and learning – while more dangerous varieties of produce were within their reach:

Der neueste Sündenfall	*The New Fall from Grace*
Du arme Menschheit wie mir graut	Oh poor humanity, I dread
Vor deinem bösen Gestirne:	The fate you have to bear:
Kaum hast du den alten Apfel verdaut,	The apple eaten, in its stead,
So beißest Du in die Birne.	You now reach for the pear.
	(Gustav B. Schwab)[46]

Still, marriage did not necessarily imply a submission of wives to husbands. Rather, Christianity suggested to Hanseats that men and women jointly submit to a specific morality. On that basis, there was a proper role for independent women as well. The conditions and boundaries of this independence were defined by the values Hanseats shared with other Reformed Protestants, in Germany and abroad.

In the world of the predominantly Protestant German *Bildungsbürgertum*, some women could make an independent living, for example as authors or teachers. Sophie Klüpfel, née Schwab, Gustav F. Schwab's sister, was the primary author of the biography of their father, the poet Gustav B. Schwab. The sales of this book helped to augment her husband's meager salary as a professor.[47]

---

[45] Gustav F. Schwab to Eliza Schwab, Venice, March 20, 1856, MSS 434, Schwab Papers, series I, box 1, folder 33.

[46] In "Unter Vaters Papieren gefunden" ["Found among father's papers"] (manuscript notebook of unpublished poems by Gustav F. Schwab, compiled posthumously by Sophie Schwab), n.d. (before 1850), MS 434, Schwab Papers, series II, box 17, folder 213.

[47] Klüpfel, *Gustav Schwab*, while published under her husband's name, is identified by Sophie Schwab as authored by her daughter, see Sophie Schwab to Gustav F. Schwab, Stuttgart, March 21, 1857, MSS 434, Schwab Papers, series I, box 2, folder 34. For Klüpfel's salary of 1,000 fl, and the financial success of the book, see Sophie Schwab to Gustav F. Schwab, Stuttgart, August 2 (b), 1857, MSS 434, Schwab Papers, series I, box 2, folder 34, and Stuttgart, January 16, 1859, MSS 434, Schwab Papers, series I, box 2, folder 35. By contrast, Ludmilla Assing reputedly received 1,500 fl per edition of her book (see note 488).

Through her late husband, the poet, Sophie Schwab was acquainted with many female writers of her time and commented on their works in her letters. For example, she condemned what she saw as the moral laxity of Ludmilla Assing's works. Assing's edition of the spicy letters exchanged between two major figures of the German Enlightenment, Alexander von Humboldt and K. A. Varnhagen von Ense (her uncle), was a best seller. Proceeds from its sale provided Assing with the income necessary to sit out an arrest warrant for indecency in a comfortable exile in Florence. By contrast, Sophie Schwab highly praised Amalie Sieveking's autobiography. The vita of this Hanseatic philanthropist, who founded the German order of Protestant nurses, left Sophie Schwab with a "delightful resonance" of its deeply Christian spirit.[48]

To the Schwabs, independence alone was not a sign of moral laxity in a woman, nor did Christian morality preclude female independence. Both Ludmilla Assing and Amalie Sieveking were outspoken activists in matters of morality and social policy who sought to shape the role of women in Germany. But they did so from opposing ideological points of view, one committed to the German Enlightenment, the other to a pious Calvinism. Not their independence and activism, but rather the content of their philosophy was the criterion by which Sophie Schwab judged them.

Incidentally, the condemnation Mrs. Schwab passed on secular liberals was not limited to women. Even Friedrich Schiller, the literary national hero, was found lacking in his moral convictions: "Reading the Bible is something different from, and not as corrosive as, these philosophical statements," Sophie Schwab found, when pondering whether Schiller's writings were appropriate fare for her grown daughter.[49]

Gustav Schwab followed his mother's line. His view of women's rights was founded in, and limited by, his Protestant worldview. For example, on a journey through Italy in 1856, he and his travel companions refused to visit several Catholic convents when learning that women were barred from entry.[50] On two separate occasions during that journey, he encountered two women who were similar in that they traveled alone. Yet only one of them drew his ire for that sin. This was Frau von Succow, an acquaintance he successfully avoided meeting in Genoa, knowing she was in that city at the same time as he. On a pleasure trip to Italy, her carriage had overturned on a road in Switzerland. Rather than compassion, this incident elicited a reprimand from Schwab: "That woman can consider herself fortunate if nothing worse than [the accident] happens to her, roaming about unaccompanied, as she is.... I heard quite a few [other] things about her that prove that she isn't in her right mind."[51]

---

[48] Sophie Schwab to Gustav F. Schwab, Stuttgart, April 1, 1860, MSS 434, Schwab Papers, series I, box 2, folder 36. Ottilie, Ludmilla Assing's sister, was the mistress of the American abolitionist, Frederick Douglas. Ottilie Assing and Gustav Schwab drew their sympathies for abolitionism from opposing sources, the former from the Enlightenment, the latter from Calvinism. Sophie Schwab also liked the writings of Ottilie Wildermuth, an author of moral tales mostly addressed to children.

[49] Sophie Schwab to Gustav F. Schwab, Stuttgart, March 23–24, 1859, MSS 434, Schwab Papers, series I, box 2, folder 35.

[50] Gustav F. Schwab to Eliza Schwab, Naples/Rome, February 29, 1856, MSS 434, Schwab Papers, series I, box 1, folder 32.

[51] Gustav F. Schwab to Eliza Schwab, Livorno/Milan, March 12, 1856, MSS 434, Schwab Papers, series I, box 1, folder 33.

The other single lady he encountered had Gustav Schwab's enthusiastic approval. Dorothea Dix's moral credentials were impeccable, because she was a well-known social reformer in the United States, and her unaccompanied journey through Europe was justified as undertaken in her cause of the humane treatment of the insane. In the account of Helen Marshall, one of Dix's biographers, "she carried with her no letters of introduction but was always fortunate in meeting some person who would give her the assistance which she desired. 'You will not be more surprised than I am that I find traveling alone perfectly easy,' she wrote American friends."[52] She even refused the service of a maid, whether for assistance or company, writing that "a maid would only be in the way, with nothing to do; . . . I never felt desolate in my life, and I have been much alone in both populous and thinly-settled countries."[53]

Apparently, Dix's sturdy self-sufficiency impressed Schwab, who also voiced support for Dix's cause. Only his slight sarcasm betrayed a sense of unease that a woman should play such a prominent political role. Schwab wrote to his wife:

I have made another interesting acquaintance, an American lady who revealed to me today that she is the well-known Miss Dix, who has done so much good for the insane asylums in America, and who effected that the last Congress appropriated 10 Million dollars for such institutions.

In Rome, she pestered the Pope, because she found his insane asylums in a despicable state, and now, after having pressed hard the authorities here [in Austria], she is traveling to Constantinople.[54]

Where elsewhere Schwab has voiced concern that women should not travel without company, he chose not to mention to his wife that Miss Dix was likewise guilty of that sin. Perhaps he shared the sentiment of a Washington, D.C., politician who praised Dorothea Dix as "a woman's rights woman worth having, going in for their rights in the right way."[55] He may also have been eager to avoid the impression that he was granting a stranger what he refused to his own wife, who was staying at his mother's home in Stuttgart with their children, and to whom he had written a few days earlier: "Concerning your meeting me in Munich on my way back, . . . you can take along one or more female companions on our account, so that you do not have to make the journey on your own."[56]

Married or not, Hanseatic women were judged by their respectability. The criteria that defined *respectability* were largely the same for both genders. Financial independence underlaid a merchant's honor, while it did not diminish the honor of his widow or daughter. To know one's place was indispensable, even if the correct

[52] Marshall, Helen, *Dorothea Dix, Forgotten Samaritan*, Chapel Hill, NC, 1937. See 156–85 for her European journey, quote on p. 179.

[53] Cited by Francis Tiffany, *Life of Dorothea Lynde Dix*, Boston and New York, 1890, 278–9. Marshall's biography (see previous note) is largely derivative of this earlier, superior study.

[54] Gustav F. Schwab to Eliza Schwab, Trieste, March 25, 1856, MSS 434, Schwab Papers, series I, box 1, folder 33. Schwab was correct concerning the appropriation, but might have missed President Pierce's veto. See Marshall, *Dorothea Dix*, 140–54.

[55] Marshall, *Dorothea Dix*, 147.

[56] Gustav F. Schwab to Eliza Schwab, Livorno/Milan, March 12, 1856, MSS 434, Schwab Papers, series I, box 1, folder 33.

places for men and women differed. A solid Christian morality further supported claims to honor, independent of gender. In the case of moral reformers like Dix or Sieveking, women with strong Christian credentials could redefine their proper place to include high places in state and society. They could not become burgomaster or Pope, but they deserved being heard by the burgomaster and the Pope. Women like Succow and Assing, who lacked a higher calling to legitimize their independence, had to expect nothing but scorn.

Even as Hanseats expected women to seek the protection of God or of their husband, they enjoyed considerable leeway within these boundaries. Moreover, men likewise had to submit to the moral authority of deity and wife, not just of their male peers, in their commercial and other public pursuits. Women passed from generation to generation not only the fortunes that made Hanseatic success, but also the values that legitimized this success.

COMMERCIAL MORALITY

Upholding Hanseatic morality was a mutual affair between the genders. It fell to Hanseatic women to enforce in their husbands and sons the moral standards that would keep them on the righteous path in their commercial dealings. Commerce was not traditionally a highly valued activity in Christian morality. Hanseats had to reconcile their economic activities with their sense of morality embodied in the family. This successful reconciliation was what created a specifically mercantile value system, integrating family, faith, and firm. Two core notions underpinned this reconciliation: a profession that God gave and took success in business and a corresponding sense of humility in the face of one's growing wealth, exhibited chiefly by renouncing excessive enjoyment thereof.

More than once, Sophie Schwab reminded her son that "poor or rich is, even for this life, not the most important thing; because where contentment is lacking, the outwardly goods of fortune are often of little use."[57] Gustav Schwab's sister, Sophie Klüpfel, likewise, emphasized the happiness "inside the family" over worldly fortune in a note to her brother.[58] Gustav Schwab, in turn, reassured his relatives that he held to the right kind of values. His mother was pleased to "receive proof from you, that outwardly wealth does not remove you from Him who grants it, and that you have not allowed [this wealth] to weaken your compassion for suffering."[59]

Crises and financial losses, in particular, were favorite occasions for reminders of the values supposedly underlying commerce. After her son had incurred heavy losses in the Panic of 1857, Sophie Schwab wrote to him:

The Dear Lord surely does not send such trials without reason, and surely it will become clear to you, eventually, why these bad times had to come upon you. May God give that things will be better, soon; so that then, you will be able to rejoice at what you

---

[57] Sophie Schwab to Gustav F. Schwab, Stuttgart, October 17–19, 1857, MSS 434, Schwab Papers, series I, box 2, folder 34.

[58] Sophie Klüpfel to Gustav F. Schwab, Tübingen, October 22, 1858, MSS 434, Schwab Papers, series I, box 2, folder 35.

[59] Sophie Schwab to Gustav F. Schwab, Stuttgart, January 16, 1859, MSS 434, Schwab Papers, series I, box 2, folder 35.

overcame, at having experienced that feeling inside of yourself, that you can make yourself independent from the outwardly goods of fortune.[60]

Miss Engel Thiermann, whose brother's firms were involved in trade with the United States, likewise explicitly attributed the 1857 crisis to merchants' moral shortcomings. In her diary, she wrote that "a pure striving for profit leads to ruin."[61]

To a morally upright merchant, God might grant success, or he might bestow failure on him as a lesson in humility. When a merchant failed to live up to his fellow Hanseats' standards of business or personal conduct, however, he could not count on the support of either deity or mortals. Wilhelm Wilkens, of Baltimore, commented on an acquaintance who apparently had failed to pay his debts:

Driver is still here ... and he will hopefully get out of here in a while, since he does know that he is superfluous here and he must have little sense of honor[.] He boards with his brother-in-law and does not make an effort to find employment.[62]

Wilhelm Wilkens was not the only merchant to make observations on the business failures of others. The specter of failure and possible bankruptcy haunted the minds of many of his colleagues. In a letter written about the same time, Friedrich Wilkens expressed compassion for a certain Mr. Reinken, whose business apparently failed. Even as he abstained from harsh words of the kind his brother Wilhelm found for Mr. Driver, he might have implied a judgment on the moral failure of Reinken, who jeopardized the livelihood of his wife and daughters: "What is going to happen with Reinken now; will he gnaw himself through? I hear he offered his creditors 50%. The poor girls are to be pitied."[63] At least Reinken had not failed to acknowledge his financial obligations in their entirety. The honor of a person – as measured by the sincerity of his effort to meet his financial and personal obligations – determined whether merchants supported them in founding their own firms or helped them in need.[64]

The example of Mr. Reinken also shows that morality and success, family and fortune, formed a complete ideological circle: the ultimate moral end of worldly fortune was the welfare of the family, or, more specifically, of women and children. "Praise be to God that you can find joy in your dear wife, and in the development of your children, and can find rest from your worries [in them]; this is the most important thing, and business comes only after that," Sophie Schwab wrote to her son.[65]

---

[60] Sophie Schwab to Gustav F. Schwab, Stuttgart, March 14, 1858, MSS 434, Schwab Papers, series I, box 2, folder 35.

[61] Cited by Garlich, Inge, *Das Leben einer Bremer Kaufmannsfamilie im 19. Jahrhundert, beschrieben nach dem Tagebuch der Engel Maria Thiermann von 1847–1858* (Hausarbeit zur ersten Staatsprüfung für das Lehramt an öffentlichen Schulen, University of Bremen), 1982, 51.

[62] Wilhelm to Julius Wilkens, March 24, 1865, MdHS MS.439.

[63] Friedrich to Julius Wilkens, April 17, 1865, MdHS MS.439.

[64] On notions of honor and integrity informing merchants' value judgments on themselves and others, cf. Ditz, Toby, "Shipwrecked; or, Masculinity Imperiled: Mercantile Representation of Failure and the Gendered Self in Eighteenth-Century Philadelphia," *Journal of American History* 81, no. 1 (June, 1994), 51–80.

[65] Sophie Schwab to Gustav F. Schwab, Stuttgart, October 17–19, 1857, MSS 434, Schwab Papers, series I, box 2, folder 34.

THE HOUSEHOLD AS A SOURCE OF IDENTITY

To Hanseats, family, faith, and firm were part and parcel of the same complex, drawing their guiding principles from the same fount, a comprehensive ideal of mercantile morality. The consciousness of this shared ideal was the force of gravity that held this group together from within. As conscious agents of the process of capital circulation, however, Hanseats moved in a larger social context. Dispersed in different ports, they interacted with a wide range of other social groups. In relation to the latter, and in response to the centrifugal forces to which Hanseats were exposed in these relations, Hanseats set themselves apart through their life-style. Family life – specifically, domestic arrangements – played a central role in positioning Hanseats vis-à-vis other social groups.

Ever since E. P. Thompson's *The Making of the English Working Class*, historians have looked to culture, in the broadest sense, for clues as to how specific social groups acquired a particular identity and consciousness.[66] Hanseats were not a class, however, but would have described themselves as an estate. By definition, members of an estate "know their place." From such a starting point, making oneself into anything seems less of an issue than it would be for a modern class whose members are jumbled together from multiple origins.[67] Hanseats came from a place in which they could be certain of their identity. For them, the point of their cultural expressions relative to other classes was the task of maintaining this identity; in spite of changing external circumstances.

Nonetheless, it is not moot to explore in the Hanseatic case the domestic arrangements that play such a prominent role in the new social history that explores the making of classes as a process driven by the relations between individuals of different social statuses. The choice of residential location and the practices of designing domestic space provide social historians with clues to the attitudes of individuals toward social distinctions. Like the middle classes or working classes, the making of which have been studied by social historians, the Bremish mercantile estate set visible markers of its distinct station in the family home.

Whether in Germany or America, Hanseats were particularly eager to distinguish themselves from those closest to their own position in society: other upper-class members and the nobility. For example, the relationship between Bremen's elite and those of other German states remained problematic. Leading Hanseats perceived industrialists, bankers, and even merchants from the hinterland as players in a minor, more provincial league. In turn, many hinterland notables regarded Hanseats as agents of a foreign interest, undercutting German industry by peddling cheap imported goods.[68]

---

[66] Thompson, E. P., *The Making of the English Working Class*, London, 1965.

[67] Children and those merchants who came to Bremen from the provinces to become long-distance merchants had to be socialized into the Hanseatic network. For the latter, this process was helped by the fact that they usually came to Bremen at a young age. In either case, to rise successfully into the ranks of the Hanseatic elite meant to embrace its value system.

[68] Engelsing, Rolf, "England und die USA in der bremischen Sicht des 19. Jahrhunderts," *Jahrbuch der Wittheit zu Bremen* 1 (1957), 33–65. List, *National System*; Etges, *Wirtschaftsnationalismus*.

For New York, Sven Beckert has shown that a wide gulf separated mercantile from industrial capitalists until the 1860s. Their association with manual labor, their often lowly origins, and the general odor of "new money" that attached itself to industrialists made this group unfit for the salon in the eyes of the mercantile elite. Credit reports on manufacturers colorfully reflected this condescending attitude. The extant papers of New York's Hanseats confirm this picture, in that they contain not a single reference to social interaction with manufacturers.[69]

For upper-class commoners in nineteenth-century Germany, one's relation to the nobility was a key marker of distinction. Hanseats were in a particularly ambiguous position. On the one hand, they were proud burghers of a republic that did not recognize titles of nobility among its inhabitants; while on the other hand, they felt superior to the common brand of small-town merchants and other notables who made up the bulk of the bourgeoisie in the German states. In setting themselves apart from the latter, they sometimes borrowed practices from the aristocracy. When Johann Georg Graue's wife gave birth to twins, her husband decided that even though "the girl was born first, nevertheless the boy shall be the oldest; this way it is judged in ruling houses when twins are born."[70] Gustav F. Schwab displayed some measure of mercantile, republican pride when he visited Genoa and saw the splendor of the palaces that old merchant families had built. "One could give several [of these] palaces to each of the German princes, better ones than they have now, and there still would be enough left."[71] Direct interaction with noblemen created a need to police the border that separated Hanseats from aristocrats with particular watchfulness. H. H. Meier found himself almost the only commoner in the private school he attended in Stuttgart. In their letters, Meier's friends in Bremen warned him against becoming too close to aristocratic circles and adopting their values. His eighteen-year-old brother Diedrich wrote: "Incidentally, they [the aristocracy] are no better than we commoners, especially we Bremeners. Since there exists no nobility here, we could all call ourselves noble, that is, if we wanted to; but we consider ourselves to be above doing so."[72]

In the way they related to the lower classes, Hanseats most resembled other upper- and middle-class groups, in the United States and in Germany. For all these groups, the family home was a showcase of one's status and a statement of class consciousness. Interior and exterior architecture announced to the lower classes one's ability to afford what they could not and demonstrated to one's peers the mastery of the code of a refined taste.[73]

The design of Schwab's mansion, "Fort Number Eight," displayed precisely this mastery. Ship captains and merchants had always had more opportunities to lend a

---

[69] Beckert, *Metropolis*, 52–5.

[70] For proximity between traditions of the nobility and Hanseatic merchants, see Schulz, "Weltbürger," 638. Quote from Johann Georg to Heinrich Hermann Graue (in Baltimore), Bremen, January 4, 1862, MdHS MS.2826, box 4.

[71] Gustav F. Schwab to Eliza Schwab, Genua, January 27, 1856, MSS 434, Schwab Papers, series I, box 1, folder 31.

[72] Hardegen and Smidt, *H. H. Meier*, 14.

[73] Blumin, Stuart M., *The Emergence of the Middle Class: Social Experience in the American City, 1760–1900*, Cambridge and New York, 1989; Kocka, Jürgen and Allen Mitchell, eds., *Bourgeois Society in Nineteenth-Century Europe*, Oxford and Providence, RI, 1993.

particular character to their dwellings by adding exotic items acquired on their journeys. Gustav F. Schwab falls into this category. While in Italy, he was constantly watching out for opportunities to acquire decorative items for the household – oil paintings, statues, and photographs.[74]

Residential location was another general marker of distinction. For Hanseats, as for other groups in the middle class and bourgeoisie on both sides of the Atlantic, residential choices since the 1850s signal an increasing withdrawal from the multitude, driven in part by a fear of insurrection. Traditionally, the merchant's home was in the same building as his countinghouse. After 1850, this began to change. For Bremen, there was an obvious political condition for this sudden exodus beyond the boundaries of the old town. Until the 1848 revolution, only those who lived within the old town, on the right bank of the Weser River, and within the limits of the former city walls, could acquire full civic rights. The new constitution, even after receiving reactionary modifications in the years between 1851 and 1854, gave inhabitants of the new town – a walled extension of the city on the left bank, developed in the seventeenth century – and of the extramural suburbs on the right bank of the Weser River the right to acquire a status as full burghers (see Map 1).[75]

The highest civic status, the Greater Privilege, not only conferred political rights on its holder, but also was the legal prerequisite for engaging in overseas trade. As merchants now had the option to keep the Greater Privilege and to move their permanent abode out of the old town and away from the plebeian hustle and bustle within it, they availed themselves of this option in droves. H. H. Meier moved into his new villa, on the corner of Meinken- and Kohlhökerstraße, in 1850. The Graue and Wilkens families moved into new houses on Kohlhökerstraße as well. The first address in the new eastern suburb (*Östliche Vorstadt*) was the Contrescarpe, where the country estates of Theodor Gerhard Lürman, an uncle of Baltimore's Gustav Lürman, and burgomaster Johann Smidt occupied prominent spots. The Contrescarpe is a street facing the park that occupied the spot where the city fortifications had stood. A view of the greenery along the elongated lakes that had taken the place of the former moat created an idyllic setting within walking distance of the countinghouses, city hall, and the stock exchange. Meinkenstraße ran northeastward from the Contrescarpe, linking it with Kohlhökerstraße. Although lacking the view of the park, the villas and townhouses along Kohlhökerstraße still offered ample garden space, making them the second best thing to a villa on the Contrescarpe (see Map 1).[76]

Architectural histories of Bremen prominently feature the buildings that were erected by merchants during this period. Stately, three- to four-story mansions with representative parlors, surrounded by spacious walled gardens, these new buildings

---

[74] Gustav F. Schwab to Eliza Schwab, Palermo, February 9, 1856 (folder 32), Rome, March 6, 1856, and Livorno/Milan, March 12, 1856 (folder 33), MSS 434, Schwab Papers, series I, box 1, folder as given in brackets. See also Hancock, *Citizens of the World*.

[75] Marschalek, Peter, "Der Erwerb des bremischen Bürgerrechts und die Zuwanderung nach Bremen um die Mitte des 19. Jahrhunderts," *Bremisches Jahrbuch* 66 (1988), 295–305. See also Garlich, *Das Leben einer Bremer Kaufmannsfamilie*, 52–60. For New York, see Beckert, *Metropolis*, 52–5. For this process in Bremen, generally, see Schulz, *Vormundschaft*.

[76] Hardegen and Smidt, *H. H. Meier*; Eleonore to Julius Wilkens, Bremen, December 19, 1862, MdHS MS.439.

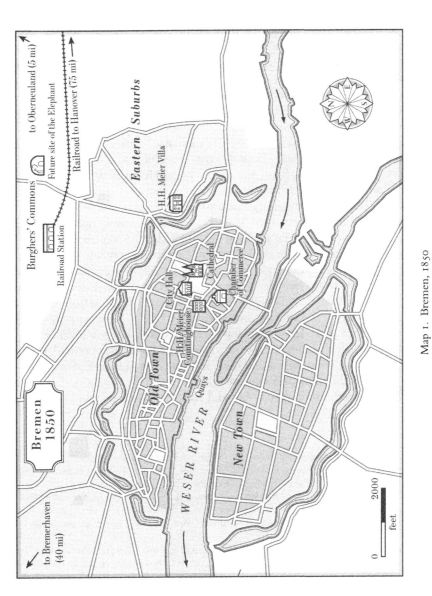

Map 1. Bremen, 1850

were markers of distinction. They signified withdrawal from those urban masses that had previously, in 1848, left such a frightening impression on the mercantile elite. Ironically, it had been the pressure exerted by these urban masses that had created the political conditions for the removal of full burghers from the city in the first place.[77]

Even as the political changes in Bremen contributed to the urban flight of the merchant elite, Hanseats in Baltimore and New York followed the same, global trend. Albert Schumacher constructed his mansion in Baltimore's elite Mount Vernon neighborhood toward the city's northern edge in the 1850s.[78] Heinrich Wilkens, likewise, moved into a house away from the port, in the countryside surrounding Baltimore. There he enjoyed working in the large garden for recreation. His letters to his brother Julius are filled with detailed descriptions of the country home and its grounds. He boasted of a new garden parlor (*Laube*), an orchard filled with plentiful fruit, lawns dotted with flower beds, an herb garden tended by his children, and a monkey to entertain the family. In this "comfortable" (*gemüthlich*) setting, Wilkens enjoyed "Sunday afternoons, [when] Fritz Roeholl and I usually lie in the hammocks."[79] By the middle of the 1860s, when Heinrich Wilkens wrote these letters, he no longer seems to have had any qualms about conspicuous consumption.

In New York, the construction of a railroad line along the Hudson River brought the farmland in the upper half of Manhattan within commuting distance of the countinghouses located on the southern tip of the island. A step ahead of the head-long flight of the New York bourgeoisie to the suburbs, Gustav Schwab was lucky to acquire a prime piece of real estate, fifteen acres on a hilltop overlooking the Harlem River.[80] In letters to his mother, he frequently reveled in the splendor and idyllic setting of his new home. To Sophie Schwab, however, a life apart from the city and one's place of work was still an alien notion. "I cannot form an image of your arrangements there, even less so of your plans to build at such a great distance from the city," she wrote after learning of her son's plans.[81] She feared for her son's health on the "long journey," especially in the short and cold days of winter, when he would travel into the night hours, and suggested that he spend weeknights in town, where he could lodge with his brother-in-law and associate, Hermann von Post.[82]

---

[77] Stein, Rudolf, *Klassizismus und Romantik in der Baukunst Bremens*, 2 vols. (Senator für das Bildungswesen, ed., Forschungen zur Geschichte der Bau- und Kunstdenkmäler in Bremen, vols. 4 and 5), Bremen, 1964/1965; Marschalek, "Erwerb."

[78] Chalfant, "Calvert Station," 14; Mayer, Brantz, *Baltimore, As It Was and As It Is: A Historical Sketch of the Ancient Town and Modern City from the Foundation, in 1729, to 1870*, Baltimore, 1871, 449–52.

[79] Heinrich to Julius Wilkens (in Bremen), Baltimore, April 20, 1865 and Baltimore, June 9, 1865 (quote), MdHS MS.439.

[80] Executor of the estate of Gustav F. Schwab, settlement of account, MSS 434, Schwab Family Papers. Manuscripts and Archives, Yale University Library, series II, box 20, folder 220. In 1909, the site of Schwab's estate was bought by New York University, which then occupied a campus adjacent to Schwab's land. Today, the former site of Schwab's home is the campus of Bronx Community College. John Christopher Schwab, "Scrapbook: Family Papers, Miscellaneous, ca. 1860–1914," MSS 434, Schwab Papers, series II, box 20, folder 222.

[81] Sophie Schwab to Gustav F. Schwab, Stuttgart, March 21, 1857, MSS 434, Schwab Papers, series I, box 2, folder 34.

[82] Sophie Schwab to Gustav F. Schwab, Stuttgart, January 16, 1859, MSS 434, Schwab Papers, series I, box 2, folder 35.

The flight to the idyll of the country house presupposed the very industrial technology that drove the expansion of the city, and that created the urban proletariat from which the better sort hoped to escape. In moving to the countryside, Schwab relied on what was still a comparatively new and accident-prone technology, the steam engine. In his relatives' letters the fear of steam-powered conveyances, to both land and water, was palpable. It probably did not help to ease his mother's mind that he was on a train that was wrecked on his commuter route, even though he escaped uninjured from the incident.[83] What made it worthwhile, in Gustav Schwab's mind, was the escape from the "unpleasant crowd in the New York docks."[84]

The only way a plebeian would find his way into the refined halls of "Fort Number Eight" was as a servant or sculpture. "I bought 4 terracotta figurines of beggars and fishermen, which they make very nicely here. I will keep two for our parlor, and give two to Recknagel," Schwab wrote his wife from Palermo.[85] As witnessed in earlier letters, live beggars had previously elicited reproach from Schwab. These were not the kind of poor who were deserving of Hanseatic charity.[86] Apparently, an added benefit of an aesthetically schooled mind was the ability it conferred to sublimate misery in its artistically rendered form. Figurines of paupers superseded the proletarian menace by representing it in an inert, romanticized fashion. Like Schwab's nephews dressing up as peasants for a festive occasion (see the following text) or noblemen donning shepherds' garb for play, the appropriation of lower-class attributes reassured upper classes in a romantic view on the good and simple pauper of the past. Contentment in misery, which presumably characterized the "good peasant" and artisan, was in turn held up as an ideal to which actual proletarians ought to live up.[87]

Perhaps Schwab was reminded of his own situation by the palaces of the past Florentine mercantile elite, "whose windows gaze into our time with a sinister expression, solidly enclosed with lattice-work, showing quite well how the gentlemen who built them had to protect themselves from uprisings and other violence."[88]

Earlier generations of Hanseats had acquired country estates as safe investments and, in some cases, as a marker of their rise into the landholding elite. As late as the

[83] Sophie Schwab to Gustav F. Schwab, Stuttgart, February 26, 1860, MSS 434, Schwab Papers, series I, box 2, folder 36. For further examples of fear of steam-powered transportation, see Sophie Klüpfel to Gustav F. Schwab, Tübingen, October 22, 1858, MSS 434, Schwab Papers, series I, box 2, folder 35, and Sophie Schwab to Gustav F. Schwab, Stuttgart, November 14, 1858, MSS 434, Schwab Papers, series I, box 2, folder 35. For the slow accommodation of the public to the risks of steam-powered travel in the nineteenth century, see Schivelbusch, Wolfgang, *The Railway Journey: Trains and Travel in the Nineteenth Century*, New York, 1979.

[84] Gustav F. Schwab to Eliza Schwab, Marseille, January 14, 1856, MSS 434, Schwab Papers, series I, box 1, folder 31.

[85] Gustav F. Schwab to Eliza Schwab, Palermo, February 9, 1856, MSS 434, Schwab Papers, series I, box 1, folder 32.

[86] See in the same letter, previous note, as well as Gustav F. Schwab to Eliza Schwab, Livorno, February 1, 1856, MSS 434, Schwab Papers, series I, box 1, folder 32.

[87] Riehl, Wilhelm Heinrich, *Die bürgerliche Gesellschaft*, Stuttgart, 1861, 76–89. For examples of Hanseatic praise of organic, communal relations, see Chapter 3, especially the discussion of Wilhelm Kiesselbach's work.

[88] Gustav F. Schwab to Eliza Schwab, Livorno/Milan, March 12, 1856, MSS 434, Schwab Papers, series I, box 1, folder 33.

1810s, many merchants quit the risky business of exposing their funds to circulation as soon as they could afford rural real estate, which promised a more steady return in the form of rent and produce sales.[89]

For Gustav F. Schwab's generation, the house in the country was no longer an object of investment, but one of conspicuity. Consequently, moving to a country estate, and away from the masses, created an ideological problem for the Hanseats' self-image. If modesty was a key value, was the construction of such a home objectionable as a flaunting of wealth? As if to placate any fears that she considered the construction of a country estate as an undue indulgence for a Christian merchant, Sophie Schwab gave her blessing to her son's relocation by couching it in terms compatible with her moral view: "I will be happy if . . . you have built yourself a pleasant and comfortable nest, and if the Dear Lord will let you enjoy this blessing in peace."[90] In the same spirit, she reminded her son, "that the most beautiful houses cannot entice me [to visit you], just the people who live in them can, and they would entice me even if they lived in a lowly hut."[91]

As the 1850s progressed, even as more and more Hanseats moved into representative villas outside of the port cities, they nevertheless insisted on constructing the country estate as the moral center of family life. Here they presented to the world their wealth and their pious, if comfortable, domestic life. In their minds, the unity of family, faith, and firm remained unaffected by the removal of their residence from the countinghouse. One way of asserting this unity was to delimit one's own group by positioning it against the "lower sorts."

Whether in the country or in town, the home was a location of class relations. Drivers and valets, who tended to the male head of the family; the office staff and apprentices in the countinghouse; and even more so, guides and carriers hired for limited time rarely are mentioned by name in family or business letters. If they are mentioned at all, it is because they failed to perform their function to the satisfaction of their employer.[92] Rudolf Schleiden relied on a valet and a clerk to fulfill his duties as Bremish minister-resident in Washington, D.C. In his letters, he never mentioned either of these men, and if it had not been for a customs declaration, they might have entirely eluded the historical record.[93]

Two groups of employees make for an exception: maids and private tutors. From Hanseatic letters, there emerges a sense that the maid played a central role for the domestic economy – not just in a narrower sense, but also in the wider sense of

[89] Engelsing, Rolf, "Bremisches Unternehmertum. Sozialgeschichte 1780/1870," *Jahrbuch der Wittheit zu Bremen* 2 (1958), 7–112. For an example, see Schleiden, Rudolf, *Jugenderinnerungen eines Schleswig-Holsteiners*, Wiesbaden, 1886, 123.

[90] Sophie Schwab to Gustav F. Schwab, Stuttgart, August 2 (b), 1857, MSS 434, Schwab Papers, series I, box 2, folder 34.

[91] Sophie Schwab to Gustav F. Schwab, Stuttgart, March 14, 1858, MSS 434, Schwab Papers, series I, box 2, folder 35.

[92] Gustav F. Schwab to Eliza Schwab, Livorno, February 1, 1856, MSS 434, Schwab Papers, series I, box 1, folder 32.

[93] Rudolf Schleiden to Hon[ora]ble General Lewis Cass, Secretary of State of the United States, Washington, DC, December 1, 1857, StAHB 4,48.21/5.E.1, Bremische Gesandtschaft in Washington, Angelegenheiten des bremischen Ministerresidenten Dr. Rudolph Schleiden (1845) 1853–1862, lists "Bernhard Bätjer, Clerk of the Legation" and "Gustav Forstberg, servant of Mr. Schleiden." In all of Rudolf Schleiden's extensive papers, this is the only document to mention his servants or clerks.

the emotional economy of the family. Margarethe, the Schwab's maid in New York, and Bärbel, Sophie Schwab's maid in Stuttgart, are frequently mentioned in letters between family members. In a hierarchy of hired help, these maids appear to have stood above the rest, surpassed only by the children's private tutors. Mr. Böckle, the tutor of Gustav F. and Eliza Schwab's children had been recommended to the Schwabs by the Meiers in Bremen, for whom Böckle had previously worked.

These three employees seem to have built close and intimate relations with the families, sharing the most important moments in the lives of family members. Sophie Schwab relied on Bärbel for her more complete and accurate memory to keep those moments alive for herself: "Not only does she remember everything that happened during your stay, but also everything that you and the children and Margarethe said, and she tells me about it every day."[94] Bärbel usually read the letters from America together with Sophie Schwab, and discussed their content with her. In particular, she seems to have provided additional reinforcement for the moral grounding of Madame Schwab's views, especially when it came to admonitions not to become intoxicated with worldly success.[95] During a long visit of Gustav Schwab and his family to his mother's house in 1856, Bärbel and Margarethe, the maids, bonded over their shared responsibilities for the different branches of the family. For as long as Bärbel remained in Sophie Schwab's service, Margarethe and she sent each other their regards by way of the letters exchanged by their employers.[96]

Mr. Böckle, the teacher, had come to Gustav Schwab's home from Bremen, by recommendation of the Meier family. His name, though, suggests Swabian origins. During the Christian holidays, which were increasingly occasions to celebrate the family, Böckle was part of the inner circle. Artistically gifted, he helped outfit the parlor in a festive way.[97]

Böckle's influence as a preceptor was considerable. In his letters home from Stuttgart, where he attended school in the 1860s, little Gustav H. ("Gussy") Schwab was afraid to mention to his parents that he was having fun with his friends on Sundays. When his parents inquired whether their son really worked even on the weekend, it became apparent that he feared the judgment of Mr. Böckle, who was in New York at that time, and who was likely to read the letters. Little Gussy's super-ego was working a bit too hard.

The special status of these three employees was grounded in their role as guardians of the family's lineage and heritage: they cared for the children and helped remember

94 Sophie Schwab to Gustav F. Schwab, Stuttgart, October 17–19, 1857, MSS 434, Schwab Papers, series I, box 2, folder 34, and April 11, 1859, MSS 434, Schwab Papers, series I, box 2, folder 35 (quote).
95 Sophie Schwab to Gustav F. Schwab, Stuttgart, March 14, 1858, MSS 434, Schwab Papers, series I, box 2, folder 35.
96 E.g., Sophie Schwab to Gustav F. Schwab, Stuttgart, May 2, 1858, August 1, 1858, and n.p., June 24, 1859, MSS 434, Schwab Papers, series I, box 2, folder 35.
97 Sophie Schwab to Gustav F. Schwab, Stuttgart, March 23–24, 1859 and December 27, 1859, MSS 434, Schwab Papers, series I, box 2, folder 35. The diminutive suffixes -le and -lin are particular to, and defining of family names in this region, surrounding Stuttgart and stretching southeast and southwest from there up the Neckar River and onto the Schwäbische Alb highland. The teacher's name is variously spelled Böcklin or Böckle by the Schwabs.

those stories that families tell to define who they are and what it is that they have in common. Considering the weight the Schwabs gave to molding their children into good merchants and merchants' wives, the influence of the personnel was of great concern to them. Thus, Sophie Schwab wrote: "I often think how glad I am to have met Margarethe, knowing the dear children so well cared for in her hands, next to maternal supervision."[98] Maternal supervision was often an afterthought in considering childcare, as it was the maids in the earlier years and the tutor in the later years who most influenced the character of mercantile offspring.

MAKING CHILDREN INTO HANSEATS

Mr. Böckle would have been pleased to know that he had implanted in little Gussy that – to use David Riesman's term – "gyropscope" of self-control so essential to a successful merchant. To instill in their children unbendable morals, firmly rooted in Christian beliefs, was a central concern to Hanseats. Everything else – success and happiness – would automatically follow, once the moral foundation of a young person's character had been laid. At the same time, the quick pace of change in the world demanded that Hanseats' children learn to adapt to new conditions. Thus, from childhood, Hanseats were primed to master the balance between commitment to tradition and innovation.[99]

To equip them for this dual task, Hanseats' children received a comprehensive education in the basics of languages and sciences, which would enable them to function in the rapidly modernizing world. German, English, French, ancient Greek, and Latin were the minimum requirements among the languages. This entailed the use of three different scripts, the Latin, the Gothic, and the Greek. For both boys and girls, mathematics and geography were added to the curriculum, which was rounded off by studies of the Bible and the modern and classic literatures in the languages learned.[100]

To prime their sons (or daughters) and heirs in the embrace of Christian virtues as well as in modern languages, sciences, and business practices was no small feat for Hanseats. Occasionally, the burden of this task can be glimpsed in the letters of parents who agonized over the prospects of their children. Sophie Klüpfel, writing to Gustav Schwab, her brother, summed up the anxiety of a parent charged with bringing up her children in accordance with inflexible moral prescriptions and concerned for their prospects in life:

May God ... let you have much joy through your children! I am delighted that they have been developing so splendidly, but you will also find that the worries multiply when they grow older. Hence I daily ask God only that he may lead my children, inwardly and

[98] Sophie Schwab to Gustav F. Schwab, n.p., April 3, 1858, MSS 434, Schwab Papers, series I, box 2, folder 35.
[99] Riesman, David, *The Lonely Crowd: A Study of the Changing American Character*, New Haven, CT, 1950; Bruford, Walter Horace, *The German Tradition of Self-Cultivation: "Bildung" from Humboldt to Thomas Mann*, Cambridge, 1975.
[100] John Christopher Schwab Scrapbooks, 1860–1864, MSS 434, Schwab Papers, series II, box 20, folder 222; Sophie Schwab to Gustav F. Schwab, Stuttgart, August 28, 1857, MSS 434, Schwab Papers, series I, box 2, folder 34.

outwardly, onto the right path of a living community with Him, so that they will submit themselves to the discipline of the Holy Spirit, in which case everything else could be anticipated with calm. While I cannot be certain in this respect, I still am generally optimistic that God will answer my prayers, even if many a battle will still have to be fought; and some small, inconspicuous beginnings prove to me that I may regard the many promises in the word of God as also directed to me, and that He who directs the hearts like streams of water will not let any of my children be lost. From this unintended ejaculation of my heart, you can gather what occupies me the most, and just how filled I am with my own powerlessness in the face of the difficulties of bringing up children.[101]

Rarely were mothers left alone with these worries. Children's characters were under close scrutiny by all relatives and by the domestic employees. Parents involved the larger family in the bringing up of their offspring. To reassure family members of their proper development, parents encouraged their children to write to other relatives, as soon as they had learned to write. Delighted over the first mail from her grandsons, Gustav H. and Hermann Schwab, Sophie Schwab wrote that she would "frame this letter in gold."[102] In Gussy, his grandmother particularly enjoyed a character trait she also recognized and encouraged in her own son, compassion. "Do you remember the beggar-boy whom he followed on the avenue when we walked up from Christophs,'" she asked her son.[103] The elders used their correspondence with the children of the family to remind them to stay on the righteous path. The family matriarch Eliza von Post in New York closed a letter to her great-grandchildren with the words, "Do not forsake Jesus!"[104]

Through these exchanges, a set of values emerges that shows as much about the Hanseats' self-image as it reflects the aims of education. Modesty, a mind-set to be pleased with whatever life deals a person, and an according ability to be grateful to God for one's possessions, no matter how meager, were highest on the list of Sophie Schwab's virtues. Repeatedly, she praises this trait in children.[105]

Diligence closely followed modesty on the list of values desired in children. After all, diligence would lead to that wealth about which one could then be modest. Sophie Schwab praised her granddaughter, Henny, "prophesying" her mother that "you will have a very diligent daughter in her," remembering the girl's eagerness to

---

[101] Sophie Klüpfel to Gustav F. Schwab, Tübingen, October 22, 1858, MSS 434, Schwab Papers, series I, box 2, folder 35.

[102] Sophie Schwab to Gustav F. Schwab, Stuttgart, November 14, 1858, MSS 434, Schwab Papers, series I, box 2, folder 35; see Sophie Schwab to Gustav H. "Gussy" Schwab, Stuttgart, February 3, 1861, MSS 434, Schwab Papers, series I, box 2, folder 37, for another example of letters exchanged between grandparents and grandchildren.

[103] Sophie Schwab to Gustav F. Schwab, Stuttgart, January 16, 1859, MSS 434, Schwab Papers, series I, box 2, folder 35.

[104] Eliza von Post to Gustav H. and Hermann C. Schwab, Fordham, April 4, 1865, MSS 434, Schwab Papers, series I, box 2, folder 39. Though blind and aged, Eliza von Post continued to take an active part in the life of the family on both continents through her correspondence. She was the grandmother of Gustav F. Schwab's wife, Eliza Schwab, neé von Post. See Sophie Schwab to Gustav F. Schwab, Niedernau, June 22, 1860, and Stuttgart, November 11, 1860, MSS 434, Schwab Papers, series I, box 2, both in folder 36.

[105] Sophie Schwab to Gustav F. Schwab, Tübingen, August 28, 1857, MSS 434, Schwab Papers, series I, box 2, folder 34.

help with domestic chores during a visit to her grandmother's house.[106] In line with his mother, Gustav Schwab's maxim was "not to despair over a person's prospects, as long as he enjoys rising early in the morning."[107]

One of the favorite cautionary tales in the upbringing of Hanseatic children was the story of the prodigal son. Many a biography of leading Hanseats contains a key moment, when the overconfident young man squanders a substantial part of his, or a relative's, fortune in speculation. These narratives function to acknowledge the temptation of a merely profit-maximizing attitude, while assuring the audience that the young man had learned his lesson for life and had become a truly responsible, truly Hanseatic merchant.[108]

Even though class or estate consciousness was not an officially endorsed value for the education of the Schwab's children, they nevertheless seem to have acquired some measure of it along the way. For Christmas, Sophie Schwab wanted to dress up her grandchildren in "Swabian peasant costume." This project greatly upset little Gustav Klüpfel, "who feared that he would have to remain a peasant boy," and was only convinced to model the lowly garb for the occasion, when he was given permission to speak in dialect while thus clad.[109]

Parents were ultimately responsible for the way their children turned out. Nevertheless, the shaping of the next generation was a collective task. It enlisted many different strands of Hanseatic family networks. This collective task was an exercise in mutual social control that involved domestic employees and relatives in distant cities. This shared burden of priming children for their future roles helped to perpetuate the family network. Moreover, the journeys undertaken by young Hanseats in the pursuit of knowledge not only reinforced the ties within and between families, but also established new ones among the next generation.

Travel and the exposure to different cultures were considered a prerequisite for young Hanseats. This puts them in one camp with much of the European nobility and wealthy Americans, who also sent their young abroad. Yet the journeys young Hanseats undertook for their education were not quite the classical grand tour. Rather, a desire to put children in suitably Calvinist surroundings and, when they had chosen a mercantile rather than academic career, to give them firsthand experience in the main branches of trade, informed the choice of destinations for these journeys.

For the first years of their general education, Hanseatic children were privately tutored. When it was time to go to grammar school, the choice often fell on one not

---

[106] Sophie Schwab to Gustav F. Schwab, n.p., April 3, 1858, MSS 434, Schwab Papers, series I, box 2, folder 35.

[107] Sophie Schwab to Gustav F. Schwab, Stuttgart, February 12, 1859, MSS 434, Schwab Papers, series I, box 2, folder 35.

[108] Hardegen and Smidt, *H. H. Meier*, 32–3; Emmy Schwab to Gustav F. Schwab, Stuttgart, August 2, 1857, MSS 434, Schwab Papers, series I, box 2, folder 34, in which Emmy Schwab subtly admonished her brother not to boast of his wealth; Lürman, Stephan, "Brief an meine Kinder aus 2. Ehe," manuscript, 1813, in folder "2 Nachrufe für Stefan Lürman," StAHB 7,128, Lürman [family papers], box 1. The latter is an advice letter by a merchant to his children from his second marriage. It begins with the words "Die größte Belohnung für überstandene Miß-Geschicke ist Erfahrung." ["The greatest reward for failures one has mastered is experience."]

[109] Sophie Schwab to Gustav F. Schwab, Stuttgart, December 27, 1859, MSS 434, Schwab Papers, series I, box 2, folder 35.

located in the hometown. Gustav Lürman, for example, attended a boarding school in Bückeburg, in the principality of Schaumburg-Lippe. H. H. Meier enrolled in the lyceum of Württemberg's capital, Stuttgart, where Gustav B. Schwab, the poet, taught Latin and Greek. Later generations of children from the Schwab and Meier families followed in their footsteps. The defining commonality of Bremen, Schaumburg-Lippe, and Württemberg was the dominance of Calvinism in these states.[110]

Whereas Hanseats looked inland for general learning, they traveled across the Atlantic for their mercantile education. Nearly every son of the major Hanseatic traders spent at least a few years in New York or Baltimore, and less often Boston, or other American seaports of lesser importance to Bremen. There they learned the ways of the Yankee and the ins and outs of the commodity markets, including the crucial detailed knowledge required to judge the quality of staples like cotton and tobacco.[111]

From the vantage point of Hanseats moored on the Atlantic's western shore, the journey took them in the opposite direction. Gustav Schwab's children attended the same lyceum that had once seen their grandfather and now, in the 1860s, saw their uncle, Christoph Schwab, as a teacher, and that their father had attended as a pupil. To round off their mercantile qualifications, they spent some time in Bremen countinghouses, before eventually returning to New York to establish themselves in their father's firm.[112]

Daughters were not given a mercantile education, but otherwise enjoyed the same kind of learning as their brothers. H. H. Meier's sister, Betty, attended school in Stuttgart during the same time that her brother was at the lyceum. The four sisters von Post – among them Eliza and Emily, who were to marry the Schwab brothers – were sent to Bremen from New York to receive an education.[113] Gustav F. Schwab's daughters attended a private school for girls in lower Manhattan.[114] Rudolf Schleiden's mother, Elisabeth Van Nuys, had received a comprehensive classical education. Schleiden recalled discussions of Greek philosophy and literature with her, more often than not conducted in Greek.[115]

The educational journeys of young people confirmed the bonds between families in the present generation and laid the foundation for those between the coming generation, as family or friends of the family provided housing for

[110] John Christopher Schwab Scrapbooks, 1860–1864, MSS 434, Schwab Papers, series II, box 20, folder 222.

[111] Beutin, *Bremen und Amerika*, 34–9, 68–75.

[112] Henny Schwab (daughter of Gustav Schwab) to Gustav H. Schwab, Fordham, April 4, 1865, MSS 434, Schwab Papers, series I, box 2, folder 39. Graves, Ralph H., "Many Duties of Gustav [H.] Schwab," *New York Evening Post*, June 26, 1909, in MSS 434, Schwab Papers, series II, box 20, folder 222.

[113] Oelrichs & Co., *Caspar Meier and His Successors*, 32.

[114] John Christopher Schwab, "Scrapbook: Family Papers, Miscellaneous, ca. 1860–1914," MSS 434, Schwab Papers, series II, box 20, folder 222.

[115] Klüpfel, *Gustav Schwab*, 125–6; Hardegen and Smidt, *H. H. Meier*, 6–7; White, Lucy Sophia, née Schwab, *Fort Number Eight. The Home of Gustav and Eliza Schwab. Compiled by their daughter Lucy Schwab White for their Grandchildren and Great-Grandchildren that they may know something of the Rock whence they are hewn*, New Haven, CT, 1925, MSS 434, Schwab Papers, series II, box 17, folder 212; Schleiden, *Jugenderinnerungen*, 16.

youths who attended school away from home.[116] Hanseatic children grew into a well-established network. Their parents had built this extensive and dense web of mutual obligations on their own childhood acquaintances and on the additions that courtship and business had brought into its orbit. They might have hoped that the ties their own children formed would one day furnish them with the same kind of transnational connections and that they would renew the complex of families, firms, and faith that held together this network.

CONCLUSION

As a group of merchants, Hanseats seem first and foremost defined by their economic activity. They only became a distinct, transnational social group in the space of the Atlantic economy by virtue of the trade they conducted. This Atlantic economy, however, was characterized by instability. Communication remained haphazard before the establishment of a transatlantic telegraph (1866), in spite of the establishment of mail-steamer lines since the 1840s. "Buying cheap and selling dear" was not the most reliable way of valorizing capital, and the uncertain trustworthiness of many business partners added another moment of risk to transatlantic ventures. Wars exacerbated this instability. The Napoleonic Wars, in particular, had been devastating for German and American merchants.

The networked character of Hanseatic business enterprises lent a necessary element of stability to their ventures. Family ties and a shared morality, in turn, were essential in knitting this network. The firm belief in the everyday applicability of Calvinist tenets was reflected in the watchfulness of both genders over the conduct of the other. The mercantile moral economy upheld by men and women woven into this dense web of mutual social control invested Hanseatic business interests with a sense of higher calling. Close family ties between different merchant houses mitigated competition between different firms. Outside the immediate family circle, ties of friendship that, in some cases, dated back decades, established obligations that suggested a cooperative mode of business transactions. Even in such relations between men that were unmediated by female influence, a shared value system helped to take the edge out of competing interests. This value system rested on the convictions of both genders.

The importance of mothers, wives, and sisters for upholding the moral economy of the Hanseatic household gave women a role much more decisive than their usual absence from the countinghouse or the legislature might suggest. The basic unit of Hanseatic commerce was the household, and in it, women's power over the financial and ideological resources rivaled that of men. The

---

[116] For several examples, see Brandes, Erika, "Der Bremer Überseekaufmann in seiner gesellschafts-geschichtlichen Bedeutung im 'geschlossenen Heiratskreis,'" *Genealogisches Jahrbuch* 3 (1963), 25–48; Hardegen and Smidt, *H. H. Meier*; Sophie Schwab to Gustav F. Schwab, Stuttgart, March 21, 1857, MSS 434, Schwab Papers, series I, box 2, folder 34; Sophie Schwab to Gustav F. Schwab, Stuttgart, March 23–24, 1859, MSS 434, Schwab Papers, series I, box 2, folder 35; Sophie Schwab to Gustav F. Schwab, Stuttgart, April 1, 1860, MSS 434, Schwab Papers, series I, box 2, folder 36; Sophie Schwab to Gustav F. Schwab, Stuttgart, April 9, 1861 (Klüpfels' and Bruns' children) and May 9, 1861 (Johanne Noltenius), MSS 434, Schwab Papers, series I, box 2, folder 37; White, *Fort Number Eight*.

willingness of male Hanseats to defend the legal standing and financial independence of their wives and children reflects their awareness of the centrally important role the women of their estate played in its collective success. The gender arrangements in the Hanseatic household were a matter of tradition, not an outflow of a modern sense of women's rights. Women's status was threatened by the modernization of the legal code. For this elite, progress meant a threat to women's independence.

Even as Bremen's merchants in all ports were linked to one another by intermarriage to an extraordinary degree, they were nonetheless not all part of the same family, nor had they all been apprenticed in the same firm. Hence, competition between different Hanseatic "clans," or clusters of firms, could have been just as fierce as that between Hanseats and other groups of merchants. But it was not. Beyond the family, the state of Bremen served to tie together the different clans and companies in a shared political framework. Bremen's status as an independent player in the concert of states allowed it to pursue policies that served the interest of Hanseats worldwide. These policies were set by political institutions dominated by merchants and scholars who hailed from mercantile families.

Overseas, the development and enforcement of Bremish policies were supported by a dense consular network, whose functionaries were drawn from mercantile circles. In addition, Bremen's newspapers, which were circulated to foreign ports along with the commodities traded by Hanseats, kept those who did business overseas in touch with the political affairs of the free city. Through these venues of communication, a peculiar Hanseatic ideology, neither all traditionalist nor all liberal, was kept fresh in the minds of Hanseats in Bremen and abroad. The state of Bremen posited a political interest common to all members of her mercantile elite, whether at home or abroad. This shared political interest, together with the ideology of cosmopolitan conservatism, formed the third, equally indispensable pillar of the transatlantic Hanseatic network.

3

Cosmopolitan Conservatives

Hometown Traditions and Western Ideas in Bremish Politics, 1806–1860

TRADITION AND MODERNITY

Hanseatic politics present a seeming paradox for the study of political ideas in the nineteenth century. In their role as free traders and pioneers of transatlantic trade, Bremen's elite appears to be on the radical liberal fringe of the Western political spectrum. In their role as hometown burghers committed to the traditions of an estate, it appears to be a part of the Central European forces of reaction against the achievements of the French Revolution.

Historical scholarship offers little to resolve this seeming paradox. The Hanseatic mercantile elite occupies a marginal position in the national histories of Germany and the United States, in spite of its active involvement in transatlantic trade, as well as in German and American politics.

In the American context, these Hanseats have hardly been noticed outside of a specialized field of "ethnic" history.[1] Within the history of German liberalism and the middle class, Hanseats have only recently begun to attract attention as a peculiar local case.[2] Where German or American historians have noticed Hanseats, the view of Bremen's elite as part of the left wing of German liberalism dominates, not least fueled by the self-image promoted by postwar Bremish historians.[3] German historians of America and of German-American relations followed the received view of

---

[1] E.g., Cunz, Dieter, *The Maryland Germans: A History*, Princeton, NJ, 1948, 293–315. Sven Beckert does not examine the relevance of the German background of 23% of the members of his sample group of New York bourgeois (p. 147); subsuming them into his, otherwise excellent, study of an important and neglected aspect of U.S. history in his *The Monied Metropolis: New York City and the Consolidation of the American Bourgeoisie, 1850–1896*, Cambridge, MA, 2001. A notable exception is Mustafa, Sam A., "The Role of the Hanseatic Cities in Early U.S.–German Relations," *Maryland Historical Magazine* 93, no. 3 (Fall 1998), 265–87.

[2] Schulz, Andreas, "Liberalismus in Hamburg und Bremen zwischen Restauration und Reichsgründung (1830–1870)," in *Liberalismus und Region. Zur Geschichte des deutsche Liberalismus im 19. Jahrhundert*, ed. Lothar Gall and Dieter Langewiesche, Munich, 1995, 135–60; idem, *Vormundschaft und Protektion. Eliten und Bürger in Bremen, 1750–1880* (Stadt und Bürgertum, vol. 13), Munich, 2001.

[3] Two important contributions: Beutin, Ludwig, *Bremen und Amerika. Zur Geschichte der Weltwirtschaft und der Beziehungen Deutschlands zu den Vereinigten Staaten*, Bremen, 1953; Engelsing, Rolf, "England und die USA in der bremischen Sicht des 19. Jahrhunderts," *Jahrbuch der Wittheit zu Bremen* 1 (1957), 33–65.

the Hanseats, fitting them into a larger picture of transatlantic democratic ties among these two countries.[4]

At the same time Hanseats were "modernizers" and conservatives; committed to their ancient traditions and the revolution of international trade; and hometown particularists and transatlantic cosmopolitans. We have seen that Bremen's elite relied on traditional practices in their business ventures and in their family life, and that their success as merchants in a rapidly changing world market was founded on their very traditionalism.

In developing their political ideas, and in building the institutions of the state of Bremen, Hanseats likewise negotiated contradictory desires: to preserve a traditional politics of deference and to make Bremen's institutions efficient tools for facilitating world trade. The ideological and institutional framework they developed was capable of containing these contradictions and of realizing both these conflicting desires.

With Hegel, we can understand the form in which contradictions can move toward a synthesis as a dialectical relation.[5] With Marx, we can add an awareness that this relation depends on particular social and economic conditions.[6] The form that allowed Hanseats at the same time to criticize and realize modern, capitalist social relations, including a capitalist world market, and the form that allowed them simultaneously to deny and to affirm the traditional, communal values of an early-modern hometown was *modern conservatism*. Hanseats' intense trading ties to the Atlantic World, and their exposure to its political ideas, added a cosmopolitan dimension to this form, resulting in a peculiar brand of cosmopolitan conservatism.[7]

The political positions at which Bremen's merchants arrived by the mid-nineteenth century put them in a transnational political current that has as much, if not more, in common with an emerging posttraditional conservatism, as it does with classical liberalism. This new Western conservatism was a response to the French Revolution that did not want to turn back the clock to absolute monarchy, but that also rejected democracy.[8]

At a time when German proponents of a market society and a constitutional state were not yet sharply differentiated into camps of liberals and conservatives, Hanseatic adherence to liberal ideas was at best selective and driven by particular interests. Hanseats' primary allegiance was to tradition, order, and estate. Not unlike

---

[4] E.g., Adams, Willi Paul, "German Translations of the American Declaration of Independence," http://chnm.gmu.edu/declaration/adams2.html (accessed June 7, 2004); Dippel, Horst, *Die amerikanische Verfassung in Deutschland im 19. Jahrhundert. Das Dilemma von Politik und Staatsrecht*, Goldbach, Germany, 1994; Moltmann, Günter, *Atlantische Blockpolitik im 19. Jahrhundert. Die Vereinigten Staaten und der deutsche Liberalismus während der Revolution von 1848/49*, Düsseldorf, 1973.

[5] Hegel, G. W. F., *Elements of the Philosophy of Right*, trans. H. B. Nisbet, Cambridge, 1991.

[6] Marx, Karl, "Theses on Feuerbach," in *The Marx-Engels Reader*, ed. Robert C. Tucker, New York and London, 1978, 143–5.

[7] Engelsing, "England und die USA," 47, cites Heinrich Smidt, son of Burgomaster Smidt, as saying that the commercial relations between Bremen and the United States were a step toward the fulfillment of the "as yet unrealized ideals of the cosmopolitans."

[8] When Bremen's burgomaster, Arnold Duckwitz, witnessed the campaign for the Northern German Reichstag in 1867, the first election in the Hanseatic city that was conducted under the rules of universal, equal, male suffrage, he remarked that "this election business here is becoming American." See Engelsing, "England und die USA," 55.

conservatives in the United States, they were willing to adapt some of their institutions and practices to the exigencies of an emerging industrial capitalism, but strove to contain potentially threatening consequences of this modernization by preserving corporatist traditions and a hierarchical social order.

Moreover, as participants in U.S. politics, Bremen's merchants contributed to the transatlantic scope of this brand of modernization. Although, at first sight, Hanseatic politics may appear as stubbornly local and particularistic, we will find that they were part of a transnational bourgeois alternative to liberalism and democracy, drawing their inspirations from Burke rather than Rousseau, preferring Adam Müller to Hegel, and having more in common with John C. Calhoun than with John Stuart Mill.[9]

In locating Hanseats within the spectrum of political ideas in Germany and the United States, we will first turn our attention to Bremen. This chapter will lay out the governmental system of the city, and the political ideas it reflected.

Bremen enjoyed its independence as a function of the restoration of a European order based on custom and divine right by the Congress of Vienna. Its standing in the international system was tied to its status as a member of the German Confederation that encompassed the German monarchies and free cities. The state of Bremen used its power to make treaties for giving its merchants access to foreign markets. It also created the transportation infrastructure and the laws that laid the foundation for Hanseats' engagement in world trade.

Within Bremen, the mercantile elite enjoyed a legally privileged status. As the highest class of burghers, holders of the Greater Privilege, they maintained a firm grip on the institutions of the city-state. They used this power to perpetuate a corporatist social order that shielded the artisans and laborers from the pressure of capitalist competition. While foreign trade was free trade, guild-like arrangements governed the markets for all commodities within the city, even for import and export staples.[10]

Bremish politics formed a bond among all Hanseats in Bremen, Baltimore, and New York. Through Bremen's consular network and numerous newspapers, the channels of political communication between Hanseats in all these ports complemented family correspondence in an essential way. They tied together the different family groups, creating a transnational public sphere in which Hanseats could formulate their shared interests.

Where Hanseats engaged with merchants, politicians, or intellectuals beyond their network, this transnational public sphere intersected with the political life of both the United States and Germany. These varied influences on the Hanseatic political mind left their imprint on the writings of one of Bremen's most prolific scholarly authors, Wilhelm Kiesselbach, an "organic intellectual" of Bremen's elite.[11]

Through Kiesselbach, we can understand the political ideology that allowed Hanseats to synthesize the contradictions of their existence laid out in the preceding

---

[9] Johann Smidt, Bremen's arch-conservative burgomaster, saw the city's "friendship" with the United States as a possible source of support for maintaining the city's independence. See Engelsing, "England und die USA," 46–7.

[10] Marschalek, "Bürgerrechts."

[11] Even as Antonio Gramsci's term applies in its literal sense – as an intellectual of his class – the pun is intended, in that Kiesselbach was an advocate of organicism.

text. In his engagement with American and Bremish institutions and ideas, Kiesselbach developed a theory of a "social-economic state." In essence, what he meant by this was an estatist order that preserved deference in the political realm, while allowing for capitalist social relations. For his ideas, Kiesselbach was indebted to an Anglo-American conservatism that had arisen as a response to the French Revolution and the Enlightenment.[12]

A COSMOPOLITAN PLACE

The Hanseatic network served as a continuous conduit for political ideas. Hanseats in the United States remained involved in Bremen politics in two ways: by following the Bremen press and by making demands on the state of Bremen through the consuls. Information thus flowed both ways, in print as newspapers and prices current, and handwritten as letters and as consular correspondence, mainly based on local mercantile sources. The interlocking of political and economic channels of decision making and information is illustrated by the common practice of forwarding consuls' reports to the Bremen *Handelskammer* (chamber of commerce).[13]

The transoceanic, semipublic sphere Hanseats created for themselves relied not just on written communication, but also on face-to-face interaction. In a letter to his brother Gustav in 1861, Christoph Theodor Schwab relates a conversation he had with merchants in Bremen about the debates over the abolition of guilds, then taking place in the *Bürgerschaft* (see Chapter 4). During this conversation, the wine merchant Mr. Platinius told Christoph Schwab about a discussion he had regarding the same issue in Bordeaux, involving Hanseats residing there, as well as one Bremish merchant from California, Heinrich Loening. The latter had bought advertising space in Bremen's papers to publish a statement in support of the abolition of guild prerogatives. Merchants and artisans in Bremen had responded to Loening's statement.[14]

Hanseatic social clubs in American ports were sites of the transoceanic conversation in which Bremen's merchants debated their political interests. These clubs had numerous German newspapers delivered, most of them from Bremen. We can safely assume that these papers were read for information on prices and ship movements, but

---

[12] Bremen's elite carried out in practice what Kiesselbach developed in theory. For this, it is immaterial whether they took his views as a blueprint, or whether Kiesselbach systematized the views prevalent among his peers. Kiesselbach's main works were published around 1860, but give meaning to Hanseatic politics throughout the era between the Congress of Vienna and the German and American domestic wars of the 1860s.

[13] E.g., Hermann Wätjen could write his *Frühzeit des Nordatlantikverkehrs*, a history of foreign trade, based almost exclusively on the diplomatic records in the Bremen State Archive. On the abundance of letters written by emigrants, see Kamphoefner, Walter D., and Wolfgang Helbich, eds., *Germans in the Civil War: The Letters they Wrote Home*, trans. Susan Carter, Chapel Hill, NC, 2006; and Kamphoefner, Walter D., Wolfgang Helbich, and Ulrike Sommer, eds., *News from the Land of Freedom: German Immigrants Write Home*, Ithaca, NY, 1991.

[14] Christoph Theodor Schwab to Gustav F. Schwab (in New York), Stuttgart, April 9, 1861, MSS 434, Schwab Papers, series I, box 2, folder 37. I call the space in which these conversations took place a "semipublic sphere," because it functioned like Habermas's public sphere, without meeting the criterion of being open to general participation. Habermas, Jürgen, *The Structural Transformation of the Public Sphere: An Inquiry into a Category of Bourgeois Society*, Cambridge, MA, 1989.

political information was no less relevant for business in the nineteenth century than it is today. The correspondents of Baltimore Hanseat Julius Wilkens took it for granted that he followed the local news from Bremen. His sister Eleonore wrote, "I cannot think of anything else to tell you, you will read the regular city news in the *Courier [an der Weser]*" – the daily paper catering to the merchant elite and especially covering shipping and trade. Eleonore Wilkens's husband-to-be, Wilhelm Knoche, mentioned another paper, which covered more continental news and was read by the middle class. He wrote in reference to the war against Denmark in 1864, "you will be well informed about these matters by the *Weser Zeitung*."[15]

In similar clubs in Bremen, one would have looked in vain for American papers. Hanseats had a variety of these delivered directly to their countinghouses. When they arrived at a club like the Museum or the Erholung on a day that the newspapers arrived from the United States, they could expect to be on the same page as their peers. American politics and business news mattered just as much to Hanseats as did intelligence from the continent.[16]

Still, for Hanseats in Bremen and America, Bremen remained the reference point for their shared political ideals that reflected their peculiar existence as cosmopolitans who were rooted in a community with claims to a centuries-old tradition. In personal letters to his friend and brother-in-law, Julius Wilkens, Wilhelm Knoche frequently invoked this shared tradition, in almost identical wording: "Otherwise all is as it used to be and even the old Roland still stands on the market square."

If Knoche had looked for a more apt symbol of permanence and the particularity of a place, he would have been unlikely to find one in Bremen. The eighteen-foot stone statue of the legendary knight, Prince Roland, has been standing on the market square, in the very heart of the city, since 1404. The statue depicts a standing knight in armor, holding a drawn sword in his right hand and a shield with a double-headed eagle by his left arm. Above his bare, curly-haired head, a canopy rises another ten feet, giving him the appearance of a guard post. He is flanked to the north by city hall, the seat of the *Senat*, and to the south by the *Schütting*, the home of the *Handelskammer*. Yet, his watchful gaze faces east, toward the cathedral.

The symbolism of Roland statues is traditionally that of an emblem of justice. He stands in the market square not by accident, but as a reminder to the moral embeddedness of commerce. The distance between the points of his characteristic, pointed pieces of knee-armor measures a Bremish yard (ca. 83 cm.), serving as a yardstick to buyers and sellers in the literal as well as the figurative sense. In his defiant stance toward the church, Roland's statue represents the claims to power of the medieval commune of burghers, which had wrested control of the city from the bishop. Based on these initial symbolic meanings, the statue came to embody

---

[15] Eleonore to Julius Wilkens, December 19, 1862; Wilhelm Knoche to same, February 27, 1864, MdHS MS.439. A sampling of the Weser-Zeitung for 1856 showed that the paper published correspondents' reports from the United States, and carried almost daily reports on that country. Some of these correspondents may have been merchants, which would make the newspaper a two-way medium, as well. Future research might be directed at establishing the professions of these writers. See Weser-Zeitung, StAHB, Mikrofim FB 311; Engelsing, Rolf, *Massenpublikum und Journalistentum im 19. Jahrhundert in Nordwestdeutschland* (Wolfram Fischer et al., eds., Studien zur Wirtschafts- und Sozialgeschichte, vol. 1), West Berlin, 1966, esp. 212–29, on mercantile journalism in Germany.

[16] Engelsing, *Massenpublikum*.

mercantile tradition, pride, and political independence, as the mercantile estate became the ruling group in the city.[17]

The *Schütting*, to the Roland's south, is adorned by the motto of the merchants' guild, "buten un binnen, wagen un winnen" – "without and within, venture and win." City hall, to his north, was often more inclined to follow the prescription borne by St. Ansgar's Gate, "Bremen wes gedhechtig; laß nicht mehr ein, als Du bist ihrer mechthig" – "Bremen be prudent; do not admit more than you can support."[18] Like the Roland, Bremen's merchants were situated between tradition and progress, between venturing out into the world and keeping a closed society at home. They negotiated the demands of both in a unique and often ingenious way.

The state of Bremen based its claims to legitimacy on its upholding of tradition in economic, political, and social life. Hanseats clung to a restrictive citizenship in Bremen, to a constitution that tied political rights to membership in an estate, and to a politics of deference. In their view, even if individuals had enjoyed perfectly equal, contractual rights in the marketplace, social and political equality did not logically follow from this. Unlike liberals, for whom the contract is the basis of human relations, Hanseats held the conservative view that the individual gains rights and duties only as a consequence of his station in society. They recognized as social equals men of standing and their wives, and as political equals men who had bought the Greater Privilege, which alone conferred full civic and economic rights in Bremen.

Hence, understanding the state of Bremen as a political entity is important not only because it provided a source of coherence to Hanseats who were active in different parts of the world, by representing their shared interest and their common beliefs, but also to avoid the trap of characterizing Hanseats as liberals, by way of a short-circuited conclusion that assumes that liberalism, capitalism, and cosmopolitanism form a package deal under a label of *modernization*.

When Wilhelm Knoche invoked the Roland in his letter to Julius Wilkens, he was invoking the particularity of a place, Bremen, which undergirded Hanseats' activities across the space created by world trade. True, Hanseats were in many essential ways cosmopolitans. Yet their cosmopolitanism was rooted in a particular local tradition. This tradition was the foundation, not just of their political ideas, but also of their economic ventures and their family bonds.

BREMEN IN THE INTERNATIONAL SYSTEM

Its long history as an independent, mercantile city-republic lent the force of tradition to Bremen's role in international politics and to the elite's role in Bremen's politics. It

---

[17] Wilhelm Knoche to Julius Wilkens, June 7, 1865 (direct quote); Wilhelm Knoche to Julius Wilkens, February 3, 1859, both MdHS MS.439. Schwarzwälder, Herbert, Geschichte der Freien Hansestadt Bremen, 4 vols., Hamburg 1987, vol. 1; for the Roland legend and the symbolism of Roland statues, see Gathen, Antonius David, *Rolande als Rechtssymbole. Der archäologische Bestand und seine rechtshistorische Deutung*, West Berlin, 1960.

[18] Both inscriptions are in Lower German. The English translations are by this author. The former was coined by Otto Gildemeister (1823–1902), a poet and author who translated Byron and Shakespeare into German, and who served as senator (from 1857) and burgomaster (intermittently, 1871–86), the phrase was inscribed on the façade of the building in 1899. Prüser, Friedrich, "Gildemeister, Otto," *Neue Deutsche Biographie* 6, Berlin, 1964, 395–6.

also helped shape the ideology held by that elite. Within a system of states founded on the idea of divine right, Bremen, along with its Hanseatic sister cities of Hamburg and Lübeck, had a republican governmental system that dated back to the Middle Ages. Even if this form of government made Bremen suspicious to the rulers of the territorial monarchies in Germany, there was nothing inherently progressive about Hanseatic republicanism.

At the beginning of the nineteenth century, Bremen's constitutional system was based on elite rule. The aldermen were handpicked from the merchants' guild, and the majority who lived in the lower rungs of the corporatist structure was excluded from political participation. Sovereignty rested with the government, until 1822 officially called *Rat* (council), but publicly referred to as the *Senat*, whose members were called into that body by way of co-optation. The burgomaster was chosen from amidst the members of the *Senat* and technically remained a *primus inter pares* who represented the city as a whole. Until 1848, both the burgomaster and the *Senatoren* served in their offices for lifetime terms.[19]

Before 1806, Bremen had been a Free Imperial City, not under the domain of a secular territorial ruler or a bishop, but under the immediate, if entirely nominal, rule of the emperor. In 1806, as a result of Napoleon's victories over Prussia at Jena and Auerstädt and over Austria at Austerlitz, the Holy Roman Empire of the German Nation ceased to exist and Bremen's political status was called into question. *Senator* Johann Smidt bemoaned that the "free burghers of the *Reich*" had been turned into "republican outlaws" overnight.[20]

French dominance over the German states affected Bremen's economy, in that the Continental Blockade made all commerce with England illegal. As Bremen's merchants engaged in brisk smuggling ventures with British traders located on the island of Heligoland, the city increasingly ran afoul of French interests.[21] In 1810, in order better to enforce the blockade, France annexed the Northern German seaboard, making Bremen the seat of a French Département, named "Bouches de Weser."[22]

With Napoleon's defeat in 1813, Bremen was "liberated," but her political status remained unsettled. Ultimately, the arrangements made by those states that emerged from the war as the Great Powers would determine the fate of the city. The Congress of Vienna created the German Confederation as the loose framework that would comprise the German states. There would no longer be an emperor, but rather a council of sovereigns (*Bundesrat*) at the head of this federation. The member states of the confederation retained the right to form alliances with foreign countries independently, unless they were directed against other member states. The individual states had full control over their armed forces. Only along the Rhine were formed a few federal fortresses, in which soldiers from several states were combined under the command of

---

[19] Schulz, *Weltbürger*, 642–8.
[20] Johann Smidt, as quoted in Möller, Kurt Detlev, "Zur Politik der Hansestädte im Jahre 1806," *Zeitschrift des Vereins für Hamburgische Geschichte* 41 (1951) (Festschrift für H. Reincke), 330–52, quote p. 337; Bippen, Wilhelm von, *Johann Smidt, ein hanseatischer Staatsmann*, Stuttgart and Berlin, 1921, on Smidt in general.
[21] Schleiden, *Jugenderinnerungen*, 51.
[22] Schwarzwälder, *Geschichte*, 14–20; Rössler, Horst, *Hollandgänger, Sträflinge und Migranten. Bremen-Bremerhaven als Wanderungsraum*, Bremen, 2000, 73.

the confederation. If the whole confederacy was to declare war, the member states were obliged to send fixed contingents. The *Bundesrat* had the right to pass laws; however, these would not become effective in any of the states, unless enacted by its sovereign. For all practical purposes, the different states retained full sovereignty, including the right to enter into treaties and levy tariffs.[23]

Of the many Free Imperial Cities that had existed in 1789, only Hamburg, Bremen, Lübeck, and Frankfurt survived the end of the old Holy Roman Empire of the German Nation, the territorial arrangements of the Napoleonic Wars, and the Congress of Vienna. There had been 1,789 sovereign entities in the empire in the year 1789. After the Congress of Vienna, there were just two dozen left. Under the circumstances, it was no small feat for Bremen's representative at the congress, *Senator* Johann Smidt, to have secured Bremen's independence.

Johann Smidt embodied in his politics the sensibilities of Bremen's elite. He was an arch-conservative in domestic matters, while embracing liberalism and free trade in international politics. Bremen's merchant elite left their political affairs mostly to legal and religious scholars of their fellow Calvinist faith. Smidt fit that description well. Born in 1773, he was the son of a Reformed minister. He studied theology in Jena and received his ordination as a minister in Zurich. While in Jena, Smidt had befriended Johann Gottlieb Fichte and mixed with other figures of the German Enlightenment. After his return to Bremen, Smidt had been elected into the *Senat* in 1800. His biographers paint a picture of Smidt as a sharp-witted intellectual who was convinced that Bremen could play a leading role in world trade. The city's political elite must have realized Smidt's gift – his age at the time of his election was twenty years below the average for new *Senatoren*.[24]

While a delegate to the Congress of Vienna, Johann Smidt used his diplomatic talent and influence for a cause equally important to him as Bremen's sovereignty: the exclusion of Jews from the city. Under French rule, Jews had been allowed to settle in Bremen. The spirit of reform that gripped Prussia during the wars against Napoleon had resulted in Jewish emancipation in that kingdom. The liberal ideal of a citizenry composed of equals, rather than a people divided into privileged orders and estates, was the dominant principle in German political thinking in the period from 1810 to 1818. Prussia, with its comparatively enlightened ministries during this brief reform period, was perceived as the bellwether of a general trend contemporaries believed would shape the constitutions of the German Confederation and its member states. Smidt, dedicated to a vision of community based on tradition, was not about to allow this liberal trend to become a reality.[25]

A provision in the founding document of the German Confederation under discussion in Vienna stated that "Jews receive full civic rights in the states of the Confederation." Cunningly, Johann Smidt worked behind the scenes to have the word *in* replaced with the word *by*. Instead of an obligation to emancipate Jews,

[23] Lemnitzer, Jan Martin, "'A few burghers in a little Hanseatic town' – Die Bremer Seerechtskampagne von 1859," *Bremisches Jahrbuch* 83 (2004), 87–111.

[24] Bippen, *Johann Smidt*; Möller, "Politik der Hansestädte."

[25] Wippermann, Wolfgang, *Jüdisches Leben im Raum Bremerhaven. Eine Fallstudie zur Alltagsgeschichte der Juden vom 18. Jahrhundert bis zur NS-Zeit* (Burchard Schepeler, ed., Veröffentlichungen des Stadtarchivs Bremerhaven, vol. 5), Bremerhaven, 1985, 37–52.

states would be given the discretion to do so. Smidt's lobbying efforts were successful, and the final document contained the change in wording he had desired. Jewish emancipation in Germany was thus deferred for another thirty-three years. Free to revert to the exclusive criteria for citizenship, Bremen's government quickly moved to exclude Jews from the city. Those Jews who had settled in Bremen under French law were expelled.[26]

Arguably, Jews were not the only ones excluded. Catholics were equally unwanted in the Hanseatic city, and even Lutherans found it hard to be accepted into Bremish society. On the one hand, Smidt's anti-Judaism was merely an affirmation of the general principle of communal exclusivity and homogeneity. On the other hand, Smidt went to great lengths to have the principle confirmed specifically for Jews, and in practice, no other group was as systematically purged from the city.[27]

In 1821, in recognition of his achievements, Johann Smidt was elected burgomaster. As such, he pursued a particularistic policy, directed against nationalism and popular participation. If Bremen found herself aligned with German liberals on occasion, it was due to a convergence of interests on questions of trade. After 1830, however, the liberal-nationalist mainstream increasingly favored a protective tariff, to which Bremen's merchants did not subscribe.[28]

During his thirty-six years at the head of the government, Smidt put into practice his vision for Bremen as a city of world trade. He systematically created the conditions that put Bremen's merchants in the position to engage competitively in trade with the United States. In the 1820s, he secured by treaty with the neighboring Kingdom of Hannover a piece of land by the mouth of the Weser River, on which the deep-sea port of Bremerhaven was built. In 1827, he signed the

[26] Quote from Möller, "Politik," 337. For Smidt in Vienna, see Baron, Salo, *Die Judenfrage auf dem Wiener Kongress*, Vienna and Berlin, 1920; Bippen, *Johann Smidt*, 158–78; Hundt, Michael, "Die Vertretung der jüdischen Gemeinden Lübecks, Bremens und Hamburgs auf dem Wiener Kongreß," *Blätter für Deutsche Landesgeschichte* 130 (1994), 143–90; Rüthnick, Richard, *Bürgermeister Smidt und die Juden (Bremens Judenpolitik 1803–1848)*, Bremen, 1934. The latter is an anti-Semitic treatment of the subject. Mustafa, "Hanseatic Cities," errs when he writes that "the Hanseatic cities ... were ... tolerant of religious minorities – Catholics and Jews – who were allowed to participate freely in the economic life," 268. This was true of Hamburg, not of Bremen, where residential restrictions against Jews and Catholics were not abandoned until 1849. See Toury, Jacob, "Die Revolution von 1848 als innerjüdischer Wendepunkt," in *Das Judentum in der deutschen Umwelt, 1800–1850. Studien zur Frühgeschichte der Emanzipation*, ed. Hans Liebeschütz and Arnold Paucker, Tübingen, 1977, 359–76, 367. Emancipation in Bremen was rescinded with the 1854 constitution, and finally reintroduced only in 1863. See Wipperman, *Jüdisches Leben*, 51–2.

[27] Marschalek, "Bürgerrechts"; Wippermann, *Jüdisches Leben*. Before French rule, Catholics had been excluded from residence, while Lutherans faced restrictions on occupation and office holding. Bremen was a Calvinist community.

[28] Baasch, Ernst, "Hamburg und Bremen und die deutschen wirtschaftlichen Einheitsbestrebungen von der Begründung des Zollvereins bis zum Anschluß Hannovers (1854)," *Hanseatische Geschichtsblätter* 47 (1922), 115–69; Best, Heinrich, *Interessenpolitik und nationale Integration 1848/49. Handelspolitische Konflikte im frühindustriellen Deutschland* (Helmut Berding, Jürgen Kocka, and Hans-Ulrich Wehler, eds., Kritische Studien zur Geschichtswissenschaft, vol. 37), Göttingen, 1980; Krieger, Adolf, *Arnold Duckwitz, hanseatischer Staatsmann und Reichshandelsminister von 1848 im Kampf für eine deutsche Wirtschaftsordnung. Wirtschaftspolitische Aufsätze* (Abhandlungen und Vorträge herausgegeben von der Wittheit zu Bremen, vol. 15, no. 1, August 1942), Bremen, 1942.

trade treaty between Bremen and the United States. In the 1830s, he lent his support to merchants' efforts to attract German emigrants to the port of Bremen. Further strengthening the ties between the Hanseatic city and the hinterland, a railroad line connecting Bremen to Hannover was completed in 1848, with the financial backing of the Bremish state. In the 1840s, Smidt made sure that Bremen would be among the first continental ports to establish a direct steamship connection with the New World. In 1853, he further cemented the ties to the United States by appointing Rudolf Schleiden as Bremen's first professional diplomat in Washington, D.C.[29]

Smidt's record is one of aggressive modernization, applied selectively to turn Bremen into a major player in international trade. If his modest world-historical fame rests on his anti-Judaic record, Johann Smidt's image in Bremen remains that of a man revered for a prudent foreign policy that propelled the city from a regional trading center to an *entrepôt* of world trade. Where modernized laws or infrastructure did not serve this purpose, the city's mercantile elite avoided them. Thus Bremen refused to join the German Customs Union, created in 1833, until 1888. The abolition of tariffs on trade between its member states was not worth the impediment to foreign trade – especially the considerable reexport trade – of the high external tariff barriers set up by the customs union.[30]

These, then, were the political conditions that made it possible for Hanseats to become the cosmopolitan community of transatlantic merchants that thrived in America. The state of Bremen maintained not just the legal and institutional infrastructure of global trade that put Bremen on the map. It also built a network of consulates in the New World, whose functionaries were recruited from Bremen's merchant houses in American ports. Through this network, Bremen projected abroad its – admittedly modest – power as a state. Its consuls served judiciary functions for ship crews, negotiated with customs officials, helped hunt down deserters, and labored to create public goodwill toward the immigrants who arrived on Bremish vessels. Through the consuls, Bremen also received crucial intelligence about the economic and political situation abroad. As consuls tended to come from well-established Hanseatic families, Bremen's diplomatic service immediately reinforced the connections established by families and firms. Yet the Hanseatic bid for a slice of a modern commercial system rested on a political and economic structure at home that remained vigorously committed to tradition.[31]

[29] Schwarzwälder, *Geschichte*, 73, 121–34.
[30] Ibid., 221–2. Today, one of the four bridges across the Weser River in Bremen is named after Smidt. Arnold Duckwitz to Rudolf Schleiden, Bremen, June 16, 1853, StAHB 7,116 [Rudolf Schleiden Papers], folder "Briefwechsel Rudolf Schleiden mit Senator Arnold Duckwitz, 1854–1879," third of five unnumbered and unlabeled boxes.
[31] Rösing, Johannes, "Schleiden, Rudolf" *Allgemeine Deutsche Biographie* 54, Munich, 1908, 33–41; Steinsdorfer, Helmut, "Zur Erinnerung an Rudolf Schleiden (1815–1895) – Diplomat, Politiker und Publizist aus Schleswig-Holstein," *Die Heimat (Husum)* 102, no. 9/10 (September–October 1995), 201–15; Fink, Georg, "Diplomatische Vertretungen der Hanse seit dem 17. Jahrhundert bis zur Auflösung der Hanseatischen Gesandtschaft in Berlin 1920," *Hanseatische Geschichtsblätter* 56, Lübeck, Germany, 1932, 112–55; Graßmann, Antjekathrin, "Hanse weltweit? Zu den Konsulaten Lübecks, Bremens und Hamburgs im 19. Jahrhundert," idem, ed., *Ausklang und Nachklang der Hanse im 19. und 20. Jahrhundert* (Hansischer Geschichtsverein, ed., Hansische Studien, vol. 12), Trier, Germany, 2001, 43–66.

BREMEN AS HOMETOWN

In domestic politics, Johann Smidt presided over the dismantling of the Napoleonic Code in Bremish law and the reintroduction of customary laws. At the center of this traditional legal order stood a tiered system of citizenship that made participation in the political and economic life of the city a matter of acquired privilege, rather than of rights. It was in a memorandum Smidt wrote during the occasion of the Congress of Vienna, that he summed up the _modus operandi_ of Bremen's governmental system: "In states this small, the constitution is but the framework of an extended family life, where the bond is only held by mutual trust."[32] As much a normative as a descriptive statement, Smidt affirmed here his firm belief in a communal basis of government and his opposition to liberal theories of society.

After 1813, the _Senat_ had reinstated a corporatist structure of city government. Not unlike the "hometowns" of central Germany described by Mack Walker, Bremen's political and social institutions intertwined to uphold a precapitalist form of society. Its cornerstone were the guilds, bases of civic identity and cultural expression, as well as institutions with an economic function – that of limiting the markets for labor and commodities, in the service of providing all market participants with a "just price." Limits on residency and citizenship restricted occupational mobility within and the movement of outsiders into the city.[33]

The institutions of civic government represented layers of power, emanations of particular estates, created under specific historical circumstances, and hence invested with the aura of tradition.[34] They had come into being over the course of centuries, as more and different groups came to lay claims to participation in the governance of the city. The _Senat_ represented the oldest layer of communal rule. The _Kaufmannskonvent_ (merchants' convention) and its organ, the _Handelskammer_, embodied the claims by merchants to participate in city government, historically often in conflict with the _Senat_. The _Bürgerschaft_ was the youngest layer, a body incorporating artisans and their guilds into city government alongside the mercantile representatives.[35]

The 1848 revolution in Bremen was the first successful attack from within on the political principle behind this tangle of institutions. The brief reign of the democrats – supported by the lower and middling classes of the city, but constantly sabotaged by the _Senat_ – brought universal male suffrage and a formal separation of powers among the _Senat_ (as government), the _Bürgerschaft_ (as legislature), and the judiciary. However, it left the corporatist social structure unaffected.[36]

Burgomaster Smidt's course of action during the revolutionary upheaval of 1848 can be regarded as an apt expression of the peculiar mix of conservatism and

---

[32] Smidt, Johann, "Denkschrift über die Judenfrage in Bremen," as paraphrased by Baron, Salo W., _Die Judenfrage auf dem Wiener Kongreß_, Vienna and Berlin, 1920, 105. In 1920, Baron found this document in the Vienna State Archive. I could not establish the present location.

[33] Cf. Walker, Mack, _German Home Towns: Community, State, and General Estate, 1648–1817_, Ithaca, NY, and London, 1971. See also Chapter 4 for the demise of the guild system in the early 1860s.

[34] Cf. Niehoff, Lydia, _550 Jahre Tradition der Unabhängigkeit. Chronik der Handelskammer Bremen_ (Handelskammer Bremen, ed.), Bremen, 2001, 101.

[35] For terminology, please see the glossary.

[36] Biebusch, Werner, _Revolution und Staatsstreich. Verfassungskämpfe in Bremen, 1848–1854_ (Veröffentlichungen aus dem Staatsarchiv Bremen, vol. 40), Bremen, 1974.

innovation that characterized Bremen's mercantile elite at home, and helped shape the behavior of its merchants abroad. Smidt had been called by the revolutionary German parliament, the Frankfurt National Assembly, to serve as foreign minister in the revolutionary German government, but declined. Instead, he encouraged his protégée, *Senator* Arnold Duckwitz, to accept an appointment as minister of commerce. This sent a signal that Bremen was with the revolutionary movement, in case it won; yet it made sure that the Hanseatic presence at Frankfurt was conservative enough not to forego future cooperation with crowned heads, in case these stayed on their bearers' shoulders.[37]

Within Bremen, Smidt made sure that the popular movement demanding the extension of citizenship rights to the unpropertied was kept in check. A new *Bürgerschaft*, elected in 1848 with universal male suffrage, had a democratic majority. The *Senat*, however, remained in office, its existing members confirmed in their lifelong tenure. Only newly elected *Senatoren* were to be restricted to a twelve-year term. The revolutionary *Bürgerschaft* had the chance to replace one *Senator* who died in 1849, but otherwise the *Senat* remained an institutional safe haven for reactionaries, who could bide their time until an opportunity presented itself to restore the traditional political order.[38]

Senator Diedrich A. Meier displayed a sense of disgust at the state of affairs in a letter to Gustav B. Schwab. From the point of view of this Hanseat, democracy was primarily a nuisance hindering good government by the elite:

We would be happier and more joyful here if we did not have the democrats, because these make our life difficult and one engages in public affairs, from which one cannot withdraw here, but with annoyance and grudgingly, but in our station one cannot help but deal with these things.[39]

Fortunately for Meier, Smidt, and their allies, help was on the way. By 1851, the revolution in Germany had been defeated. Prussian and Austrian bayonets had restored the German Confederation and the power of the monarchs. Johann Smidt secretly appealed to the restored council of German sovereigns (*Bundesrat*) for a law that threatened with force any member state of the confederation that retained a democratic constitution. Once that law had been passed, the *Senat* used the threat of an armed intervention by the confederation to bypass the *Bürgerschaft* and to enact a voting law that considerably restricted the suffrage (1851; see Table 9). Once the first election under the new law had purged the democrats from the parliamentary body, Smidt successfully pushed for a constitution that reinstated the rights of the estates, yet left the separation of powers partially in place (1854).[40] Completing the reactionary backlash, the leader of the democrats, pastor Rudolf Dulon, was defrocked and incarcerated. Smidt, the theologian, did not pass the opportunity to cite religious as well as political grounds for his prosecution. Dulon eventually went to the United States.[41]

---

[37] Bippen, *Johann Smidt*; Krieger, *Arnold Duckwitz*; Schwarzwälder, *Geschichte*, vol. 2, 181–214.

[38] Schwarzwälder, *Geschichte*, vol. 2, 181–214; Biebusch, *Revolution*.

[39] D. A. Meier to Gustav B. Schwab, Bremen, December 11, 1849, MSS 434, John Christopher Schwab Family Papers. Manuscripts and Archives, Yale University Library, series I, box 1, folder 29.

[40] Jurisprudence, in particular, remained in the hands of a separate branch of government, where it had been an executive function before 1848.

[41] Schwarzwälder, *Geschichte*, vol. 2, 207–14.

TABLE 9. *Representation in the* Bürgerschaft *under the 1851 Voting Law*

Class	Members of the Bürgerschaft	Eligibility	No. of Voters	Voters per Member of the Bürgerschaft
I	16	Scholarly Estate★	141	14.1
II	48	Mercantile Estate★	776	16.2
III	24	Artisanal Estate★	138	5.8
IV.a.	10	Residents of Bremen, >500 Thaler taxable income	886	88.6
IV.b.	10	Residents of Bremen, 250–500 Thaler taxable income	1,754	175.4
IV.c.	10	Residents of Bremen, no taxable income (i.e., <250 Thaler)	2,460	246.0
V.a–c	6	Residents of Vegesack (3 voter classes @ 2 members each)	475	79.2
VI.a–c	6	Residents of Bremerhaven (three voter classes @ 2 members each)	375	62.5
VII.	10	Agricultural Estate★	750	75.0
VIII.	10	Other rural population	2,355	235.5
	150	TOTAL	**9,224**	average 61.5

Source: Herbert Schwarzwälder, *Geschichte der Freien Hansestadt Bremen,* 4 vols., Hamburg 1987, vol. 2, 217–18. Classes marked by an asterisk (★) represent proper estates, each electing a chamber to represent their members. The individual members of an estate, and its chamber, jointly picked the *Bürgerschaft* members for that class.

Numbers reflect the population in 1852. Only one-eighth (12.5%) of the total population of the state of Bremen were able to vote under any of the categories. Many inhabitants were excluded from voting because of their age, others because they did not have a status as burghers. Even in the 1867 Reichstag elections, however, in which every male from age 25 could vote, only 18,636 persons (16.3%) out of 114,000 inhabitants could vote. Assuming gender parity among the population, this would suggest that a share of up to two-thirds of the population was below 25 years of age. See Krieger, Adolf, *Bremische Politik im Jahrzehnt vor der Reichsgründung* (Schriften der Bremer Wissenschaftlichen Gesellschaft, Reihe F [früher A★], Friedrich Prüser, ed., *Veröffentlichungen des Archivs der Hansestadt Bremen,* vol. 15), Bremen, 1939, p. 90, note 2, and p. 118, note 1.

THE CORPORATIST ORDER OF THE 1850S

The economic side of the corporatist order had not been affected by the revolution of 1848. Where, in other German states, free labor (*Gewerbefreiheit*) was high on the revolutionary agenda, Bremen's democrats had a strong base among the crafts and therefore left the guilds alone.[42] Guild-like arrangements in the mercantile profession, supported by a solid consensus among the elite, likewise survived

[42] Ibid., 193, 203, 227. While literally translating into "freedom of trades," *Gewerbefreiheit* was discussed as a matter of the right of individuals to choose their profession freely. Its proponents and opponents alike used the term *free labor* (*Freiheit der Arbeit*) in the debates, and I have chosen to use this term to describe the idea behind the project of the abolition of the guilds. Trade in this sense does not describe commerce (as in "free trade agreement"), but artisanal production (as in "the tools of the trade").

1848 virtually unaltered. For example, the right to become a long-distance merchant remained tied to the purchase of the Greater Privilege.[43]

Under the 1854 constitution, a person's station in society was once again defined by his or her economic function. Every occupation had a place in a corporate order. A cobbler was a member of the shoemakers' guild qua his profession, which he held as a quasipublic office; at the same time, a person desiring to work as a cobbler would have to be a member of the shoemakers' guild in the first place. All traditional trades and professions were organized in this corporate manner. Providing services or selling commodities was reserved by law to those organized in a guild. Only nontraditional occupations, such as cigar making, and laborers outside of the transportation business were exempt from these regulations.[44]

The two venues of admittance to most of the artisanal guilds, and hence to market participation as a producer in that craft, were apprenticeship and inheritance (in the case of masters' widows). For mercantile professions, access could be bought, in that the Greater Privilege entitled its bearer to engage in foreign trade, whereas the Lesser Privilege came with the right to trade commodities domestically. Some professions were further limited, in that the law provided for only a limited number of *Senat*-appointed office holders. Such was the case for lawyers and notaries public, but it was also the case for brokers and agents, subdivided by types of commodities: stock, bonds, bills of exchange, specie, and, finally, ships. These professions, unlike the guilds, lacked bodies of self-government. Their practitioners were answerable to the community at large, through *Senatorial* supervision.[45]

Until the 1860s, then, there was not a fully free market for labor or services. Neither was the labor power of the working class turned into a commodity to be bought or sold at will, nor were professionals free to practice their occupation at their own discretion. Labor and exchange within the city remained deeply embedded in a traditional ethos of household, estate, and community.

Among the traditional institutions of corporate society that survived into the 1860s, those governing financial matters were particularly remarkable. In a study of Bremish financial markets, Hanseatic economic historian Ludwig Beutin argues that, where other German states had resorted to externalizing money lending and exchange from the Christian community by allowing it to Jews, Bremen had created the brokers' corporation for these purposes. Brokers were required to be of the Reformed creed and were forbidden to conduct any business on their own account. Merchants, in turn, were obliged to conduct their monetary transactions through the brokers.[46]

[43] Marschalek, Peter, "Der Erwerb des bremischen Bürgerrechts und die Zuwanderung nach Bremen um die Mitte des 19. Jahrhunderts," *Bremisches Jahrbuch* 66 (1988), 295–305.

[44] Schwarzwälder, *Geschichte*, vol. 2, 227–30.

[45] Beutin, Ludwig, *Bremisches Bank- und Börsenwesen seit dem 17. Jahrhundert. Von der Wirtschaftsgesinnung einer Hansestadt* (Abhandlungen und Vorträge herausgegeben von der Bremer Wissenschaftlichen Gesellschaft, vol. 10, no. 4, December 1937), Bremen, 1937; Böhmert, Victor, *Beiträge zur Geschichte des Zunftwesens* (Preisschriften, gekrönt und herausgegeben von der fürstlich Jablonowski'schen Gesellschaft zu Leipzig, IX.), Leipzig, 1862 (1859).

[46] Beutin, *Bank- und Börsenwesen*; Ahrens, Gerhard, "Staatsschuld und Anleihenpolitik der hanseatischen Stadtrepubliken im frühen 19. Jahrhundert," *Blätter für Deutsche Landesgeschichte* 134 (1998), 361–406.

Mandated by law, the balancing of accounts between merchants had to be administered by two brokers, appointed by the *Senat*. On two weekdays, at a set time, the brokers compared outstanding accounts and calculated balances. The merchants then settled their accounts with each other in specie. The evident benefit of this procedure was to lower the amount of money needed in circulation. This venerable system had been in place essentially unaltered since 1626.[47]

The brokers were expressly forbidden from engaging in banking activities on their own account. They could not give credit. Their revenue came exclusively from the commission fees they received from the merchants.[48] Still, the broker system made possible a credit system. In the eighteenth century, merchants within Bremen began to draw bills of exchange for three or six months – much longer than the thirty days usual even in the mid-nineteenth century – on each other. By doing so, they expanded the amount of available capital. Beutin contended that the fragility of this system, caused by the right of every merchant to demand payment at the due date, was counterbalanced by the closely knit structure of the merchant community, based on mutual trust.[49] Whether trust or interest constituted a stronger bond, the system worked. Most likely, a strong family network supplied both trust and interest as incentives to make it work.

Beutin correctly points out that, apart from facilitating circulation, the broker system fulfilled the function of keeping the market of Bremen closed to foreigners. Noncitizens of Bremen were not allowed to do business with each other within the city. Wholesale trade was legally reserved to holders of the Greater Privilege, which could be bought for four hundred Thaler Gold and for which a security deposit and a minimum amount of property were required. The Lesser Privilege, which came with more restrictive economic rights, went for fifty Thaler Gold. The brokers enforced trade restrictions. Bremen's market was thus a closely watched, closed society. As the brokers supervised the marketplace, the *Senat* supervised the brokers.[50] The traditional ethos of this economy continued to decry interest as usury throughout the first half of the nineteenth century, although the use of bills of exchange expanded.[51]

Taxation remained governed by tradition as well. Among the general population, an income tax was collected by the *Senat*. The holders of the Lesser Privilege and the Greater Privilege, however, who contributed most of the tax revenue, enjoyed the privilege of self-taxation. With their civic oath, they had sworn to contribute an annual amount of taxes, dependent on their wealth. This amount was paid in cash, anonymously deposited in city hall on a set day of the year. As late as 1866, a special tax to finance the cost of the Six Weeks War was collected in this way.[52]

Individuals – in as far as we can speak of individuals under a system that defines a person first and foremost in relation to his or her station – enjoyed political rights

[47] Beutin, *Bank- und Börsenwesen*, 8.

[48] These fees were: 1% of their value for bills of exchange, 1/8% of the coverage sum for insurance contracts, and 1/36% Thaler Gold (2 Grote) per Last (literally, "load," a cubic measure) for the commissioning of cargo; Beutin, *Bank- und Börsenwesen*, 10.

[49] Ibid., 18.

[50] Ibid., 21, 50–1; Beutin, *Bremen und Amerika*, 120–1.

[51] Beutin, *Bank- und Börsenwesen*, 25–30.

[52] *Verhandlungen der Bremischen Bürgerschaft im Jahre 1866*, 20. Sitzung, July 7, 1866, 301–8. From here on, I will cite the Bürgerschaft minutes in the following abbreviated format: VdBBü [YEAR]/ [SESSION No.], [SESSION DATE], page numbers.

through their membership in corporations. The 150 members of parliament, the *Bürgerschaft*, were elected in eight different voter classes, each class defined differently, but all defined by the economic standing and social function of its members (Table 9).

The first class consisted of sixteen members, representing the scholars' estate. All those who held a doctorate were eligible as voters in this class. The second, and largest, individual class was jointly elected by the members of the Merchants' Convention (*Kaufmannsconvent*) and the *Handelskammer*. Voters in this class had to hold the Greater Privilege and engage in some form of overseas trade. Class three comprised the representatives of the artisans' guilds. Its twenty-four members were elected jointly by the Trades' Convention and the Chamber of the Trades. Finally, freeholders of farmsteads, together with the Chamber of Agriculture, sent ten men into parliament. These four groups represented proper corporate bodies, or estates. A total of 1,805 persons were represented through these estates. Another 8,305 persons had voting rights in the remaining four voter classes, defined by taxable income and place of residence. Bremen's most recent chronist, Herbert Schwarzwälder, has estimated that seven-eighths of the population, or another seventy thousand persons, were completely disenfranchised under the 1851 voting law.[53]

This system of representation was evidently uneven. It was also deliberately confusing. To make matters more complicated, only half of the members delegated by each voter class were elected every three years, for a six-year term. The other half were elected for the same duration of term, but at an interval three years removed. To American readers, this principle should be familiar. It is essentially the same mechanism as that by which the U.S. Senate is elected, with the difference that the latter is divided into three cohorts, rather than two. As in the U.S. Constitution, its purpose in Bremen was to limit the impact of an "undesirable" election outcome. The desired effect of the eight-class voting system was to discourage broad popular participation. After its introduction, less than one in ten eligible low-income voters participated in elections.[54]

No amount of support for democrats among "the many" would have been able to change the central fact of this system – it was an instrument of mercantile political dominance. Short of another revolution, any changes to that system were thus to be "reforms from above," originating within the mercantile estate. This estate, however, saw the corporate mode of popular representation as a keystone to a good social order and a well-run polity. While the Hanseats' support for this system of government was consistent, none of them justified it as elaborately as Wilhelm Kiesselbach.

WILHELM KIESSELBACH: ORGANIC INTELLECTUAL OF BREMEN'S ELITE

Practical politicians are not as prone to develop a coherent theory of their own interests as are intellectuals. The latter can afford an honest appraisal, where the former might be limited by tactical considerations.[55] In spite of the standing quip of

---

[53] Schwarzwälder, *Geschichte*, vol. 2, 217–18.
[54] Ibid. This same class had been the main force behind the 1848 revolution.
[55] I am following Eugene Genovese in this argument. See his *The World the Slaveholders Made: Two Essays in Interpretation*, New York, 1969, 163.

outsiders that Hanseats suffered from a narrowness of intellectual perspective induced by their fixation on commercial pursuits, Bremen's elite did produce some original thinkers. Most remarkable among them was Wilhelm Kiesselbach, an organic intellectual in the double sense, as a theorist for his estate and as a proponent of an organically ordered, corporatist society.

An academic with a nationwide audience, Wilhelm Kiesselbach was recognized by his contemporaries as a Hanseatic theorist.[56] In his works, he provided the theoretical justification for combining a corporatist political order with a liberal economic order. Merchants participating in public debates in Bremen resonated Kiesselbach's arguments, familiar to them from his writings, as well as personal interaction. Born in 1824, Kiesselbach stemmed from a well-established Hanseatic family and was part of the circle of intermarried elite members.[57] He taught history at Heidelberg, but, after the death of his wife, retired to Bremen in 1862, where he died in 1872.[58]

Although Kiesselbach's most important publications date from the early 1860s, they illuminate the world of ideas that informed the generation of Hanseats who had made Bremen into a center of world trade in the preceding decades. Kiesselbach's oeuvre represents the sum of experience of Bremen's elite, systematizing the opinions generally shared among his estate and affirming convictions formed and solidified over time. One reason these Hanseatic ideas were never developed as extensively earlier might be that they had never been as vigorously under attack from the forces of industrialization, nationalism, and democracy as they were in the 1860s. At that point, Bremen's elite needed a Kiesselbach to represent to the world what they already knew to be true.

Kiesselbach's writings place him squarely at the center of the transatlantic nexus that informed political debates in Bremen. He was one of the first Germans to write on the subject of the U.S. Constitution, the Declaration of Independence, and the *Federalist Papers*.[59] Epitomizing the Hanseatic interest in the United States, Kiesselbach wrote:

Over the couch in father's study, there hung a lithography of the American Declaration of Independence, of July 4th, 1776; surrounded by the portraits of Washington, Hancock, and Jefferson, and the coats-of-arms of the old thirteen states of the Union. As a boy, I often stood in front of this tableau, asking myself how this confederation of states had been ordered. When, after the early death of the father, I was allowed to take

[56] E.g., when Marx alleged the inability of merchant capital to grasp the essence of the political economy of industrial capitalism, he cited Kiesselbach as the leading example. Marx, Karl, *Capital*, vol. 3, Moscow, 1974 (Progress Publishers), 327, note 46. Likewise, on p. 339 of the same volume of *Capital*, Marx refers to Kiesselbach's study *The Course of World Trade in the Middle Ages* (Der Gang des Welthandels im Mittelalter, Bremen 1860) to illustrate his point that the "purely mercantile cities" live in their glorious past, and utterly lack all comprehension of modern capitalist times.

[57] Cf. Brandes, Erika, "Der Bremer Überseekaufmann in seiner gesellschaftsgeschichtlichen Bedeutung im 'geschlossenen Heiratskreis,'" *Genealogisches Jahrbuch* 3 (1963), 25–48.

[58] Kiesselbach's brother, e.g., was married to the daughter of Mayor Duckwitz. Lührs, Wilhelm, "Kiesselbach, Wilhelm (1867–1960)," *Neue Deutsche Biographie* 11, Berlin, 1977, 599–600. While treating the nephew of the Wilhelm Kiesselbach discussed here, Lührs's article contains valuable biographical information on his uncle. See also Engelsing, "England und die USA," 57.

[59] Kiesselbach, Wilhelm, *Der amerikanische Federalist. Politische Studien für die deutsche Gegenwart*, 2 vols., Bremen, London, and New York, 1864.

the frame, the dear image of the deceased merged with my scholarly studies, which I had ceaselessly conducted in my youth, under this great document, now looking at me from the wall.[60]

This display of sentimental attachment to the founding documents of the United States and his praise for "the proud accomplishment of Washington"[61] have led German historians of the United States to consider Kiesselbach a liberal. The late Willi Paul Adams claimed that Kiesselbach desired a democratic state in Germany. Horst Dippel credits Kiesselbach with locating the principles of the Declaration of Independence in their North American context, yet blames him for missing their universal content.[62]

Both characterizations miss the mark. Kiesselbach was an opponent of democracy, and he was well aware of the "universal" – in his own words, "abstract" and "French" – content of the Declaration of Independence. The point was that he rejected this content and welcomed the Constitution as an overdue rectification of the dangerously revolutionary situation created under the Articles of Confederation.[63]

In Kiesselbach's worldview, the "abstract state of law"[64] had to be complemented by elements of a "social-economic state." He identified the former with the French model of "drawing straight lines from the center of power to the atomized individual in society" and blamed this type of state for what he regarded as the unhealthy dominance of the bureaucracy over society.[65]

His ideal of the "social-economic state" may best be characterized as corporatist or rather estatist. Unlike other conservative proponents of a corporatist, "organic" social order, however, Kiesselbach was not an enemy of capitalism by any means. This set him apart from both German reactionaries and the Southern Conservative tradition in the United States.[66] At the same time, Kiesselbach shared with these latter contemporaries the view that the person is more than a bearer of abstract rights.[67] Overall, his views most closely resembled those one might find among

---

[60] Kiesselbach, *Federalist*, vol. 1, iii. Kiesselbach further mentions that he received a copy of the *Federalist*, when his brother brought one back with him from the United States.

[61] Idem, iv.

[62] Adams, "German Translations"; Dippel, Horst, "Die Unabhängigkeitserklärung in Deutschland: Betrachtungen über politische Kultur und gemeinsame Werte," http://www.dhm.de/magazine/unabhaengig/dippel_d.htm (accessed June 7, 2004).

[63] Other Hanseats found the rights of states the most appealing feature of the U.S. Constitution. See Engelsing, "England und die USA," 62–4.

[64] He uses the term *Rechtsstaat* throughout.

[65] Kiesselbach, Wilhelm, *Socialpolitische Studien (Nach den in der Deutschen Vierteljahrsschrift veröffentlichten Aufsätzen des Verfassers zusammengestellt und neu durchgearbeitet)*, Stuttgart, 1862, 117. The notion of bureaucracy that informs Kiesselbach assumes a unified civil administration that makes decisions based on abstract principles.

[66] Riehl, Wilhelm Heinrich, *Die bürgerliche Gesellschaft*, Stuttgart, 1861, e.g., pp. 174–5; Genovese, *The World the Slaveholders Made*, esp. part II on George Fitzhugh, whose thought has a strong resemblance to both Riehl's and Kiesselbach's; idem, *The Slaveholders' Dilemma: Freedom and Progress in Southern Conservative Thought, 1820–1860*, Columbia, SC, 1992; Gentz, Friedrich von, *The French and American Revolutions Compared*, translated by John Quincy Adams (1800), in *Three Revolutions*, ed., Stefan T. Possony, Chicago, 1959.

[67] For the roots of this position in German Enlightenment and Romantic thought, see Harada, Tetsushi, *Politische Ökonomie des Idealismus und der Romantik. Korporatismus von Fichte, Müller und Hegel* (Volkswirtschaftliche Schriften, vol. 386), West Berlin, 1989. A shared ancestor of English,

Whigs in the United States.[68] Within Germany, he remained a unique figure, reflecting the peculiar position of Hanseats in the society of the German states.

As a member of the Hanseatic elite, Kiesselbach was proud of the accomplishments of (merchant) capital. He described the state as a mere "skeleton," to which "mobile property"[69] adds "muscles," and "drives rolling money as blood through the veins it has created." He viewed the absolutist state as mostly concerned with war, an enterprise detrimental to trade interests. Eventually, he believed, the body politic created by mobile property would be able to do without the "belligerent bone structure of the state." The Kantian vision of world peace brought about by harmonious, mutually beneficial commerce among nations, shared by so many Hanseats, echoed strongly in this view and might excuse the awkward image of this utopian world as a body without bones.[70]

Not unlike the American Founding Fathers, and even not unlike democrats, Kiesselbach believed in the ability of society to govern itself. The key difference between Kiesselbach's thought and the liberal and democratic tradition was their different views of what actually constitutes a "society."

For Kiesselbach, the basis of self-government was not the individual endowed with political rights, but a society organically constituted by the mutual bonds of economic interdependence and cooperation among its members. His usage of the term *organic*, however, deserves a closer look, lest he be subsumed with those conservatives who regarded traditional institutions as an immediate expression of (human) nature or divine will. Kiesselbach emphasizes that both the state and the city are "*made*," once there arises, from an increase of the division of labor, a need for firmer social structure. Before the medieval commune of burghers, or the feudal state, there was nothing but the "corrosive republicanism of agriculture." This rural society was "a group of people that was *not yet* socially *organic*."[71]

Once states were established, trade remained the driving force behind progress and civilization. International law, for example, is a child of international trade. Between states that do not engage in foreign trade, there would not even be any international politics in a proper sense – that is, other than mere military clashes over territory. Kiesselbach's pride in the civilizing mission of merchant capital contrasts starkly with the anticommercialism of agrarian conservatives.[72]

German, and American proponents of this view was Burke, Edmund, *Reflections on the Revolution in France*, London 1986 (1790).

[68] See Ashworth, John, *"Agrarians" and "Aristocrats": Party Political Ideology in the United States, 1837–1846*, London and Atlantic Highlands, NJ, 1983; Howe, Daniel Walker, *The Political Culture of the American Whigs*, Chicago and London, 1979.

[69] *Bewegliches Eigentum*, as opposed to immobile, landed property, includes both trade and trades.

[70] Kiesselbach, *Studien*, 35; see also p. 46, where he praises the liberating qualities of circulation.

[71] Ibid., 41; my emphasis. The quip against Jefferson may well be intended.

[72] Ibid., 58. For examples of anticommercialism directed against the Hanseatic cities: Möller, Kurt Detlev, "Zur Politik der Hansestädte im Jahre 1806," *Zeitschrift des Vereins für Hamburgische Geschichte* 41 (1951) (Festschrift für H. Reincke), 330–52; Böhmert, Victor, "Die Stellung der Hansestädte zu Deutschland in den letzten drei Jahrzehnten," *Vierteljahrsschrift für Volkswirthschaft und Cultur* 1 (1863), 73–115. For an important American example, see Taylor, John, *An Inquiry into the Principles and Policy of the Government of the United States*, London, 1950 (1814), esp. pp. 230–353. Cf. Chapter 5.

The philosophical core of Kiesselbach's ideas was a kind of estatist materialism, resonating with the idea of "sober business sense" so highly valued in mercantile circles:

The struggle for the daily bread, i.e., that labor which supports the individual's existence, is the condition of all human activity. The natural division of labor not only puts man in a particular place in the general structure of society; but the kind of his work also has an inescapable effect on the development of his individuality.[73]

The individual attains importance not as an abstract person, but as a member of a group defined by its economic activity. This embeddedness of the individual serves to counteract a second, negative impact of money: its tendency to level people by making them equals in the marketplace. Kiesselbach considered the French tradition of statecraft and constitutionalism and its precursor, Roman Law, as "the law of a pure money-economy."[74] This legal tradition "separates person, labor and property from one another," where they ought to be considered inseparable moments of a whole.[75]

Evidently, mercantile activities depended on the interaction of legally equal partners to contracts in the marketplace. The ubiquity of contractual relations in their own social sphere, however, did not necessarily lead merchants to assume that the contract could serve as a general model for political relations in society at large. The contract between merchants is never an abstract legal interaction, but is embedded in the moral economy of the estate. Barriers to admission to the estate, the market, or both, assure the honor of the parties to the contract.[76]

This might explain why the Rousseaudian idea of a social contract appeared as an absurdity to Kiesselbach.[77] A contract can only come to be between agents who are equal by virtue of their station; the mere establishment of a contractual relation, however, does not render both parties equal.

That said, Kiesselbach does come down on the side of free competition in the marketplace for commodities and labor. He wants to see both trades and land-ownership opened up to all interested parties. In other words, he supports the abolition of primogeniture and entail and the scrapping of guild exclusivity.[78]

Kiesselbach wants the individual to be free to establish himself in any branch of economic activity. Once, however, a person has settled for a calling, his political rights should be derived from his social position. It is here that Kiesselbach explicitly recommends the Bremish example as a model for the political constitution of Germany:

The mercantile state of *Bremen* proves that a social organization of the state is possible, and that it has the best consequences for a vibrant political life. . . . Bremen held to the

---

[73] Kiesselbach, *Studien*, 118. This passage echoes James Madison's *Federalist* No. 10, a text Kiesselbach praised for its insights (see p. 201 of this study).

[74] Ibid., 125.

[75] Ibid.

[76] H. H. Meier expressed this consciousness in his defense of the broker system, see Chapter 4, 224. For the assumption that contractual relations do not entail social equality in the United States, see Stanley, Amy Dru, *From Bondage to Contract: Wage Labor, Marriage, and the Market in the Age of Slave Emancipation*, New York, 1998; and Richardson, Heather Cox, *The Death of Reconstruction: Race, Labor, and Politics in the Post–Civil War North, 1865–1901*, Cambridge, MA, and London, 2001.

[77] Kiesselbach, *Studien*, 129.

[78] Ibid., 180.

estatist principle of citizenship in her constitutional organs. The *Senat* is formed from the scholarly and mercantile estates in a particular proportion; the "Bürgerschaft" – that is, parliament – likewise is not formed by timocratically constituted voter classes, but is elected by the different great incorporated branches of labor in the city; in it [the Bürgerschaft], the difference between the scholarly, mercantile, artisanal, and agricultural estates reappears. *This institution has immediately sprung from [social] conditions*; it is a natural product of Bremish society.[79]

Kiesselbach emphasizes that the healthy, organic, corporatist order of his hometown can exist in spite of the overwhelming dominance of mobile property in this community, which easily could have led to the development of a "pure state of law and abstract citizenship." It did not, because the estatist consciousness of Bremen's inhabitants made this impossible. Their corporatist institutions are so well entrenched that the French model never made any inroads.[80]

Kiesselbach's account of the Bremish constitution is remarkable for what it does not reveal. He does not mention that the majority of those citizens who enjoyed the right to vote were represented in taxation-based classes, rather than by estate. Likewise, he ignores that the eight-class voting system had been established – against the wishes of the *Bürgerschaft* – by a *Senat* wielding the threat of an armed intervention by the German Confederation in 1851, rather than "following immediately from circumstances." In brushing over these uncomfortable bits of history and facts, Kiesselbach's account may well, however, reflect accurately the view Bremen's merchants held of their political institutions. To them, Bremen was a commonwealth governed by tradition, organically reflecting society in its concreteness – and not subject to the political influence of money or abstract theories.

There are, for Kiesselbach, limits to the corporatist way of running a society. "Man does not belong to the state merely as a worker; his general human relations go beyond his station."[81] For those relations that do not fall within the immediate purview of economic activity, Kiesselbach regards the principles of "abstract law" somewhat better suited.

Rather than submitting the peasant to a patrimonial court, or having an artisan judged by the guild, Kiesselbach prefers equality before the law, regardless of a person's station. He wants an independent judiciary to mete out justice according to uniform standards. Similarly, he wants taxation and military duty to be uniformly exercised across all strata of society.[82]

Kiesselbach manages to strip the estates of their actual, traditional content – their economic and legal function – while assigning them a novel, political function as institutions that mediate popular representation. Without economic exclusivity, and without an internal justice system to enforce it, an estate – whether the nobility or the guilds – becomes an empty shell. Traditionalist conservatives would not have taken this Hanseatic version of estatism as the real item.

---

[79] Ibid., 180–1. Italics: my emphasis; other: original emphasis. Note that unlike Hegel, who proposes a corporate scheme of representation in the Philosophy of Right (§311), Kiesselbach considers this legislative body an immediate expression of society.

[80] Ibid., 181.

[81] Ibid.

[82] Ibid., 181–2.

Nevertheless, to Hanseats, these remnants of estatism were important enough to defend until 1918. What remains of estates in Kiesselbach's scheme is, first, an elaborate model for political representation that avoids the "head-count consti-tution" favored by democrats, and potentially favoring the dispossessed; second, an attempt to preserve tradition and an "organic," hierarchical order; while, third, giving "abstract law" its due in limited spheres of social life. This modernized estatism formed a key component of Hanseats' political identity – it is the core of Kiesselbach's project, just as it was the core of Hanseatic politics.

KIESSELBACH AND AMERICA

In this view, Kiesselbach finally appears as a writer positioned squarely in a trans-atlantic discourse on democracy; albeit not quite in the same fashion as imagined by the historians of Hanseatic liberalism. As much as he despises the French example, he considers the British model of "self-government" worthy of emulation.[83] The English constitution is, for him, "the product of English society," as opposed to that of abstract legal or logical premises.[84]

What Kiesselbach likes about America is the very conservatism of its Founding Fathers, inspired by the English tradition. He particularly praises the tenth and fifty-first essays of the *Federalist Papers* in his discussion of that document:

No. 10 provides a brilliant example of the clarity of Madison's thinking as a statesman; in it, he documents an insight into the nature of the republican system of representation, which far surpasses the dominant ideas of his times.[85]

Kiesselbach quotes Madison's – now classical – discussion of divergent social interests:

A landed interest, a manufacturing interest, a mercantile interest, a moneyed interest, with many lesser interests, grow up of necessity in civilized nations, and divide them into different classes, actuated by different sentiments and views, . . .[86]

and comments on it in enthusiastic agreement:

These are glorious words! For the first time in modern political science, they shift the center of attention in statecraft to the harmonious balance of the different social forces. . . . Note that the author openly states, that a purely democratic constitution . . . must lead to majority rule, with its revolutionary consequences; whilst only theoreticians can delude

---

[83] Ibid., 117. Kiesselbach uses "self-government" in the English original throughout his works. Rather than rendering it in Latin script, as was customary for foreign words, he uses the Gothic!

[84] Ibid., 129. Kiesselbach follows Burke, either directly, and/or through Burke's reception in Adam Müllers Elementen der Staatskunst, see Harada, *Politische Ökonomie*, 72–3.

[85] Kiesselbach, *Federalist*, vol. 1, 283. Kiesselbach's nephew became a noted jurist in the tradition of the historical (or sociological) school of law, which develops legal standards from a basis of interests and ends, rather than concepts and principles. The man who is considered the father of this tradition of legal scholarship, Rudolf von Jhering (1818–92), was the main inspiration for Charles Beard's reading of the *Federalist*, for which numbers 10 and 51 play a central part. See Beard's *An Economic Interpretation of the Constitution of the United States*, New York and London, 1965 (1913), note 1 to p. 14.

[86] Madison, James, "No. 10," Hamilton, Alexander, James Madison, and John Jay, *The Federalist Papers*, New York, 1961 (1787–8).

themselves to believe, that an equal distribution of rights among the public can lead to an equality of property, opinions, or passions.[87]

The "revolutionary consequences of majority rule" that Madison had in mind were partisan or sectarian dominance, but more importantly, a redistribution of property undertaken by the have-nots.[88] Kiesselbach shared this concern, but, unlike Madison, believed that only a hierarchically ordered society – a "social-economic state" – in which people knew their proper station could provide a permanent safeguard against democratic, egalitarian designs.

In Kiesselbach's view, the American experiment had failed, in spite of the brilliant statesmanship of Madison and his fellow Founding Fathers. It is as a bad example, rather than as a model "for contemporary Germany"[89] that Kiesselbach discussed American political institutions.

Jefferson and Jackson had forever shattered a quiet world where the masses had deferentially followed the leadership of enlightened notables.[90] As a result, 1860s America was characterized by a "restless striving for profit, whereas an actual humanity of existence has yet to take roots.... On average, Americans lack true human culture," evidenced by their "antiquated religious ceremonies, and their ridiculous cult of womanhood.... Particularly for the Yankees, the ethical improvement of the individual's worth counts for nothing," while "a loosely structured state gives broad leeway to political arbitrariness."[91]

Neither side in the great conflict between North and South could lay any claim to moral superiority. The North, completely "beholden to pure business life," fights to enslave the South to its industrial system. The South is driven by opposing interests: free trade and the perpetuation of its agrarian aristocracy.[92] Nonetheless, Kiesselbach favored a strong, or rather, "structured" state over the loose civic bonds allowed by agrarian republicanism and its theorist. This places him much closer to the Hamiltonian tradition of Whigs and Republicans, than to Jeffersonian republicanism or Jacksonian democracy.

From the beginning, Kiesselbach argues, the most important flaw in the American state had been the "mathematical" delimitation of political entities, from the township on upward. Partitioning the land along longitudes and latitudes rather than following natural boundaries created abstract spaces, unable to instill their inhabitants with a warm sense of home. Any "social, cultural, and moral accomplishments among the many," however, presuppose communities that organically fit into the natural geography of a place.[93]

Like the French *arrondissements* and *départements*, which cut "straight lines" through the historical provinces, the American political space embodied in the territorial form of the state represents the idea of society as an amassment of atomized

---

[87] Kiesselbach, *Federalist*, vol. 1, 284.
[88] Ibid., 285; Madison, "No. 10."
[89] The subtitle of his 1864 book on the *Federalist* was *Politische Studien für die deutsche Gegenwart*; literally "political studies for the German present."
[90] Kiesselbach, *Federalist*, vol. 1, 422–6
[91] Ibid., 419.
[92] Ibid., 438.
[93] Ibid., 417.

individuals, assembled on an equal plane, imagined as equidistant from the focal point of governmental power. This double meaning of the image of straight lines is intentional: in its political and geographical sense, it evokes an empty geometric space, a grid or matrix, ready to be filled by power emanating from the bureaucracy.[94]

This original sin of American state making, the oblivion to place and difference, in Kiesselbach's view, had come back to take revenge on the Union at the moment of the Civil War. From its inception, the Union had "carried in its lap several unborn embryos of nationality." The armed conflict showed Kiesselbach that "the time of the Union may soon be over, and the time of the formation of particular states, following the given geography, will follow from there – [this is] a physical process of history, impervious to the ethical or political free will of the individual!"[95]

Moreover, the equality and disembeddedness of individuals in this empty, geometric space of the state had given the mass of the people the wrong ideas about their rights. Specifically, in the absence of a warm sense of home in hierarchical, deferential conditions, it had created democratic aspirations. These aspirations, in turn, had led to the moral decay Kiesselbach logically associated with democracy. The American example stood before 1860s Germany, not as a model for emulation, but as a dire warning. The voices that had first sounded that warning, and which Kiesselbach channeled, had been those of American conservatives. These conservatives could point to some of the Founding Fathers' writings to back up their positions.[96]

TRANSNATIONAL CONSERVATISM

At first, Kiesselbach's corporatism might appear to bear a mark of provinciality. After all, he believes that the practices of his hometown can serve as a universal model. If we consider the full range of ideas that informed his position, however, we can recognize Kiesselbach as part of a transnational discourse on capitalism and democracy that owes more to Western influences than to Continental ones. Rather than a backward-looking small-town burgher, he is part of a transnational strand of modern conservatism that was at the cutting edge of modernization on both sides of the Atlantic.

Alexander Hamilton's heirs, American Whigs and Republicans, promoted transportation infrastructure, industrial growth, and the development of a capitalist financial system. They were thus modernizers, in the same fashion as Johann

---

[94] Kiesselbach, *Studien*, 117. Andreas Schulz suggests that Bremen's elite looked to France as a political model. He bases his argument on the structural similarity between the social and political order under the Bourbon monarchy and in the Hanseatic city. In both places, an undemocratic government drew legitimacy from providing for the welfare of the people and from increasing the wealth of society. On this level of fairly abstract comparison, Bremen and France do look similar. Schulz does not, however, present evidence that Hanseats considered France a model. Evidence abounds that Bremen's elite considered the principle of representation based on wealth, rather than on estates, as too close to the democratic mode of representation they despised. Kiesselbach's writings display animosity toward France for this very reason. See Schulz, *Vormundschaft*, 336–7.

[95] Kiesselbach, *Federalist*, vol. 1, 439–40.

[96] Howe, *American Whigs*.

Smidt and his estate. Moreover, Hanseats, like these American conservatives, were deeply skeptical of democracy and concerned over the moral implications of an economy built on self-interest, as opposed to cooperation in the spirit of brotherly love and charity.

To make sense of Hanseats' politics, we have to follow their lead in looking across the Atlantic, to the "great sister Republic" on its western shore.[97] This is not to deny that Hanseats were also shaped in and by a German cultural space. With its peculiar cosmopolitan conservatism, however, Bremen's elite ill fits into the broad currents of German bourgeois politics, let alone of German liberalism. Hanseats shared their dislike of democracy with grand-bourgeois liberals of their time, like the Rhenanian bourgeoisie. Unlike the latter, however, Hanseats' willingness to apply the prescriptions of political economy to their own activities was limited, betraying a continued investment in a traditional order.[98] Not unlike Hanseats, southwest German democrats held to certain aspects of an older corporatist order for much longer than Rhenanian liberals. Yet their vision of a republic of small producers had little in common with the type of society envisioned by Hanseats, either. Moreover, Hanseatic opposition to democracy put them in a camp different from that of southwest German democrats.[99]

Almost the only factor uniting these different political currents among the German populace was their opposition to absolute monarchical rule. From that point of view, they all appear as "progressives" of some sort, and a general label of liberalism seems out of place. The reputation of Bremen as a hotbed of radicalism, acquired since the days of mercantile opposition to Bismarck and confirmed by a half-century of Social-Democratic rule after World War II, may have clouded our view of the political philosophies that converged in the peculiar world of mid-nineteenth-century Hanseatic politics. In reconstructing this world, we should restore to conservatism its due place. In looking for its origins, we should turn our eyes toward the Atlantic, rather than to Bremen's hinterland.

In the United States, Hanseats knew a purely bourgeois state from firsthand experience, but they did not necessarily like what they saw. There, under conditions of universal white male sufferage, the differentiation of bourgeois politics into a conservative and a liberal camp, as consciously distinct political currents, had already taken place. When looking across the Atlantic, therefore, Bremen's merchants could draw upon a broader range of political expressions for their interests. In his critique of the artificiality of American governmental institutions; in his dismissal of democracy, and of the moral decay it engenders; and in his predictions for the imminent demise of the failed experiment, Kiesselbach betrays his indebtedness to a broader, transatlantic current of political thought.

---

[97] [Schleiden, Rudolf], "Facts in Relation to a Direct Steam Communication Between the United States and Germany" (leaflet distributed to members of the U.S. Congress), Washington, DC, August 1856, StAHB 2,B.13.b.1.a.2.b.I., document no. 5, quotes pp. 1 and 3. English in the original.

[98] Cf. Boch, Rudolf, *Grenzenloses Wachstum? Das rheinische Wirtschaftsbürgertum und seine Industrialisierungsdebatte, 1814–1857* (Bürgertum. Beiträge zur europäischen Gesellschaftsgeschichte, vol. 3), Göttingen, 1991. See also Chapter 4.

[99] Cf. Nolte, Paul, *Gemeindebürgertum und Liberalismus in Baden, 1800–1850. Tradition–Radikalismus–Republik* (Kritische Studien zur Geschichtswissenschaft, vol. 102), Göttingen, 1994.

With Burke, Kiesselbach admired some aspects of the American Revolution, but came to loathe the path the Union took from there. Both believed that the French Revolution marked the point when abstract rights – undermining solid, reasonable statecraft – appeared on the political stage.[100] Nevertheless, American conservatives had to work with what they had been dealt, if they did not want to abandon their polity to the Jeffersonians and Jacksonians. Even as America was lost to a proper order, let alone estatism, nothing would prevent political actors from trying to restore as much of a good, hierarchical social order as possible. Whether this would be achieved by limiting the impact of the popular vote, or by using it to elect conservative candidates, was a question of expediency.

The Whig Party was based on the latter strategy, and it was among that party that Hanseats found their most important allies in the United States. The Whigs' was a bourgeois conservatism, rather than a traditional, legitimist conservatism based on divine right.[101] It is the former brand of conservatism that informs Kiesselbach's prose, drawing not just on an Anglo-American tradition (Burke), but also on its German reception (Müller) and its retranslation into an American context (Gentz through Adams).[102] It is this same Western conservatism that influenced politically active Hanseats in Bremen, the German states, and the United States.

To know that Bremen remained a safe spot in a changing world in which the imperturbed gaze of the Roland rested on a community that expressed the Hanseats' political wishes in its social and political order was a source of strength and unity for these merchants. Yet the benefit of being members of a transatlantic network supported on a sovereign state was more than simply a matter of ideological comfort or group identity. It provided Hanseats with a governmental framework that allowed them to posit their shared interests through a state that enjoyed international diplomatic recognition. Part of these shared interests was a modernization of the fields of shipping, commerce, and communication. Hanseats hoped to preserve an Atlantic economy dominated by commerce, rather than wishing to create a national political economy characterized by industry, let alone a national polity based on popular participation in politics. Within that Atlantic economy, however, any step toward an accelerated turnover of capital would find Hanseatic support.

The state of Bremen played a crucial role for Hanseatic projects of modernization that served this end. Hence, where Hanseats most visibly played a role as "modernizers," they were acting from a basis that was most "traditionalist." At the same time, American Whigs' schemes of internal improvement harmonized with the Hanseats' wishes. A shared conservative outlook added to the Hanseats' ability to work with their allies in the United States, through diplomatic and domestic channels. Between the United States and Bremen, these two conservative groups helped to bring about a revolution in transatlantic commerce.

[100] Burke, *Reflections*.
[101] Ashworth, *"Agrarians" and "Aristocrats"*; Howe, *American Whigs*.
[102] Harada, *Politische Ökonomie*; Gentz, *French and American Revolutions Compared*.

PART II

Exchanges in a Transnational World

4

Free Labor and Dependent Labor

From Patronage to Wage Labor and Social Control, 1810–1861

FREE LABOR AND IMPROVEMENT

In 1850s America, "free labor and free soil" was the slogan of those who opposed the expansion of slavery into the Great Plains. The contradictions of both parts of this slogan were readily apparent to many contemporaries, and readily exploited by apologists for slavery.[1] Often, to keep the soil "free" meant to keep it free from blacks, not just free of enslavement. Ohio and Illinois, strongholds of the emerging Republican Party, barred African Americans from settling within their borders. And by "freedom of labor," its proponents meant a system of social production in which the relation between a worker and his master was based on a contractual agreement.[2] Politically aware members of the working class pointed out that in order to have to enter into such an agreement, the worker also had to be free from the ability to make a living by other means.[3]

Nonetheless, the promise of "freedom" had a strong appeal; perhaps the more so, the more ambiguous its meaning. Armed with Adams Smith's theoretical foundations for a free market, Republicans in the United States, and Liberals in Britain and Germany, considered the transformation of all relations of production into free wage-labor relations a virtue. To them, constitutional (if not republican) government, civil liberties enshrined in the Bill of Rights, free trade, and free labor emanated from the same first principles, the rights that man possesses in a state of nature, preceding the formation of societies and states.[4]

Scholars of German-American relations have long known that political actors on both sides of the Atlantic felt themselves united in the knowledge that they shared this set of ideas we call liberalism. Just as Americans looked with enthusiasm toward Europe in 1830 and 1848, so too did European liberals look to America in 1861. The Union, first in fighting slavery, and from late 1862 in adapting abolition as its

[1] Ashworth, John, *Slavery, Capitalism, and Politics in the Antebellum Republic*, 2 vols., vol. 1: *Commerce and Compromise, 1820–1850*, Cambridge, 1995.
[2] Stanley, Amy Dru, *From Bondage to Contract: Wage Labor, Marriage, and the Market in the Age of Slave Emancipation*, New York 1998.
[3] Marx, Karl, *Capital*, 3 vols. (Karl Marx and Friedrich Engels, Werke, vols. 23–5), Berlin, 1979 [1894].
[4] Hamerow, Theodore S., *The Social Foundations of German Unification: Ideas and Institutions*, Princeton, NJ, 1969; Hobsbawm, Eric, *The Age of Capital, 1848–1875*, London, 1975.

official war aim, represented the cutting edge of a worldwide movement to increase and expand human freedom.[5]

Contemporaries were well aware that the abolition of slavery meant not just an expansion of personal freedom, but a revolution in labor relations. For that reason, German liberal nationalists who wished to establish a free market for capital, commodities, and labor across all German states pointed to America as a sign that their own demands were in accordance with the general march of progress. To abolish the guilds, they argued, meant to bring free labor (*Freiheit der Arbeit*) to Germany. To restore to the working man the natural state of freedom that an artificial system (of guilds) had taken from him became a cause of equivalent moral force as the abolition of slavery in America.[6]

But the proponents of "freedom" were not the only political current that had a transnational flow. The defenders of slavery in the United States and the defenders of guilds in Germany used virtually identical arguments in countering the revolution in the labor relations that they faced. Slaveholders claimed that slavery was the last refuge of the good old days, where masters had been benevolent patriarchs who took care of the whole person of their subordinates – morality, livelihood, and all.[7] Defenders of the German guilds, likewise, stressed the harmonious relationship among master, journeyman, and apprentice. Both contrasted these forms of dependent labor with a view of capitalism as an inherently amoral social system; one based on cold cash, utility, and self-interest, all to the detriment of the weakest members of society – the working people.[8]

As Eugene Genovese pointed out, slavery did shield Southerners of both races from the full force of capitalist social relations. What Genovese forgot in his late oeuvre, however, was that to those facing coercive exploitation it is by no means preferable to the contractually mediated kind. That slavery was a coercive system and that the self-image of benevolence cultivated by slaveholders was a lie was evident not just to slaves, but also to most unprejudiced observers. To most workers on both sides of the Atlantic, likewise, the cozy relations within the craft were beginning to look less benevolent by the day. Yet the claim to represent a non-capitalist, and thus less coldly exploitative, social arrangement had more truth to it in the artisan's "whole house" than in the "big house" of the plantation.

Bremen's mercantile elite did not fit comfortably on either side of the divide between proponents of free or dependent labor. Hanseats dealt heavily in the products of slave plantations, but they also relied on the immigrants who flocked

---

[5] Biefang, Andreas, *Politisches Bürgertum in Deutschland, 1857–1868. Nationale Organisationen und Eliten* (Kommission für Geschichte des Parlamentarismus und der politischen Parteien, corp. ed., Beiträge zur Geschichte des Parlamentarismus und der politischen Parteien, vol. 102), Düsseldorf, 1994; Etges, Andreas, *Wirtschaftsnationalismus. USA und Deutschland im Vergleich (1815–1914)*, Frankfurt and New York, 1999; Evans, Richard J., and Hartmut Pogge von Strandmann, eds., *The Revolutions in Europe, 1848–1849: From Reform to Revolution*, Oxford, 2000; Gall, Lothar, and Dieter Langewiesche, eds., *Liberalismus und Region. Zur Geschichte des deutsche Liberalismus im 19. Jahrhundert*, Munich, 1995; Langewiesche, Dieter, *Nation, Nationalismus, Nationalstaat in Deutschland und Europa* (Beck'sche Reihe, vol. 1399), Munich, 2000.

[6] See p. 242, for use of this argument in debates in Bremen.

[7] Genovese, Eugene D., *The World the Slaveholders Made: Two Essays in Interpretation*, New York, 1969.

[8] Riehl, Wilhelm Heinrich, *Die bürgerliche Gesellschaft*, Stuttgart, 1861. See also p. 243 for this side of the argument in debates in Bremen.

to the free-labor society of the industrializing North. At home, Bremen's political system rested on a corporatist structure whose bedrock were the guilds, yet the free flow of capital and commodities was as important to the city's merchants as the livelihood – and thus political cooperation – of the lower orders of society.

Ultimately, Bremen's elite resolved these contradictions in a familiar fashion – by selectively applying liberal and traditionalist solutions, case-by-case. Between 1810 and 1861, the story of Bremen's increasing engagement in world trade is one of increasingly capitalist social relations between workers and their masters. For more and more groups in the city's social fabric, the modernization of Bremen's commercial relations meant the dissolution of the customary communal ties of "patronage and protection," and their replacement with wage-labor relations and policies of social control.

In the 1810s, sailors were the first group to be removed from the legal bounds of a traditional, communal order and to be placed under a modern wage-labor regime. From the 1830s onward, emigrants who entered Bremen on their way abroad constituted another group that was no longer contained within traditional communal arrangements. In the 1860s, artisans followed suit, as a majority of the mercantile elite forced an abolition of the guild system.

As Hanseats introduced legal and technological changes that opened the door to capitalist social relations within Bremen, they also strove to shore up the moral foundations of a good order based on deference and firm ethics. This meant three things: first, they limited the effects of "modernization" to the lower orders of society, while keeping in place their own privileged position; second, they applied a liberal economic program while following a conservative political course; and third, they substituted social control and repression for the paternalistic integration of the lower classes.

In following this path to modernization, Hanseats closely resembled the American Whigs, and to a certain extent their Republican successors. This resemblance formed the basis for affinity and cooperation, both in the United States, and in advancing schemes of international improvement. The relationship between Whigs and Hanseats was not free of contention. The Whigs' advocacy for a protective tariff and opposition to immigration, however, did not outweigh the more fundamental affinity established by the values and the general outlook on the world they shared with their Bremish counterparts. By exploring the Hanseats' policies in Bremen, this chapter lays the groundwork for a discussion of the relations between Hanseats and Whigs that will be the subject of Chapter 5.

SAILORS AND EMIGRANTS

The very spirit of improvement that drove American Whigs, broadly conceived, also inspired Hanseats. Both groups embraced the material progress unleashed by the Enlightenment, while rejecting its philosophical foundations and political implications. The Hanseats' most ambitious venture in the second quarter of the nineteenth century, the construction of the deep-sea port of Bremerhaven, illustrates that their commitment to a society and state based on a union of markets, machines, and morality was second to no comparable Whig schemes in the United States.[9]

---

[9] Drayton, Richard, *Nature's Government: Science, Imperial Britain, and the "Improvement" of the World*, New Haven, CT, and London, 2000; Mintz, Steven, *Moralists and Modernizers: America's Pre–Civil*

Where better to put into practice a political and social vision, then in a city that is built from scratch? The City by the Sea corresponded with the City upon a Hill, long before the first vessels crossed the Atlantic from New York to Bremerhaven. Here, Hanseats built a community that, while new, was designed to be as "organic" as Bremen. They were driven to undertake this project by the commercial impetus to "venture abroad."[10]

Nature, as in most schemes of "improvement," was an obstacle to progress in its unhewn state, but an ally to mankind once subjected. Waterways and their shores were the parts of nature most relevant to Hanseatic modernizers. Bremen is located sixty kilometers inland from its mouth on the Weser River. After the Congress of Vienna, the city controlled a territory stretching some forty kilometers along the river and extending up to ten kilometers into the countryside away from its banks. The forty kilometers of the river between the city and the open sea were not under its territorial control. The left bank belonged to the Grand Duchy of Oldenburg and the right bank to the Kingdom of Hannover, then ruled in personal union by the British kings.[11]

Thus nature and politics threw obstacles in Bremen's path to the sea. Its slow pace led the Weser River to silt up, and the shipping channel frequently changed its course, as sandbanks changed their shape and location. Deep-sea vessels could travel only as far as Brake, located on the left bank. From there, cargo had to be reloaded onto barges. The Grand Duchy of Oldenburg charged a toll on vessels passing the town of Elsfleth, halfway between Brake and Bremen. In 1825, Oldenburg began to treat Bremish vessels anchoring at Brake for the purpose of transshipment as if they had been destined to, or originated in, that port. The Hanseatic city seemed in danger of losing its status as an overseas port (see Map 2).

Under its British rulers, Hannover was less hostile to Bremish interests. The *Senat* had been trying since the 1790s to gain a territory by the mouth of the river, on the right bank, for the construction of a deep-sea port. From there, Bremen could be reached through Hannoverian territory by highway – avoiding tolls, fees, and harassment imposed by Oldenburg – or by barge, at least avoiding transshipment in Brake. The Grand Duchy's changed policy in 1825 spurred Burgomaster Johann Smidt to revisit these plans. It took nearly two years of intense, secret negotiations before a treaty was signed. In this treaty, Hannover sold to Bremen 342 Morgen of land, for a price of 74,000 Thaler.[12] Bremen received sovereignty over some of the territory and de facto sovereignty over the rest, but had to grant Hannoverian

---

War Reformers (Stanley I. Kutler, ed., The American Moment Series, unnumbered vol.), Baltimore and London, 1995; Walters, Ronald G., *American Reformers, 1815–1860*, New York, 1997 (1978).

[10] Schwarzwälder, Herbert, *Geschichte der Freien Hansestadt Bremen* (4 vols.), vol. 2, Hamburg, 1987, 121–34; Kellner-Stoll, Rita, *Bremerhaven, 1827–1888. Politische, wirtschaftliche und soziale Probleme einer Stadtgründung* (Burchard Scheper, ed., Veröffentlichungen des Stadtarchivs Bremerhaven, vol. 4), Bremen, 1982; Oberg, Jan, "Strange Sailors: Maritime Culture in Nineteenth-Century Bremen," in *Bridging Troubled Waters: Conflict and Co-operation in the North Sea Region since 1550*, ed. David J. Starkey and Morten Hahn-Pedersen (7th North Sea History Conference, Dunkirk 2002) (Fiskeri- og Sofartsmuseets Studieserie, vol.17), Esbjerg, Denmark, 2005, 113–33.

[11] Entholt, Hermann, "Bremens Handel, Schiffahrt und Industrie im 19. Jahrhundert (1815–1914)," in *Die Hansestädte Hamburg/Bremen/Lübeck*, ed. O. Mathies, H. Entholt, and L. Lichtweiss (Die Deutsche Wirtschaft und Ihre Führer, vol. 5), Gotha, 1928, 131–244, here pp. 148–9.

[12] 1 Morgen equals 0.6 to 0.9 acres.

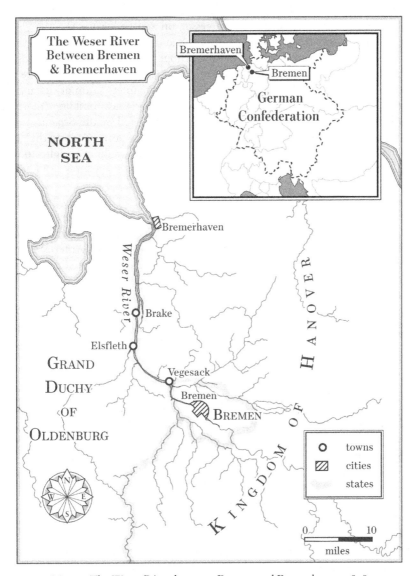

Map 2. The Weser River between Bremen and Bremerhaven, 1848

subjects equal access and rights in the entire area. Military sovereignty was excepted and remained with Hannover.

Construction on the new port of Bremerhaven began in the spring of 1827 – the same year that Bremen signed its first trade treaty with the United States. Dutch specialists were leading in hydrological engineering. A group of Dutch contractors under twenty-seven-year-old Johann Jacob von Ronzelen submitted the winning bid to complete the project for 833,000 Dutch Gulden. They delivered a port whose main dock measured 752 by 58 meters, at a depth of 5.5 meters. The lock measured 42 by 26 meters, with gates that could accommodate ships up to a breadth of 22 meters. The installations were finished in late summer of 1830. The first ship to enter the new port was an American vessel, on September 12, 1830.

Bremerhaven was a *faite d'un prince*, through and through. The planned city that was to surround the port first existed on a lithograph that laid out the roads. The population-to-be was designated as "colonists" or "settlers." Land plots were given out by the state for a yearly sum of ground rent. At the intersection of city and port, panoptically placed on top of the inner levee, a neoclassical building housed the administration of the territory. Its officers were appointed by the *Senat* in Bremen and enforced laws passed in Bremen. Revenues from the port went into the general budget of the Bremish state. The new population had no traditional rights to which it could appeal. A city without history has no traditions. In making and enforcing laws for Bremerhaven, the *Senat* worked with a *tabula rasa*.[13]

The irony of Bremerhaven is that it looked a great deal like Kiesselbach's foil of American spatial arrangements: a blank grid, filled up by the power of the central bureaucracy, in this case emanating from Bremen. This similarity was not lost on contemporary German observers who compared the city to an American frontier town: a place without roots and soul.[14] In Hanseats' minds, this comparison was unfounded. The difference between their new city and an American city was that Bremen's elite used its power to recreate from scratch an organically ordered community, inspired by a vision of good order. Not his namesake, Captain John Smith, but the pious John Winthrop was the American founder of settlements closest in spirit to Johann Smidt in this endeavor (see Map 3).

TRANSIENTS AND RESIDENTS

The laws of German hometowns revolved around one main purpose: maintaining social cohesion (see Chapter 3). Strict residency restrictions and a high barrier to the inclusion of new burghers served that purpose. Even the territorial German states had no unified statuses of citizenship. Rather, subject status (*Staatsangehörigkeit*, or "belonging to the state") was conferred to those who were recognized as indigenous by a locality. As hometown constitutions regarded the livelihood (*Nahrung*) of an individual as a central concern, communities offered charity to the resident poor. By excluding nonmembers of the community from these benefits, residency rights limited the mobility of the poor and discouraged migration.[15]

In the United States, communities had never had comparable control over citizenship. For a society based on immigration, the hometown model would have been

---

[13] To the present day, port revenue in Bremerhaven benefits the general budget of the State of Bremen. In the 1970s, the local Liberal politician Manfred Richter, who went on to become a mayor of Bremerhaven in the 1990s, threatened to appeal to the United Nations' De-Colonization Committee for redress.

[14] Kellner-Stoll, *Bremerhaven*, 424–31.

[15] Brubaker, Rogers, *Citizenship and Nationhood in France and Germany*, Cambridge, MA, 1992; Gosewinkel, Dieter, *Einbürgern und Ausschließen. Die Nationalisierung der Staatsangehörigkeit vom Deutschen Bund bis zur Bundesrepublik Deutschland* (Berding, Helmut et al., eds., Kritische Studien zur Geschichtswissenschaft, vol. 150), Göttingen, 2001 (Habilitationsschrift, Freie Universität Berlin); Walker, Mack, *German Home Towns: Community, State, and General Estate, 1648–1817*, Ithaca, NY, and London 1971.

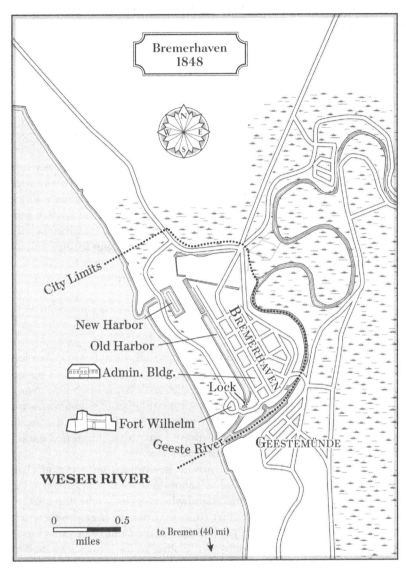

Map 3   Bremerhaven, 1848

dysfunctional. Nonetheless, American states and municipalities maintained vagrancy laws, which were built on the assumption that every person had a "natural" place of residence. As in Germany, relief for the poor was a major concern informing such laws. Indigent immigrants threatened the solvency of local charities and led to recurrent backlashes against immigration.[16] As a countermeasure, Hanseatic merchants were among the first to institute charities specifically catering to needy immigrants in

---

[16] Rockman, Seth, *Welfare Reform in the Early Republic: A Brief History with Documents* (Bedford Series in History and Culture, unnumbered vol., Boston and New York, 2003.

American ports. The poor who travel were thus, from the beginning, a concern that Hanseats and their American peers shared and had to deal with in practice.[17]

Whereas Bremen's institutions, like those of other German towns, were traditionally bent on preventing the population from migrating, Hanseats' shipping interests dictated a policy that encouraged some people to do just that. But how do you tell a migrant from a vagrant?

The status was a matter of a person's utility: paying passengers and working sailors were encouraged to come to Bremerhaven, but not to linger. Vagrancy was a trespass that followed when an individual lost his usefulness by refusing to go away when no longer needed and by becoming a burden on charity.

Throughout Germany, the large number of people drawn to cities as workers in the new industrial economy clashed with the rigid traditional limits on immigration maintained by urban communities. Although industrial workers settle in a place, many of the people drawn to Bremerhaven were transients. This made it easier for the authorities to maintain a closed society for those who had a permanent residency status. Laws that addressed the presence of sailors and emigrants focused on ensuring that these groups would remain transient. Thus emigrants were screened for their ability to support themselves in transit, and sailors were limited to a four-week sojourn in Bremerhaven.[18]

PATRIARCHS GONE BAD

From the earliest days of the port's construction, social control of the labor force set in motion by the ambitious project was on the top of the *Senat*'s agenda for Bremerhaven. The laborers who excavated the port's basin and built the new city were recruited from abroad, as were an increasing number of sailors who served on Bremish ships. The state's dealings with both groups show that the authorities perceived them as an unruly, morally depraved mass that threatened good order and stability. But their presence was a necessary evil.[19]

For both groups, publicly licensed private institutions were put in charge of ensuring their smooth transit and good behavior. Emigrants who arrived in Bremen had been solicited by agents in the hinterland who worked for the ship brokers. The three Bremish ship brokers, as distinct from shipowners, were publicly licensed officials, working for set fees. As a public office farmed out to private citizens, the ship brokerage functioned analogously to the office of the money broker. The ship brokers had extended their activities into soliciting immigrants as a matter of broadening their income base. Their success, and the tacit official recognition they received for this activity, made them into de facto, full-time emigration agents.

---

[17] Wätjen, Hermann, *Aus der Frühzeit des Nordatlantikverkehrs. Studien zur Geschichte der deutschen Schiffahrt und deutschen Auswanderung nach den Vereinigten Staaten bis zum Ende des amerikanischen Bürgerkrieges*, Leipzig, 1932, 133–81; Hennighausen, Louis P., *History of the German Society of Maryland*, Baltimore, 1909; Beutin, Ludwig, *Bremen und Amerika. Zur Geschichte der Weltwirtschaft und der Beziehungen Deutschlands zu den Vereinigten Staaten*, Bremen, 1953, 92, 293.

[18] Oberg, "Strange Sailors."

[19] Rössler, Horst, *Hollandgänger, Sträflinge und Migranten. Bremen-Bremerhaven als Wanderungsraum*, Bremen, 2000, 118; Oberg, "Strange Sailors"; Kellner-Stoll, *Bremerhaven*, 54–66. "Abroad," during this period of time, refers to all states outside of Bremen, including other German states.

Their offices in the German states sold tickets to prospective emigrants, who would thus arrive in Bremen with the bulk of their travel expenses already covered.[20]

While waiting for their passage, emigrants relied on private lodgings. Increasingly, these small inns and guesthouses came under official scrutiny. On the one hand, a significant part of the population of Bremen and Bremerhaven relied on emigrant boarders for their income . Hence, mandating that emigrants stay in government-operated dorms would have hurt the local economy. On the other hand, landlords were prone to fleecing the strangers. Reports of fraudulent practices that would reach the villages inland, as well as the foreseeable American hostility to immigrants who arrived in the New World without means, were likely to hurt the emigration business, overall. The state responded by licensing private landlords to operate official immigrant lodgings under supervision by the authorities.[21]

Sailors, likewise, relied on private boardinghouses for their lodgings while in port and faced the same problems as emigrants did. Tavern keepers who housed sailors would ask that their guests deposit their entire funds with them. Landlords deducted the costs of lodging, food, drink, and personal services directly from their boarders' accounts. More often than not, they overcharged for these items. Many landlords doubled as hiring agents. Sailors whose accounts had become depleted were at the mercy of their landlords, who frequently signed hire-contracts on their behalf. The first installment of the hire then went to settle the sailor's account. Destitute sailors made willing crew members. Hence, the excesses of the innkeepers against sailors were not checked to nearly the same extent as those against emigrants. An ordinance passed in 1832 did, however, mandate the separation of boardinghouses and hiring agencies, and required that both be licensed. Still, supervision remained sporadic.[22]

Both sailors and emigrants were essential for Bremen's mercantile business. The primary function of laws passed to regulate their behavior was thus to ensure the availability of a pool of cheap maritime wage labor, on the one hand, and a constant supply of reasonably solvent passengers, on the other. If the law had stopped there, one might argue that it followed a sheer interest of profit maximization. Yet regulations for emigrants and sailors went beyond the immediate demands of business to include a wide variety of moral commandments. Alcohol and prostitution were the main targets of the moral regulations the *Senat* decreed over these transient populations.[23]

Two ordinances, passed in 1832, formed the legal framework for Bremen's handling of sailors and emigrants, respectively. Emigrants were required to register with the police upon their arrival in Bremen. If they could not prove that they owned sufficient funds to continue their trip to the United States, they were deported.

---

[20] Engelsing, Rolf, *Bremen als Auswandererhafen, 1683–1880* (Karl H. Schwebel, ed., Veröffentlichungen aus dem Staatsarchiv der Freien Hansestadt Bremen, vol. 29), Bremen, 1961. For the brokers' office, see Chapter 3.

[21] Before the completion of a railway line from Bremen to Bremerhaven in 1862, emigrants who arrived in Bremen had to wait for connecting transportation downriver, thus supporting a considerable emigrant business in both towns. See Beutin, *Bremen und Amerika*, 87–96, 144; Engelsing, *Auswandererhafen*.

[22] Oberg, "Strange Sailors."

[23] Engelsing, *Auswandererhafen*; Oberg, "Strange Sailors"; Gerstenberger, Heide, and Ulrich Welke, *Vom Wind zum Dampf. Sozialgeschichte der deutschen Handelsschiffahrt im Zeitalter der Industrialisierung*, Münster, 1996, 45–50.

The owners of emigrant ships leaving Bremerhaven were required to uphold minimum standards for their passengers. Rudolf Engelsing found that the emigrant ordinance of 1832, which demanded that shipowners store ninety days worth of provisions on their westbound journey and prove the seaworthiness of their vessels, was "an almost literal copy of a U.S. passenger law passed in 1819."[24]

Bremen continued to follow the American legal example for as long as it remained an independent state. Horst Rössler found that the *Senat* gave drafts of emigrant ordinances to the American consul in Bremen, and made the consul's suggestions into law without further changes. Compliance with U.S. standards would ensure that immigrants who disembarked from Bremish ships would not run afoul of the law in America. Moreover, Bremen looked to the United States for inspiration when it came to regulating the flow of transient populations, for which the German legal tradition held no useful precedent. Hamburg, treating emigrants as vagrants under German laws, had hurt its interests by outlawing emigration altogether in the 1840s.[25]

Sailors, unlike emigrants, had held a place in customary German law. We are indebted to Heide Gerstenberger and Ulrich Welke for their pathbreaking study of maritime labor relations in the transition from the early-modern Atlantic to the nineteenth-century capitalist world market. This account of Bremish dealings with sailors is based on their findings and on the work of Gerstenberger's student, Jan Oberg.

Gerstenberger and Welke found that early-modern German sailors had not been a transient population at all. Not unlike the artisanal household, the ship was a communal workspace governed by traditional privileges and mutual obligations between crew members, including captains and officers. Until roughly 1815, ship crews had been composed of men drawn from the same villages, who relied for governance on the social control assured by mutual familiarity. Ventures were communal endeavors, where the crew signed an agreement to sail out, at the beginning of the shipping season, to a specific port and back. A captain's authority was based on his navigational skills and his respect for traditional rights and obligations. These rights included the *Führung*, the right of sailors to transport a certain amount of cargo on their own account.[26]

Kiesselbach would have found these arrangements a fine example of healthy communal relations between superiors and their dependents. Unfortunately, these legal traditions stood in the way of Bremen's participation in transatlantic trade. To make worthwhile voyages to America, merchants wished to extend the length of sailors' engagements beyond customary, seasonal limits and to gain full control over vessels and cargoes as their property.

---

[24] Engelsing, *Auswandererhafen*.

[25] Ibid., 131; Rössler, Horst, *Hollandgänger, Sträflinge und Migranten. Bremen-Bremerhaven als Wanderungsraum*, Bremen, 2000, 203–7, and notes 23 and 27 (pp. 254–5). When Heinrich Smidt, Burgomaster Smidt's son, wrote in 1832 that "we can only learn from America," he might have referred to emulation of the kind evident in Bremish emigrant laws. See Engelsing, "England und die USA," 53–4.

[26] Gerstenberger and Welke, *Vom Wind zum Dampf*, 30–50, esp. p. 35. Führung may best be translated as "(captain's) privilege" in English. It is presently unclear to me to what degree, or at what time, sailors' rights to conduct petty trade had been abolished in the Anglo-American Atlantic. The experience of Olaudah Equiano, however, suggests that this right was still practiced in the 1780s. See Equiano, *The Interesting Narrative of the Life of Olaudah Equiano, or, Gustavus Vassa, the African*, New York, 2004.

In reaching these goals, Bremen's elite received welcome assistance from a "foreign aggressor." The French had slashed sailors' customs along with all other traditional German laws when they had governed Bremen. Significantly, amidst the rhetoric of restoration that had followed on the French defeat of 1813, the *Senat* had refused to restore the traditional rights of sailors. In their place, a new maritime labor regime was constructed, in which sailors were made into wage laborers and captains made into commanders. Captains were no longer backed in their control over their workforce by customary authority based on personal honor and skill, but by positive law, upheld by special courts in port. In a legal framework that defined ship and cargo as nothing but property, under the undivided control of their respective owners, the *Führung* was specifically outlawed.

Hire-contracts were now made, not for a specific route, but "to some port *and a market*," allowing for transatlantic journeys of indeterminate duration. Desertion became a crime under this new regime. Sailors had to agree to the new laws when they signed the muster-roll, which they had to do in front of the *Wasserschout* – the novel Admiralty Court-cum-administration. Sailors were no longer part of a communal venture, but were turned into individuals in a wage-labor relation.[27]

The function of the new maritime labor laws was to enable a practice of shipping that allowed for longer and more frequent journeys. Whereas, under the old customs, crews had been absent from home only during the summer, they now could be offshore for several years, without a right to terminate their employ. The shipping season was extended, sailing dangerously close to the forbidding conditions of wintertime navigation, and in some cases right through them. Layover times in port were dramatically reduced. In 1840, transatlantic ships on average spent as little as sixteen days in the port of Bremerhaven. Bremish participation in world trade came at the price of a general speed-up in maritime transportation, a process Gerstenberger and Welke call "the industrialization of sail."[28]

The brawling, boozing, whoring sailor, whose "homeland was the sea" was made by these new laws.[29] The collapse of communal work relations, embedded in the coastal village, made seafaring men, in the words of one Bremish merchant, into the "reckless and clumsy" strangers who were "often helpless and at a loss like a child," and who therefore became a charge of the "authorities, as to be guided by strict paternal justice."[30] This "paternal justice," however, was no longer the paternalism of the organic community. It was a system of social control designed to cushion the consequences of the destruction of communal customs – Toennies's communal patriarchy gone bad.[31]

The transition from paternalism to social control – so familiar from the social history of American and German artisans – affected emigrants too.[32]

[27] Gerstenberger and Welke, *Vom Wind zum Dampf*, 32.

[28] Oberg, "Strange Sailors," 5; Gerstenberger and Welke, *Vom Wind zum Dampf*.

[29] In the words of the popular German singer and actor Hans Albers, known for movie roles as a sailor.

[30] Delius, Friedrich Adolph, in 1850, as cited by Oberg, "Strange Sailors," 11. Delius was a shipowner and transatlantic merchant in Bremen.

[31] Tönnies, *Community and Civil Society*, 26–7.

[32] Cf. Stürmer, Michael, ed., *Herbst des Alten Handwerks. Meister, Gesellen, und Obrigkeit im 18. Jahrhundert*, Munich, 1986; Johnson, Paul E., *A Shopkeeper's Millennium: Society and Revivals in Rochester, New York, 1815–1837*, New York. 1978.

Hanseats brought this same paternalistic attitude of a state that takes charge of a "lower class" of people to emigrants and sailors alike. In 1852, the *Handelskammer* claimed:

In the past, the emigrant was considered a commodity, which should provide the ship-owner with the highest gain possible. In Bremen, one began to treat him like a human being, namely as a human being in particular need of assistance, whose exploitation by speculation ought to be shown into limits which ensure that his well-being is maintained, and that he may flourish in his new homeland, to his own blessing, and, if possible, also to that of his fatherland.[33]

In the early 1830s, at the point when emigration and, with it, the maritime labor market experienced an explosive growth, the *Senat* laid down a framework of regulations that stressed the "helplessness" of these two groups of transient strangers. Upholding their morality was at the core of the ordinances passed at that time. Hanseats perceived their moral guidance of the helpless as the offer of a hand up into a useful, and therefore blessed, life of "industry."[34]

Like Whigs and Social Reformers in the United States, Hanseats substituted Calvinist stewardship for a moral economy embedded in communal customs. Instead of a right to livelihood (*Nahrung*), they offered uplift, sobriety, and prayer.[35] Soon, however, it became clear that the aim of making available a sufficient supply of emigrants and sailors tended to conflict with that of molding the behavior of these groups. Individual voices began explicitly to reject the aim of betterment: "immigrant ships cannot be model institutions," one merchant remarked in 1856.[36]

As a result, the paternalistic approach to emigrants and sailors was bifurcated: on board the ships at sea, a strict discipline that criminalized alcoholism, lewdness, and insubordination predominated for both sailors and emigrants; in port, the two groups were spatially segregated from each other, and jointly from the resident population. For emigrants waiting in port for their passage, close supervision prevailed. In Bremerhaven, the construction of heavily policed emigrant dorm buildings facilitated a tight moral regime.

Jan Oberg found that for sailors in Bremerhaven, unlike for emigrants, moral standards were relaxed. Providing a safety valve and a source of income to locals, prostitution and drinking became unofficially tolerated. The establishments that served alcohol and housed prostitutes were still subject to police supervision. Now, however, the object of that supervision was to prevent a spillover of immorality into the resident population. In 1851, the marching band of the revolutionary German Navy gave a concert in the largest bordello in Bremerhaven, owned by one Friedrich Freudenthal. This still caused a scandal in Bremen, but it reflected the praxis in Bremerhaven. Significant parts of the town had been turned into a port district, where other moral standards applied.[37]

---

[33] Cited by Engelsing, *Auswandererhafen*, 132–3.
[34] See Schulz, Andreas, "Weltbürger und Geldaristokraten. Hanseatisches Bürgertum im 19. Jahrhundert," *Historische Zeitschrift* 259 (1994), 637–70.
[35] Ibid.
[36] Engelsing, *Auswandererhafen*.
[37] Oberg, "Strange Sailors," 9.

The toleration toward sailors' habits practiced by the *Senat* in Bremerhaven was by no means a departure from Hanseats' principled commitment to morality and good order. Oberg shows that the same merchant (F. A. Delius) who called for "strict paternal justice" in 1850, had believed in 1839 that the right sort of laws "would not impair the independence of the proper sailor at all, but improve the one who is messy and raffish, but otherwise capable."[38] Oberg concludes that over the course of the 1840s, Delius, along with many of his peers, had given up on sailors as a group that could be "improved." Spatially segregating them from other groups of the population reinforced the moral standards for everyone else, as the exception that proves the rule. Hanseats still held sailors to be a group requiring close "paternal" attention, albeit one that had turned down the helping hand offering betterment, thus forcing the benevolent authority to mete out punishment.[39]

Oberg finds that repression and the concern with penal institutions in Bremerhaven increased, as the attempts to improve sailors failed to show results. Violence and riots became a main concern of the local authorities and were met with imprisonment. By contrast, Oberg observed that personal damages were "punished far less heavily than any offence which endangered the effectiveness and the safety of the transportation system." Property and (hire-)contracts now became the main focus of criminal prosecution. For example, Oberg found that, in 1837, members of the crew of an American ship that had sold some of its cargo to the local population were sentenced to three years in prison.[40]

Contract mindedness and a respect for property were essential marks of a civilized member of society to those on both sides of the ocean who held a broad concept of "improvement."[41] Where education, refinement, sobriety, and piety failed to produce the values that made a person into a functioning participant in the labor market, however, repression could step in to compensate for the lack of those values. Seth Rockman has shown that vagrancy legislation in the early American republic followed this very logic. It ensured directly, by means of repression, what gentle moral persuasion and schemes of betterment had failed to achieve, without, however, giving up on the rhetoric of improvement.[42] If conformity to the rules of a capitalist market is the substance of the cake and if morality is the icing, it still takes both to make a complete pastry. In running their city by the sea, Hanseats were following the same recipe book as contemporary American reformers.

Although a "modern," capitalist regime of wage labor, contractual relations, and sacrosanct property ownership guided Hanseats' dealings with sailors and migrants in Bremerhaven from an early point on, their approach to the lower orders in the city of Bremen remained characterized by a wish to maintain a closed market and society. An economy based on *Nahrung* bought the consensus from the resident

---

[38] Ibid., 11–12.

[39] Ibid. For a similar shift in the United States from considering the lower orders of society as objects of uplift, to regarding them as "irredeemable," see Beckert, Sven, *The Monied Metropolis: New York City and the Consolidation of the American Bourgeoisie, 1850–1896*, Cambridge, MA, 2001, 76.

[40] Oberg, "Strange Sailors," 10, 12.

[41] Stanley, *From Bondage to Contract*; Richardson, Heather Cox, *The Death of Reconstruction: Race, Labor, and Politics in the Post–Civil War North, 1865–1901*, Cambridge, MA, and London, 2001.

[42] Rockman, *Welfare*.

population in Bremen – a consensus for which the elite did not have to ask the transients who came through Bremerhaven.

In Bremen, the guilds continued to serve as integral parts of a community that included the elite as well as the broad mass of burghers and subjects. These "idyllic relations," however, came under increasing pressure as industrialization took off in 1850s Germany.[43]

FREE LABOR VS. GUILD LABOR

Until the early 1860s, socially and economically, the city of Bremen retained many of the quaint forms of an embedded exchange uncharacteristic of a liberal, capitalist society – at least for merchants and craftsmen. As the 1850s progressed, a growing number of Hanseats came to see the institutions of their hometown as anachronistic. They were determined to adjust to the changing times, and not let the "factory towns" overtake them.

By the late 1850s, a majority of merchants had begun to view many corporatist limitations on economic activity as harmful to the competitiveness of their city, as well as to the general welfare and education of its burghers. Yet, those merchants who became the leading modernizers, most prominently H. H. Meier, picked selectively from the liberal economic program. They had no intention of applying it to their own activities – long-distance trade was supposed to remain a closed shop. Moreover, Hanseats were virtually unanimous in their refusal to change the political and constitutional structure of their state.

Inconveniently, the constitutional and social structure that had resulted from the revolution of 1848 and the reaction of the years 1851–4 was a delicately balanced edifice of corporatist and liberal building blocks. Any changes to one part would inevitably upset other parts. Because of the linkage between economic and political rights – voting rights were based on membership in an estate, which is an economically defined social grouping – Bremen's constitution appeared especially inimical to any reform that would try to extend economic liberties, while leaving political privilege in place.[44] Moreover, unlike sailors and migrants, artisans were citizens of Bremen, represented in the *Bürgerschaft*. The majority of artisans was vehemently opposed to "free labor" and wished to see the guilds maintained.

The task of mercantile reformers was thus threefold: first, they had to invent ways of changing the economic structure of society without upsetting the political order that rested immediately on it; second, they had to maintain consensus among the merchant class, so as not to jeopardize their dominance of the *Bürgerschaft*; and third, they had to preserve mercantile hegemony over the other social groups. For even if the formal political influence of artisans and the middle class was negligible, there remained a fear of revolution, kept awake by the recent memory of 1848. As the 1860s dawned, the Hanseatic elite had to demonstrate that it was up to this task.

Victor Böhmert was a leading promoter of free labor. From 1856 to 1860, the economist served as editor of Bremen's *Handelsblatt*, the internationally circulated

---

[43] Marx, Karl, and Friedrich Engels, "Manifesto of the Communist Party," in *The Marx-Engels Reader*, ed. Robert C. Tucker, New York and London, 1978, 473–500.

[44] See Chapter 3.

daily catering to the mercantile interest. His views, laid out in an 1859 prize essay, eloquently restated the classical arguments of political economy: guilds inhibited innovation by insisting on traditional techniques and styles, stifled competition by setting prices, kept men from unfolding their talents by restricting access to the trades, and so on.[45] In 1860, Böhmert was rewarded for his efforts with the prestigious job of *Zweiter Syndikus* (head lawyer) of the *Handelskammer*. By hiring this nationally renowned champion of free labor, the core institution of Bremen's merchants had made a clear policy statement.[46]

British political economy was a staple of Hanseatic mercantile education. Although free trade had long been a key component of the ideology of Bremen's elite, and the basis of Bremen's foreign policy, adherence to tradition, and a desire to keep social relations at home harmonious had led merchants to strengthen the guilds as late as in the 1851 trades law (*Gewerbeordnung*).[47] H. H. Meier had argued in 1851 that free labor was theoretically right, and that he wished its introduction, but that he was willing "to take existing conditions into account." At that time, many of his fellow merchants were not yet ready to follow him even that far. By 1857, in debating a bill for the abolition of the guilds, Meier publicly declared that "competition is the drive behind the energy of the individual." He hoped for free labor to regain markets for Bremen's trades, "so that no longer will one have to buy one's furniture in Berlin," where factories were readily producing such items for a mass market, and in the newest fashion. Against the defenders of guild prerogatives, who feared being crushed by foreign competition once stripped of exclusive market access, Meier marshaled the vision of an unfettered Bremish industry, itself setting out to conquer markets abroad.[48]

In the 1850s, industrialization within Bremen, and in the immediate vicinity, was still a far cry from the centers of German industrialization in Saxony and the Rhineland. Yet, as Meier's example of furniture bought in Berlin shows, the rise of industry in general, even if elsewhere, changed the rules of the game throughout the German states. Where free foreign trade, even if slightly skewed by Bremen's absence from the German Customs Union, introduced a growing number of non–guild-made items into the local market, the erosion of guild privilege had already become a fact.[49]

The problem of social control of the producing majority of the population by the merchant elite was fundamentally altered by the rise of industry. A proletariat removed from the paternalistic bonds of the artisanal home/workplace, shared by

[45] Heyde, Ludwig, "Böhmert, Karl Viktor," *Neue Deutsche Biographie* 2, Berlin, 1955, 394–5. Böhmert, Victor, *Beiträge zur Geschichte des Zunftwesens* (Preisschriften, gekrönt und herausgegeben von der fürstlich Jablonowski'schen Gesellschaft zu Leipzig, IX.), Leipzig, 1862; this essay was awarded a prize on January 30, 1860, and was written during 1859.

[46] Heyde, "Böhmert."

[47] Schwarzwälder, *Geschichte*, vol. 2, 228.

[48] Hardegen and Smidt, *H. H. Meier*, 156, 158. In this context, "foreign" means from "states other than Bremen," not necessarily outside of Germany.

[49] Bremen did not join the German Customs Union until 1886, and had been completely surrounded by customs union territory since 1854, when Hannover and Oldenburg had joined that organization. See also a statement by the *Senat* cited in VdBBü 1861/7, March 20, 1861, 107. For the conscious emulation of successful, foreign examples, see Engelsing, Rolf, "England und die USA in der bremischen Sicht des 19. Jahrhunderts," *Jahrbuch der Wittheit zu Bremen* 1, 1957, 33–65, esp. pp. 36–8.

a master, his family, and his apprentices and journeymen could no longer be integrated into the community in the same way that artisans had been through the guilds. As a means for creating political and social harmony, the guilds were becoming increasingly useless.[50]

In 1857, the first attempt to legislate away the guilds had failed. This only served to spur modernizers' determination. The balance of power between trade traditionalists and advocates of free labor did not change much in the *Bürgerschaft* that convened in 1858, yet when the 1860 election results had been tallied, it became clear that the new *Bürgerschaft*, to be in session on January 1, 1861, would have an insurmountable majority *against* free labor.[51]

In this situation, the mercantile modernizers, lead by Meier, made a desperate effort to force a new trade law through the old *Bürgerschaft*, before the newly elected members joined it. Unexpectedly, they were successful, in spite of the bitter resistance of every single member elected from the guilds. On December 29, 1860, the *Bürgerschaft* passed the *Gesetz, die Gewerbekammer betreffend* with a five-vote majority.[52]

In the debate that surrounded the passage of the 1860 trade law, modernizers sold free labor as a step toward more liberty, reiterating Smithian political economy. State Archivist Dr. Meinertzhagen was representative for this group, when he declared that "industry will be unfettered, . . . [and no longer will anyone be] dragged into court for exercising a right [to work], which he could have lost only because of [the] unnatural [guild system]."[53]

Most of the defenders of the guilds were either democrats or craft traditionalists.[54] A few representatives of these latter two groups were merchants or academics, whose views had convinced them to run for office in one of the lower orders. One of them was Dr. Karl Theodor Oelrichs, brother of the Baltimore and New York Oelrichs, head lawyer of the *Gewerbekammer* (Chamber of the Trades), and a staunch defender of guild tradition. Leader of the democrats was Johannes Rösing, a linen merchant and banker.[55] His group, however, was entirely marginal among the elite.

The democrats in the *Bürgerschaft* regarded an unfettered market for labor and commodities as a guarantee for social upheaval. Where modernizers pointed to foreign countries with a wish to emulate their success, their opponents saw the danger of social disharmony. Johann M. Wulftstein, a representative for the middle rank of Bremen's voters, stated this argument most starkly, if not clearly:

You pointed to larger countries, in which one could presumably observe the blessing of free labor. If we look more closely at these countries, we [see] filled almshouses and correctional institutions; a numerous proletariat on the streets – always prone to be

[50] Schwarzwälder, *Geschichte*, vol. 2, 229, 233–4.

[51] Ibid., 228–9.

[52] Ibid., 228.

[53] VdBBü, 1861/7, March 20, 1861, 100.

[54] For key speeches by opponents of free trade, see VdBBü, 1861/7, March 20, 1861, 98 (Georg Wilhelm Leppert), and 99 and 104–5 (Johann M. Wulftstein).

[55] For Oelrichs: VdBBü, 1861/7, March 20, 1861, 92. For Rösing: "Rösing (I.)," in Bippen, Wilhelm, *Bremische Biographie des 19. Jahrhunderts*, Bremen, 1905; [Freie Hansestadt Bremen], *Bremischer Staatskalender auf das Jahr 1861*, Bremen, 1861, 40.

made rebellious by some eggheads, since where there is free labor, the greater number of workers will remain on a lower level of education; finally, the recurrent plague of hunger, all these are not signs of blessing. Those gentlemen who wish to bring such blessings to Bremen will soon see them turned into a terrible curse. They drive the workers down the road of beggary, crime, and vice.[56]

Among the representatives of the mercantile estate, Wilhelm E. Backhaus was one of the few who shared Wulfstein's views. To Backhaus, the modernizers were abandoning the compact between the social classes and were "divid[ing them] into hostile camps." Free competition was "nothing but the arbitrary domination of the weak by the strong." "What we need," Backhaus tried to convince the *Bürgerschaft*, "is not an extension of economic freedom, but its restriction, so that the exploitation of one individual by another will not become the only, dominant moral law."[57]

But Backhaus was not merely a disappointed traditionalist. He had come to side with the democrats because he saw in equal voting rights a remedy for class conflict. Like American Democrats, he argued that a politically empowered populace could end class legislation in favor of the few. If the mercantile class did not dominate the polity, it could not pass legislation that only benefited them.[58]

In spite of their legislative victory, modernizers had reason to be uneasy. The menacing alliance between traditionalists and democrats contributed to their fear of losing political power to the have-nots. "We do not have a democratic majority in the Bürgerschaft *yet*, but, alas, the party is strong enough to cause all kind of discontent," Burgomaster Duckwitz stated with some resignation.[59]

It soon became clear that by introducing free labor into the Bremish economy, the mercantile modernizers had removed a keystone of the constitutional order, and, therefore, potentially, of their own privileged position. The *Handelskammer*, like the Chamber of Trades, drew its legitimacy from a corporatist worldview. The opponents of free labor in the *Bürgerschaft* were eager to exploit the contradiction of liberalizing craft production, while keeping mercantile professions closed shops.

To democrats, the "liberty" heralded by modernizers seemed to imply the full-scale implementation of the democratic political program, along with the liberal economic one. If the state was no longer to recognize "station" or "estate" for one group of burghers, the same certainly should apply to all burghers. If the Chamber of Trades no longer embodied an officially recognized, exclusive social group, how could it continue to claim representation of that group in the *Bürgerschaft*? If all burghers were to become equals in the market, why should they not also become citizens, that is, equals in politics? Free competition for the Thaler logically called for a free competition for the popular vote.[60]

The mercantile elite – not even the most committed modernizers in its ranks – never granted that logical connection. They were ready to prop up the estatist

[56] Ibid., 104–5. Wulfstein represented voter class IV.b., see Table 9, 170.

[57] Ibid., 106.

[58] Ibid., 106–7.

[59] Arnold Duckwitz to Rudolf Schleiden, January 30, 1861, Nachlaß Rudolf Schleiden, 5 unnumbered boxes, folder "Briefwechsel Rudolf Schleiden mit Senator Arnold Duckwitz, 1854–1879," Staatsarchiv Bremen, Sig. 7,116, my emphasis.

[60] See VdBBü, 1861/7, March 20, 1861, 98 (Leppert), and 106–7 (Wilhelm E. Backhaus).

constitution by replacing the corporatist keystone, which they had just removed, with a construction that proved stable enough to last fifty-seven years, with remnants still in place to this day.[61] Membership in the guilds became voluntary. Every person practicing a trade could now vote for the Convention of the Trades, which continued to elect the Chamber of the Trades. As before, the Chamber of the Trades and Convention of the Trades still jointly selected the twenty-four members of the *Bürgerschaft* that were reserved for artisans. Thus the estatist mode of political representation was assured. In essence, this construction put artisans in a position analogous to that of merchants: to be engaged in trade meant to be represented in the Merchants' Convention, and thus meant to enjoy political rights qua one's economic activity.[62]

This was an ingenuous solution. For even if a capitalist economy can do without democracy, it still had seemed a contradiction to leave an estatist political order in place while removing its "organic," corporatist, economic essence. In effect, the new model of the chambers preserved the deferential spirit of the corporatist world and transformed it into an institutionally based political expression of that proper sense of social hierarchy that the Hanseatic elite wished to uphold. This was Kiesselbach's political theory put into practice.

Although the modernizers had managed to avoid a spillover of the spirit of liberty that had been unleashed by their economic reforms into the realm of political representation, they were much less successful in defending their own monopolies in the economic sphere. Between 1861 and 1863, the broker system was stripped of its essential functions, the Lesser Privilege and Greater Privilege were abolished for one general status of citizenship, and the fee for naturalization was lowered. As a result, the mercantile profession became much less exclusive.[63]

Restrictions on most economic activities were abandoned. For example, the handling of cargoes, formerly an exclusive privilege of stevedores specializing in different goods, was now open to free competition. The broker system lost its communal exclusivity through its reform. Now, non-Christians could nominally also become brokers, and foreigners were allowed to do business with one another in Bremen. Devoid of its main rationale, the broker system for commodities was completely abandoned in May 1867. Any person taking an oath under the law was now allowed to call himself a broker and mediate business transactions. As a financial institution, the brokers remained in charge of settling balances among merchants twice weekly, but this procedure was no longer mandatory.[64]

The laws that scrapped these remnants of corporatism in the economic order of Bremen were introduced by democrats and were openly designed to taunt the

---

[61] The Handelskammer and the Chamber of Trades were complemented in 1921 with a Chamber of Workers (Arbeiterkammer) and a Chamber of Clerks (Angestelltenkammer), representing wage workers and salaried workers, respectively. In 2001, the latter two were merged to form the Chamber of Employees (Arbeitnehmerkammer). These chambers are still based on mandatory membership. They retain seats on *Bürgerschaft* committees, where their delegates enjoy all the rights of regular members, except for voting rights.

[62] Schwarzwälder, *Geschichte*, vol. 2, 227–30; Niehoff, *550 Jahre Tradition*, 101–5.

[63] Beutin, *Bank- und Börsenwesen*.

[64] Beutin, *Bremen und Amerika*, 53–7. Beutin, *Bank- und Börsenwesen*, 120–1. Because subjects of Bremen, such as the unpropertied, were not necessarily citizens, those, too, had been excluded from the broker system, and thus from the right to do business.

mercantile mainstream. Johannes Rösing's democrats and their allies hoped to unmask the rhetoric of "free labor" merchants wielded against the guilds as a mere smokescreen for a class-based attack on the rights of working people. In putting the axe to mercantile privilege, some traditionalists furthermore hoped for a chance to exact revenge on those merchants who had abolished the guilds.[65]

Now the roles of the earlier debate on free labor were virtually reversed. H. H. Meier took to the rostrum to defend the limitations and privileges of the brokers' office:

> We have a corporation of brokers that is, as a whole, respectable, and different from what one can find in any other mercantile city. The standing of the brokers ... contributes in essential ways to the solidity of Bremen's commerce.... I strongly wish that we will not change the brokers' office, and the mercantile interest at large shares this wish.... [Abolishing the brokers' office] is not a consequence of free labor, since brokers are not engaged in a trade. Their position can be compared to that of notaries-public, who are under oath, and whose word and signature can be trusted. This would not be the case if brokers were entirely free.[66]

When it came to their own exclusive institutions, it became quite clear that even the most committed modernizers among Hanseatic merchants embraced liberal policies only in a very selective fashion – as their democratic opponents were quick to remind them. The point Rösing and his democrats missed, however, was that H. H. Meier and his allies had at no point committed themselves to a full implementation of the liberal economic program. Their selective adaptation of individual liberal policies was not a matter of inconsistency, but followed from the Hanseats' overall worldview.

RELUCTANT MODERNIZERS

Competition with "other mercantile cities" in a capitalist world market contributed both to H. H. Meier's desire to improve the existing, good order, and to his ongoing investment in its moral economy. This competition created an impetus to emulate the most successful model. In transportation and production, this meant to follow a path to capitalist wage-labor relations. While the *Bürgerschaft* debated the merits of guilds, the Civil War raged in North America, radicalizing and popularizing the critique of slavery. There, the Northern elites were rapidly moving to make a virtue out of the necessity of wage labor. In so doing, they were beginning to reformulate their social creed to posit the necessity of wage labor as a virtue. The use of the term *free labor* by the enemies and defenders of guild privilege in Bremen suggests an awareness that this social transformation was a transnational process.[67]

---

[65] See VdBBü, 1861/13, May 29, 1861, 220–5; Schwarzwälder, *Geschichte*, vol. 2, 230. I am indebted to Dr. Lydia Niehoff for bringing to my attention that some of the friends of Johannes Rösing Sr. in the mercantile elite were among the supporters of the campaign for the protection of private property at sea (see Chapter 6). Apparently, for some Hanseats, support for free trade was compatible with a reluctance to embrace free labor. Bringing different standards to domestic and international politics was consistent with the traditional Hanseatic approach outlined here.

[66] VdBBü, 1861/13, May 29, 1861, 220–1.

[67] Ashworth, John, *Slavery, Capitalism, and Politics in the Antebellum Republic*, 2 vols., vol. 1: *Commerce and Compromise, 1820–1850*, Cambridge, 1995; Beckert, *Metropolis*.

In spite of his role as Bremen's leading "modernizer," H. H. Meier's language betrays his continued investment in the ethos of his estate. His is not the language of a man committed all-out to unfettered, capitalist relations, but of a traditionalist wanting to preserve the ethos of a communal order by improving upon it. If this meant dissolving communal social relations for the lower sorts, he was willing to bite this sour apple. To Meier and his peers, the ethos of honor and mutual trust within their own estate still appeared as an asset in the competition with other cities, giving Bremen's market a "solidity" that assured the continued patronage of buyers.[68]

But the competitive advantage it conveyed was not the only reason for Hanseats to remain committed to their communal nexus of families, firms, and faith. This was the way of life that they were used to, and they were not about to abandon time-honored traditions lightly. While H. H. Meier defended the brokers' office in the Bürgerschaft, the coherence of his estate was already beginning to crumble, as subsequent chapters (Chapters 7–9) will show. To effect this process of dissolution, however, it would take foes more formidable than Bremen's democrats.

The initial drive to engage in the world market the exigencies of which now transformed Bremen's society had emanated from the customary communal ethos that had governed Bremen. By the 1860s, as the price for "venturing and winning" on a changing world market, Bremen was faced at its gates with "more than [it could] support" within its traditional social structure.[69] Not just migrants, but also industrially manufactured commodities – Marx's "heavy artillery of capital" – were asking for admittance.[70] Opening the doors to either of them meant to change the customary arrangements in Bremen. Hanseats took the clues for the laws and ideas that replaced these customary arrangements with modernized ones from the West, especially from the United States.

---

[68] In the 1850s, an unnamed liberal visitor to Bremen from the German hinterland attested to the success of Bremen's attempts at modernization and linked it to the city's trade relations: "The influence of the uninterrupted and cordial intercourse with the youthful North America has had a vitalizing and stimulating effect on Bremen, and on its development and importance." Cited by Engelsing, "England und die USA," 60.

[69] For the inscriptions on the façade of the Schütting and St. Ansgar's Gate, see p. 178. For a discussion of the relation between community, society, and commerce, please see pp. 49–53.

[70] Marx and Engels, "Manifesto," 473–500, here: p. 477. See also Chapter 3.

5

International Improvement

Hanseats, Hamiltonians, and Jacksonians, 1845–1860

The nature of political parties in the United States has long been a matter of disagreement among American historians. Were parties driven by ideology, economic interest, ethnocultural identity, or some combination thereof?[1] In whittling down to two tickets an infinity of preferences and choices based on individual understandings of the world, shaped by material and cultural life, parties in the United States were always impure creatures. Yet, in the 1840s, at the height of the Second Party System, we find that Democrats and Whigs offered clear alternatives. Both offered consistent visions that combined fundamental political, economic, and cultural commitments into a coherent whole. Bourgeois parties both, they differed in their approach to the political management of a capitalist economy. Democrats represented a liberal-democratic tradition that stressed the empowerment of the common man as a corrective to the power of the moneyed few. Whigs represented a modern conservative tradition that wished to maintain hierarchy and social control, with the better sorts firmly in charge in state and society. Neither party was entirely determined in its political choices by its fundamental nature. But that this division was what told these parties apart, and that this division was not an exceptional feature of the American political landscape, but rather a local variant of global political currents, is visible in the interaction among Democrats, Whigs, and Hanseats.

HANSEATS IN AMERICAN POLITICS

On June 15, 1846, the U.S. Senate voted on an amendment to the Post Office Department appropriations bill. Connecticut Democrat John M. Niles had moved

[1] Formisano, Ronald P., *The Birth of Mass Political Parties, Michigan 1827–1861*, Princeton, NJ, 1971; idem, *The Transformation of Political Culture: Massachusetts Parties, 1790s–1840s*, New York and Oxford, 1983; Holt, Michael F., *Political Parties and American Political Development from the Age of Jackson to the Age of Lincoln*, Baton Rouge, LA, and London, 1992; Formisano, Ronald P., "The 'Party Period' Revisited," 93–120; and Holt, Michael F., "The Primacy of Party Reasserted," *Journal of American History* 86, no. 1 (June 1999), 151–7; Kohl, Lawrence F., *The Politics of Individualism: Parties and the American Character in the Jacksonian Era*, New York, 1989; McCormick, Richard P., *The Second American Party System: Party Formation in the Jacksonian Era*, Chapel Hill, NC, 1966; Pessen, Edward, *Jacksonian America: Society, Personality, and Politics*, Homewood, NJ, 1969; Schlesinger, Arthur M., Jr., *The Age of Jackson*, Boston, 1945.

to "appropriate $25,000 for the establishment of steam mail service, between New York and Bremen." For Bremen's special envoy, Carl Theodor Gevekoht, the success of his mission hinged on the passage of this amendment. We might imagine that he anxiously watched from the gallery, as one by one the legislators were called to give their vote. Passage was by no means assured, and the yeas went head to head with the nays throughout the roll-call vote. The amendment had managed to whip up a storm of debate that followed the sectional and party rifts characteristic of the Second Party System. The Whigs, clearly the weaker party with twenty-three out of fifty-six senators, had been the strongest supporters of the measure. Infrastructural, or "internal," improvements had been a key plank in the party's platform since its inception in the 1830s. Both parties understood steamer subsidies as an extension of this policy overseas. Thus the strong opposition to mail steamer subsidies in the South and West was based on the principled Democratic hostility to federal spending on internal improvements and "chartered monopolies." Whigs from those regions would be unlikely to support this unpopular measure. Not a single senator from outside the northeastern states had spoken in support of the subsidies. Some of the northeastern supporters, however, were Democrats. Gevekoht could take some comfort knowing that one of them had given enthusiastic support to the amendment – its author, John M. Niles of Connecticut. Niles had been postmaster general under President Van Buren and now served on the Committee on Post Offices and Post Roads. Another nine Democrats were to join him in the final vote: five from the northeast, two from Gulf Coast states, and one each from Virginia and Arkansas. In the end, party discipline trumped sectional interest only for the minority party. Four Whigs from interior states abstained, allowing the rest of their caucus to pass the amendment with the help of the ten Democrats who put a policy of "improvement" over party doctrine. By a majority of three votes, the amendment passed. Thus the path was cleared for the first American mail steamer line to Europe to be subsidized by the federal government. That its eastern terminus was to be Bremerhaven, Bremen's young outpost on the mouth of the Weser River, was not an accident.[2]

European Americanists have emphasized that the United States serves as a plane for Europeans' projections. Old-world liberals and conservatives can pick and choose from American political life to support their own views.[3] In Hanseats' interactions with Americans, we see that this mechanism works both ways. Bremen could be imagined as a place where their social vision had been realized by both Whigs and some Democrats. But the cooperation between Hanseats and their American allies was not just a matter of imagined commonalities. These

---

[2] *Congressional Globe*, vol. 15, 29th Cong., 1st Sess. (1845–6), 973 (vote), 943–5 (Senate debate), and 722–5 (House debate).

[3] See, e.g., Barclay, David E., and Elisabeth Glaser-Schmidt, eds., *Transatlantic Images and Perceptions: Germany and America since 1776*, Cambridge and New York, 1997; Gaehtgens, Thomas W., and Heinz Ickstadt, eds., *American Icons: Transatlantic Perspectives on Eighteenth- and Nineteenth-Century American Art* (Julia Bloomfield, Kurt W. Forster, and Thomas F. Reese, eds., Issues and Debates. A Series of the Getty Center Publication Program, vol. 2), Santa Monica, CA, 1992.

political actors knew to a large extent who they were dealing with, and they realized their shared interests.[4]

The American advocates of improvement could see in Hanseats like-minded men. These were Germans equally opposed to mob rule as America's republican elites, yet untainted by any association with monarchical regimes in Europe. Whigs and Hanseats agreed that the march of technological and moral progress was the calling of the nineteenth century, and that they were executing a divine design in furthering such progress. Markets, machines, and morality made for the gradual improvement of a fundamentally good society. This trinity of improvement was the respectable answer to the terror of the French Revolution. If men of standing and sound morals managed to break the spell of medieval superstition and feudal dominance over mankind, the rabble that had frightened the better sorts in the 1790s, and again in 1830, might well be turned into a populace diligently and prudently laboring for their own betterment. As long as the masses accepted these terms, their superiors would gladly lend them a hand up.[5]

Orthodox Jacksonian Democrats did not share this vision of "improvement." To them, a republic was safest in the hands of an empowered citizenry, whose equality before the law and at the ballot box formed a bulwark against the usurpation of their power by any class with aristocratic pretensions. More committed than Whigs to free, unfettered competition on the marketplace, Democrats believed that private enterprise supported by government was the first step onto a slippery slope that led back to a society in the thrall of a privileged order. However aware orthodox Democrats may have been that Hanseats were just such a privileged order in their hometown, the support these foreign merchants showed for government-funded corporations would have been proof enough that they were on the side of "aristocracy."[6]

In spite of the party line, a few internationally minded Democrats were among the strongest allies that the Hanseats had in Washington. Most important among them was Ambrose D. Mann. In 1846, he had just returned from Bremen, where he had served as American consul since 1842. Although Mann was solid in his Democratic convictions, his politics reflect an earlier strand of Democratic thinking. In the image of an early John C. Calhoun, or even Jefferson, Mann held to both emanations of the strong belief in reason fostered by the Enlightenment: the

---

[4] Engelsing, Rolf, "England und die USA in der bremischen Sicht des 19. Jahrhunderts," *Jahrbuch der Wittheit zu Bremen* 1, 1957, 33–65, here 45, claims that the United States barely noticed the Hanseatic cities, and therefore left them to their own devices in transatlantic trade. Although Bremen was not as important to American foreign policy as England or France, or even as Spain or Prussia, its commercial importance was not lost on contemporary Americans, as even Engelsing's own sources show. When Andrew Jackson compared the Hanseatic cities to "chicken" whom the American "horse" refrained from crushing out of sheer compassion, he not only showed that he had noticed the Hanseats, but that he was none too fond of them. This sentiment was shared by many in his party.

[5] Cf. Chapter 4; Howe, Daniel Walker, *The Political Culture of the American Whigs*, Chicago and London, 1979; Ashworth, John, *"Agrarians" and "Aristocrats": Party Political Ideology in the United States, 1837–1846*, London and Atlantic Highlands, NJ, 1983; idem, *Slavery, Capitalism, and Politics in the Antebellum Republic*, 2 vols., vol. 1: *Commerce and Compromise, 1820–1850*, Cambridge, 1995.

[6] Cf. Chapter 3; Sellers, Charles, *The Market Revolution: Jacksonian America, 1815–1846*, New York and Oxford, 1991; Taylor, John, *An Inquiry into the Principles and Policy of the Government of the United States*, London, 1950 (1814).

betterment of mankind through science and its application in technology, and the ability of the people to govern themselves democratically. This was a vision of modernization quite unlike the notion of improvement shared by Hanseats and Whigs. As with his intellectual ancestors, Mann's convictions, too, reached their limits when it came to slavery. Thus he became a steamship promoter specifically with a view to making the slaveholding South independent of northern commerce. As a diplomat, his postings reflect this transition: after serving as consul to Bremen, he returned to the continent once more in 1849–50 to support the democratic revolutions in Germany and Hungary. His final mission took him to Paris in 1861, as an agent for the Confederacy.[7]

There were some Democrats who, once in positions of influence, adopted the policies initially associated with Hamilton. Embracing tariffs, banking, and infra-structural measures designed to create a denser and more extensive marketplace, John M. Niles was a perfect specimen of this current. His orthodox colleagues in Congress despised him for this reason and alleged that he was not in full possession of his mental powers.[8] Ever since his tenure as postmaster general, Niles had been a champion of a developmental vision compatible with that of the Whigs, without, however, abandoning his belief in the Democratic politics of equality. To Niles, working with the Hanseats made sense, because these Bremish merchants could deliver a mail steamer line that promised to extend American commercial relations at a comparatively modest price.

Hanseats, too, knew their American counterparts and their political views. They were pragmatic in building a coalition for their aim of securing mail subsidies for a line to Bremen. Whigs' preference for a strong tariff and Democrats' advocacy of popular participation in politics made for points of contention between Hanseats and both major parties. As long as a congressman was willing to vote for a Bremen line, however, these differences mattered little.

Beyond questions of practical policy, however, Hanseats had a deep affinity with Whigs based not only on their shared vision of "improvement," but also on their fundamental agreement on social and political values. By contrast, Bremish mer-chants brought a basic dislike to their interactions with Democrats, whom they regarded as the party of mob rule.[9]

Their interactions, disagreements and affinities, with Hanseats place the main currents of the Second Party System in a transnational context. In this context, the debates that define the antebellum United States no longer appear as exclusive or exceptional to the New World. Instead, Democrats and Whigs can be recognized as specifically American political currents that correspond with two major variants of Western, bourgeois politics – one liberal-democratic, the other conservative-elitist. Bearing on the debates in American historiography on the nature of Democratic and Whig politics, we can realize that their main disagreement was not over

---

[7] Beutin, Ludwig, *Bremen und Amerika. Zur Geschichte der Weltwirtschaft und der Beziehungen Deutschlands zu den Vereinigten Staaten*, Bremen, 1953, 284, note to p. 57; "Mann, Ambrose Dudley," *Dictionary of American Biography* 6, New York, 1933, 239–40.

[8] "Niles, John M.," *Dictionary of American Biography* 7, New York, 1934, 522–3; Sellers, *Market Revolution*.

[9] Cf. Chapters 3 and 4.

whether capitalist social relations were a desirable goal, but rather over the political and ideological arrangements that were to accompany capitalist modernization. With Hanseats, Whigs envisioned a union of markets, machines, and morality to buffer the disruptive consequences of capitalism. American and European democrats, by contrast, demanded an empowerment of the populace to counter the growing clout of the elites who steered the social transition to industrial capitalism.

THE POLITICAL ECONOMY OF TRANSATLANTIC COMMERCE AND COMMUNICATION

To judge not only the merits of Democrats' and Whigs' positions in the debate over mail steamers, but also the assumptions underlying these positions, we will have to take a detour into the history and political economy of ocean navigation. Democrats demanded that international shipping be left to the free play of market forces. Whigs insisted that the free market was unable to deliver steam-driven ocean liners.[10] The historical record supports the Whigs' claim.

Even if both parties had been able to agree on the facts of the matter, however, the political question would have remained open: did the United States really need its own mail steamers, and who would benefit from them? Whigs argued that expedited mail delivery was in the public interest, and that, hence, government subsidies would serve the common good. Orthodox Democrats disagreed. Letter writing was a private luxury, practiced by few.[11] If these few wanted their correspondence to travel more quickly, they ought to pay for it. Hence, the essential question at stake in this debate was the role of the state vis-à-vis society.

To complicate matters, as a new technology that captured the public imagination, ocean steamers were ideologically overdetermined. On April 22, 1838, the first transatlantic steamship, the *Sirius*, had arrived in New York from Cork. A day later, a vessel owned by a rival British company, the *Great Western*, joined her there, after a passage of fifteen days from Bristol, beating the eighteen-day passage of the rival vessel, which had had to cover less distance.[12] The sudden realization that it was possible for an Atlantic crossing to be made by a vessel relying mainly on steam power set off two conflicting, equally emotional responses: the hope for universal progress through technology and the fear that this technology would give a rival nation – specifically, Britain – a decisive advantage in war and commerce.[13] In both cases, contemporaries assumed that ocean navigation had been changed radically

---

[10] Cf. note 444.

[11] See the remarks by Rep. William W. Payne, 275.

[12] Tyler, David Budlong, "Steam Conquers the Atlantic," PhD diss., Columbia University, New York and London, 1939, 52; John G. B. Hutchins, *The American Maritime Industry and Public Policy, 1789–1914: An Economic History* (i.e., Harvard University, inst. ed., Harvard Economic Studies, vol. 71), Cambridge, MA, 1941, 343–4, erroneously claims the *British Queen*, rather than the *Sirius*, had been the first transatlantic steam vessel to arrive in New York.

[13] Auxiliary steam engines had previously been used on some transatlantic packet boats (see Tyler, "Steam," 54–5). The novelty of these two vessels, and those that were to follow, was their capacity to cross the ocean by steam power, alone. This capacity was just that, however, and throughout the 1840s, 1850s, and 1860s, steam vessels remained fully rigged as sailing vessels, because steam was too unreliable.

overnight. Steamers would cruise to a fast and inevitable victory over sail, in Christian seafaring and in naval battles.

To this day, the hubris contemporaries of the nineteenth century brought to steamships remains a standard feature in histories of this transportation technology. In works like *Steam Conquers the Atlantic* or *The Great Atlantic Steamships*, the titles betray a great deal of romanticization.[14] The heroic story of daring entrepreneurs who embraced a technology of the future, and wielded it as a tool in titanic struggles between competing, equally glorious, steamship lines will be familiar to anyone who has ever been fascinated by this mode of transportation. Especially in the past decade, maritime scholarship has been making great strides toward debunking this well-entrenched myth, even if its impact on the popular literature so far has been negligible.[15]

The "technology of the future" was anything but efficient. Early steamers were side-wheelers, rather than screw-driven vessels. The inefficiency of paddle wheels was evident even to contemporaries.[16] The upward motion of the paddles, and the friction of the paddles as they enter into and leave the water, counteracted the forward motion of the ship. In gales, one paddle wheel might be submerged too deeply to have any motive impact, while the other would stick out of the water, with the same result. The low efficiency of the paddle wheels was only exceeded by that of early steam engines. Combined, these two technological components required a tremendous amount of coal to keep the vessel moving, leaving little if any space for the transportation of cargo. If steamships were going to be useful, it was going to be for goods that were high in value, but low in volume, as well as for passengers and mail. Their benefit was to be found in a fairly abstract quality: speed.[17]

---

[14] Tyler, "Steam"; Fox, Steven, *Transatlantic: Samuel Cunard, Isambard Brunel, and the Great Atlantic Steamships*, New York, 2003.

[15] Three works that stand out as sober accounts of early steam navigation: Sloan, Edward, "Collins versus Cunard: The Realities of a North Atlantic Steamship Rivalry, 1850–1858," *International Journal of Maritime History* IV, no. 1 (June 1992), 83–100; Gerstenberger, Heide, and Ulrich Welke, *Vom Wind zum Dampf. Sozialgeschichte der deutschen Handelsschiffahrt im Zeitalter der Industrialisierung*, Münster, 1996; and Hutchins, John G. B., *The American Maritime Industry and Public Policy, 1789–1914: An Economic History*, London and Cambridge, MA, 1941 (Harvard Economic Studies, vol. 71). Common to these works is their attention to the role of the state in setting the parameters for international trade and shipping, and to the character of steamship lines as capitalist business enterprises. This distinguishes them from most maritime literature, whose authors tend to focus on technology and lore.

[16] One of the doubters was Dr. Dionysius Lardner, a natural scientist, engineer, and member of the British Association for the Advancement of Science. His assertion, made in 1827, that a steamship "voyage directly from New York to Liverpool" was as likely as "a voyage from New York or Liverpool to the moon," earned him lasting ridicule. Nevertheless, Lardner's assumption that the maximum range of a steamer was 2,550 miles was based on a realistically pessimistic assessment of the problems with coal consumption, engine efficiency, and paddle-wheel technology that were to plague early steamers. See Tyler, "Steam," 4, 33–4, 40–1.

[17] Ibid., 38, 40. Steam-engine technology made a significant breakthrough in the 1880s, with the development of compound engines that better utilized the steam. Even before that, the introduction of the propeller screw in the 1850s increased the efficiency of steam engines, although early screw steamers were slower than side-wheelers. Side-wheelers were still built in the 1860s, but the share of propeller-screw vessels increased steadily. See Gerstenberger and Welke, *Vom Wind zum Dampf*; [North German Lloyd Steamship Company, Bremen], *70 Years North German Lloyd Bremen, 1857–1927*, Berlin, 1927, 32–8.

Although steamers provided for speed, they did so at a price of human lives. Even after decades of their use in industry and transportation, steam engines remained a dangerous technology. A boiler explosion on a riverboat was a deadly disaster, but survivors would still stand a chance if they reached the shore. Not so onboard a vessel on the high seas. The risk of fire on steamships was considerable, even short of a boiler explosion. On her very first trip, a fire broke out in the boiler room of the *Great Western*, while still on the River Thames. Isambard K. Brunel, the director of the company that owned the ship, had to risk his life, and was incapacitated for weeks, after an attempt to quell the flames. He survived the fall from a ladder in the smoke-filled boiler room because he came to land on his fellow director, Captain Claxton. Though the damage to the ship was minor, all but eight of the passengers fled the vessel as it anchored off Bristol, preferring the slower but safer passage on a sailing packet.[18]

Under these conditions, transatlantic steamers remained unprofitable for decades. A number of companies went out of business after a few years of operation. Few steamer lines ever paid dividends, and the stock prices of nearly all steamship companies plunged by as much as 90 percent at some point in their career. The losses of the pioneering *Great Western* were covered by the parent company, the Great Western Railroad, and even she remained in service for only eight years. Those steamship companies that became known as success stories relied heavily on government subsidies, paid under mail contracts. Without these subsidies, private capital would have stayed away from steamship schemes. Not capital in search of valorization, but governments in pursuit of accelerated communication and naval advantages in war kept the first transatlantic steamers afloat.[19]

Merchants had a vested interest in convincing states to pay for mail-steamer service. The speed of communication is an essential factor for trade. Capital remains tied up in transit, when bills of exchange, contracts, and orders cross the ocean to reach their destination. The faster the documents that represent it, the shorter the turnover time of capital. Traditionally, merchant capital draws its largest profits from arbitrage – buying cheap to sell dear. The pursuit of arbitrage profits tends to pit one merchant against all others. Whoever learns first about market conditions abroad can react first by shipping a certain type of cargo or withholding another. Even as late as 1860, we still find private and business letters displaying the excited tone of men who wanted to be the first to profit from uncommon opportunities.

---

[18] This account is based on Tyler, "Steam," 49–50. Innumerable other examples of steamship disasters exist. On average, one in two steamships appears to have been lost at some point during her service. One of the most dramatic incidents of the 1850s was the sinking of the Hamburg-Amerika Packetfahrt-Actiengesellschaft's *Austria* in 1858, which killed five hundred. See Tyler, "Steam," 255; Sophie Schwab to Gustav F. Schwab, Stuttgart, November 14, 1858, and Sophie Klüpfel to Gustav F. Schwab, Tübingen, October 22, 1858, both MSS 434, John Christopher Schwab Family Papers. Manuscripts and Archives, Yale University Library, series I, box 2, folder 35. For the shortcomings of the first steamers between New York and Bremerhaven, see Wätjen, Hermann, *Aus der Frühzeit des Nordatlantikverkehrs. Studien zur Geschichte der deutschen Schiffahrt und deutschen Auswanderung nach den Vereinigten Staaten bis zum Ende des amerikanischen Bürgerkrieges*, Leipzig, 1932, 36; for those of Fritze's and Lehmkuhl's venture (see p. 283), ibid., 56–7. For other examples, see Arnell, J. C., *Steam and the North Atlantic Mails: The Impact of the Cunard Line and Subsequent Steamship Companies on the Carriage of Transatlantic Mails*, Toronto, 1986, 107–24, 239, 241, 243–4.

[19] See the literature cited in notes 12–18 to this chapter.

When the market for hops was undersupplied in Bremen, Johann Georg Graue wrote to his brother in Baltimore: "Have first-grade commodity bought <u>right away</u>; I expect the price [in Baltimore] has risen, but that is immaterial, I must have some."[20]

Regular venues of communication tend to even out informational advantages, as "prices current" – printed lists of commodity prices – from foreign ports arrive on a dependable schedule and become available to all merchants through daily newspapers. Hence, merchants' private interests to be first to know add up to a collective interest to speed up communication. This is a collective interest established, first, among the merchants in one port against those of all other ports, because the more and the faster information and goods are available in one place, the greater its competitive advantage over others.[21]

Since the 1820s, regularly scheduled sailing packets had gone a long way toward making the transatlantic flow of information more reliable.[22] Within months of the arrival of steam service, however, mail migrated to these newer vessels. Steamers made the passage from the English Channel to New York in as little as two weeks. Especially on the westbound journey, a sailing vessel could not beat this time. It took the average sailing ship forty-three days to travel from Bremen to New York. Even the fastest vessels rarely made the voyage in less than twenty days. Steamships were not only faster, but also kept their schedule more reliably, provided they did not run into engine trouble. Given the common interest of merchants in accelerating the speed of communication, it is not surprising that they favored steamers over sailing packets.[23]

But merchants were unable to shoulder the cost of the new transportation technology – particularly not the gigantic operating losses. By the mid-1840s, the lesson that steam navigation was not a good investment opportunity had become generally acknowledged. Not even in a city like New York would the collective interest of merchants in expedited communication have sufficed to bring them to finance a steamship venture. Private capital was not going to be attracted to any steamship schemes, unless government subsidies guaranteed a return on investments (see Table 10).

From the start, ocean steamers were tokens in international rivalry. Britain had begun in 1840 to subsidize the Cunard Line, for the transportation of mail between Liverpool and British North America. Cunard steamers called at Boston on a regular schedule. Especially in the winter, Canadian mail was transported through the

---

[20] Johann Georg Graue to Herman Henrich Graue, Bremen, October 22, 1860, Maryland Historical Society, MSS 2826, Graue, H. H., Papers, 1834–1871, 4 boxes, box 4, 1855–1871. Strong emphasis in the original. H. H. Meier spoke for Bremen's merchants when he said that "speed of movement in trade and exchange is becoming more and more important." Cited by Bessell, Georg, *1857–1957: Norddeutscher Lloyd. Geschichte einer bremischen Reederei*, Bremen, 1957, 16.

[21] Cf. Chapter 1.

[22] Arnell, *Steam*, 20.

[23] StAHB 2,B.13.b.3, *Hanseatica. Verhältnisse der Hansestädte mit den Vereinigten Staaten von Nordamerika. Hanseatische diplomatische Agenten, Konsuln usw. bei den Vereinigten Staaten von Nordamerika und Korrespondenz mit denselben*. In New York, 1815–1868; file no. 15, "Consulat zu Newyork, F. W. Keutgen, 1859 Novb. 1–1861; Gustav Schwab 1862. –. Enthält No. 1- 89. 1859 Nov. 1–1868 Okt. 28," document no. 15 of 89, "Bericht des Bremischen Consulats zu Newyork für 1860, Juni 1861," 24; Wätjen, *Frühzeit*, 50.

TABLE 10. *Unprofitability of Steamers: Average Expenses and Income for a Steamer Round-Trip, New York–Liverpool, ca. 1850*

Expenses	US$	Income	US$
Fuel	8,600	Revenue	12,065
Repairs	9,215	Subsidy	19,250
Insurance	8,900		
Overhead	21,600	Operating Loss	17,000
Total	**48,315**	Total	**48,315**

Based on Cunard's estimates for Collins's vessels, as cited by Fox, *Transatlantic*, p. 125. With all cabins fully booked, a Cunard steamer could make $38,000 and an OSNC steamer $35,280 in passenger revenue on a round-trip. See Wätjen, *Frühzeit*, p. 34. Subsidy amount based on the 1845 U.S. Law, see Arnell, *Steam*, p. 173. Judging from Fox's and Wätjen's figures, a subsidized steamer could break even, if 76% to 82% of available passages were sold. At $60 (OSNC, 3rd class) to $190 (Cunard) per one-way ticket, steamer passages were not affordable to all but a handful of emigrants, and the steamers were rarely sold out. The occupancy rate of 33% suggested by Fox's figures seems realistic for Collins's vessels.

United States, as the Saint Lawrence River became unnavigable.[24] For their correspondence with Britain and Europe, U.S. merchants had to depend on these British mail steamers. The considerable amount spent on transatlantic postage, although by itself insufficient to support a steamer line, nonetheless benefited British interests, exclusively. Moreover, Cunard's mail contracts stipulated that the steam vessels had to be made available to the Royal Navy in case of war, and naval officers routinely received training on board Cunard's vessels.

If the United States wanted its own mail steamers, it would have to pay subsidies. Mercantile interest, national defense, and cosmopolitan hopes coalesced to lead increasing numbers of American politicians to advocate an emulation of the British example. As advocates of an active government role in providing for infrastructural improvements, Whigs were more likely than Democrats to support such subsidies. Their defeat in the 1844 election spurred them to a last-minute effort. The passage of a bill authorizing the postmaster general to award contracts to American companies for carrying the mail by steamer to foreign countries was one of the last acts of the 28th Congress, and President Tyler signed it into law during his last hours in office in early March 1845.[25] The foundation for American mail steamers had been created. Now it remained up to financiers to avail themselves of the option.

The involvement in shipping of the federal government somewhat complicated the political interest of merchants. Whereas merchants in one port tend to be united in their wish to have an informational advantage over merchants of all other ports, mail steamers provided a potential common interest between merchants in all port

[24] Arnell, *Steam*, 39–56, 78, 82–9, 136–54.
[25] Tyler, "Steam," 142. Whether Bremen's inclusion in the list of European ports that the law listed as prospective Eastern termini for steamer lines was already the result of a lobbying effort on Hanseats' part, or whether it reflected a recognition by the bill's authors of Bremen's importance as a port for American trade, is unclear.

cities within a country. U.S. merchants shared the interest that the federal government provide for mail steamers. A local, mercantile competition for speed was thus
partly displaced by international rivalry.

Due to the cost of steamers, however, not every port could have its own line. If
the federal government was to get into the steamer business, it had to decide on *one*
terminus, creating a new kind of intercity competition to become that terminus.
This intercity competition had a new quality: it no longer pitted every port against
every other, but involved only those under the domain of one particular territorial
state. By assuming responsibility for steamer service, the federal government had to
become the arbitrator of local mercantile interests in determining transoceanic mail
routes.

This explains both the interport rivalry for becoming the end point of the new
mail-steamer lines, as well as the eventual, although grudging, assent of congressmen favoring lines between ports other than Bremerhaven and New York to the
proposed subsidy for the Ocean Steam Navigation Company (OSNC): without
unanimity among those favoring "international improvement" in principle, their
opponents would have voted down subsidies, altogether, and America would have
continued to depend on Britain for its international correspondence.

For Bremen, as a city-state, the matter was less complicated. New York was the
main American port Hanseats served, and on the European side, Bremen stood in
competition with all other transatlantic ports, unmediated even in its relations with
Hamburg by a nation-state. Hence, the Hanseatic elite could apply itself with
single-minded determination to gaining the first mail contract.

THE BREMISH EFFORT TO GAIN THE FIRST EURO-AMERICAN STEAMER LINE

In Bremen, *Senator* Arnold Duckwitz, Burgomaster Johann Smidt's young protégée,
read the American newspapers attentively. Thanks to the Cunard steamers, they were
but three to four weeks old when they reached him. At the first sign that mail steamer
subsidies were contemplated, he urged the Bremish *Senat* to make use of the
opportunity.[26] Through Dudley A. Mann, the U.S. consul in Bremen, the *Senat*
offered Polk's administration the opportunity to exempt American steamers from
port fees and promised a tariff-exempt storage of coal in Bremerhaven. Mann was
recalled from his post in Bremen in 1845. He returned to Washington a convert to
Bremen's cause, equipped with 155 bottles of German wine to aid his lobbying
efforts. As a result of Mann's good rapport with Secretary of State James Buchanan
and Postmaster General Cave Johnson, Bremen moved to the top of the list of
European ports under consideration as destinations for American mail steamers.[27]

The law of March 3, 1845, authorized the postmaster general to solicit bids for
two lines of mail steamers, one offering biweekly service between New York on
the western shore of the Atlantic and either Hamburg, Bremen, Antwerp, or Le
Havre on the eastern end, with an obligation to call at an English port on the
channel; the other offering biweekly service between New York and Liverpool.

---

[26] Wätjen, *Frühzeit*, 33.
[27] Ibid., 25–6.

Contractors had to be American citizens, and the ships had to be American-built and manned exclusively by American crews. The subsidy was to amount to $20,000 per trip to Bremen or Hamburg (20 sailings, for a total of $400,000 p.a.), $19,250 per trip to Liverpool ($385,000), and $15,000 per trip to Le Havre or Antwerp ($300,000). Contracts could be made for a period of time of up to ten years, and were to contain a provision that gave the U.S. government a right to sequester the vessels in case of war.[28] As a conscientious public official, Postmaster General Cave Johnson was not about to subvert the law, even if he was not a friend of government support to private companies. Thus, in late 1845, he publicly solicited bids for contracts under the steamer law.[29]

The *Senat* knew that public opinion and congressional votes mattered in U.S. politics. It dispatched Carl Theodor Gevekoht to New York, where he was to enlist merchants in support of the cause, before going to Washington for a concerted lobbying effort. Gevekoht had been a merchant in Baltimore and was well connected in the United States. A number of important American citizens lent their names to Gevekoht's mission. Most prominent among them was John Jacob Astor. This dean of New York society had been sympathetic to Hanseatic interests for decades. His daughter was married to Vincent Rumpff, the Hanseatic Ambassador to France.[30] Hanseats in New York began publishing newspaper articles in support of a line to Bremen. Prussia's ambassador to Washington, Baron von Gerolt, joined their campaign.[31]

Three bids were entered for the mail contract, all from New York. The postmaster general picked the offer that was most favorable to the federal government, the one made by Edward Mills. Historians of American steam navigation have characterized Mills as a blank page in mercantile circles, a speculator who lacked any experience in shipping or trade. His fate before and after his involvement with the mail steamer line has eluded the historical record, lending some support to the received opinion of his importance. Mills's bid proposed a biweekly service between New York and Le Havre via Cowes on the Isle of Wight.[32] Postmaster General Cave Johnson, by now convinced that Bremen would be preferable to Le Havre, moved Mills to change his plan and to offer monthly service to Bremen and Le Havre, each, with biweekly departures from New York alternating between these two destinations.[33]

On the German side, meanwhile, Bremen had begun to create the conditions necessary for the success of the projected line. The existing dock in Bremerhaven, dating from the early 1830s, was too narrow and shallow for an ocean-going paddle wheeler. The *Senat* began construction of a new dock, which could not only accommodate the newest steamers, but whose design was based on an optimistic assessment of the future growth in overall traffic and in the size of ocean-going

---

[28] Arnell, *Steam*, 173; Hutchins, *American Maritime Industry*, 350–2.
[29] Grant, Clement Lyndon, "The Public Career of Cave Johnson," PhD diss., Vanderbilt University, 1951, esp. 221–31.
[30] Wätjen, *Frühzeit*, 29; Beutin, *Bremen und Amerika*, 30.
[31] Wätjen, *Frühzeit*, 26.
[32] Arnell, *Steam*, 175; Tyler, "Steam," 143–4; House Doc. No. 162, 29th Cong., 1st Sess.; Wätjen, *Frühzeit*, 29, claims that Mills had been a stockbroker.
[33] Tyler, "Steam," 144.

vessels (see Map 3).[34] As part of the effort to make Bremerhaven a desirable destination for American steamers, the *Senat* had also negotiated a significant reduction of transit tariffs with Hannover and the streamlining of mail transportation between Bremen and the Kingdom of Hannover, including the construction of a post office in Bremerhaven.[35]

After Mills had incorporated the OSNC, it soon became clear that no amount of government-built infrastructure would attract sufficient private capital to get the enterprise afloat. New York's financial markets remained frosty toward his company.[36] Supporters of the line began looking for other sources of capital. The limits of American federal financial commitments to the venture were set by the law of 1845. Contributions to the capital stock were explicitly not part of the contracts under that law. The state of Bremen had already committed $1 million to the new dock, and was unable to carry much more of a financial burden. Hanseatic merchants in Bremen and America had bought some stock of the new company, but by the spring of 1847, only about $200,000 of stocks had been signed, out of a total of $1 million offered. Other sources of capital were badly needed.

In this situation, the *Senat* decided to sell the scheme to other German governments. Duplicating the successful approach taken earlier in Washington, three special envoys were dispatched to the German capitals. Their mission was astonishingly successful. Prussia and Bremen each contributed $100,000; Hannover $25,000; Saxony $20,000; and a number of smaller states combined gave a total of $44,100. The smallest individual contribution came from a tiny Thuringian principality, which gave $300. The total of funds contributed by German governments came to $300,000.[37] This amount was given as a loan to Oelrichs & Co., of New York. That firm then signed $300,000 worth of OSNC stock, formally complying with the provision of the 1845 act that the mail steamer company be funded by American investors. Mills yielded control of the company to a group of established New York merchants, with Hermann Oelrichs, who was Bremen's consul in New York and an American citizen, as vice president. Mills settled for a position as "general agent" of the company.[38] Hanseats' successes in Germany and the United

---

[34] Engelsing, *Auswandererhafen*; According to Wätjen, *Frühzeit*, 33–4, the OSNC steamers were 75m in length and had a draught of 9.5m. The old dock had a depth of 5.5m and a breadth of 58m. See Schwarzwälder, *Geschichte*, 131. See also note to Table 8.

[35] Wätjen, *Frühzeit*, 26–7.

[36] The Collins line, founded to take advantage of the New York–Liverpool subsidies under the 1845 Law, was largely financed by the New York branch of Brown Bros., based in Liverpool. The reluctance of American merchant bankers to invest in steam navigation was thus not limited to the OSNC. See Sloan, "Collins versus Cunard."

[37] Wätjen, *Frühzeit*, 31. The total of $300,000 includes another $11,000 signed by other New York merchants on behalf of the state of Bremen.

[38] Tyler, "Steam," 147–8. According to Wätjen, *Frühzeit*, 29, 31. Oelrichs & Co. signed an additional $15,000 on its own account. Combined with the stock held in combination with the German loans, this would have made Oelrichs & Co. a near-majority interest in the OSNC, because, altogether, only $643,800 worth of stock was sold. Wätjen also claims, erroneously, that Hermann Oelrichs's younger brother, Edwin, became a member of the OSNC's board. See Pitsch, Franz Josef, *Die wirtschaftlichen Beziehungen Bremens zu den Vereinigten Staaten von Amerika bis zur Mitte des 19. Jahrhunderts* (Karl H. Schwebel, ed., Veröffentlichungen aus dem Staatsarchiv der Freien Hansestadt Bremen, vol. 42), Bremen, 1974, 125.

States represented a triumph of Bremish diplomacy, which relied exclusively on mercantile connections.[39]

Getting Congress to pay the bill for the subsidies proved a harder task than convincing the German governments to contribute to an American business enterprise. By the time Congress debated the appropriations bill, E. K. Collins of New York had made a bid for a contract for mail service to Liverpool. Some congressmen preferred this line over one that sailed to a relatively small German port, and many did not believe that two lines were sustainable, in spite of the provisions of the law of 1845. Most Democrats were hostile to the plan of mail-steamer subsidies, on principle. It did not help much that one of their own party, John M. Niles of Connecticut, was the main advocate of the measure. In the end, it was decisive that Hanseats and their allies were able to build a majority based on a shared commitment to "improvement."

WINNING FRIENDS IN CONGRESS

Congressional proponents of the subsidies stressed their importance for trade and war. For John M. Niles, the arrival of ocean-going steamers had shrunk the world. It had brought the United States "nearer to Europe," and had thus resulted in increased commerce and communication. This expansion of opportunities, however, came to benefit a "rival nation," which had made "international correspondence . . . subservient to the advancement of her commercial interests." Because Niles attributed to ocean steam mail service "a connexion with, and influence upon, the commerce of the country, and . . . advantages for naval defense in case of war," command of the new technology would be of decisive importance for American success in her ongoing rivalry with Britain.[40]

Note that Niles assumed a crucial role of correspondence for commerce, even though it was unfeasible to transport any but "light and valuable goods" on the new steamers. He saw the main benefit for trade of mail service in "affording facilities for commercial transactions." Not the transportation of goods, as such, but the ease of the commercial *transactions* that set these goods in motion was his main concern. Commodities were bought, transported, and sold, because merchants wrote contracts, bills of exchange, orders, powers of attorney, and a wide range of general business correspondence. Without these documents, not a single hogshead of tobacco or bale of cotton would ever leave the American shores. Britain treated the provision of the communication infrastructure that underlay commercial relations as a responsibility of government, because it understood the importance of the

---

[39] Mustafa, Sam A., "The Role of the Hanseatic Cities in Early U.S. – German Relations," *Maryland Historical Magazine* 93, no. 3 (Fall 1998), 265–87; Fink, Georg, "Diplomatische Vertretungen der Hanse seit dem 17. Jahrhundert bis zur Auflösung der Hanseatischen Gesandtschaft in Berlin 1920," *Hanseatische Geschichtsblätter* 56, Lübeck, Germany, 1932, 112–55; Graßmann, Antjekathrin, "Hanse weltweit? Zu den Konsulaten Lübecks, Bremens und Hamburgs im 19. Jahrhundert," in *Ausklang und Nachklang der Hanse im 19. und 20. Jahrhundert*, ed. idem (Hansischer Geschichtsverein, ed., Hansische Studien, vol. 12), Trier, Germany, 2001, 43–66.

[40] *Congressional Globe*, 29th Cong., 1st Sess., Appendix, 986.

flow of information for trade. For Niles, this British policy was "worthy of our imitation."[41]

Niles could argue that "government has no interest in the freights," at least not in providing for their transportation, because he assumed that trade would follow routes of communication, rather than vice versa. Mail service was "changing the course of trade, and freights are taking that direction." Allowing the British to dominate this new mode of transportation would, therefore, serve to reinforce the existing domination of American trade by Liverpool. This seemed especially dangerous at a time when "every year the proportion of our importations in foreign vessels is increasing." Bremen promised an alternative to American dependence on Britain. The provision of a communication infrastructure, however, was essential for realizing this promise.[42]

Advocates of the steamer subsidies also embraced the darker side of steam navigation – the possibility of using this new technology for a naval advantage in case of war. Unlike many of his colleagues, however, Niles did not treat national defense as a problem of technology alone. Instead, Niles displayed a broader view of international security, in which it mattered almost as much, if not more, to have friends abroad, as it did to have steamers at home. Britain, America's "jealous rival," had placed herself in a menacing position, blocking the young republic from unimpeded access to its natural friends, and thus from its potential allies in that very rivalry:

At present, all communication, all intelligence from this country, reaches the continent through England, and has a British taint or odor given to it. The people of the continent know nothing about this country [the United States], except what passes through English channels; and, as a rival nation, jealous of our growing prosperity and greatness, there exists a natural disposition to pervert or misrepresent everything concerning our institutions and the character of our people, and the rising prosperity of this country.[43]

Hence, mail steamers promised to realize the hope of cosmopolitanism, a world in which mutual understanding, fostered by commerce and communication, guaranteed peace.[44] England appeared as the main obstacle on the path to such a world.

By contrast, when Americans looked to continental Europe in the antebellum period, they saw peoples eager to shake off aristocratic tyranny, and to embrace "government by the people." In the 1830s, the struggles for independence in Poland and Greece had confirmed American observers in this hopeful gaze. The

---

[41] Ibid., 987. An economic historian of the transportation industry supports Niles's take: "These [mail steamer] services, by improving transport relations between England and the area touched, had an active influence on the localization pattern of world trade rather than the passive effect of tramp sailing vessels. It was, therefore, a matter of some importance to the United States that the ocean transportation was being so organized with its hub in Great Britain." Hutchins, *American Maritime Industry*, 348.

[42] *Congressional Globe*, 29th Cong., 1st Sess., 943, and Appendix, 985–7.

[43] Ibid., Appendix, 986.

[44] For the importance of this argument in A. D. Mann's lobbying effort with Postmaster General Cave Johnson, see Tyler, "Steam," 143–4.

revolutions of 1848 would serve further to reinforce it.[45] It was this hope that Europeans were potential republican allies that promoters of the mail-steamer subsidies appealed to when they praised the steamer lines as venues for "the diffusion of a knowledge of American institutions" abroad.[46] Learning about these institutions meant wanting to emulate them.

Hanseatic lobbyists successfully appealed to these American hopes. Bremen's representatives in the United States cast the "very small" city-state as a natural ally of "her great sister-republic," the United States. The appeal to the perpetual peace among republics was a major selling point. When Bremen's Minister Resident, Rudolf Schleiden, lobbied Congress for a renewal of steamer subsidies in 1856, he would claim that "Bremen, being a small republic was not likely to be ever involved in any war, . . . her institutions, inclinations and habits are more like those of the United States."[47]

As the Senate debated the mail-steamer subsidies, the United States was already at war with Mexico. In a situation like that, good diplomatic ties even to aristocratic European governments might have looked like a valuable gain, in their own right. Prussia had given strong support to Bremen's lobbying effort, and Niles made explicit that this concerted campaign had left an impression on him:

There are connected with [the line] numerous political advantages. To the people of Germany and Prussia the enterprise was of great importance. The Prussian Minister [Baron von Gerolt] took a deep interest in it, and a special agent [Gevekoht] had been sent from Bremen for the express purpose of aiding in the completion of this work of commencing a direct communication between the United States and the German States, which would so materially enlarge the commercial and political intercourse, and extend the relations of both countries.[48]

Opposition to the subsidies shows that Democrats were treating this issue as a battle over principles. William Allen of Ohio led the charge. Allen had been a stalwart of the Jacksonian party line in Congress since the 1830s. During the Polk administration, he was instrumental in assuring congressional approval of the appropriation

---

[45] Herzstein, Robert Edwin, "New York City Views the German Revolution 1848: A Study in Ethnicity and Public Opinion," in *Consortium on Revolutionary Europe 1750–1850: Proceedings 1976*, 102–20; Roberts, Timothy M., and Daniel W. Howe, "The United States and the Revolutions of 1848," in *The Revolutions in Europe, 1848–1849: From Reform to Revolution*, ed. R. J. W. Evans and Hartmut Pogge von Strandmann, Oxford, 2000, 157–80; Roberts, Timothy M., *Distant Revolutions: 1848 and the Challenge to American Exceptionalism*, Charlottesville, VA, 2009.

[46] *Congressional Globe*, 29th Cong., 1st Sess., 722 (Rep. Hilliard, W-AL).

[47] [Schleiden, Rudolf], "Facts in Relation to a Direct Steam Communication between the United States and Germany" (leaflet distributed to members of the U.S. Congress), Washington, DC, August 1856, StAHB 2,B.13.b.1.a.2.b.I., document no. 5, quotes pp. 1 and 3. English in the original. When taking his office in Washington in 1853, Schleiden had said that "[Bremen] is in many regards like an American port; and even the banner of the ancient little Republic shows the same stripes, though not the stars, as the ensign of the larger sister Republic on this side of the ocean." From "Speech delivered by Mr. R. Schleiden on the occasion of his presentation in the character of Minister Resident of the Republic of Bremen to His Excellency the President of the United States of America, on the 8th day of July 1853," StAHB 4,48.21/5.E.1, Bremische Gesandtschaft in Washington, Angelegenheiten des bremischen Ministerresidenten Dr. Rudolph Schleiden (1845) 1853–1862.

[48] *Congressional Globe*, 29th Cong., 1st Sess., 943.

of funds for the Mexican War. His word carried some weight with his fellow Democratic legislators.[49] Other Democratic figureheads, like Thomas Hart Benton and John C. Calhoun, were also strong opponents of the mail-steamer plan.[50] To Allen, however, fell the role of representing the pure Jacksonian position.

Ever watchful of the "evils" of "joint-stock concerns," Allen "wished to keep this Government clear of all manner of connexion with human combinations – especially moneyed combinations" and the "immense patronage" inherent in this entanglement. The line to Bremen was but the beginning of a universal "system" of mail-steamer lines. The idea of "systems" was highly fraught in the Jacksonian mind, and evocative of paper money, tariffs, and chartered monopolies. What these systems had in common was their purpose of redistributing wealth from the "citizens in the interior" to "particular companies of men," by setting up monopolies and "removing competition."[51]

In the less genteel debating culture of the House of Representatives, Alabama Democrat William W. Payne called by name the "particular companies of men" who were to be the beneficiaries of this system:

Who was benefited by the Post Office Department? Was it not those who were engaged in writing letters? And if so, ought they not to bear the burden of its expenses? Instead . . . , you require individuals in the country, who perhaps do not write one letter a year, to pay their equal proportion to meet the expenditure of this Post Office Department. In other words, we taxed the coat, the salt, the shirt, of the laboring man, to pay the postage upon the letters written by the commercial men of the country.[52]

For Payne, mail-steamer subsidies were yet another scheme of "taxing the laboring classes for the benefit of the merchants of Boston, New York, Philadelphia, Baltimore, &c."[53]

Mainstream Democrats' view of international politics was determined by their commitment to western expansion, and a resulting indifference to relations with European powers. By the time the post office bill had reached the Senate, war with Mexico had commenced. In the light of this event, Thomas Hart Benton – one of the main war hawks – agreed that the United States should build war steamers. Still, he doubted that the vessels built under the contract with Edward Mills would be fit for such a use. Benton preferred vessels produced by "navy yards, with proper workmen" to "a scheme of getting the ships built by a kind of partnership" with private capital. In a resounding statement of national sovereignty, he exclaimed that "the Government was committed to nothing in this matter; and if it were, he would violate the obligation [to Mills] at all hazard, rather than embark in such an enterprise." From Benton's point of view, making friends in Europe was apparently not a high priority for a self-sufficient, well-armed nation.[54]

---

[49] McGrane, Reginald Charles, William Allen, *A Study in Western Democracy*, Columbus, OH, 1925, esp. pp. 74–5, 86–7, 103–25.
[50] *Congressional Globe*, 29th Cong., 1st Sess., 945 (Benton) and 973 (Calhoun).
[51] Ibid., 943.
[52] Ibid., 723–4.
[53] Ibid., 724.
[54] Ibid., 945.

Niles's explicit support for an emulation of British policies raised a particularly red flag for Democrats. They had considered Britain's original Navigation Act as part and parcel with the corruption of that country's polity. Under government protection, and only under it, special interests thrived and private enterprise withered.[55] The very idea of copying Great Britain's policies, hence, was anathema to them. Benton thundered:

As well it might be contended that this nation should be involved in a debt of nine hundred millions, because the national debt of Great Britain amounted to that sum, as propose to establish steam lines because Great Britain had done so.[56]

Behind the "scheme" to inaugurate a "steamer system," Jacksonians like Benton saw lurking the entirety of "aristocratic," Hamiltonian politics – and, rhetoric aside, their suspicion was not entirely unreasonable.

INTERNATIONAL TRADE, NATIONAL PRINCIPLES, AND LOCAL INTERESTS

Besides the principled Jacksonian argument against steamer subsidies, Bremen's friends in Congress had to fight against those who preferred a line to Liverpool, which had been proposed by the merchant E. K. Collins of New York. As it was unclear whether more than one of the proposed lines could be realized, merchants with trading ties to different ports were pitted against each other. International competition for steamer business thus found a mirror in intercity competition within the United States. Nonetheless, for proponents of "improvement," the national interest in keeping up with British competition overruled local jealously toward New York.

T. B. King, a Whig representative from Georgia who later would join A. D. Mann as a Confederate agent in Europe, said that although "he had no feeling of hostility to the route recommended; he had his doubts in relation to it." When Alabama Whig Henry W. Hilliard took offence at King's lack of enthusiasm for the proposal, King hastened to declare that he "was not opposed to this system [of mail-steamer subsidies]; he was as anxious as [Hilliard] to see such a line of ships established on American capital, and by American skill and industry." In the end, King gave his vote for the measure.[57]

Congressmen were aware that the federal government had to allocate a competitive advantage to some particular city in positioning the nation as a whole more favorably on the world market. Hanseats' friends therefore appealed to the competing shipping interests to accept that New York "was the proposed terminus of the line, because her [i.e., New York's] [commercial] position made her so." In serving as the United States' most prominent port, New York was furthering the common good.[58]

---

[55] Cf. Taylor, *Inquiry*.
[56] *Congressional Globe*, 29th Cong., 1st Sess., 945.
[57] Ibid., 722–3.
[58] Ibid., 945 (Senator Dix, D-NY).

While New York's importance for American commerce was obvious even to the city's rivals, the case for Bremen as the eastern end of the line was more difficult to make. Opponents and supporters of the OSNC agreed on the analysis that American commerce was dependent on Liverpool, but disagreed whether a steamer line to a continental port could offer a remedy or questioned whether a remedy was needed at all. T. B. King doubted the use of a line to Bremen. For his home state of Georgia and its cotton-producing economy, "Liverpool was the great commercial point, and if we sent letters to Cowes, they must go to Liverpool afterwards."[59]

Niles's fellow senator from Connecticut, the Whig Jabez W. Huntington, "was opposed to the Bremen line, [which] would be attended with sundry disadvantages." He "would go for the Liverpool line, [and] thought the time had not arrived for two lines." Justifying why he nonetheless voted for the Bremen line, Huntington explained that, "if the contract [with Mills] was obligatory, having been fairly made, he would not hesitate in authorizing it."[60]

New York's congressional delegation shared Huntington's preference for Liverpool. For Manhattan's Nativist representative, W. W. Campbell, Britain was the main commercial competitor. By subsidizing its mail steamers, "Great Britain ... was destroying our trade, and interfering with the enterprise of our people."[61] In the Senate, Democrat John A. Dix echoed this concern: the Cunard Line had a de facto monopoly on passenger and mail service between Liverpool and the U.S. East Coast. If Cunard was to put into effect an existing plan to extend service to New York, the costs for entering the New York–Liverpool market would be increased for any newcomers. Hence, there was some urgency to Collins's project. Funding a line to Bremen while leaving Cunard alone on the line to Liverpool meant sidestepping the real problem.[62]

Even so, Dix acknowledged that the Hanseatic city might be on the way to becoming a significant foreign market in the future: "Bremen-Haven ... furnishes access into the heart of northern Germany, [and is] the chief outlet for the maritime commercial communications of the Zoll Verein [Customs Union] States.... We carried to the Hanse-Towns 46,460 hogsheads of tobacco, and only 26,111 hogsheads to England."[63] Gevekoht's efforts apparently had made an impression even on skeptics like Dix.

Without the massive opposition to the subsidies by orthodox Democrats, the coalition that passed Niles's amendment may well never have come to be. In the face of such opposition, however, representatives of all conflicting shipping interests realized that they had to win the fundamental battle over the principle of international improvement first, before they could bicker over the particulars. Supporters of the Liverpool and Bremen lines, and spokesmen for other American ports, agreed that the government had a responsibility for promoting commerce by providing the infrastructure for communication. A vote for Bremen was a vote for that principle and against Jacksonian opposition to "improvements." For furthering a

---

[59] Ibid., 722.
[60] Ibid., 944.
[61] Ibid., 724.
[62] Ibid., 944–5.
[63] Ibid., 944.

commercial, transatlantic expansion of American interests, rather than a military expansion of American territory, Bremen looked like a promising ally. Hence, apart from the Jacksonians, every single one of the doubters cited here voted for the OSNC subsidies.

BREMISH AMERICAN STEAMER LINES BETWEEN
1846 AND 1860

The steam vessels that began to plow the waves, propelled by international rivalry, cosmopolitan hopes, and government subsidies, heralded a revolution in international communication and transportation. Financially, however, steamer companies remained in shallow waters until the 1860s, when the search for a more efficacious use of steam power on the seas led to technological improvements.[64] Yet none of the supporters of mail-steamer subsidies had ever claimed that these lines would be a great financial success. They were a fiscal burden that had to be assumed to reach other, more important political goals.

When it began operations, the OSNC was celebrated on both sides of the ocean. On June 19, 1847, the steamer *Washington* arrived at Bremerhaven, completing the first trip from New York of the new mail-steamer line in seventeen days. One of the immediate benefits of the line was the establishment of the first postal convention entered into by the United States. Mail transported on the OSNC steamers was conveyed to and from the states of the German Confederation, as well as the parts of Austria and Prussia located outside of its borders, for fixed postage rates well below those charged for letters sent via Britain.[65]

The new steamer line gave the United States a valuable bargaining token in its rivalry with Britain. The kingdom at first reacted with punitive measures to the new competition. The Royal Post Office charged letters arriving via Cowes with the full transatlantic postage that would have been due for their transportation by a Cunard steamer. First Assistant Postmaster General Major R. S. Hobbie went to London to negotiate a postal convention with Britain that avoided this dual postage. His mission failed and, for about a year, the United States and Britain became locked in an escalating struggle over the mails. When the United States blocked the Canadian mail from traveling through the United States, Britain gave in. Both countries signed a postal treaty that went into effect in January 1849. A central foreign policy goal stated by the Hanseats' friends in Congress had thus been achieved.[66]

In other respects, too, the Bremen line lived up to the expectations of its supporters, vindicating the Hanseatic-Whig alliance. Mail volume between New York and Bremerhaven grew from 79,637 annual letters in 1848 to 354,470 in 1852. Commerce between the two places grew at a slightly slower pace. In terms of commerce and communication, the United States had become more independent

---

[64] cf. note 459; Gerstenberger and Welke, *Vom Wind zum Dampf.*

[65] Wätjen, *Frühzeit*, 35, lists the rates: sea postage 24c; U.S. inland postage 5c (10c above 300 miles); German inland postage 10c (none to Bremen, and reduced to 5c to Hannover, Oldenburg, and Hamburg). A letter from Baltimore to Bremen would have cost a total of 29c, from New York to Berlin 34c, from St. Louis to Vienna 44c.

[66] Arnell, *Steam*, 176–9.

of Britain. It had only been able to do so because American politicians had been willing to engage in transnational cooperation.[67]

For the ten years that the United States paid lump sums to mail-steamer lines, the OSNC survived as a business enterprise. Partly because of the disruptions caused by the revolution of 1848, the company was unable to pay dividends until 1852. Even then, dividend payments to American investors were only made possible because the German governments forfeited interest payments on the loans they had given to Oelrichs & Co. in New York. In 1852, the mail subsidy contract was renewed for another five years, thanks to the exertions of Bremen's diplomats and their friends in Washington. After 1853, the OSNC finally turned a profit.[68]

Then, effective in 1857, Congress abandoned lump-sum subsidies for a system that paid steamship lines only the postage for the letters they actually transported. In 1856, Rudolf Schleiden had attempted to convince a majority in Congress to continue subsidizing the OSNC, but this time Hanseatic diplomacy failed.[69] The 1851 and 1856 debates in Congress over the renewal of the contract with the OSNC were exact replicas of the one in 1846. Perhaps the animosity between the camps had become sharper in 1856, but the basic arguments remained the same.[70]

Between 1846 and 1857, the political economy of ocean steam navigation had changed as little as the fundamental outlooks of American politicians in the Jeffersonian and Hamiltonian traditions. What had changed were the political conditions in the United States, where an increasingly assertive Democratic Party returned to its Jeffersonian roots in economic policy, as it remade itself into an organization more and more committed to the defense of slavery. Men like Niles were increasingly rare among its ranks. After Buchanan's election to the presidency, federal financial commitment to the internal or international improvements that nourished the rival political economy of the North fell victim to this increased vigor of Jeffersonian doctrine.[71]

In 1846, the Second Party System still organized Americans into political, not sectional, camps. Whigs and Democrats could legitimately represent free and slave states. In 1856, this was no longer the case, as slavery became the defining issue. Yet as the Realignment of 1854–56 and the emergence of the Republican Party upended the Second Party System, the political concepts Democrats and Republicans employed in the half-decade leading up to the Civil War remained as firmly rooted in the same old Jeffersonian-Hamiltonian divide as ever, if not more so.

Unable to meet expenses without full subsidies, the OSNC was dissolved, and its steamers sold to the British government to be used as troop transporters in the Crimean War. After liquidation, stockholders recuperated a mere third of their

---

[67] Wätjen, *Frühzeit*, 34, 36. See also Chapter 1, Graph 3.

[68] Tyler, "Steam," 241–2, claims that OSNC stock had been on par only for a brief period of time, in 1854. This is technically correct, but not exactly true. Wätjen, *Frühzeit*, 37–45, discusses the financial situation of the OSNC, and states that OSNC stock rose above par after 1854 (p. 40). While OSNC stock was valued at below 10% in the summer of 1853, it closed the fiscal year of 1853 – in which the German governments forfeited interest payments – with a net profit of $112,465.05 and was able to pay a 7% dividend, and 10% thereafter (pp. 39–40).

[69] [Schleiden] "Facts in Relation to a Direct Steam Communication."

[70] *Congressional Globe*, 34th Cong., 3rd Sess. (1856–7), 107, 196, 908, 915, 993, 997, 1103–7, 1112.

[71] See the debates over the renewal of mail-steamer subsidies in ibid., esp. pp. 1103–12.

initial investment. Other steamer lines did not fare much better. From 1853 to 1855, the Bremish firms of Fritze & Co. and Carl Lehmkuhl jointly ran steamers between Bremerhaven and New York. They bought two decommissioned vessels of the defunct German navy, which sailed on alternate weeks from the OSNC steamers. On Rudolf Schleiden's request, the U.S. Postmaster General promised to pay a subsidy to the line on the same terms as those granted to the OSNC if its vessels managed to keep a regular schedule. Although the Fritze and Lehmkuhl steamers apparently carried some mail, technical difficulties and the resulting reluctance of the traveling public to entrust their lives to these vessels, made the line a failure, and it never met the postmaster's standards. Fritze and Lehmkuhl were glad for the opportunity to sell their ships, too, to the British government for use in the Crimean War.[72]

In 1857, the American Vanderbilt Line took over the mail route to Bremerhaven previously served by the OSNC. Immediately, its vessels encountered the same difficulties that had plagued every other steamer line. Schleiden attempted to capitalize on the hostile press reaction to the unreliability and unsafe state of the Vanderbilt vessels, but his effort to convince the postmaster general to strike Vanderbilt's vessels from the list of official mail carriers did not bear fruit. Service improved after 1858, but the line never became profitable. In 1860, it was unceremoniously abandoned.[73]

In 1858, H. H. Meier's North German Lloyd began to compete with Vanderbilt for mail and passenger business between Bremerhaven and New York. The Lloyd remained unprofitable for the remainder of the decade. H. H. Meier's stubbornness, persuasiveness, and entrepreneurial skill in leading the Lloyd kept investors and creditors of this line pacified through these doldrums. Only in the mid-1860s did the company turn the corner to profitability. Financial backing by the state of Bremen, including the continual extension of the port infrastructure in Bremerhaven, from which the Lloyd profited most, played a crucial role in keeping the Lloyd afloat during its first decade. "Improvement" still required some state to shoulder its costs – for the time being, the United States was no longer that state.[74]

HANSEATS, DEMOCRATS, AND WHIGS: THE TRANSNATIONAL SECOND PARTY SYSTEM

The history of American mail-steamer subsidies has broad implications for our understanding of the Second Party System. It shows that Democrats and Whigs were much more in touch with developments outside of the United States than we commonly assume. There were many American politicians, in both parties, who were aware that they had friends, as well as foes, abroad. In achieving their policy goals, these politicians sought transnational partners. The main currents of bourgeois politics in the United States and in Europe ran along the same lines. Whigs and Democrats represented two competing paths toward capitalist modernization. The

---

[72] Wätjen, *Frühzeit*, 37–45, 56–9.
[73] Ibid., 59–63.
[74] Bessel, *Norddeutscher Lloyd*, 29–30; [North German Lloyd Steamship Company, Bremen], *North German Lloyd*, 30–8. For the North German Lloyd, see also Chapters 1 and 7.

conservative-authoritarian and the liberal-democratic paths to capitalist development were equally transnational in the extent of their followership and in their intellectual lineage. In the case of the mail-steamer subsidies, the conservative side was better prepared to cooperate transnationally, and thus to further its interests.

How much of a basis was there for cooperation between Whigs and Hanseats beyond the mail-steamer question? Strong policy disagreements between the two groups might suggest that their collaboration was founded on a momentary concurrence of interests. Whigs stood for a program of national industrialization, while Hanseats were committed to an Atlantic economy. Whigs embraced protective tariffs, while Hanseats were free traders.[75] The Whig Party became the home to American Party Nativists, whose attacks on immigration immediately hurt the Hanseats' most lucrative business. Northern Whigs had within their ranks some of the few who openly criticized slavery, whereas Hanseats traded in the produce of slave labor. And yet, in 1840, Hanseats in America had enthusiastically greeted Harrison's election to the presidency.[76]

Since at least 1832, we find Hanseats taking clear sides in the American political conflicts, and they exclusively sided with the Whigs. Caspar Meier, Bremen's consul in New York, had written to his nephew, H. H. Meier, in Bremen: "So you will have to put up with [Nathaniel Pearce, the new American consul in Bremen], at least as long as the Jackson party remains in power." Echoing Whigs' complaint over Jackson's "spoils system," Bremen's merchants were furious that Friedrich Jacob Wichelhausen, who had served as American consul to Bremen since 1796, was removed from his post, and alleged that Pearce owed money to Bremish firms in Baltimore.[77]

When *Senator* Diedrich A. Meier found democrats distasteful in 1849, he could rest assured that Hanseats' American friends had been in his shoes before.[78] Like this Hanseat, Whigs perceived democrats as a group of self-proclaimed tribunes of the lower sort, who were rousing the masses against their social betters. If only left alone by such agitators, the simple folk surely would have realized that the elite were acting in their interest and out of a selfless commitment to the public good. Could a man of standing not expect gratitude for giving his valuable time in public service? Whigs could have sympathized with a man like Meier, and vice versa.

Nativist rabble-rousers, by contrast, found the sympathies of Whigs and Hanseats to be similar. In 1854, *Senator* Heinrich Smidt, the son of Burgomaster Johann Smidt,

---

[75] Only in 1845, the Whig majority in the U.S. Senate had rejected a trade treaty with the German Customs Union that would have lowered the tariff on some German imports. Chitwood, Oliver Perry, *John Tyler: Champion of the Old South*, New York and London, 1939, 332–3.

[76] The Bremish elite had been opposed to Jacksonian Democracy from the beginning. As early as 1832, Caspar Meier, Bremen's consul in New York, had written to his nephew, H. H. Meier, in Bremen: "So you will have to put up with [Nathaniel Pearce, the new American consul in Bremen], at least as long as the Jackson party remains in power." Echoing Whigs' complaint over Jackson's "spoils system," Bremen's merchants were furious that Friedrich Jacob Wichelhausen, who had served as American consul to Bremen since 1796, was removed from his post, and alleged that Pearce owed money to Bremish firms in Baltimore. See Beutin, *Bremen und Amerika*, 20, 33–4, 277, quote on p. 277.

[77] Beutin, *Bremen und Amerika*, 20, 33–4, 277, quote on pp. 277.

[78] See Chapter 3, 168.

approvingly restated what the American consul in Bremen had told him, that "the Know-Nothings have a justified side as a necessary reaction of intelligent and provident Americans against the blind despotism of numbers of immigrants, in as far as they [the immigrants] are merely tools of political agitators."[79] Many of these "tools of agitators" had sailed to the United States on Bremish vessels, and their passages paid Hanseats' bills. Still, Hanseats applied the same criteria to the handling of emigrants, as Nativists brought to their interaction with immigrants.[80] In both cases, the migrant was treated as a suspicious stranger whose permanent settling in the community Nativists in New York and Baltimore wanted to avoid as much as Hanseats in Bremerhaven. Maintaining an exclusive community of respectable Protestant citizens was just another common concern between Bremen's merchants and their American friends.

The tariff question was a serious policy issue that could have divided Hanseats and Whigs. As much as Hanseats were committed to free trade, though, they had to suffer fairly little from the tariff barriers around the United States – under the 1827 treaty with the United States, Bremen's merchants enjoyed a most-favored-nation status. Besides, some Hanseats were willing to grant that a modest, differential tariff might be a legitimate tool of trade policy. They were in favor of free trade only if it relied on a mutual agreement between the two sides involved, not as a unilaterally applied open-door policy.[81]

Still, it remains ironical that in the alliance between Whigs and Hanseats, American protectionists and Bremish free traders were working hand in hand to "improve" international commerce and communication. Without the underlying agreement on their political values and their social vision, this alliance would have seemed an absurdity. If, however, we take into account the basic outlook of these two groups, their cooperation makes perfect sense.

As we have seen in the writings of Wilhelm Kiesselbach and in Bremish policies in Bremerhaven, Hanseats looked to America for inspiration. They owed a debt to Whig thinkers and practitioners not only for their conceptual tools for judging democracy, but also for the legal and administrative techniques for handling those transient populations for which German law held no precedent. They shared with Whigs their apprehensions and perhaps a sense of nostalgia as they "improved" the world. Neither of these sentiments weighed too heavily to be placated by ideas such as those of Wilhelm Kiesselbach. He told Bremen's merchants what he needed to believe as much as they did: that by changing the world beyond all recognition, they had stayed true to time-honored traditions. This is the classical ideological operation of modern conservatism.

From this perspective, Burgomaster Johann Smidt's programmatic statement on the future of the Hanseatic cities, made in 1806 under the immediate impression of

---

[79] Cited by Beutin, *Bremen und Amerika*, 294. The American consul to Bremen at that time was William Hildebrand, ibid., 277.
[80] See Chapter 4.
[81] Arnold Duckwitz to Rudolf Schleiden (in Freiburg i. Brsg.), Bremen, January 20, 1878, February 16, 1878, and February 23, 1878, StAHB 7,116 [Rudolf Schleiden Papers], folder "Briefwechsel Rudolf Schleiden mit Senator Arnold Duckwitz, 1854–1879," third of five unnumbered and unlabeled boxes; Beutin, *Bremen und Amerika*, 25–6, 30–1, 62–3.

the collapse of the Holy Roman Empire of the German Nation, appears in a new light:

[The Hanseatic Cities] have not abandoned the hope to become ... generally respected asylums of peace and quiet in the midst of the world's storms .... They will stand justified before the world, by striving for the highest not only in cosmopolitan regard, but also, in a patriotic respect, by striving to salvage from the ruins of the Roman Empire of the German Nation that character which it, although it was its most noble one, has hitherto sought to assert in vain, its Holyness.[82]

The Kantian, cosmopolitan vision of world peace that reverberates in this statement has as its complement the enforcement of good order and morality (*Polizey*). The latter is directed against the "lower sorts," so that the "better class" may devote their energies to the higher ideals they salvaged from the lost, preindustrial world. Together, both can then "improve" the world, fulfilling a destiny that is perhaps less manifest than the continental expansion favored by American Democrats or German nationalists, but no less tangible or preordained in the minds of its advocates.[83]

Like their Hanseatic allies, Bremen's friends in Congress were aware that they operated in a larger world. They saw political friends and adversaries in foreign places who closely resembled those they knew at home. Whigs and Hanseats shared a vision in which the state, under the stewardship of elites, pursued the moral and material improvement of society. In Bremerhaven, with its mixture of modern commerce and social control, Whigs could have seen their ideals of an improved society realized.

Markets, machines, and morality formed the constellation that guided the political course Whigs steered in the United States and Hanseats followed in Bremen. To both groups, the founding of a mail-steamer line with the support of governments was a logical extension of their fundamental political commitments. In working for an extension of commerce, Whigs and Hanseats saw themselves as offering extended opportunities for wage labor to the lower orders of society, thus presenting a practical remedy to the dangerous radical ideas prevalent among democrats.

The Whigs were also the "Christian party in politics," the Evangelicals and reformers whose vision of improvement linked inseparably technological progress and the moral betterment of individuals.[84] The Whig program thus included an excessive dose of an ideology that overdetermined the state as a source of good

---

[82] Johann Smidt to the Rat of Bremen, September 1806, StAHB B,5.e, quoted in Möller, "Politik," 348.

[83] Governmentally and ideologically, we can understand this transnational correspondence between Whigs and Hanseats both as a continuation of the Calvinist Axis described in Chapter 2, from Bremen via Bremerhaven to New York, and as an extension of Hanseats' political preference for a hierarchically ordered society described in Chapter 3. Bear in mind, too, that Hanseats drew a line where it came to the traditions of their own estate, which were not up for modernization (cf. Chapter 4). Finally, the idea implied by Smidt, that the better sorts ought to be privileged practitioners of higher ideals, foreshadows Andrew Carnegie's arguments in his "Gospel of Wealth."

[84] Ely, Ezra Stiles, *Discourse Delivered on the Fourth of July, 1827*, quoted in James, Bessie Rowland, Anne Royall's U.S.A., New Brunswick, NJ, 1972, 192.

policy and morality, not just of legal protection and financial support for the creation of a national market.[85] Public schools that imbued children with piety and a patriotic respect for republican institutions; laws that encouraged temperance and the observation of the Sabbath; reforms of penal institutions, hospitals, and asylums, which kept deviant parts of the population under close supervision; public libraries, which offered workingmen the tools required for understanding their proper place in society and for perfecting their skills; professional police and fire departments that removed rowdy elements from city streets; and the discouragement of the immigration of undesirable groups, most of all Catholics, formed the main items on the Whig agenda.[86]

In their Calvinism and in their stewardship over the Bremish population, Hanseats found common ground with Whigs. Bremen's elite had always considered the mass of the population as their charges, maintaining a tight lid on any stirring of demands for popular participation. Like Whigs, Hanseats envisioned for themselves the role of the benevolent guardian toward a materially and morally bright future of a populace who had yet to live up to the promise of their own perfection contained in the plan of their Divine Creator. In this view, theorized by Wilhelm Kiesselbach, maintaining a hierarchical, paternalistic society was the best framework for allowing this populace to improve itself, so that they might attain their promise. Like the Whigs, Hanseats moved gradually from a paternalistic relation with the common folk to one of social control as the century progressed.

Hanseats and Whigs rejected the liberal idea of the individual as driven by rational self-interest. Instead, they held to a pessimistic anthropology informed by the idea of original sin. Therefore, they believed, in the words of one Whig legislator, in "the rule of law and of morals," to be upheld by government over whatever individuals might come to regard as right or true in the arbitrariness of their will or conscience.[87] This idea of the state is the exact opposite of the classical liberal formulation, in which society and the individual rights of its members precede the formation of the state, and in which the state is the creation of society for the very protection of the individual rights of the members of society.[88]

While Democrats stood in the Enlightenment tradition of trust in the individual and his capacity for reason and self-government, the Whig Party was committed to an essentially illiberal state, one that Wilhelm Kiesselbach might have recognized as the warm home of the organically rooted person.[89]

Only a minority of Democrats – among them Ambrose D. Mann – realized what Whigs had seen: that they, too, had friends abroad. But Mann picked strange

---

[85] Mintz, Steven, *Moralists and Modernizers: America's Pre–Civil War Reformers* (Stanley I. Kutler, ed., The American Moment Series, unnumbered vol.), Baltimore and London, 1995.

[86] Ashworth, *"Agrarians" and "Aristocrats"*; Wilentz, Sean, *Chants Democratic: New York City and the Rise of the American Working Class, 1788–1850*, New York and Oxford, 1984; Howe, *American Whigs*.

[87] Reed, William B., *Daily Pittsburgh Gazette*, January 26, 1836, 2. Reed was a state representative from Philadelphia. For a contemporary portrayal of Reed's position, see Poulson's *American Daily Advertiser*, January 19, 1836. There, Reed's views are qualified as representative for the Whigs. See also Mueller, Henry R., *The Whig Party in Pennsylvania* (Columbia University Studies in the Social Sciences, vol. 230), New York, 1969 (1922), 24, 225, note 1.

[88] Ashworth, *"Agrarians" and "Aristocrats"*; Howe, *American Whigs*.

[89] Cf. Chapter 3.

bedfellows, building his alliance with an estate that would drive out of town in 1851 those in its hometown whose ideas would have made them a perfect match for American Democrats. Had congressional Jacksonians been less provincial, they might have discovered that the *Bremische Bürgerschaft* had in its ranks those who rejected the vision of "improvement" championed by the Hanseatic elite. They might have learned that in the very same year that they questioned the wisdom of a steamer line to Bremerhaven, democrats in the *Bürgerschaft* were mounting a strong challenge to the *Senat*'s near-absolutist control over the port town.[90]

It is difficult to imagine that Mann was not aware of these democratic stirrings in Bremen, where he had spent four years. Perhaps he put his sectional interest over his political predilections. Or, perhaps, he was afflicted with the syndrome that has brought many progressives, in their desire to see a world full of allies, to imagine all kinds of foreign political actors as kindred spirits, no matter how much their actual politics were opposed to their own.[91] In either case, he sided with the Hanseatic elite, not with its democratic opponents.

THE IRONY OF MODERNIZATION

Unable or unwilling to realize their affinities with their Bremish counterparts, orthodox Democrats drew their arguments against mail steamers from a familiar source, the critique of Hamiltonian politics developed by John Taylor of Caroline and popularized by Jefferson and Jackson.[92] These Democrats knew what they were up against: a comprehensive worldview that combined the logic of market morality with technological progress in a political program that called for an active, good government. This program still appeared as a cosmopolitan endeavor in the service of the betterment of humanity – often including the abolition of slavery. By the 1850s, however, it was clear to observers that this same program laid the ground-work for the takeoff of industrial capitalism, now well under way in the United States and in Germany, alike.[93]

The late Atlantic economy rested on the new types of regimes of social control that American Whigs set up in cities like New York and Baltimore, and that their Hanseatic allies inaugurated in Bremerhaven and on their vessels. As schemes of improvement – furthering markets, machines, and morality – ocean steamers, port facilities, and the laws and institutions that molded populations into market participants and wage-labor forces are points on a continuum.[94]

---

[90] Kellner-Stoll, Rita, *Bremerhaven, 1827–1888. Politische, wirtschaftliche und soziale Probleme einer Stadtgründung* (Burchard Scheper, ed., Veröffentlichungen des Stadtarchivs Bremerhaven, vol. 4), Bremen, 1982, 149–56.

[91] The enthusiasm of the Western left for Palestinian nationalism is a case in point.

[92] Taylor, *Inquiry*, esp. pp. 230–353.

[93] Beckert, Sven, *The Monied Metropolis: New York City and the Consolidation of the American Bourgeoisie, 1850–1896*, Cambridge, MA, 2001; Ashworth, *Slavery*; Genovese, Eugene, *The World the Slaveholders Made*, New York, 1969.

[94] Wilentz, *Chants Democratic*; Rockman, Seth, *Welfare Reform in the Early Republic: A Brief History with Documents* (Bedford Series in History and Culture, unnumbered vol., Boston and New York, 2003; Johnson, Paul E., *A Shopkeeper's Millennium: Society and Revivals in Rochester, New York, 1815–1837*, New York, 1978.

To their promoters, these schemes meant the betterment of mankind by combining the material blessings of progress with the spiritual blessings of a Christian tradition. The function of "improvement," however, was the creation of the conditions that made possible an industrial world economy. The logic of competition and profit maximization that drove this world economy undermined what remained of local, communal particularity, or "organic customs."[95]

On both sides of the ocean, democrats appeared as defenders of the social substance and the moral economy of local particularity. When Democrats accused Whigs of destroying or exploiting the communal world of honest, hard-working small commodity producers, and when Bremen's artisans accused the Hanseatic elite of abandoning them to the vagaries of free competition, they alleged that the function of "improvement" was the real, hidden intent. This allegation misses the mark.

Whigs and Hanseats were just as disturbed as Democrats by the disruptive consequences of forging globally linked societies from disparate communities. The former, however, differed from the latter, in that they attempted to rescue from the lost communal world of the early-modern period that Tönnies described, not the embeddedness of production and exchange, but the shared, binding morality that rested on tight social control. Aware that morality was no longer made binding as a function of immediate personal ties among the members of a community, these modern conservatives put government in charge of exerting social control over the members of a society.[96]

In a simple teleological account of modernization, the liberal-democratic vision of the state is held to be the political theory most compatible with a capitalist society. If we presume that personal freedom and political equality are essential elements of a capitalist society, the Whigs would not appear to be a "capitalist party." In historical practice, however, making populations into functioning wage workers and contract-minded individuals almost always involved a coercive effort.[97]

The transnational strand of conservatism represented by Hanseats and Whigs, and the policy of international improvement it pursued, was therefore a contradictory affair. While Whigs spoke a language presumably incompatible with a liberal-capitalist state, they nonetheless expressed in that language the policies that turned the American populace into functioning members of a capitalist society and that made the financial and transportation infrastructure required for creating such a society. This same irony holds true for Hanseats. They were busy building a world – technologically, legally, and economically – that would unleash the furies of democracy, nationalism, and liberal capitalism that would undermine their independence as an estate.

[95] Cf. Chapters 3 and 4.
[96] Cf. Chapters 3 and 4; and Ashworth, *"Agrarians" and "Aristocrats"*; Wilentz, *Chants Democratic*; Howe, *American Whigs*; Sellers, *Market Revolution*; Johnson, *Shopkeepers Millennium*.
[97] Rockman, *Welfare*; Stanley, Amy Dru, *From Bondage to Contract: Wage Labor, Marriage, and the Market in the Age of Slave Emancipation*, New York, 1998; Richardson, Heather Cox, *The Death of Reconstruction: Race, Labor, and Politics in the Post–Civil War North, 1865–1901*, Cambridge, MA, and London, 2001; Ashworth, *Slavery*.

The making of an industrial world market was not exclusively the work of private enterprise. It required an active role for governments to provide the nerves of communication that set in motion the bone and muscle of industry and to mold populations into willing, useful, and morally firm market participants. These processes changed the world in dramatic ways.

Still, "improvement" was not just a smokescreen for a program of capitalist change – it was the real content of a program that resulted in such change, but that created a world quite different from the one its proponents had envisioned. The view of the state held by conservative modernizers did offer a moral justification for strengthening government to a point where it could assume the burden of improvement; and measures of improvement did create the necessary conditions for the development of an industrial capitalist world market. However, they were the outcome of a political process, whose results were contingent. It is therefore not surprising that the motivations of the actors in that political process, and the results of their actions, did not always correspond.

Recent scholarship on the idea of "improvement" has emphasized both the role of the state for putting it into practice and the continuity between repressive government policies directed in the name of this idea against domestic and colonial populations. In the work of Richard Drayton, the enclosure movement in Britain, that original sin of primitive accumulation, appears as an immediate ancestor to the administration of the Other in Britain's colonial empire.[98] A concept of improvement and attention to the role of government are indispensable for understanding the transnational conservatives who made the modern industrial world economy. Chapter 6 is devoted to exploring, through the lens of the Hanseatic worldview, how improvement squared off with ideas about races, nations, nation-states, and empires.

---

[98] Drayton, Richard, *Nature's Government: Science, Imperial Britain, and the "Improvement" of the World*, New Haven, CT, and London, 2000, esp. p. xvi; Marx, Karl, *Capital*, 3 vols. (Karl Marx and Friedrich Engels, Werke, vols. 23–5), vol. 1, Berlin, 1979 [1894], Chapter 27.

6

Nations, Races, and Empires

Hanseats Encounter the Other, 1837–1859

ESSENTIAL ASSUMPTIONS

An older generation of Hanseatic historians has claimed that Bremish merchants gradually but consciously advanced the cause of German unification through their activities in commerce and international politics. More recent scholarship has followed this characterization of Hanseats as promoters of national unification.[1] The year 1871, when Bismarck unified Germany, clouds the view of the decades that preceded this watershed. All previous history appears to run along straight lines that culminate in the *telos* of German unity, much like the history of the antebellum United States remains under the shadow of the Civil War.[2] Even as a transnational approach calls into question such national history, we would engage in the same rewriting of history to fit our present sensibilities, if we were to dismiss every national sentiment uttered by Hanseats during the first two-thirds of the century.

[1] Hardegen, Friedrich, and Käthi Smidt, *H. H. Meier, der Gründer des Norddeutschen Lloyd. Lebensbild eines Bremer Kaufmanns 1809–1898*, Berlin and Leipzig, 1920; Wätjen, Hermann, *Aus der Frühzeit des Nordatlantikverkehrs. Studien zur Geschichte der deutschen Schiffahrt und deutschen Auswanderung nach den Vereinigten Staaten bis zum Ende des amerikanischen Bürgerkrieges*, Leipzig, 1932; Krieger, Adolf, *Arnold Duckwitz, hanseatischer Staatsmann und Reichshandelsminister von 1848 im Kampf für eine deutsche Wirtschaftsordnung. Wirtschaftspolitische Aufsätze* (Abhandlungen und Vorträge herausgegeben von der Wittheit zu Bremen, vol. 15, no. 1, August 1942), Bremen, 1942; idem, *Bremische Politik im Jahrzehnt vor der Reichsgründung* (Schriften der Bremer Wissenschaftlichen Gesellschaft, Reihe F (früher A*), Friedrich Prüser, ed., Veröffentlichungen des Archivs der Hansestadt Bremen, vol. 15), Bremen, 1939. Remarkably, the latter, based on Krieger's dissertation, is one of the few texts that gives significant room to those Hanseats who continued to oppose national unification, either on principle or under Prussian leadership. Bessell, Georg, *1857–1957: Norddeutscher Lloyd. Geschichte einer bremischen Reederei*, Bremen, 1957, 13. Schwarzwälder, Herbert, *Geschichte der Freien Hansestadt Bremen*, 4 vols., Hamburg, 1987, vol. 2, 274–7; Schulz, Andreas, *Vormundschaft und Protektion. Eliten und Bürger in Bremen, 1750–1880* (Gall, Lothar, ed., Stadt und Bürgertum, vol. 13), Munich, 2002 (Habilitationsschrift, Universität Frankfurt [Main], 2000), 683–4, who claims that there was "no alternative" to an alliance between Bremen's elite and Bismarck; and Biefang, Andreas, *Politisches Bürgertum in Deutschland, 1857–1868. Nationale Organisationen und Eliten* (Kommission für Geschichte des Parlamentarismus und der politischen Parteien, corp. ed., Beiträge zur Geschichte des Parlamentarismus und der politischen Parteien, vol. 102), Düsseldorf 1994, show Bremen as a stronghold of the nationalist movement, specifically the *Nationalverein* (National Association, see Chapter 8), and suggest that the Bremish elite in the 1860s favored national unification. See Chapter 8 for a discussion of this claim.

[2] Evidently, if we take seriously the metaphor of the watershed, the course of history should be running toward World War I from 1871 up, and toward the French Revolution from 1871 down.

The point is to understand the meanings that Hanseats attributed to the nation before the 1860s, in all their nuances. When Hanseats encountered strangers, did they make nationality a criterion for socializing or doing business with them? Did nationality structure the way Hanseats thought about culture and civilization? Was the nation-state a political project to which Hanseats lent their support, and if so, what constitutional and social foundations did they envision for a unified Germany? Were their demands on states for the provision of infrastructure, law, and order dependent on those states becoming *nation*-states?

As an ideology that posits essential, inherent differences between people, based on culture or biology, the idea of race is a close kin to that of the nation. Hence, Hanseatic reactions to encounters with non-Europeans can serve as a test case for the worldview of Bremish merchants. A reconstruction of this worldview – of their basic assumptions about peoples and nature, culture and civilization – will show that a wide range of intellectual influences beyond nations and races competed with and often overruled essentialist assumptions in the Hanseatic mind. Most importantly, the cosmopolitan elitism of their estate made most Hanseats reluctant to embrace nationalism and racism.

THE ELEPHANT ON THE COMMONS

Racism is the elephant in the room of any history that sets out to construct a positive line of tradition for the nation. This is particularly true for German history. Only between 1933 and 1945 did Hanseatic historians proudly stress the race consciousness of their subjects. Rewriting the history of Bremen, Richard Rüthnick celebrated Johann Smidt's anti-Semitism, Adolf Krieger praised Arnold Duckwitz's "struggle for a German economic order," and Herman Wätjen discovered the civilizing role Germans played in conquering the American West.[3]

Bremen's elite had led the way for this reevaluation of the transnational ties of its ancestors. Already in 1932, Hanseats commemorated the glory of German colonialism by erecting the statue of a thirty-foot-high brick elephant next to the burghers' commons (*Bürgerweide*), within view of the main train station (see Map 1). For the decades that followed World War II, this elephant was conventionally agreed to not be there. Only in 1990 did the city complement it with a placard some thirty feet from the statue, explaining the latter as a symbol of colonialism. At the center of this placard is a hole in the shape of the African continent, inviting the visitor to contemplate the elephant through this hole. By making visible again the elephant on the commons through a silhouette of Africa – present by virtue of its absence – the complementary exhibition strives to confront and come to terms with the city's racist past.[4]

---

[3] Rüthnick, Richard, *Bürgermeister Smidt und die Juden (Bremens Judenpolitik 1803–1848)*, Bremen, 1934; Krieger, *Arnold Duckwitz*; Wätjen, Hermann, *Der deutsche Anteil am Wirtschaftsaufbau der Westküste Amerikas*, Leipzig 1942.

[4] In 1990, the elephant was officially rededicated as an "Anti-Colonial Monument," in the presence of Sam Nujoma, President of the Republic of Namibia. In 1932, the main speakers at the dedication of the monument had been Eduard Achelis, the head of one of Bremen's major merchant houses, and General von Lettow-Vorbeck, the military leader of the massacre of the Herero and Nama in German South-West Africa in 1906–7. See Gustafsson, Heinz, *Namibia, Bremen und Deutschland*.

In the sources that illuminate the Hanseats' world pre-1860, race is a conspicuous absence. The few exceptions, however, allow for some extrapolation. Germany did not acquire colonies until the 1880s, and although the Hanseats did trade with Africa and Asia throughout the century, they were not yet the commercial hand-maidens of a German imperial power. Bremen's trade relied largely on the products of slave labor, but the slave-owning Hanseat was a rare exception. Not tainted with the direct political or economic exploitation of non-Europeans, Bremen's merchants could consider themselves as cosmopolitans, not involved in imperial domination, but in building a morally and materially brighter future for all humanity by peaceful trade.[5]

Hanseatic trade and foreign policy operated within the framework of a global free-trade regime dominated by the British Empire. The Atlantic World was but the busiest sector in this global space. Race has been read back into the making of the West, and of Britain in particular, by recent scholarship. Even the most "civic" – that is, not based on ethnic homogeneity – projects of European nation building had a subtext of race, in that the emergence of European modernity materially rested on the exploitation of extra-European peoples. To reap the benefits of empire, it was not necessary to buy into the ideology of race.[6]

Still, notions of race began to enter the minds of Hanseats at the same time as they were making up these minds on the national question. Many of those nonwhite peoples drawn into the Anglo-American world created by the British Empire crossed paths with Hanseats and helped shape their thinking about themselves, and about their place in the world. Even so, as late as the 1850s, Hanseats brought to their encounters with the Other the same mercantile mind-set that allowed them to keep an open mind toward different nations. The refined and respectable nonwhite person could socialize with Hanseats on equal terms, while the dark-skinned plebeians received an equal helping of scorn as did their white counterparts.[7]

SHIPS' NAMES AS CULTURAL AND POLITICAL STATEMENTS

If we look for evidence of national imagery in Hanseats' world, we need to look no further than to the names Bremen's merchants gave to their vessels. The first two steamers built by the OSNC were the *Washington* and the *Hermann*. They were named after the founders of the nations they connected – General Washington for the United States, and Arminius, the leader of the Cheruskans, the tribe who

Ein steiniger Weg zur Freundschaft, Delmenhorst, Germany, 2003; Gebel, Thomas, "Schwachhausen und die SWAPO," *taz [Die Tageszeitung]* Bremen, no. 6639 (January 2, 2002), 23; Achelis, Eduard, Meine Lebenserinnerungen aus 50jähriger Arbeit (photocopy of typescript), Bremen 1935/1936, StAHB, call number 135.Ai, esp. p. 23.

5 Cf. McBride, David, Leroy Hopkins, and C. Aisha Blackshire-Belay, eds., *Crosscurrents: African Americans, Africa, and Germany in the Modern World*, Columbia, SC, 1998.

6 Drayton, Richard, Nature's *Government: Science, Imperial Britain, and the "Improvement" of the World*, New Haven, CT, and London, 2000; Gilroy, Paul, *The Black Atlantic: Modernity and Double Consciousness*, Cambridge, MA, 1993; idem, *There Ain't No Black in the Union Jack: The Cultural Politics of Race and Nation*, London, 1987; Bolster, W. Jeffrey, *Black Jacks: African American Seamen in the Age of Sail*, Cambridge, MA, and London, 1997.

7 This pattern of status trumping race is supported by the findings of Cannadine, David, *Ornamentalism: How the British Saw Their Empire*, London, 2001.

defeated Varus's Roman legions in Northern Germany in 9 A.D., for Germany. The first North German Lloyd steamers on the line to New York were christened *Hudson* and *Weser* – after the rivers flowing through New York and Bremen, respectively.[8]

The names of these steamers appeal to different types of nationalism, but they all invoke nationality. In the imagination of romantic nationalists, landscapes and peoples formed an organic whole. In 1848, the nationalization of landscapes through their representation in art and literature was already well established, and rivers played a particularly central role in the nationalist imagination. The Hudson had come into its role as the stream whose image defined American nationality. The Weser, on the other side of the ocean, carried less of a strong symbolic meaning. The "German River" is the Rhine, and only a much later Bremish steamer would be named for it. Nonetheless, as a river, it invoked romantic imagery.[9]

The two "fathers of their nation," Washington and Arminius, stand for two major currents of nationalism in the modern age. Washington represents the civic nation – Friedrich Meinecke's *Staatsnation* – defined by the political framework of a constitution that guarantees rights and representation to the citizen. Arminius, by contrast, represents the ethnocultural nation, the *Kulturnation*, based on the shared ethnic or cultural characteristics of its members.[10] Unlike Washington, Arminius did not set out to build a nation when he beat the Romans. He was claimed as a founding father only in retrospect, by ethnocultural nationalists who, during the Napoleonic Wars, made a case for the perpetuity of German ethnic homogeneity and difference from, mostly, the state-peoples of France and its forerunner, Rome. By 1848, the image of Arminius as a tribal, Germanic ancestor of the modern German nation was familiar to all educated Germans.[11] But Washington was not an empty symbol to Germans either. Even before the revolution of 1848, the first American president was venerated by German liberals and radicals, who held up the revolution that Washington had defended as a model for their own hopes.[12] Thus the names of the OSNC steamers appealed, with alternate visions of nationality, to Germans and Americans.

The simultaneous appeal to romantic, ethnocultural, and civic nationalism betrays a certain opportunism toward potentially conflicting visions of both nations, not a firm commitment to one vision of the German nation alone. Their invocation of nationality does not necessarily mean that Hanseats believed in the nation as a

---

[8] Wätjen, *Frühzeit*, 33, 36 (OSNC), and 67 (Lloyd).

[9] Andree, Rolf, and Ute Rickel-Immel, *The Hudson and the Rhine. Die amerikanische Malerkolonie in Düsseldorf im 19. Jahrhundert*, Kat. Ausst. [Exhibition Catalog], Düsseldorf, Kunstmuseum, 1976.

[10] Meinecke, Friedrich, *Weltbürgertum und Nationalstaat* (Hans Herzfeld, Carl Hinrichs and Walther Hofer, Friedrich Meinecke. Werke, Bd. 5), Munich, 1962 (1911). Meinecke's work was an attempt by a liberal in late imperial Germany to defend the German Enlightenment against its nationalist critics. See also Brubaker, Rogers, *Citizenship and Nationhood in France and Germany*, Cambridge, MA, 1992.

[11] Dörner, Andreas, *Politischer Mythos und symbolische Politik. Sinnstiftung durch symbolische Formen am Beispiel des Hermannsmythos*, Opladen, 1995 (also PhD diss., Universität Essen, 1994); Flacke, Monika, "Deutschland. Die Begründung der Nation aus der Krise," in *Mythen der Nationen. Ein Europäisches Panorama*, ed. idem, Munich and Berlin, 1998, 101–28, esp. pp. 102–7.

[12] Moltmann, Günter, *Atlantische Blockpolitik im 19. Jahrhundert. Die Vereinigten Staaten und der deutsche Liberalismus während der Revolution von 1848/49*, Düsseldorf, 1973.

uniform cultural entity, that they made nationality their criterion for judging others, or that it drove their political initiatives and desires. The idea of Germany as a "mere geographical concept," in the words of Prince Metternich, or as cultural space, moreover, does not necessarily entail a commitment to a nation-*state*.

For naming the second set of its steamers, the OSNC tapped into yet a different discourse. These vessels bore the names of men of science, *Humboldt* and *Franklin*. Although contemporaries saw Alexander von Humboldt and Benjamin Franklin as eminent representatives of their respective nations, their achievements also belonged to humanity at large. In naming steam vessels after scientists, Hanseats appealed to the hope for technological progress evoked by this new technology. It might have been an added benefit that Franklin was also known as a champion of a Protestant work ethic. As a teacher of frugality and self-discipline, and as a contributor to material progress, Franklin embodied the sense of improvement Hanseats held so dear. As a developmental vision, this notion of improvement resonated with a cosmopolitanism that had dominated German intellectual life in the Enlightenment, and that still mattered for Hanseats.[13]

An important reason for the subordinate status of the nation in Hanseats' thinking was that their sight was set toward the Atlantic. This ocean was a transnational space. It was so not least because the British Empire, the state-entity that dominated the Atlantic World, was more than just an extended nation-state. The context of empire for the making of the nation was invoked by the names of the first two OSNC steamers in ways that may not have been apparent to those who christened them. Washington's unification of the British colonies against the motherland could be likened to Arminius's unification of the warring Germanic tribes against Rome. Both men were military leaders. Both had previously been in the military service of the empire they defeated. They were recruited in the peripheral dominions of that empire, policing its marches against the barbarian outside world – Washington as an Indian fighter in the Transappalachian west, and Arminius as a Roman ally in the borderlands between Rome and the unromanized Germanic north.

If the stories of both leaders would be incomplete without their relation to the overbearing imperial power of the time, so would that of the OSNC and the relation between America and Germany it established and embodied. The British Empire set the framework of a political economy in which these subsidized mail steamers operated, in which Hanseats plied their trade, and in which German and American nationalism were made. This framework, moreover, extended beyond the Atlantic, to establish a global regime of free trade and European domination.

Britain likewise set the cultural tone of the age that we call the Victorian Era. It defined respectability and refinement as universal middle-class values, but it did so in positing civilization as the opposite to the barbarism of Others. It placed the Western bourgeoisie in one cultural camp, and the barbarian Other in an opposing one. The cultural difference thus became the basis of racial ideas that emerged in the same process.[14] While Hanseats moved in this Victorian, cultural space, the main

---

[13] Wätjen, *Frühzeit*, 38. The Humboldt and the Franklin were built for the Bremen line, but never used as intended. Instead, they ran on the New York–Le Havre Line, partly owned by the OSNC.

[14] For the global character of Victorian culture, see Young, Linda, *Middle-Class Culture in the Nineteenth Century: America, Australia and Britain*, New York, 2003.

point of reference for their judgments remained the mercantile ethos of their own estate.

SOCIALIZING WITH THE OTHER

In early 1856, Gustav F. Schwab went on an extensive trip to Europe. He had made the crossing from New York with his family. In Paris, just after the New Year, he said good-bye to his wife, Eliza, and their young children, whom Eliza took with her to Stuttgart for an extended stay with Sophie Schwab, Gustav Schwab's mother. An accomplished Hanseatic merchant in New York, Schwab planned to inspect firsthand the places in Sicily from which his firm, Schwab & Recknagel, received sumac and sulfur. On the journey through France and Italy, he wanted to combine business and edification, visiting several business partners and experiencing the treasures of antiquity along the way. Throughout the trip, Schwab shared his impressions with Eliza, in a constant stream of detailed letters. In April, he reunited with his loved ones in Stuttgart, where the entire family spent the spring, before returning to New York via Bremen.

The trip took Schwab onto unknown terrain, inviting him to reflect upon his encounters with strangers and strangeness and to make decisions with whom to socialize or do business. What criteria did he bring to these encounters? One might expect him to hold a fixed set of assumptions about the "national character" of "Others" (Hegel). Instead, we see Schwab apply a range of differentiated criteria to cultures and individuals, which allowed him to revise and develop his views as his journey progressed. Travel makes us learn more about ourselves than about the places we visit, so from Schwab's judgments of Others there emerges an image of his view of himself and of his place in the world relative to Others. This image is not one of ethnic or cultural nationalism. It is one of an elite cosmopolitanism that set clearly defined, yet open and flexible, boundaries between the world of one's peers and the world of outsiders.

As a true cosmopolitan, Schwab was a stranger nowhere. He discovered that most of his new acquaintances shared some mutual friends or business partners with him. In one letter, he remarked, "I hardly meet any person with whom I do not already have some kind of relation."[15] A case in point was a soirée in the house of the merchant Adolf Gruber in Genoa. "It turns out that young Pagenstetter, who came to our counting-house the past spring, had previously been in Gruber's counting-house for several years, and was well-liked there. Further, [Gruber's associate] Herr Weyermann has a brother in New York in Spies' counting-house. We will have an opportunity to return to him the hospitality I have received here."[16]

Hanseats moved in a global class of merchants. With others in that class, they shared the habit of assessing the worth of an individual based on "character" and refinement. Hanseats were groomed from childhood to develop these essential

---

[15] Gustav F. Schwab to Eliza Schwab, Palermo, February 9, 1856, MSS 434, John Christopher Schwab Family Papers. Manuscripts and Archives, Yale University Library, series I, box 1, folder 32.

[16] Gustav F. Schwab to Eliza Schwab, Genua, January 27, 1856, MSS 434, Schwab Papers, series I, box 1, folder 31.

qualifications for moving among the better sort.[17] Yet, as much as Hanseats might have liked to believe that refinement was an inherent characteristic, they, along with anyone who made a claim to an exalted station, knew that cultural tastes, social skills, and commercial and political knowledge were acquired. Because anyone with the necessary means and connections could acquire them, a solid command of the habits that signaled refinement did not necessarily indicate that a person was inwardly a gentleman. For social intercourse, this fine distinction might not have mattered as much.[18] For business transactions, however, Hanseats liked to be on firmer ground before deciding that a counterpart could be trusted.

Within their own network, Bremen's merchants knew with whom they were dealing. Personal acquaintance, or at most two degrees of separation, ensured credibility (Chapter 1). In the port towns where Hanseats were active, non-Hanseatic merchants were still no strangers to them. For better or worse, one's character was known to those who mattered. When Julius Wilkens planned to "establish himself" in Baltimore in a firm of his own, his brother Friedrich offered him a word of warning about his prospective associate: "If I were you, I would think twice about Crichton's proposal, the burned child fears the fire, yet you know best."[19] In exchanges like these, merchants evaluated each other's credibility.

The further away from familiar ground Hanseats ventured in establishing business connections, the more important this kind of secondhand advice became. Especially in the fast-growing and fluctuating world of the American bourgeoisie, credit-rating agencies came to play a central role for replacing firsthand knowledge about a person's character with anonymous standards. In the 1850s and 1860s, credit ratings were still largely based on assessments of the character of an individual, gained by interviewing those of standing who knew him. Ratings agencies filled in the gaps that emerged where merchants could no longer acquire first- or even secondhand knowledge about prospective business partners, but they applied the same standards to which a merchant would have held them if he had known them in person.[20]

Outside of the United States, merchants could not depend on the help of ratings agencies. To an extent, second-degree connections as described by Schwab could help to establish a basis for trust. A recommendation by Gruber might have carried some weight for Schwab. Schwab received frequent requests for help from young Germans who hoped to establish themselves in America, and most of these came with references from Bremen or Württemberg.[21]

---

[17] Bushman, Richard, *The Refinement of America: Persons, Houses, Cities*, New York, 1992. For Hanseats' education, see Chapter 2.

[18] Halttunen, Karen, *Confidence Men and Painted Women: A Story of Middle-Class Culture in America, 1830–1870* (Yale Historical Publication, Miscellany, vol. 129), New Haven, CT, and London 1982.

[19] Friedrich to Julius Wilkens, January 18, 1864, Wilkens, Julius, 1838?–1898, Papers, 1849–83, MdHS MS.439.

[20] Beckert, Sven, "Merchants and Manufacturers in the Antebellum North," in *Ruling America: A History of Wealth and Power in a Democracy*, ed. Gary Gerstle and Steve Fraser, Cambridge, MA, 2005, 92–122.

[21] Sophie Schwab's letters provide numerous examples. See, e.g., Sophie Schwab to Gustav F. Schwab, Stuttgart, August 21, 1858 (35), November 28, 1859 (35), January 9, 1860 (36), June 29–30, 1860 (36), and May 9, 1861 (37); and Christoph Theodor Schwab and Sophie Schwab to Gustav F. Schwab, Stuttgart, September 28, 1859 (35); MSS 434, Schwab Papers, series I, box 2, folder: as indicated in parentheses.

Where these means of ascertaining the character of a counterpart were absent, merchants were forced to rely on their own judgment. Schwab's letters show that nationality, religion or creed, and race were criteria in his preliminary judgments, or prejudices, of strangers. Nevertheless, he was able to reflect on these criteria and to revise the images he formed under first impressions. When in doubt, he fell back on the same standards he employed in judging business partners.

Nationality was a criterion that allowed Schwab a first, rough sorting of the strangers he encountered on his journey. Schwab was more likely to give Germans, Britons, and Americans the benefit of the doubt, while he would approach Frenchmen and Italians with a prejudicial caution. In Genoa, Schwab was introduced to a Mr. Parodi-Köster, whom he found to be "a crook, like all Genoese."[22] In the same vein, he felt comfortable in Livorno, where he "enjoy[ed] dealing with proper German and English houses, rather than French and Italian ones."[23]

These attitudes were not based on a fully fledged ethnocultural construction of the nation. His positive or negative prejudice about either nation did not determine Schwab's attitude toward all of their individual members. For himself, Schwab at times seemed to be filled with a sense of his own inadequacy, rather than superiority, in dealing with Italians and Frenchmen. Much of this unease had to do with language.

In Genoa, Schwab turned down an invitation to a grand ball, "so as not to reveal my ignorance of the Italian language."[24] In Milan, as in most places before that, Schwab chose an English speaker for his companion in his tourist activities, a lieutenant of the U.S. Navy, so that he could share his impressions in a familiar tongue.[25] On another occasion, Schwab hints that he made progress with his French, but was not yet confident that he had mastered the language.[26] As long as his French and Italian counterparts did not speak English or German as well as he did, Schwab would have found it difficult to carry on a conversation that would allow for the subtleties of refinement to be communicated, and thus to evaluate the character of his counterparts, independently. Where he met English-speaking Frenchmen, he had nothing but kind words. On a carriage ride to Rome, Schwab shared the coach with two Frenchwomen, whom he praised as educated and modest – models of feminine virtue in spite of their national background.[27] On another occasion, he found a Mr. de Bonneville to be an "interesting person," with whom he enjoyed an animated debate over religion on a train ride through France. When Schwab came to Rome, he even sought to meet de Bonneville there, but was disappointed to find that he had already departed. But Schwab's interaction

[22] Gustav F. Schwab to Eliza Schwab, Genua, January 27, 1856, MSS 434, Schwab Papers, series I, box 1, folder 31.

[23] Gustav F. Schwab to Eliza Schwab, Livorno, February 1, 1856, MSS 434, Schwab Papers, series I, box 1, folder 32.

[24] Ibid.

[25] Gustav F. Schwab to Eliza Schwab, Livorno/Milan, March 12, 1856, MSS 434, Schwab Papers, series I, box 1, folder 33.

[26] Gustav F. Schwab to Eliza Schwab, Paris, January 11, 1856, MSS 434, Schwab Papers, series I, box 1, folder 31.

[27] Gustav F. Schwab to Eliza Schwab, Naples/Rome, February 29, 1856, MSS 434, Schwab Papers, series I, box 1, folder 32.

with de Bonneville was not just facilitated by a shared, foreign language. The Frenchman also qualified as a "person with whom I ... already have some kind of relation" – "Theodor Pressel of Tübingen ... had been the private tutor of [de Bonneville's] sister" and Pressel was an acquaintance of Schwab's brother-in-law, Karl Klüpfel.[28] These connections put de Bonneville squarely in the same group of people as Adolf Gruber, the German merchant in Genoa – a cosmopolitan elite.

Just as Schwab did not consider all Frenchmen as essentially inferior, neither did he assume that all Germans, Americans, or Britons were essentially his peers. In spite of his general affinity for the United States, Schwab once uttered "surprise" at a number of recent transactions in New York that had brought him into contact with "honest" American counterparts.[29] The sense that a shared nationality did not establish much of a commonality emerges from Hanseatic attitudes toward hinterland Germans. Dealing with non-Hanseatic German elites, *Senator* Gabain, when attending a conference on commercial law in 1857, remarked upon the absence of "higher mercantile experience and intelligence" among the delegates from other German states, and found the bankers and industrialists from the hinterland characterized by the "narrowness of their vision." In the early 1860s, Burgomaster Arnold Duckwitz complained in similar terms about the Prussian ministerial bureaucracy, whose members were recruited from the landed nobility.[30] One way in which Hanseats marked their distinctness from these provincials was that they often spoke English among themselves, especially in Bremen.[31]

Hanseats might have moved with most ease in the worlds of the Anglo-American Atlantic and the German Confederation, but they remained, in their own view, a group apart from either of these worlds. Against Anglo-Americans, they held the suspicion that self-interest overruled morality in their business ethics. Hanseats shared this prejudice with nationalist Germans, who made the same accusation of crude materialism against Hanseats.[32] From other Germans, Hanseats felt themselves distinct by the breadth of their cosmopolitan vision, as opposed to the provincial narrowness of the hinterland. In both cases, as far as Hanseats were concerned, nationality could not serve as an automatically assumed basis for

[28] Gustav F. Schwab to Eliza Schwab, Marseille, January 20–21, 1856, MSS 434, Schwab Papers, series I, box 1, folder 31; and Naples/Rome, February 29, 1856, MSS 434, Schwab Papers, series I, box 1, folder 32.

[29] As quoted in Sophie Schwab to Gustav F. Schwab, n.p., April 3, 1858, MSS 434, Schwab Papers, series I, box 2, folder 35.

[30] Gabain quoted in Schnelle, *Handelsgesetzbuch*, 34; Arnold Duckwitz to Rudolf Schleiden, Bremen, January 17, 1862, StAHB 7,116 [Rudolf Schleiden Papers], folder "Briefwechsel Rudolf Schleiden mit Senator Arnold Duckwitz, 1854–1879," third of five unnumbered and unlabeled boxes.

[31] Engelsing, Rolf, "England und die USA in der bremischen Sicht des 19. Jahrhunderts," *Jahrbuch der Wittheit zu Bremen* 1 (1957), 33–65, here p. 51.

[32] Engelsing, "England und die USA," esp. pp. 40–3, 57–8, quote on pp. 40–1, cites the Bremish merchant Friedrich Adolph Delius, who, "in the 1840s," wrote: "On the one hand, England is the most dangerous enemy of an economically independent Germany and the epitome of all self-interested trade policy; on the other hand, English trade policy gives the best practical instruction as to how Germany, in responding to England, must conduct herself vis-à-vis foreign countries." See Chapter 4 for Delius's ideas on the social control of itinerant populations, which seem to reflect a change of heart that parallels that of British liberals over the 1840s.

socializing or conducting business with others. In social interaction between individuals, refinement and character trumped nationality.

If nationality was not a firm criterion for the recognition or rejection of Others as equals, we might suspect that religion or creed was – after all, Calvinism was such an integral part of Hanseats' identity (cf. Chapter 2). In Naples, Gustav F. Schwab expressed delight at meeting "countrymen" – and then went on to list men and women from Bremen and Württemberg, two solidly Protestant states.[33] The nations Schwab found more trustworthy than others were predominantly Protestant, whereas those he distrusted were predominantly Catholic. Yet, Schwab's account of his acquaintance with de Bonneville – "an ardent propagandist for Catholicism" – shows that he could look beyond religious differences, if a person was otherwise a gentleman.[34]

In dealing with the general Italian population, however, Schwab was initially led by solid anti-Catholic presumptions. The further south he traveled, the more frequent and dismissive his remarks about Catholicism became. In Palermo, at first, his anti-Catholicism reached new heights. Schwab explained the backwardness of the Kingdom of Both Sicilies, and the poverty of its general population, on religious grounds: "Monks and priests rule the land and bleed it dry. Imagine, there are 20 to 30 thousand monks and nuns in Palermo alone, a city of 160,000 inhabitants. Such an army of idlers is even worse than one of soldiers, and Sicily has an abundance of the latter, in addition."[35]

The image of benighted despotism Schwab invokes resonates with the anti-Catholicism then prevalent among Nativists and Evangelicals in the United States. In the view of these groups, there existed a linkage among liberty, industry, and faith that explained American success. This trope, so familiar to American Protestants in the 1850s, would also come to inform patriotism in the German Empire of the 1870s, and we can see in Schwab's depiction of the Two Sicilies a nucleus of that later ideology.[36]

Perhaps Schwab's initial view of the Sicilians was informed by the opinions of his acquaintances, most of whom were Germans residing in that port as merchants.

---

[33] Gustav F. Schwab to Eliza Schwab, Naples, February 6, 1856, MSS 434, Schwab Papers, series I, box 1, folder 32.

[34] Gustav F. Schwab to Eliza Schwab, Marseille, January 20–21, 1856, MSS 434, Schwab Papers, series I, box 1, folder 31.

[35] Gustav F. Schwab to Eliza Schwab, Palermo, February 9, 1856, MSS 434, Schwab Papers, series I, box 1, folder 32.

[36] On the United States, see Knobel, Dale T., *America for the Americans: The Nativist Movement in the United States*, New York, 1996; Baker, Jean H., *Ambivalent Americans: The Know-Nothing Party in Maryland*, Baltimore, 1977; Lipset, Seymour Martin, and Earl Raab, *The Politics of Unreason: Right-Wing Extremism in America, 1790–1977*, Chicago and London, 1978 (1970). On Germany, see Fischer, Fritz, "Der deutsche Protestantismus und die Politik im 19. Jahrhundert," in *Probleme der Reichsgründungszeit 1848–1879*, ed. Helmut Böhme, Cologne and Berlin, 1972, 49–71; Flacke, "Deutschland," 111–15; Hübinger, Gangolf, *Kulturprotestantismus und Politik. Zum Verhältnis von Liberalismus und Protestantismus im wilhelminischen Deutschland*, Tübingen, 1994; Becker, Frank, "Konfessionelle Nationsbilder im Deutschen Kaiserreich," in *Nation und Religion in der deutschen Geschichte*, ed. Heinz-Gerhard Haupt and Dieter Langewiesche, Frankfurt and New York, 2001, 389–418; Kuhlemann, Frank-Michael, "Pastorennationalismus in Deutschland im 19. Jahrhundert – Befunde und Perspektiven der Forschung," in ibid., 548–86.

Among his companions in Palermo were also two British merchants who were en route to China, where they were established. Schwab undertook his sightseeing tours of the environs in the company of these Britons, to whom he referred as "the Chinese." He invited them to join him and his German acquaintances at the local German enclave – a beer pub run by Sicilian monks in a convent's cellar. Surely the irony was not lost on Schwab.[37]

If the judgments of his local acquaintances had been the base of Schwab's first impressions of Sicily, he was ready to question them after gaining firsthand experience. After a few days in Palermo, Schwab consciously began to question his assumptions about the linkage between Catholicism and idleness, and eventually discarded them. He had discovered that the land on a steep hillside, which he climbed to gain the view from the mountaintop, was cultivated almost all the way to the summit. "I have to revise my opinion of the Sicilians," he conceded. "It takes no small amount of diligence, after all, to cultivate these small patches of land, some thousands of feet above the valley, so difficult to access, and under so hot a sun." These cultivators were clearly Catholics. In Schwab's eyes, they had redeemed their nation and their creed through their industry. In this case, all it took to gain Gustav F. Schwab's respect was the embrace of a Protestant work ethic, not of the Protestant creed.[38]

Religion and nationality might have served Schwab as *a priori* criteria for his judgments, but they were not in any way fixed and immutable. Considerations like character, refinement, and work ethic modified or overruled religion and nationality, not just in the case of individuals with whom he interacted, but also in Schwab's opinions of "the many," whatever their nationality may be. He looked at individuals, merchants or not, with an eye that judged the qualification of his counterpart as a business partner. He also assessed the worth of a country with the gaze of someone who asks for its value as a partner in foreign trade. The rational core of this approach is the concern with profit. Schwab would give credit where it was due, to countries or individuals alike. The conscious moral root of Schwab's attitude, however, was his commitment to the Calvinist-mercantile ethos that was founded on the existence of Bremen's mercantile estate as a cosmopolitan community.

RACE AND EMPIRE

The true test for the universality of their mercantile values would be whether Hanseats were willing to apply them to non-Europeans. If we assume that refinement and civilization emerge in the nineteenth century as generically "Western" attributes functioning as complements to an increasingly dismissive view of the racialized Other, we should find that Hanseats brought racist assumptions to their encounters with nonwhites. Indeed, racist ideas had taken root in Hanseats' minds. Not unlike their views on nationalism and religion, however, Hanseats were able to question and revise their racist assumptions. In actual encounters with, and in

---

[37] Gustav F. Schwab to Eliza Schwab, Palermo, February 9, 1856, MSS 434, Schwab Papers, series I, box 1, folder 32.

[38] Ibid.

policies directed toward non-Europeans, Hanseats could look beyond the racial construction to detect, not a uniform Other, but both unwashed masses and gentlemen in dark skin.

When Haiti gained its independence from France, the United States refused to grant diplomatic recognition to a state founded on the rebellion of slaves. Bremen, by contrast, approached the new nation with the same attitude it had brought to the United States. Here was a former colony, now open to direct trade with the continent. This was good for business, and the Hanseatic City established two consulates in Haiti.[39]

In 1837, Bremen joined the anti–slave-trade treaty that had been made between Britain and France in 1835. The main concern that drove the *Senat* to this step was the danger that Bremish emigrant ships would be seized as slavers. The criteria laid down in the Franco-British treaty for telling a passenger vessel from a slave-trading one were based on the amount of space allotted to each passenger. A ship that could be densely packed with humans, by the layout of the steerage quarters or by the amount of provisions carried, was automatically suspicious. In itself, an emigrant vessel could not easily be distinguished from a slaver. Being a party to the treaty gave Bremen more leverage to protect its vessels from seizure.[40]

A secondary consideration was to prevent Africans from coming to Bremerhaven. Britain and France had agreed to capture any and all slave-trading vessels. Under the treaty provisions, liberated Africans would be sent to the home port of the vessel. By joining the treaty, Bremen was able to prevent this clause from being applied to any Bremish ships that might be seized by either of the treaty powers. Article 3 of the agreement by which the Hanseatic cities joined the Anglo-French treaty states that liberated slaves are to disembark in French or English ports, "because the disembarkation of Negroes in the above-mentioned [Hanseatic] ports would be accompanied by great inconvenience."[41] It would be a mistake, however, to read this clause as motivated simply by racism.

Blacks, like migrants and sailors, were a group Hanseats treated with a "paternal" attitude. Neither of these groups could expect to receive recognition as equals from Bremen's merchants. All of them were equally unwelcome to remain on Bremish territory for any prolonged stay. Within these limits, blacks did not receive special discriminatory treatment based on race. As illegally traded slaves, they were just another group in a larger, transient population that posed a problem to law and order, and that had to be dealt with by administrative means. The *Senat* took care that freed slaves should not stay for any prolonged period of time in Bremerhaven, let alone settle there; but it did the same with sailors and migrants. In the case of all three groups, the main objective was to keep strangers from becoming permanent

---

[39] Graßmann, Antjekathrin, "Hanse weltweit? Zu den Konsulaten Lübecks, Bremens und Hamburgs im 19. Jahrhundert," in *Ausklang und Nachklang der Hanse im 19. und 20. Jahrhundert*, ed. idem (Hansischer Geschichtsverein, ed., Hansische Studien, vol. 12), Trier, Germany, 2001, 43–66, here p. 61.

[40] StAHB 2,C.4.g.1.II, *Beitritt der Hansestädte zu den zwischen England und Frankreich zur Unterdrückung des Sklavenhandels abgeschlossenen Verträgen 1837. Generalia et diversa 1836–1868.* This file contains a printed form that allows Bremish authorities to declare that the purpose of the journey of a specific vessel is not related to slaving.

[41] Ibid.

residents who might become a charge to public charity, or a problem for the maintenance of order. To be sure, to fear that these groups would end up indigent if they stayed on Bremish territory meant to assume that their individual members lacked the necessary "industry" to prosper. This assumption, however, was based on a class prejudice. It might have been an essentialist assumption – that certain groups were inherently incapable of bettering themselves – but not one primarily based on a notion of race.[42]

On the issue of black slavery in the United States, Hanseats were largely silent. American blacks are rarely mentioned in their letters. In this respect, enslaved blacks formed a blind spot not unlike the personnel who served Hanseats in their homes and countinghouses.[43] When slaves did appear in correspondence, it was as commodities alongside tobacco and cotton. Bremen's consul in Richmond, Eduard Wilhelm deVoß, dutifully listed the prices of slaves in that market in his annual reports.[44] Here, too, Hanseats' attitude toward slaves mirrors the one they took toward immigrants and sailors, who were mostly important as factors on the balance sheet.[45]

The cotton merchant Ludwig Kirchhoff was an exception. Of Bremish origin, Kirchhoff served as consul for Lübeck in New Orleans. There he had married the daughter of a plantation owner, a Mr. Welham. When his father-in-law died and Kirchhoff inherited the plantations, it did not take long for the news to reach Rudolf Schleiden and Gustav F. Schwab. It is more than a little likely that Welham had owned slaves who worked on his estates. Schleiden and Schwab agreed that Kirchhoff should sell the plantations. Schleiden based this opinion on Kirchhoff's precarious health. He had learned about Welham's death after Lincoln's election, which had put slavery on the national agenda. Yet Schleiden's only reference to slavery was his remark that "the current situation may not be especially favorable for a sale of the old man's plantations." This was a decidedly pragmatic take on the issue of slavery.[46]

Hanseatic newspapers followed the mounting tension in the United States over slavery during the last half of the 1850s. In March of 1856, the *Weser Zeitung* ran a series of articles that debated the pros and cons of slavery, without, however, favoring one position over the other. In its columns, correspondents' reports from the United States were printed without regard to their tint. One correspondent in

---

[42] By contrast, Jews were explicitly excluded from Bremish territory as a "nation" and as a religious group. See preceding, Chapter 3, and Wippermann, Wolfgang, *Jüdisches Leben im Raum Bremerhaven. Eine Fallstudie zur Alltagsgeschichte der Juden vom 18. Jahrhundert bis zur NS-Zeit* (Burchard Scheper, ed., Veröffentlichungen des Stadtarchivs Bremerhaven, vol. 5), Bremerhaven, 1985, 46–52.

[43] See Chapter 2.

[44] StAHB, 2,B.13.b.10, *Hanseatica. Verhältnisse der Hansestädte mit den Vereinigten Staaten von Nordamerika. Hanseatische diplomatische Agenten, Konsuln usw. bei den vereinigten Staaten von Nordamerika und Korrespondenz mit denselben.* Konsulate Richmond etc., contains the annual reports for 1854–7 and 1861. There is no evidence to determine whether deVoß owned any slaves.

[45] Gustav F. Schwab was a rare case where we can discern strong antislavery sentiments. See note 86 to this chapter, as well as Chapter 8.

[46] Rudolf Schleiden to Gustav F. Schwab (in New York), Brattleboro, VT, August 29, 1860 and August 31, 1860, and Washington, DC, November 24, 1860, MSS 434, Schwab Papers, series I, box 2, folder 38.

New York described the conflict in Kansas as a confrontation between "abolitionists and friends of law and order." A different correspondent called the Fugitive
Slave Law "horrible" and described its devastating consequences for escaped
slaves.[47] Editorials ignored the issue. Apparently, Hanseats were not ready to side
with either party to the conflict. Their religious leanings might have drawn them
toward abolitionism, while their commercial interests in cotton and tobacco would
have given them an interest in seeing slavery maintained. Neither of these conflicting interests seems to have outweighed the other strongly enough to have driven
Hanseats toward an active stance on slavery.

If Hanseats largely ignored slavery, the defenders of the "peculiar institution" did
not ignore Hanseats. In his opinion, concurring with U.S. Chief Justice Rodger
B. Taney's Dred Scott decision, Justice John A. Campbell pointed to Bremen law.
Campbell stressed the contrast between German Law, which confers freedom to a
person by virtue of his presence in a specific territory, and the American legal
situation. Campbell, who would later become assistant secretary of war in the
Confederate States of America, held that the principle of Bremish law, that "city
air makes free," was not a valid precedent for American jurisprudence.[48]

If Hanseats were color blind in their condescension and paternalism toward the
"lower sorts," they were equally open to accept non-Europeans as peers if they
passed the test of refinement and character. An encounter of Gustav F. Schwab's
stands as an impressive example. On the journey from Paris to Marseille, Schwab
became friends with a fellow train passenger. His account reveals a surprisingly
open-minded flirt with the Other, while showing the strong roots racial stereotypes
had in Schwab's thinking. Schwab wrote to his wife:

I have to tell you about an acquaintance I have made on the way. On the station in Lyon
I met a man who had drawn everyone's gaze upon himself, and who was a mystery to
everyone. A tall, handsome man, almost as black as a Negro, a fine physiognomy, a
marvelous turban on his head, woven from silk and gold, and with oriental garments
under his coat. By chance, I came to sit in the same compartment as he; he was
accompanied by a very well-educated Frenchman and his mother, and since these
people spoke English, we soon began a conversation. By and by I found out that the
man was a Hindoo, and a Khan of the belligerent and famous tribe of the Mahrattas,
whose history is still fresh in my mind from Macauly's essays. He speaks perfect English,
and must have lived in the nobility in London and Paris. We had the most interesting
conversation, and we soon became such good friends, that he told me just minutes ago
how much he regrets having to leave here tomorrow or the day after tomorrow, and
that we cannot make the journey through Italy, which he also plans to make, jointly....

There is nothing new under the sun; just imagine, an honest Swabian and a Hindoo
Khan arm in arm! Although he is of a belligerent tribe, you do not have to think that he
could suddenly twist my neck; he is a very gentle and refined man, and on the train,
when I offered him some of my excellent raspberry schnapps, he made a face like our
children did when they first tried to drink beer. Since he is very well-informed and

---

[47] Bremen *Weser Zeitung*, January 3, 1856, February 14, 1856, March 6, 1856, and March 7, 1856.
[48] See *Dred Scott v. Sandford*, U.S. Supreme Court, Mr. Justice Campbell concurring, in http://www.
   tourolaw.edu/patch/Scott/Campbell.asp (accessed October 1, 2005) (Touro College Law Center,
   Project P.A.T.C.H.).

curious, we have very good conversations, and today he, Louis Gmelin, and I walked around for several hours, through the city [of Marseille] and the port, where we were onboard the *Great Republic*, which has anchored here to load bombs for the Crimean. . . .

The Hindoo had invited me for breakfast, and Louis also took part, and was very useful to the people for his knowledge of travel opportunities and of this place [Marseille] in general. Afterwards, we went for the walk I already mentioned. . . . For tomorrow, I have invited the Khan and his companions to lunch.[49]

"Refinement" trumped race in Schwab's assessment of the man who as yet remained the anonymous "Khan." Not that Schwab lacks in racial stereotypes that would suggest a condescending attitude. The Other can be childlike and cruel at the same time. In describing him to Eliza, his wife, he paints the Khan as the nonthreatening, docile, and childlike Other, while addressing a concern that would be on the mind of both spouses: is this man a threat?

Having established the Khan's fundamentally benign disposition, Schwab can then grant him the honor and dignity that makes him one of his peers. The Hindoo speaks English and associates with nobles. Now Schwab can feel justified in expressing unabridged admiration – he and the Other walk "arm in arm." Apparently, the feeling was mutual:

On Tuesday, I brought my friend, Azimullah Khan, to his steamer. I hope to meet him again in Rome. He wanted to make me King of India, with a salary of 50,000 pound sterling; what do you think about that, maybe for a year? His companion, Msr. de Bonneville of Paris, a very interesting man, and an ardent propagandist for Catholicism, wanted to know the address of Theodor Pressel of Tübingen, who had been the private tutor of his sister. Since I did not know it, I gave him Klüpfels' address, and he might send them a letter for Pressel. . . .

Louis and I have had a lot of fun with his majesty, the Khan, who urgently invited me to visit him in India, where he promised to take me on the hunt for lions and tigers. You will find this clearly evident.[50]

After a few days, the Khan had ceased to be a mere specimen of his kind, and had become a person with a name, even a "friend." He is established as yet another "person with whom I already have some kind of relation" – in this case, four degrees of separation from Sophie Klüpfel, Gustav F. Schwab's sister. The offer to come to India seems worth toying with for Schwab. What gentleman would decline an invitation to hunt wild game?

Eliza Schwab shared her husband's enthusiasm. He answered her, that "I am glad that you felt pride over my acquaintance with the Khan. I will tell him when I see him in Rome." She had even sent his letters to Bremen, so that friends and relatives could read them. Apparently, Schwab could expect his Hanseatic friends to be equally proud of his encounter.[51] Still, as a good Hanseatic wife, Eliza Schwab had

---

[49] Gustav F. Schwab to Eliza Schwab, Marseille, January 14, 1856, MSS 434, Schwab Papers, series I, box 1, folder 31.

[50] Gustav F. Schwab to Eliza Schwab, Marseille, January 20–21, 1856, MSS 434, Schwab Papers, series I, box 1, folder 31.

[51] Gustav F. Schwab to Eliza Schwab, Genua, January 27, 1856, MSS 434, Schwab Papers, series I, box 1, folder 31, and Rome, March 6, 1856, folder 33.

to ask Faust's question, "how do you think about religion?" Her husband could assure her that "the Khan is a Mohametan, although he holds Christianity to be the true religion, and he knew much about it." Apparently, matters of belief had been among the subjects of conversation among Schwab, Azimullah, and de Bonneville. Schwab had learned that he was not dealing with a "Hindoo" and had discovered de Bonneville to be an ardent Catholic. Their religious differences, and what appears to have been a candid debate about the merits of their respective beliefs, did not diminish Schwab's respect for either of the two men. Among gentlemen, the boundaries for tolerance were wide.[52]

Sadly, for Schwab, by the time he made it to Rome, Azimullah and de Bonneville had already left. They "have traveled on to the Holy Land, but I still met Monsieur de Bonneville's mother here in my hotel." This was the last Gustav F. Schwab saw or heard from Azimullah Khan.[53] Or was it?

We do not know with certainty what further information Schwab received about his friend's world-historic role, or how he judged this information. Schwab never mentions Azimullah again in his extant correspondence. But he had read Macauly, and he might have read future publications on India. He certainly read the German and American newspapers, which would have covered the story of the "Sepoy Mutiny," which became the Indian Rebellion of 1857.

Did Azimullah take him into his confidence about his plans? Did he mean it, when he invited Schwab to take a post in the government of India? Azimullah was in no position to make such an offer, and Schwab must have known this. When Schwab met him, Azimullah had just spent two years in London, lobbying futilely on behalf of his lord, Nana Sahib. This adopted prince was not recognized by the British as a legitimate heir to Peshwa Baji Rao, the last ruler of Oudh. They thus denied the adopted son the lavish stipend that had been granted his father.[54]

When Azimullah left London, he was disenchanted with the British, and a plan to gain independence for India was beginning to form in his mind. From Rome, he traveled to Constantinople and spoke to representatives of the Sublime Porte in the hope of forming an alliance. From there, he visited the Crimean battlefields in order to gain insight into military tactics. It was there, so some of his biographers claim, that he became convinced India could win an armed struggle for independence.[55]

Considering his active efforts during this trip to win allies, was Azimullah testing the waters with Gustav F. Schwab? Would he have been ready to fight arm in arm against the British? We cannot know. Conventional wisdom suggests that Gustav F. Schwab would have sided with the empire, with the white Protestant side, against the Other, once that Other dropped the childlike meekness and showed his bloodthirsty self.[56]

[52] Gustav F. Schwab to Eliza Schwab, Naples, February 6, 1856, MSS 434, Schwab Papers, series I, box 1, folder 32.

[53] Gustav F. Schwab to Eliza Schwab, Naples/Rome, February 29, 1856, MSS 434, Schwab Papers, series I, box 1, folder 32.

[54] Hibbert, Christopher, *The Great Mutiny: India 1857*, New York, 1978, 173.

[55] Hamid Hussain, "The Story of the Storm – 1857," *Defence Journal* (India) May 2002 (online edition), http://www.defencejournal.com/2002/may/storm.htm (accessed January 15, 2005).

[56] Incidentally, one of the Fritze/Lehmkuhl steamers that had been sold to the British was used as a troop transporter in squashing the rebellion. See Wätjen, *Frühzeit*, 59.

In British accounts of the Indian Rebellion of 1857, Azimullah is personally held responsible for what is considered the cruelest act of violence committed by the Indian side. In Kanpur, the outnumbered British garrison, besieged by Nana Sahib's forces, was offered safe passage in a note written by Azimullah. The British agreed to his terms for their surrender. At Satichaura Ghat on the River Ganges, however, as the disarmed soldiers and their families embarked boats that were to take them to Allahabad, Nana Sahib's troops opened fire. There was a single survivor.[57]

After the British had crushed the first struggle for Indian independence, Azimullah accompanied the Nana Sahib into exile in Nepal, where both men presumably died of a fever in 1858. Still, rumors of Azimullah's survival, periodic appearances of self-styled descendants of the Khan, and the discovery of what turned out to be a forged diary of Azimullah's as late as the 1950s, suggest his elevation to the status of a martyr and national hero within India. Both the British and Indian sides agreed that Azimullah was a mastermind of the Indian Rebellion of 1857. Schwab's account, as well as others, suggests that he would have had the skills to be such a leader, though the need of both sides to create a master villain, or a heroic leader, might have created a tendency to overemphasize his role.[58]

Azimullah did not lack admirers in the West, as a British officer had to discover to his annoyance:

While searching over the Nana's Palaces at Bithur, we found heaps of letters directed to that fiend "Azimula Khan" by ladies in England . . . written in the most lovable manner. Such rubbish I never read. . . . How English ladies can be so infatuated. . . . You would not believe me if I sent home the letters.[59]

Whatever Gustav F. Schwab's feelings about his friend might have been after learning of his role in the rebellion, at the time of their encounter this Hanseatic merchant was perfectly willing to admit Azimullah to that global class of refined gentlemen among which Bremen's merchants counted themselves.

NATION AND CULTURE

If refinement and character trumped race and nationality for Hanseats in personal encounters, their views of culture and nature, in general, were influenced by the romantic nationalism that had become a dominant strain of Western thought since the beginning of the nineteenth century. Scholars of nationalism have identified art and literature as the main media that helped disseminate romantic nationalist views in the nineteenth century. With history and landscape painting, as well as novels and poetry, the medium was the message.[60]

The aesthetic of nationalism, the investment of culture and nature with essentialist meaning – something "higher," or "deeper," or otherwise "transcendent" –

---

[57] Hibbert, *Mutiny*, esp. pp. 177–90.
[58] "History Disproved?," *Deccan Herald*, June 30, 1953; i.e., "From our Files, 50 Years Ago," *Deccan Herald*, June 30, 2003, http://www.deccanherald.com/deccanherald/jun30/files.asp (accessed January 15, 2005).
[59] Roberts, Earl, Field-Marshal, *Letters Written during the Indian Mutiny*, London, 1924, 120, quoted in Hibbert, *Mutiny*, note 16 (to p. 173), 412.
[60] See note 11 to this chapter.

was at the core of the intellectual movement of romanticism. In Germany and elsewhere, romantic nationalists actively constructed their nations in the image of the *Kulturnation*.[61] Nevertheless, romantic nationalism was not the only set of ideas informing contemporaries' views on nature or culture. A reverence for the classical world and the ideal of reason that went along with it was still available as part of the legacy of the Enlightenment. Christianity, too, continued to inform the value judgments of men and women in the nineteenth century. Hanseats were influenced by all three of these currents.[62]

German nationalism after 1871 achieved a synthesis of romanticism, classics, and Christianity. Thus, by the late nineteenth century, Germans came to believe that their new empire embodied the best of the classical heritage, while being rooted in the essential soul of the German people and completing the work of a Protestant god.[63] In the thinking of 1850s Hanseats, however, this synthesis had not been achieved. In their minds, romanticism, reason, and Protestantism still stood as competing and conflicting frameworks of interpretation for their perceptions of culture and nature. Moreover, these three discourses – neither individually, nor taken together – did not inevitably lead them to an embrace of nationality as the main organizing principle of their worldview.

The idea of the nation was of limited use to Hanseats, who relied on international trading ties that were based on the strength of their transnational community and its cosmopolitan ethos. Assured of their identity as an estate, they had perhaps less need than others to look for a spiritual or political home in a nation or nation-state.

For all their sober business sense, Hanseats were not immune to the influences of romantic nationalism. Gustav F. Schwab's father, the poet Gustav B. Schwab, had made significant contributions to this current. He was the author of a widely read travel guide to the Lake Constance region, which took the reader into a mnemonically charged Swabian landscape, invoking the presence of figures and events of historical significance for Germany. In the same vein, the poet's *Journeys across the Swabian Alb* weaved tales of local heroes and dramas into a narrative of past German glory, implying a call to contemporaries for its revival.

This move of investing what stands for the particularity of a place with a national meaning culturally transforms local artifacts into national symbols. It fills the abstract space of the nation with the spirit of particular places, in that process leeching their original content and their embeddedness in local customs. The end result of that process is the transposition of manifold local particularities into one national particularity.[64]

In itself, the romantic gaze is employable for different means. The nation is not its only possible content. Gustav B. Schwab's style, and the effect of invoking a glorious past through particular localities and the stories associated with them, resembles that of

[61] See p. 308–10 and note 10 to this chapter.

[62] See Chapter 2.

[63] See p. 318 and note 36 to this chapter.

[64] This argument follows Mack Walker, who sees the National Socialist vision of a "national community" as the result of an analogous process in the sociopolitical realm, whereby the sense of place felt by hometown burghers was appropriated for the nation by National Socialism. See Walker, Mack, *German Home Towns: Community, State, and General Estate, 1648–1817*, Ithaca, NY, and London, 1971.

Washington Irving in his *Alhambra*. Whether or not Gustav F. Schwab had read Irving, he shared his poetic sensibility, which helped shape his gaze on historic locations. Upon visiting a Moorish palace near Palermo, he fantasized that "one can imagine quite well how the Moorish beauties enjoyed their lives in this place."[65] Here, the content of the romantic mind-set is an orientalist imagination.[66]

Even more important as a medium than literature, paintings powerfully conveyed the same sense of a nationalized landscape as Gustav B. Schwab's works. Gustav F. Schwab indicates the impact that landscape painting had for conditioning his perceptions, when he complained that "I found Mt. Vesuvius more picturesque than it appears in the paintings."[67] Contemporaries explicitly considered landscape and history painting as a medium that could convey a sense of national identity. Nevertheless, the skills that went into this art form, as well as the discourse surrounding their interpretation, were made in a transnational space. Authors, painters, and their audiences shared tastes and aesthetic criteria across borders. Consumers and creators of culture who traveled and translated contributed to this dimension of romanticism as a transnational discourse.[68]

Emmanuel Leutze is a case in point. The German-American painter had come to Düsseldorf, because Wilhelm Schadow's art school had a reputation for producing the finest artists in the fields of landscape and history painting. For his project of creating works of art that expressed the essence of American nationality, Leutze turned to Germany. There he found not only the techniques, but also the themes and ideas that went into German painting at the time.[69]

Perhaps Leutze had read Gustav B. Schwab's works when he decided to travel in Swabia, the land of his birth. The painter's biographer relates that Leutze "spent months in [Swabia], enchanted by its wildly dramatic scenery and *intriguing legends*."[70] The painter's words in 1845 betray the same spirit as the poet's book in their praise of the Free Imperial Cities of medieval Swabia:

[65] Schwab, Gustav Benjamin, *Der Bodensee und das Rheinthal bis Luciensteig*, Stuttgart, 1826; idem, *Wanderungen durch Schwaben* (Das malerische und romantische Deutschland, vol. 2), Leipzig, 1837; Irving, Washington, *The Alhambra*, Philadelphia, 1832; Gustav F. Schwab to Eliza Schwab, Palermo, February 9, 1856, MSS 434, Schwab Papers, series I, box 1, folder 32.

[66] Said, Edward, *Orientalism*, New York, 1978.

[67] Gustav F. Schwab to Eliza Schwab, Naples, February 6, 1856, MSS 434, Schwab Papers, series I, box 1, folder 32.

[68] Groseclose, Barbara S., *Emmanuel Leutze, 1816–1868: Freedom Is the Only King*, Exhibition Catalog, National Collection of Fine Art, Smithsonian Institution, 1976, Washington, DC, 1976; Gaehtgens, Thomas W., and Heinz Ickstadt, eds., *American Icons: Transatlantic Perspectives on Eigteenth- and Nineteenth-Century American Art* (Julia Bloomfield, Kurt W. Forster, and Thomas F. Reese, eds., Issues and Debates. A Series of the Getty Center Publication Program, vol. 2), Santa Monica, CA, 1992, esp. Christadler, Martin, "Romantic Landscape Painting in America: History as Nature, Nature as History," 93–117; Andree and Rickel-Immel, *Hudson*; Bluestein, Gene, "The Advantages of Barbarism: Herder and Whitman's Nationalism," *Journal of the History of Ideas* 24, no. 1 (1963), 115–26; Handlin, Lilian, "Harvard and Göttingen, 1815," *Massachusetts Historical Society Proceedings* 95 (1983), 67–87; Burwick, Fred L., "The Göttingen Influence on George Bancroft's Idea of Humanity," *Jahrbuch für Amerikastudien* [West Germany] 11 (1966), 194–212.

[69] Gaethgens, Barbara, "Fictions of Nationhood: Leutze's Pursuit of an American History Painting in Düsseldorf," in Gaehtgens and Ickstadt, eds., *American Icons*, 149–54.

[70] Hutton, Ann Hawkes, *Portrait of Patriotism*: "Washington Crossing the Delaware," Philadelphia and New York, 1959, 36, my emphasis.

There [in Swabia], the romantic ruins of what were once free cities ... in which a few hardy, persevering burghers bade defiance to their noble oppressors ... led me to think how glorious had been the course of freedom from those small isolated manifestations of the love of liberty to where it has unfolded all its splendor in the institutions of our own country.... [T]his course represented itself in pictures to my mind, forming a long cycle, from the first dawning of free institutions in the middle ages, to the reformation and revolution in England, the causes of emigration, including the discovery and settlement of America, the early protestation against tyranny, to the Revolution and Declaration of Independence.[71]

Even as this might appear as a straightforward statement of American exceptionalism, it was the German landscape that triggered these reflections in the painter's mind. Put into the broader context of Leutze's oeuvre, it becomes just as much an expression of German romantic nationalism.

One of the lesser-known works by the German-American painter was a rendition of Mount Hohenstauffen, an image literally taken straight out of Gustav B. Schwab's tales.[72] Hohenstauffen had been the site of the ancestral castle of the Stauffer dynasty, who had ruled as German emperors from 1138 to 1254, presiding over a period of cultural and economic bloom in German history. Stauffer Emperor Frederick Barbarossa, who had died on crusade in 1190, was the stuff of legend. According to a widely disseminated tale, Barbarossa and his army slept inside Mount Kyffhäuser, awaiting the day when the idea of a German

---

[71] Emmanuel Leutze in 1845, cited by Howat, John K., "Washington Crossing the Delaware," *Metropolitan Museum of Art Bulletin* 26, no. 7 (March 1968), 289–99, quote on p. 295.

[72] Leutze, Emmanuel, Hohenstauffen, Württemberg, ca. 1854, see Groseclose, *Emmanuel Leutze*, 25, 86; Schwab, Gustav B., *Wanderungen*, 96–101, 247–8. Leutze's painting takes the same perspective on the bare mound of Hohenstauffen, with the Rechberg in the front, as the lithograph in Schwab's book (opposite p. 96). The painting embodies the formal language of romantic paintings. The lower three-fifths of the canvas show landscape. Below a diagonal from the horizon to the lower right corner of the painting, rugged rock represents pure nature. From a rock mound near the left side of the painting, a cross reaches up almost to the horizon. Above the diagonal, in the right half of the painting, Mount Hohenstauffen towers above the Rechberg, and reaches into the top two-fifths of the canvas, otherwise filled with sky. A funnel of dark storm clouds rises to the top edge of the painting from a point slightly to the right of the Mount, dominating the upper-right corner. The rest of the sky is filled with indirect sunlight, which illuminates the plain below the cross and gives Mount Hohenstauffen a mystic aura. The dark, billowing clouds evoke the burning of the castle during the Peasant Wars in 1525, while the aura of sunlight hints at the glory of the Stauffers. The Christian cross reaches up from the land into that aura, representing the promise of rebirth of imperial glory from the German soil. The motive of the cross on the mountain as a symbol of romantic nationalism appears in Andreas Achenbach's as well as in Carl Friedrich Lessing's works. Both were influential for Leutze. The use of sunlight and clouds to construct a sense of sublimity can be traced back to Caspar David Friedrich, who frequently uses a spatial composition that invokes a divine presence by directing the view heavenward along lines of landscape and sky. Leutze combines all these stylistic devices in his "Westward the Course of Empire Takes Its Way" (Groseclose, *Emmanuel Leutze*, 60, 96), whose 1861 version displays a cross in a similarly prominent place as the one in Hohenstauffen; as well as in a similar rendition of a German medieval tale by Leutze (ibid., 81). Note that the title of an 1850 Bremish pamphlet had expressed in words almost identical to the name of a Leutze painting the hope that America fulfill the promise of modernity: Andree, Karl, "Hin nach Westen flieht die Weltgeschichte!" Bremen, 1850, cited by Engelsing, "England und die USA," 56.

empire was ready to be revived.[73] Leutze's painting spoke directly to the romantic myth of the Stauffers.

Gustav F. Schwab actively participated in the discourse on the Stauffers when he went to southern Italy. As rulers over a Holy Roman Empire of the German Nation that encompassed the entire Italian peninsula and Sicily, the last Stauffer emperors had taken up residence in Naples. After visiting the graves of Frederick II and Henry VI, Schwab wrote: "What a strange fate it is, that we should find our great German Emperors resting here, but it is understandable that the gentlemen would have neglected their fatherland and wasted their powers on Italy."[74]

Reveling in the romantic sense of failed heroism, Schwab also went on a pilgrimage to the place where the last Stauffer, Conradin, had been beheaded after a betrayed attempt to regain the German and Sicilian crowns by force. Conradin's failure was a tale of lost grandeur, quite to the romantic taste, not unlike that of Boabdil, the last Moorish king of Granada. Disappointed not to find a marker on the unimposing market square in a rundown part of Naples where Conradin had taken his last breath, Schwab had to rely on his historical imagination alone to invest this shabby place with significance.[75] Thanks to the pervasiveness of the Stauffer myth in German art, literature, and education – but even more so, thanks to his ability to adopt the romantic gaze, which enables the viewer to see things that are not there – Schwab was amply primed for this mental effort.[76]

Travel literature assisted those who lacked an encyclopedic knowledge of romantic, historical tales by providing readers with abridged accounts of the stories popularized by art and literature that were associated with the places they described.[77] While Gustav F. Schwab was well read, when his memory was in need of being refreshed he relied on a travel guide written by Friedrich Pecht. "I have grown quite fond of Pecht's book," he wrote to Eliza. "[It] often speaks straight from my soul."[78] Written for an educated class, books like Pecht's drew on the emerging fields of history and art history, which helped shape a perception of the world in national terms. Pecht was a leading figure among writers who did just that. As an art critic in imperial Germany, he was to become recognized as the guardian of the artistic mainstream of conservative modernism.[79] Through Pecht, after climbing the cupola of the Milan Cathedral, Schwab "felt a bit of that pride,

---

[73] In his *Deutschland. Ein Wintermärchen*, Gustav B. Schwab's publicistic nemesis, Heinrich Heine, makes fun of nationalists' hopes for the return of a medieval, feudal monarch. See the translation by T. J. Reed: Heine, Heinrich, *Deutschland: A Winter's Tale*, London, 1986, 58–69.

[74] Gustav F. Schwab to Eliza Schwab, Palermo, February 9, 1856, MSS 434, Schwab Papers, series I, box 1, folder 32. Schwab's "understanding" rests on the obvious beauty of the Italian landscape and the pleasantness of the Mediterranean climate.

[75] Gustav F. Schwab to Eliza Schwab, Naples, February 6, 1856 and Naples, February 24, 1856, MSS 434, Schwab Papers, series I, box 1, folder 32.

[76] Flacke, "Deutschland," 108–11.

[77] Mark Twain, in *The Innocents Abroad*, parodies these very stories, at the same time as he engages in the discourse of travel literature in which they function.

[78] Gustav F. Schwab to Eliza Schwab, Livorno/Milan, March 12, 1856, MSS 434, Schwab Papers, series I, box 1, folder 33. Pecht, Friedrich, *Südfrüchte. Skizzen eines Malers*, 2 vols., Leipzig, 1854.

[79] Bringmann, Michael, "Pecht, Friedrich," *Neue Deutsche Biographie* 20, Berlin, 2000, 156–7.

that a German architect and German art gave Italy this, her most beautiful, cathedral."[80]

There is a certain irony in the story of travel literature in the nineteenth century. The improved means of transportation – steamships and railroads – made pleasure travel available to an unprecedented number of people. This increased mobility created a mass market for travel guides, which, in turn, inspired more tourism. Business promoters and writers often worked hand in hand in this process. Thus Gustav B. Schwab had been asked to write his guide to the Lake Constance region by a publisher connected with a company that had set up steamship service on the lake. In 1840, the opening of railway lines in the region prompted a revised edition of the work.[81]

The prevalent view promoted through the bulk of these guidebooks was one of romantic nationalism.[82] Hence, in an age in which the world was shrunk by the collapsing of space into time, nationality was reinforced as a category of perception for those who crossed national borders for the first time. By giving their vessels names that invoked nationality, the directors of the OSNC were following a broader trend. In appealing to romantic visions of the nation, they catered to the cultural tastes of the traveling public.

Yet Hanseats did not simply exploit national sentiment for gain. Qua their ties to the larger world of the German educated bourgeoisie (*Bildungsbürgertum*), and qua their presence in the transnational space in which romantic styles in art and literature emerged, Hanseats partook in the worldview romantic nationalists put forth. But an aesthetic sense, or a taste for a particular kind of art or literature, does not immediately entail a commitment to a political program. It appears that Hanseats viewed the world through the most national glasses when they dealt with cultural artifacts.[83] In social interaction, and in politics, they continued to rely on their estatist cosmopolitanism throughout the 1850s. Nonetheless, it remains ironic that their transnational activities led Hanseats to help promulgate nationalist perceptions.

The nationalist discourse on aesthetics and nature to which the names of the OSNC vessels appealed was not the only worldview available to Hanseats. Like others in the broader world of educated elites around the Atlantic, Bremish merchants were conversant in multiple, often-conflicting approaches to the world. An Enlightenment tradition that revered the classical world and puritan reservations about its rational content competed with each other and with the romantic nationalist view in shaping their perceptions of the world.

---

[80] Gustav F. Schwab to Eliza Schwab, Livorno/Milan, March 12, 1856, MSS 434, Schwab Papers, series I, box 1, folder 33. Pecht, Südfrüchte.

[81] Klüpfel, Karl [and Sophie], *Gustav Schwab. Sein Leben und Wirken*, Leipzig, 1858, 127.

[82] E.g., Gustav B. Schwab's Wanderungen durch Schwaben appeared in a series of travel guides to Germany, *Das malerische und romantische Deutschland* [Picturesque and Romantic Germany].

[83] One might also include "nature" among such artifacts, to the extent that the landscape in romanticism receives its meaning as the site of particular human activities, be they the reverence for particular places, the tilling of the soil, or the general investment of a region with spiritual significance for a people; just as the spirit of a people is rooted in the land. Hence, the opposition between "nature" and "culture," itself a relic of the one-sidedly rational mind for the Romantic, is transcended. Cf. Schiller, Friedrich, *On the Aesthetic Education of Man: In a Series of Letters*, trans. Elizabeth Wilkinson and L. A. Willoughby, Oxford, 1967 (1793–5).

Gustav F. Schwab's letters from Italy displayed the simultaneity of, and the conflict between, the different habits of perceiving art and nature that were available to him. On visiting a Greek temple to Poseidon, he reveled in its metaphysical properties: "There is nothing mysterious there, everything is crystal-clear and yet there is such a calm majesty and power [in this building], that it becomes incomprehensible after all, what it is that thus animates these colossal stones."[84] Is it the rational clarity and simplicity of the form that conveys the sense of majesty, or is it an ontological essence – divine or otherwise – behind the appearance? Does reason stand on its own merits, or is it the mechanism through which God effects his plan? Schwab's view of the temple embodies the unresolved tension between his affinities for Christianity and the Enlightenment.

Schwab's father, the poet, had had a similarly guilty and conflicted love affair with antiquity. He confided to a friend:

When I am with my Ancients and the "eternal Latin", as Flemming calls it (albeit without any sarcasm), I often have feelings of uncanniness. Through the constant contact with these ingenious unbelievers, I often feel a strange and uncanny paganizing breeze that carries doubts and coldness against that which surely still lives in my innermost self as that which is the most holy and the most true [i.e., Christianity].[85]

Gustav F. Schwab's views were characterized by the same tension. Yet antique artifacts posed a challenge to this Hanseat's moral views not just because of their philosophical and political content, but also because of their sensual form. Philosophically, the skeptical and rational spirit that Hanseats admired in antiquity was the same that they feared in modern socialism and radical liberalism, especially in its democratic variant. Aesthetically, the nudity of ancient statues represented pure humanity, yet invoked an image of indecency. The sight of mass-produced antique representations of the human body in the former private residences of the city of Pompei troubled Schwab: "There is abundant evidence that the Pompeians' morals were not very pure, even though most obscene images etc. have been taken to a cabinet at the museum, where they are not shown."

In assessing Pompeians' morality, a general sense of their decadence contributes to Schwab's verdict: "A certain degree of luxury is common to all [these houses]. Everywhere, one sees painted walls or mosaic floors, and one has to be surprised about this waste of labor."[86] Whether he judged present Sicilians or past Pompeians, the bedrock of Schwab's convictions was a sound work ethic, geared toward maximum productivity. On the foundation of "industry," morality would thrive; just as sufficient industry was an indicator of the morality of a person or a people.[87]

---

[84] Gustav F. Schwab to Eliza Schwab, Naples/Rome, February 29, 1856, MSS 434, Schwab Papers, series I, box 1, folder 32.

[85] Gustav B. Schwab to Ullmann, n.p., December 3, 1819, quoted in Klüpfel, *Gustav Schwab*, 104.

[86] Gustav F. Schwab to Eliza Schwab, Naples, February 24, 1856, MSS 434, Schwab Papers, series I, box 1, folder 32. Schwab would have been aware that the labor that built and decorated these houses was slave labor. Hence, his comment might reflect an association among slave labor, lack of productivity, and decadence/decay.

[87] See also Chapter 2.

Greek art, and the Renaissance sculptors who strove to imitate it, found a warmer reception by Schwab. On visiting the Uffici in Florence, he commented on the statues in the gallery:

First, [I saw] the Venus of Medici [*sic*], about which I had earlier read that she was coquettish; hence she couldn't make too deep an impression; I preferred the capitalinian [*sic*] Venus, since she is more majestic. . . . Opposite, there is the grinder, a slave and barbarian, who lies on one knee, grinding a knife, looking up and listening; here, there is wonderful life in the marble and pure nature. . . . Finally, the eye rests on the last and probably oldest statue, an apollino, or young Apollo from the school of Praxiteles, who radiates the eternal youth of Greece, incarnate; it is impossible to imagine a simpler thing, he leans on a tree trunk, one arm above his head, the other hanging, with a beauty and grace that is incomparable. . . . Among the painters, Titian deserves the price, who painted his maîtresse truly ugly-beautifully, nude.[88]

Here, Schwab's struggle to tell the pure and plain from the indecent is evident. To tell nudity in the image of sinful Adam and Eve from nudity that represents humanity, Schwab's main criteria are the absence of coquettish expression and the presence of simple majesty. His sense of aesthetics allows for sensuality, but not for sexuality. On this basis, he can admit to a vivid nocturnal fantasy: "I dreamt until half past nine the next morning of all the statues, come to life, and not a single flea dared to disturb me in my sleep."[89] Even pesky nature honored his right to these dreams.

While Christianity could conquer inner nature, outer nature required reason to be mastered. Hanseats had to rely on reason to "improve" the world with steamships, railroads, telegraphs, and other technologies that relied on science. Hence, they had to expose themselves to the "uncanny, paganizing breeze" of ancient learning and the rationality that came with it. At the same time, they had to safeguard against the lure of that culture by erecting a bulwark of deeply ingrained, inner-directed Christian morality. As Gustav B. Schwab had put it: "Franklin wrested the lightning-bolt from the hands of Heaven, and the scepter from those of tyrants: believe me, this was one and the same business!" Now that Franklin's heirs had power and science in their hands, they had to learn to use them wisely – not least to avoid that, in turn, less respectable elements would wrest them from their hands.[90]

For Gustav Schwab, being on the cutting edge of technological advances was a value in itself. While he professed his ignorance of industrial technology, he was eager to close the gaps in his knowledge and willing to give these machines the benefit of the doubt.[91] At the same time, Schwab bemoaned the loss of the immediate experience of nature brought about by modern modes of transportation: "When we stepped from the carriage in Marseille at 10 o'clock in the evening, I was surprised to breathe a very mild, balmy air; a change that I had not felt in the

---

[88] Gustav F. Schwab to Eliza Schwab, Livorno/Milan, March 12, 1856, MSS 434, Schwab Papers, series I, box 1, folder 33.

[89] Ibid.

[90] In "Unter Vaters Papieren gefunden" (notebook), n.d. (before 1850), MS 434, Schwab Papers, series II, box 17, folder 213.

[91] Gustav F. Schwab to Eliza Schwab, Marseille, January 14, 1856, MSS 434, Schwab Papers, series I, box 1, folder 31.

heated car."[92] Like many of his contemporaries, Schwab resolved his ambivalent feelings about the Industrial Revolution by selectively embracing some of its benefits, while cognitively separating them from most of its less desirable consequences. Art and aesthetics provided venues through which one could virtually recreate the experience of nature that had been lost, as immediate experience, in the process of industrialization.[93]

Since the Enlightenment, the German educated bourgeoisie (*Bildungsbürgertum*) had felt a special claim to the heritage of antiquity. In the mind of German Enlightenment thinkers, modern Germany could fulfill the promise of a reconciliation of beauty and intellect that had been implied in Greek culture and had been lost in the ascent of Roman culture. In this view, the essence of German national particularity was that this nation embodied this universal promise, and that it could bring it to fruition for the benefit of all humanity. Germans traveling to Italy who looked for traces of universal truth and beauty in the ruins of the peninsula could, hence, perceive these strange artifacts as part of their own heritage. This German calling, however, had been associated with the absence of a strong unitary German state. Political powerlessness became a virtue in that it gave Germans a cosmopolitan, philosophical perspective on the world.[94]

Hence, major representatives of the German Enlightenment, like Goethe and Wilhelm von Humboldt, reacted with disgust to the emergence of romantic nationalism during the Napoleonic Wars. Humboldt complained in 1814 about the growing number of people who "confuse being German with Christianity and knighthood." Goethe echoed this sentiment in 1829, hoping that "our contemporaries . . . may be cured from their pious knightliness."[95] Humboldt and Goethe still rested their hopes for such a cure on the classical legacy of reason. As the nineteenth century progressed, Germans were increasingly primed to perceive art and nature through glasses tinted with a romantic nationalist perspective. This perspective was entirely different from the notion of "being German" that Humboldt had in mind.[96]

For Gustav F. Schwab, the cosmopolitan universalist view of Italian art treasures was still competing with the romantic nationalist view. The claim to universalism had not yet been reconciled with romantic nationalist ideas in a reformulated German nationalism. Moreover, both the romantic nationalist and cosmopolitan universalist views were mediated by, and sometimes conflicted with, a Calvinist

[92] Ibid.

[93] Schivelbusch, Wolfgang, *The Railway Journey: Trains and Travel in the Nineteenth Century*, New York, 1979. See also Chapter 2.

[94] Bruford, Walter Horace, *The German Tradition of Self-Cultivation: "Bildung" from Humboldt to Thomas Mann*, Cambridge, 1975; Levinger, Matthew, *Enlightened Nationalism: The Transformation of Prussian Political Culture, 1806–1848*, Oxford, 2000; Meinecke, Friedrich, *Weltbürgertum und Nationalstaat* (Hans Herzfeld, Carl Hinrichs, and Walther Hofer, eds., Friedrich Meinecke, Werke, vol. 5), Munich, 1962 (1911).

[95] Bratranek, F[riedrich?] Th[eodor], ed., *Goethe's Briefwechsel mit den Gebrüdern von Humboldt (1795–1832)*, Im Auftrage der von Goethe'schen Familie herausgegeben von F. Th. Bratranek (Neue Mittheilungen aus Johann Wolfgang von Goethe's handschriftlichem Nachlasse, part 3), Leipzig, 1876, Wilhelm von Humboldt to Goethe, March 7, 1814, 254, and Goethe to Wilhelm von Humboldt, March 1, 1829, 285–6.

[96] Levinger, Matthew, *Enlightened Nationalism: The Transformation of Prussian Political Culture, 1806–1848*, Oxford, 2000.

morality. While Schwab may have envisioned the nation as a cultural entity compatible with the idea of a *Kulturnation*, he did not rely on romantic nationalism alone to guide his experience of art or nature. Instead, he found that reason and faith were often better suited to make sense of what he found on his travels.

FOREIGN AFFAIRS

Turning to "great politics," we find confirmed that a mere taste for the occasional indulgence in romantic nationalist imagery by no means determined Hanseats' answers to questions of policy and affairs of state. When it came to diplomacy and foreign policy, even when the counterparts were the governments of other German states, Hanseats were singularly uninclined to be guided by fuzzy cultural notions of national character and culture. For protecting shipping lanes, ensuring free trade, and building infrastructure, they put their commercial interests first. If German state institutions were available to meet these interests, they were ready to make use of them. Where they were absent or unwilling, however, Hanseats relied on foreign policy and global, mercantile public opinion to enlist the help of any state willing to do what was in their best interest. While they might have wished for a German central authority to create a unified market and legal system in the hinterland, Hanseats also had reasons to be wary of a possible German nation-state. Within the national movement in Germany, democracy and protectionism enjoyed strong support. Neither one nor the other was palatable to Bremen's elite.

In the 1850s, Germany was not the only place where nationalism and protectionism were almost synonymous. Internationally, economic policy debate in the first half of the nineteenth century was dominated by the conflict between free traders and proponents of protective tariffs. The models held up by the opposing camps were, for protectionists, Napoleon's "Continental System" of European autarky, and for free traders, Britain's liberal reforms of the 1830s. We associate protectionism with a program of creating a national market based on indigenous industrial production, and free trade with a preference for an Atlantic economy and a reliance on Britain as the workshop of the world. The American manifestation of the protectionist school was the "American System." While it went back to Hamilton as a set of policies, it owed its theoretical basis to Friedrich List – the southern German economist who also inspired German protectionists.[97]

Since the 1830s, the primary tool of protectionists for creating a unified German commodity market had been the Prussian-led Customs Union (*Zollverein*). Bremen had not joined the *Zollverein*, mostly because a significant share of the city's trade relied on the reexport of commodities to other, non-German markets. The high tariff barriers surrounding the *Zollverein* lands made an inclusion of the Hanseatic city undesirable to its merchants. Nationalists, however, regarded the *Zollverein* as an important step toward a nation-state. To them, Bremen's refusal to join smacked of a lack of patriotism.[98]

---

[97] List, Friedrich, *The National System of Political Economy*, trans. Sampson S. Lloyd, London, 1928 (1841); Etges, Andreas, *Wirtschaftsnationalismus. USA und Deutschland im Vergleich (1815–1914)*, Frankfurt and New York, 1999. See also Chapter 5 for the Hamiltonian program.

[98] Böhmert, Victor, "Die Stellung der Hansestädte zu Deutschland in den letzten drei Jahrzehnten," *Vierteljahrsschrift für Volkswirtschaft und Cultur* 1 (1863), 73–115.

Their critics may have been justified in saying that the creation of a national industry was not a priority for Hanseats. Bremen's merchants took an interest in the economy of the interior only in as far as it served as a market for their wares, and as a point of origin for the emigrants they carried. For both imports and emigration, Bremen competed with other ports, especially Le Havre and Antwerp, which provided shorter routes to the United States for most of southern Germany, one of the main sources of emigration. Hanseatic agents in Württemberg and Baden worked hard to attract emigrants to Bremen. In doing so, they actively played the national card. By emphasizing the ill treatment Germans received on French, Belgian, and English vessels, Hanseats slowly increased the number of passengers who chose their ships.[99]

Arnold Duckwitz, who served as Minister of Commerce in the revolutionary government of 1848, had had to negotiate the conflicting demands of his home-town and of the interior interests. In his government role, he had attempted to find a formula for satisfying both international trade and national production. He found it in advocating modest protective tariffs only on some manufacturers, a system of free-trade *entrepôts*, and the use of tariffs against nations who denied free trade. Because the revolutionary government and parliament did not last long enough to create a framework of economic policy, his ideas were never put to a test. Still, he had learned to represent Bremen's interests to the interior in a sufficiently national light. His publications during the 1850s were characterized by the attempt to sell Bremen as the "German port" to Germans who held protectionist, if not anti-commercialist leanings.[100]

Hence, in both trade and emigration, Hanseats engaged in a national rhetoric to counter anticommercialist attacks, and to increase their share of business. Where it really counted – in questions of trade treaties and tariffs – Hanseats contested the nationalist assertion that an *economically* unified Germany was preferable under all conditions to a collection of independent states. Bremen, unlike the *Zollverein*, enjoyed recognition under international law as an entity that could enter into treaties. On that basis, the city had built a system of treaties that gave its merchants the benefit of a most-favored-nation status in many countries.[101] The *Zollverein*, not unlike the German Confederation, was a loose treaty system between sovereigns. Its existence was contingent on the continued support of these sovereigns. Its recognition as an entity capable of entering treaties under international law was far from

---

[99] Engelsing, Rolf, *Bremen als Auswandererhafen, 1683–1880* (Karl H. Schwebel [Hg.], Veröffentlichungen aus dem Staatsarchiv der Freien Hansestadt Bremen, vol. 29), Bremen, 1961. See also Chapter 1.

[100] Krieger, Arnold Duckwitz; Arnold Duckwitz to Rudolf Schleiden (in Freiburg i. Brsg.), Bremen, January 20, 1878, February 16, 1878, and February 23, 1878, StAHB 7,116, Nachlaß Rudolf Schleiden, 1 of 5 unnumbered boxes, folder "Briefwechsel Rudolf Schleiden mit Senator Arnold Duckwitz, 1854–1879." See also Engelsing, "England und die USA," 38–9; Best, Heinrich, *Interessenpolitk und nationale Integration 1848/49. Handelspolitische Konflikte im frühindustriellen Deutschland* (Helmut Berding, Jürgen Kocka, and Hans-Ulrich Wehler, eds., Kritische Studien zur Geschichtswissenschaft, vol. 37), Göttingen, 1980.

[101] Fink, Georg, "Diplomatische Vertretungen der Hanse seit dem 17. Jahrhundert bis zur Auflösung der Hanseatischen Gesandtschaft in Berlin 1920," *Hanseatische Geschichtsblätter* 56, Lübeck, Germany, 1932, 112–55; Graßmann, "Hanse weltweit?"

assured. Yet, in establishing and maintaining trade relations, what mattered most were stability and continuity. Bremen had demonstrated that it could provide for both, whereas the *Zollverein* offered no guarantees that it could do the same. Therefore, giving up Bremen's established standing in foreign capitals and ports for the *Zollverein* was a step prudent Hanseats resisted.[102]

In the early 1850s, Arnold Duckwitz, who was increasingly seen as the likely successor to the aging Johann Smidt, justified Bremen's refusal to join the *Zollverein* with the inability of the latter to create lasting foreign-trade relations. To hinterland Germans, Duckwitz nonetheless held up the prospect of Bremen's integration into some form of a unified German economic space. The conditions he listed under which such integration could take place, however, could not be satisfied by the institutions existing in the 1850s. In 1853, he demanded that the German sovereigns yield complete authority to an interstate institution that was to set economic and trade policy. Bremen's ports were to be guaranteed *entrepôt* status by this institution. Eventually, a representative body, composed of delegates from state parliaments, was to set the policies of that interstate institution. It was clear that monarchs who had only just asserted their right not to yield any sovereignty, let alone to parliaments, would not agree to such conditions. The payoff, and possibly the purpose, of Duckwitz's statements was purely political: he confirmed Bremen's commitment in principle to German economic unity, thus deflecting criticism from the city's continued existence as a free-trading, mercantile state with a separate foreign policy.[103]

In 1854, after both Hannover and Oldenburg had joined the *Zollverein*, Bremen had become completely surrounded on land by high tariff barriers. Still, the city remained outside of the union. The *Senat* did, however, negotiate the creation of a *Zollverein* customs office in Bremen, where formalities could be settled in one place, thus reducing the bureaucratic friction.[104] Even if Hanseats, along with a majority of their contemporaries, considered the *Zollverein* as a step on the road toward a nation-state, they did not want to be a part of it.[105]

To achieve its foreign policy goals, Bremen continued to look for allies not in Germany, but across the sea. Bremen's reliance on, and commitment to free trade led the *Senat* toward a foreign policy that looked to international mediation and agreements, not a strengthened German authority, for creating the rules and regulations that governed the Atlantic economy. Building on the strength of its own diplomatic ties, which strongly relied on merchants as consuls in foreign ports, Bremen enlisted the help of her merchants' foreign peers for influencing the policies of different states in a way that was beneficial to the shared interests of a global mercantile class.[106]

Repeatedly in the late 1850s, Hanseats turned to this multilateral approach. Early in 1856, it looked as though Britain and the United States might go to war over the

---

[102] Krieger, *Arnold Duckwitz*.
[103] Ibid.
[104] Schwarzwälder, *Geschichte*, 231–3; Krieger, *Bremische Politik*, 21–2, shows that the office only opened in 1857.
[105] Etges, *Wirtschaftsnationalismus*, 68–78, 114–26; Heine, *Deutschland*, 31–2.
[106] Graßmann, "Hanse weltweit?"

recruitment of filibusters in the Caribbean by British agents. The *Weser-Zeitung* echoed the position Hanseats took on this conflict:

The Hanseatic cities have a deep and unquestionable interest to see these two great commercial powers reconciled, and have every reason to be concerned when questions are brought up which might, if dealt with ineptly, lead to a break between these two powers. . . . May it be permitted to remind them of Mr. [Joshua] Bates [who had chaired an Anglo-American reparations commission after the War of 1812] and suggest a similar procedure? . . . It would be hard to find a more clear-sighted and disinterested man than this champion of London's mercantile world. . . . This way the whole commercial world would have the certainty . . . that the honour of both countries, both of which Mr. Bates is a part of, in a sense, would be entirely preserved.[107]

The *Weser-Zeitung*'s commentary suggests that merchants were ideal guardians of the common good among states. This point of view reverberated with the Kantian idea that increasing commerce would contribute to "perpetual peace." For merchants, every armed conflict was a threat to free trade, and thus to local prosperity. The depiction of Joshua Bates as a citizen of two states reflects the cosmopolitan orientation of Bremen's mercantile community during the 1850s. Rather than embracing a "German" point of view, they identified their interests with a global class of merchants.[108]

We find that Bremen's elite had a long memory for significant events in this Atlantic World. In Hanseats' views, apparently this world had not fundamentally changed in the decades since Bates first played a role as a merchant diplomat. A cosmopolitan reliance on mercantile diplomacy was and continued to be the guiding principle of Bremish foreign policy. This policy found its most remarkable expression toward the very end of the 1850s. Apparently, Hanseats saw in the enlistment of privateers by the British government a particular case of a more fundamental problem: the threat to private property at sea represented by war-making states.

Jan Lemnitzer, in a groundbreaking study, explored a Bremish initiative to "protect private property at sea." To reach their aim, Hanseats made an extraordinary appeal to world public opinion, seeking to mobilize that global class of merchants whom they knew through decades of interaction. They proposed an international convention guaranteeing the safety of private trading vessels by prohibiting their seizure by belligerent parties. Hanseats circulated their call for a ban on economic warfare in all major mercantile centers along the shores of the Atlantic, relying on their private connections to foreign merchants. Within a few months, hundreds of signatures in support of the proposal had been collected. The chambers of commerce of Baltimore and New York threw their support behind the measure.[109]

---

[107] *Weser-Zeitung*, February 12, 1856, Abendausgabe, StAHB, Microfilm FB 311. Apparently the United States had accused the British envoy Crampton of hiring freebooters among the U.S. population.

[108] Kant, Immanuel, *Zum ewigen Frieden* (1795), in Akademieausgabe, Werke, vol. 8.

[109] Lemnitzer, Jan Martin, "'A few burghers in a little Hanseatic town' – Die Bremer Seerechtskampagne von 1859," *Bremisches Jahrbuch* 83 (2004), 87–111, here p. 102; Hardegen, Friedrich, and Käthi Smidt, geb. Meier, *H. H. Meier, der Gründer des Norddeutschen Lloyd. Lebensbild eines Bremer Kaufmanns, 1809–1898*, Berlin and Leipzig, 1920, 144–7; Arnold Duckwitz to Rudolf Schleiden, Bremen, November 18, 1859, StAHB 7,116, Nachlaß Rudolf

By the time the campaign for the "protection of private property at sea" had reached its furthest extent, the Civil War in the United States had begun. Whereas before, the American government seemed willing to take up the cause, Secretary of State Seward now explained to Bremen's Minister Resident Schleiden that it did not seem wise to confront the reluctant British at a time when their intervention in the American conflict was feared. Although this Bremish effort at international politics was unsuccessful, it demonstrated not only the reach of Hanseats' foreign connections, but also their ability to build alliances on issues that mattered to the mercantile class of the Atlantic World.[110]

An appeal to the German Confederation, or to a hypothetical German nation-state, would have been pointless to achieve the Hanseats' goals. In refusing to join the customs union and in pursuing international agreements, Hanseats showed that they did not yet consider their interests well served by creating a German nation-state. Moreover, any attempt to create such a German nation-state would almost inevitably have led to war – precisely what Hanseats hoped to avoid. Politically and culturally, Hanseats were comfortable to fill their niche in the Atlantic space created by the British Empire.

Even close to home, in addressing Danish impediments to free trade, Bremen relied not on the German Confederation but on the United States for help. Denmark leveled a tariff on vessels passing the Sound, the strait between Denmark and Sweden that connects the Baltic with the North Sea. Since the days of the medieval Hanseatic League, Danish control of this strait had been a point of contention between the Scandinavian Kingdom and German traders. In 1855, Hanseats saw a chance to get rid of the nuisance once and for all. Their wish to see the Sound Tariff abolished fell on open ears in Washington. American foreign policy had long made unimpeded commerce a central principle, demanding that rivers, ports, and sea lanes be accessible to vessels from all nations.[111]

American demands for an abolition of the Sound Tariff had a strong ally in Minister Resident Schleiden. As an official in the Danish government bureaucracy in the 1840s, Schleiden had been put in charge of legitimizing the Danish position. Hence, in the late 1850s, as the author of the official policy documents and legal memoranda that supported the Danish position, and as a man fluent in Danish, Schleiden was uniquely qualified to make the case against the tariff in the service of his new Hanseatic employers and in the interest of his host country, the United States. After intense pressure from the United States, Denmark agreed in 1857 to abolish the tariff in exchange for a one-time payment.[112]

Schleiden, 1 of 5 unnumbered boxes, folder "Briefwechsel Rudolf Schleiden mit Senator Arnold Duckwitz, 1854–1879."

[110] Lemnitzer, "'A few burghers,'" 107.

[111] Beutin, Ludwig, *Bremen und Amerika. Zur Geschichte der Weltwirtschaft und der Beziehungen Deutschlands zu den Vereinigten Staaten*, Bremen, 1953, 122–3; *Weser Zeitung*, March 25, 1856.

[112] Schleiden, Rudolf, *Erinnerungen eines Schleswig-Holsteiners. Neue Folge, 1841–1848*, Wiesbaden, 1890, 112. In 1848, as ethnic tension mounted in Copenhagen, Schleiden, along with the rest of the German population of the Danish capital, had fled to Kiel and joined the uprising in the duchies of Schleswig, Holstein, and Lauenburg against Danish rule. After Danish victory in 1849, Schleiden had fled to Southern Germany, and, in 1853, was recruited by Johann Smidt to represent Bremen in Washington, DC. See also Chapter 8.

Even in dealing with its immediate neighbor, Hannover, Bremen used its foreign connections to achieve its aims. As business in Bremerhaven boomed throughout the 1850s, the city and port outgrew the size of the initial Hannoverian cession to Bremen. Since Queen Victoria's ascent to the British throne, Hannover had been ruled by the Guelphs. The new authorities were increasingly hostile to Bremen, and frustrated most attempts of the city to enlarge her possession by the mouth of the Weser. Bremerhaven historian Rita Kellner-Stoll found that Hanseats resorted to a decidedly transnational approach to their problem. In 1861, as Hannover stalled negotiations over a further expansion of the port, Bremen withheld its ratification of a treaty to which Hannover and Britain were also parties, and in which the British government took a strong interest. Informed by Bremish diplomats that some pressure on Hannover in the territorial dispute over Bremerhaven would help speed along Bremen's signature under that treaty, the Queen's officials were happy to be of help. Under British pressure, Hannover ceded a substantial area to Bremen.[113]

The running dispute with Hannover over Bremerhaven was a thorn in the side of Bremen. The city's rulers were not necessarily adverse to the involvement of a central German authority in this conflict. In 1849, with Arnold Duckwitz serving as Minister of Commerce and Minister of the Navy in the revolutionary government, an argument of "national defense" had been Bremen's strongest trump in gaining more land for finishing construction of the new port that was to accommodate the OSNC steamers. As government minister, Duckwitz argued that the port was necessary to harbor the new German navy, then under construction. In that case, Hannover had to yield to Reich authority and had agreed to an expansion of Bremerhaven.[114]

Duckwitz was pragmatic in switching between local, national, and transnational appeals. Until 1848, as chief Bremish negotiator in the talks with Hannover over the expansion of Bremerhaven, his main argument had been that Bremen and Hannover shared an interest in international trade. In 1848, at the same time that Duckwitz used his new national appointment to force concessions from Hannover, he asked President Polk to furnish an experienced American officer to command the German navy, with the rank of admiral.[115] Bremish historian Rolf Engelsing found that while Duckwitz saw the United States as a natural ally for the new Germany, he, along with "many in Bremen, hoped that the United States would protect the city," if the new German nation-state was to adopt a centralist constitution and threaten Hanseatic independence.[116]

In the mid-1860s, many Hanseats were to entertain strong hopes that Prussia, in unifying Germany by force, would lend its power to settling the border dispute once and for all in Bremen's interest. These hopes were to prove unfounded. After

---

[113] Kellner-Stoll, Rita, *Bremerhaven, 1827–1888. Politische, wirtschaftliche und soziale Probleme einer Stadtgründung* (Burchard Scheper, ed., Veröffentlichungen des Stadtarchivs Bremerhaven, vol. 4), Bremen, 1982, p. 116 and note 646.

[114] Ibid., 98–9.

[115] Quaife, Milo Milton, ed., *The Diary of James K. Polk during His Presidency, 1845 to 1849*, 4 vols., Chicago, 1910, vol. 1, 169–71.

[116] Engelsing, "England und die USA," 42, note 2, and 63. It is likely that Ambrose D. Mann, then on a mission to Europe, was involved in this request. Cf. Chapter 4.

Prussia's annexation of Hannover, it continued the intransigent line of its predecessor. Still, these hopes show that Hanseats looked to whichever power seemed most inclined to serve their interests when they steered a course between national and international politics. In the 1850s, these interests led them away from the German nation and toward foreign allies.[117]

NATION AND DEMOCRACY

Perhaps one of the strongest impediments to the Hanseats' embrace of German nationalism was the German nationalists. Political nationalism in 1850s Germany – admittedly suppported by a small crowd – was not only predominantly protectionist, but also increasingly associated with demands for democracy. Because, as we have seen in Chapter 3, no self-respecting member of the Hanseatic elite would advocate popular participation in affairs of the state, sound gentlemanly opinion almost by default precluded an embrace of German nationalism as a political movement or ideology.[118]

Moreover, until the 1850s, Hanseats considered Bremen's independence as indispensable for their business ventures. This independence was guaranteed only by the framework of the German Confederation. Hence, business interests gave Hanseats an added stake in the reactionary status quo in Central Europe.

The year 1849 marked the point when the mainstream of the German middle class parted ways with the radicals and democrats. After the Prussian king, Frederick William IV, had turned down the crown of the German Empire, offered to him by parliament in April 1849, Hanseats, along with the right and center, had withdrawn their support of the revolution. The cabinet under Heinrich von Gagern, including Arnold Duckwitz, had resigned. H. H. Meier had quit his seat in parliament. As far as Hanseats were concerned, those who kept their posts in the revolutionary institutions were irredeemable radicals, whose defeat by Prussian troops in July 1849 they welcomed.[119]

If German unification could not be had within the framework of tradition and legitimacy, at most as a constitutional monarchy, Bremen's elite wanted no part of it. Specifically, they rejected any ideas of turning Germany into a republic. After all, the *Senat* based its authority on the power of tradition, just like the sovereign monarchs of the other German states. Authority legitimized by tradition was the bulwark against the anarchy of democracy. A German republic would have opened the floodgates of democracy by denying the validity and legitimacy of traditional authority.[120]

---

[117] Kellner-Stoll, *Bremerhaven*, 118–29.

[118] See Chapter 3 for Hanseats' rejection of democracy and Chapter 8 for examples of continued Hanseatic antinationalism even in the 1860s.

[119] Siemann, Wolfram, *Die deutsche Revolution von 1848/49* (edition suhrkamp, Neue Folge, vol. 266; as such: Wehler, Hans-Ulrich, ed., Neue Historische Bibliothek, unnumbered vol.), Frankfurt, 1985, 200–7, 216–17; Hardegen and Smidt, *H. H. Meier*, 67–77.

[120] The Bremen chapter of the *Nationalverein* (National Association, see Chapter 8), and hence the most convinced nationalists among Bremen's elite, nearly broke with their umbrella organization in 1862 over the question of whether the *Nationalverein* should demand a reinstatement of the revolutionary Constitution of 1849. The main reason for the rejection of this demand by the Bremen chapter was their objection to the democratic elections prescribed by that constitution. See Biefang, *Bürgertum*, 254–5.

In the early 1850s, Burgomaster Smidt had enlisted the help of the Reaction in rolling back democracy in Bremen.[121] His concern with fighting democracy did not stop in Bremen, however. As many liberal and radical activists of 1848 had fled to the United States, they remained under observation by Bremish representatives. When the *Senat* dispatched Rudolf Schleiden to Washington in 1853, he was instructed to keep track of the whereabouts, conduct, and tendencies of the political refugees who for some years had been migrating from the European states to the United States; as well as of the effect their efforts might have on maintaining a connection with their comrades on this side of the ocean, and among the German population of the United States. Where the honorable envoy should have had occasion to gain detailed intelligence in these matters, it was recommended that he report upon it.[122]

As Schleiden was to rely on the local consuls for the bulk of his information, we can assume that he was expected to enlist their help, as well, in spying on German refugees.

Rather than supporting those democrats and liberals who had stood by the constitution of 1848, and hence by German unity, when Frederick William IV had rejected the crown, Bremen's authorities were actively engaged in their surveillance and, where necessary, prosecution. As the national movement had turned democratic, Hanseats had turned against the national movement. Thus not only were they political opponents of the main current in 1850s Germany that promoted a nation-state, but they also made use of their transnational commercial and diplomatic network to fight it.

CONCLUSION AND OUTLOOK

To call 1850s Hanseats nationalists would do them an injustice. To be sure, they were conversant in the idioms of romantic nationalism and racial constructions. Whenever they commented and passed judgment on individuals, peoples, works of art, or natural phenomena, they employed these idioms. Nationality and race helped them to explain the world and served them to explain their actions and policies to others. But as frameworks of interpretation and as ideologies, nationality and race competed and often conflicted in Hanseats' minds with other ideas. Calvinism and classical learning stood as powerful correctives to nationalist and racist prejudices. In making sense of the world, and of their role in it, Hanseats often found God or Greece more relevant than Germany.

When it came to practical matters, whether in business or in affairs of state, mercantile interests overruled cultural notions in guiding Hanseats' decisions. A nationalist view could not help Hanseats judge their business partners in any useful way. To assess the credibility of an individual, Hanseats ultimately looked to a person's character and work ethic, not his nationality or skin color. Likewise, they

---

[121] Chapter 3.
[122] StAHB, 4,48.21/5.E.1., Bremische Gesandtschaft in Washington. Angelegenheiten des bremischen Ministerresidenten Dr. Rudolph Schleiden (1845) 1853–1862, "Instruction für Herrn M.J. Rudolph Schleiden, bei dessen Sendung nach den Vereinigten Staaten von Amerika" (May 18, 1853), 6.

judged treaties, policies, and institutions not by their benefit to the nation, but by their usefulness for business. The values Hanseats shared with others in a transatlantic mercantile class formed the basis of their convictions. The seed of nationalism had taken root in that ground, but it was still far from becoming a fully grown German oak. During the 1850s, Hanseats' reliance on their estatist-cosmopolitan identity served them well, making the offer of a national identity less appealing.

Their elite cosmopolitanism kept Hanseats at a distance from the nationalist movement in Germany. Nationalism entails the promise of equality – equality as citizens, for civic nationalism, and equality by virtue of shared blood or culture, for ethnocultural nationalism. Hanseats were not prepared to promise equality to anyone, on either ground. They recognized men of sound work ethics and character as worthy of making political and economic decisions. By default, they suspected the lower sorts of failing to live up to these standards. Consequently, Hanseats were more concerned with directing, controlling, and uplifting the many, than with giving them a say in public matters. They would learn in the future that the masses might vote for their betters, but in the 1850s, they were not prepared to offer them that chance.

For their social interactions and business connections, Hanseats relied more on the mercantile class of the Anglo-American Atlantic than on their ties to the German hinterland.[123] The global framework provided by the British Empire was more important to Hanseats – economically, culturally, politically, and militarily – than were the loose and limp skeletons of the German Confederation and the *Zollverein*. The city's standing in that Atlantic World was too important to be sacrificed for the uncertain prospects of a politically or economically unified Germany. During the 1850s, Hanseats found that many of their demands on global trade policy could be met by engaging in mercantile diplomacy within the Atlantic World. From the point of view of their trade interests, they did not perceive a strong need for a German nation-state.

In attracting customers, passengers, and cargo, Hanseats consciously appealed to nationalist sentiment. In selling pitches toward hinterland audiences, Hanseats found a language of nationalism an effective tool. Christening ships in ways that invoked the cultural tastes and habits of the paying public in America and Germany made sense in this context. To take these appeals to national myths at face value, and to interpret them as an all-out endorsement of nationalism, would mean to buy into this sales pitch without considering the entire product on its merits.

The proliferation of wars that began with the Italian War of 1859 changed things for Hanseats. Increasingly, they became convinced that a unified German nation-state was necessary to protect their vessels from hostile foreign powers. Advances in military technology, especially the development of rifled artillery, but also iron-clad war steamers, increased the fiscal threshold for successful military campaigns. The weapons that would decide future wars could only be afforded by large states, backed by large industry. As a collection of small states, with the exception of Prussia and Austria, the German Confederation looked increasingly feeble, and the neighboring countries, especially France and Denmark, appeared increasingly

---

[123] Those ties formed along the Calvinist Axis described in Chapter 2 would be an exception. Their basis was not nationality, but creed.

dangerous. The specters of French occupation (1810–13) and Danish blockade (1848–9) began to make more and more frequent appearances in the Hanseats' rhetoric.

Hanseats had often looked for support from beyond the ocean. In 1848, they had hoped for American protection against centralizing or nationalist excesses in Germany. Unfortunately, Bremen's sturdiest ally, the United States, was busy fighting a Civil War of its own. American foreign policy was occupied with the threat of British intervention. This was not a good time for international cooperation. Moreover, the warring parties in America likewise demanded that foreigners declared their allegiance, and Hanseats were split in their response.

Thus the shift toward embracing nation-states – German or American – was anything but painless or voluntary for Hanseats. In becoming national, Hanseats had to give up much of what had defined them during the golden days of transatlantic trade.

PART III

Decline of a Cosmopolitan Community

7

The End of Merchant Capital

Crisis and Adaptation in a World of Industrial Capitalism, 1857–1890

THE END OF MERCHANT CAPITAL?

The contention that merchant capital "ended" in the latter part of the nineteenth century might invite skepticism. After all, many of the old merchant families of Bremen still exist today. In their view and that of their chroniclers, they exist in an unbroken line of tradition from the nineteenth century, or even farther back.[1] Specific firms and corporations that specialize in trade continue to exist; but this "externally independent" "commodity-trading capital" is no longer the same creature as the fully independent "merchant capital" that existed prior to the rise of industrial-capitalist commodity production.

With Marx, we can understand the difference between the two as a change of function:

Within capitalist production, merchant capital is reduced from its formerly independent existence to a particular moment of capital investment in general, and the averaging-out of profit reduces its rate of profit to the general average. It now functions only as the agent of productive capital. The particular social conditions that formed with the development of merchant capital are no longer dominant; quite to the contrary, where merchant capital dominates, anachronistic conditions dominate. This is even true within a country, where, for example, the purely mercantile cities form quite different analogies with past conditions than the factory towns.[2]

Old, independent merchant capital was economically independent from producers. Here, merchants traded on their own account, buying cheap to sell dear. In lending meaning and stability to their ventures, merchants relied on family ties and mutual trust. By contrast, in fully developed capitalist relations of production and exchange,

---

[1] Mustafa, Sam A., *Merchants and Migrations: Germans and Americans in Connection, 1776–1835* (Aldcroft, Derek H., ed., Modern Economic and Social History Series, unnumbered vol.), Aldershot, UK, 2001; Niehoff, Lydia, *550 Jahre Tradition der Unabhängigkeit. Chronik der Handelskammer Bremen* (Handelskammer Bremen, ed.), Bremen, 2001; Schildknecht, Karl-Heinz, *Bremen und Baumwolle im Wandel der Zeiten*, Bremen, 1999; as well as older works by Ludwig Beutin, Hermann Wätjen, and Percy Schramm. Niehoff's is a solidly argued and researched work of scholarship, whose title (Five Hundred and Fifty Years of Tradition), however, speaks to the self-image of its corporate publisher.

[2] Marx, Karl, *Capital*, 3 vols. (Karl Marx and Friedrich Engels, Werke, vols. 23–5), vol. 3, Berlin, 1979 [1894], 339.

merchant capital becomes a functional appendix to commodity production whose independence as a separate sphere of investment is merely "external." The source of profit is no longer arbitrage, but surplus value production, a share of which devolves upon money- and commodity-trading capital by a process of averaging out the profits among social capitals. The moral and social arrangements that made traditional merchant capitalists a distinct culture are no longer required for the success of the owners of modern money- and commodity-trading capital.[3]

The history of Bremen's merchants between 1857 and 1890, which will be discussed in this and Chapters 8 and 9, appears as an illustration of Marx's findings. One by one, the foundations of this group in its economic, political, and cultural existence crumbled. Those families and individuals who emerged from the upheaval the owners of successful business concerns were no longer beholden to the communal ethos of Hanseatic merchants that had existed in the first half of the century.

A CHANGING WORLD

By the end of the 1850s, a decade of economic expansion had created a changed world. Across the Atlantic World, the Panic of 1857 had annihilated much speculative capital, but the infrastructure created by the industrial boom remained in place. Railroads, gasworks, machine-tool plants, and steamship lines returned to profitability within a year, and their collective impact was one of changing the way contemporaries perceived and experienced the world.

The new economic forms that had arisen during this time likewise continued to bloom: commodity futures, investment banking, joint-stock firms with widespread shareholdership, and the corporation, whose elevation to the legal status of a natural person was imminent in Germany and the United States. Once the economy recovered from the worldwide economic crisis, these new instruments of financial capital were ready to spring back into action and fund further growth.[4]

Improved means of communication and the growth of urban populations, increasingly composed of wage workers, led to the expansion of the public sphere to include the mass of the people. In Germany and the United States, the masses were speaking for themselves with increasing frequency and force. They put on the agenda both the inequities created by the rise of industry and the demand for an increased participation in the administration of public affairs. This democratic tendency was particularly unwelcome to German elites; while in America, where adult, white males enjoyed the suffrage, economic demands and strikes led the middle class to reevaluate their attitude toward the many. For liberals and conservatives alike, the Paris Commune of 1871 only confirmed their worst fears of the

---

[3] This section is based on those parts of Marx, *Capital*, vols. 1–3 (MEW, vols. 23–5), that pertain to merchant capital. Specifically of interest are vol. 1 (MEW 23), Berlin, 1972 [1890], 161–91; vol. 2 (MEW 24), Berlin, 1977 [1893], 31–153; and vol. 3 (MEW 25), Berlin, 1979 [1894], 278–349. See also preceding, xii–xvi.

[4] Beckert, Sven, *The Monied Metropolis: New York City and the Consolidation of the American Bourgeoisie, 1850–1896*, Cambridge, MA, 2001, 145–71.

uncouth urban rabble. The groundwork for the backlash against democracy that followed after 1871, however, had been in place since the 1850s.[5]

Technological progress and expanded industrial production also meant that weapons technology made great strides. Rifled artillery and the repeater-rifle threatened to make warfare much more ferocious and bloody. The high price of this new weaponry also meant that states saw themselves compelled to command a much larger share of the national wealth if they wanted to keep up with their competitors. Drawing on the same types of financial institutions that had funded the expansion of industry in the preceding decade, Prussia, France, and the United States borrowed heavily to ensure their success on the battlefield. Higher taxes and, therefore, an increased role of the state in shaping the economic fortunes of society, resulted. Nationalism, in turn, helped justify the increased burden on the people's resources as a sacrifice for a higher cause. In Germany, these developments rendered the smaller and even medium-size states of the Confederation increasingly ineffective as players in the international system of states. Only Prussia and Austria had the means to modernize their armies, and even they had to strain their finances in doing so.[6]

Politically, Germany remained characterized by the dualism between these rival great powers. While the heartlands of both Prussia and Austria lay within the boundaries of the German Confederation, both states ruled over extensive territories that lay outside of Germany's borders. Northern Italy, Hungary, and a variety of smaller Slavic regions belonged to the Habsburg Empire, but were not included in Germany. The same was true for the regions that had given the Kingdom of Prussia its name, the provinces of Western and Eastern Prussia. As a political entity, the German Confederation was made ineffectual by the Austro-Prussian rivalry, and by the tenuous connection between their respective interests and those of the Confederation as a whole. Only in terms of international law, the confederation played an important role as the guarantor of the independence of the several smaller member states, like Bremen.

A new political force appeared on the German scene in 1859, the National Association [*Nationalverein*]. Even as it was essentially a club of notables, this organization was willing to enlist the general population in support of its political aims. The most important of these aims was the creation of a unified German nation-state; but beyond that, the National Association's program remained vague and was only made more concrete by a string of resolutions passed toward the mid-1860s. To some German elites, the *Nationalverein* seemed to promise a venue to harness the dangerous force of the general populace for a respectable goal, and hopefully to render it inert in the process. After ten years, nationalism had once again become a respectable *political* option, not just a cultural attitude, for the better sort. Other members of Germany's elites, however, continued to fear the linkage between nationalism and democracy, and doubted the ability of the *Nationalverein* to sever this connection. These groups thought that their interests were

---

[5] Ibid., 140–1.
[6] Förster, Stig, and Jörg Nagler, eds., *On the Road to Total War: The American Civil War and the German Wars of Unification, 1861–1871*, Washington, DC, 1997.

better served by the multitude of dynastic and city-states that constituted the German Confederation.[7]

In the United States, the conflict over slavery escalated by the day. The Compromise of 1850, in which the South had relinquished sectional parity in the Senate in exchange for the Fugitive Slave Act, had not created lasting peace. Slaveholders took an increasingly intransigent position, defending the South's "peculiar institution" as a positive good. Federal institutions followed suit. In the Dred Scott decision of 1856, the Supreme Court ruled that slaves did not cease to be property even if removed into a free state. The resulting stepped-up enforcement of the Fugitive Slave Act outraged northern public opinion and contributed to the rise of the Republican Party. Technological progress and economic growth inspired confidence in Northerners in the superiority of their social and economic vision, and lent additional vigor to their opposition to slavery. An increasing number of people on both sides perceived the conflict over slavery as an unbridgeable conflict over fundamentally different visions of American society – a hierarchical society based on agriculture and slavery against an egalitarian society based on industry and wage labor. In 1859, John Brown's raid on Harpers Ferry raised sectional tension to a new high, but slaveholders and their allies still seemed firmly in power in Washington, D.C. While the Republicans had captured the House of Representatives in 1858, the Senate had remained under Democratic control throughout the decade. But in 1860, there were growing demands that the South secede from the union if Lincoln was elected president.

These conflicts and processes in both countries proved impossible for Hanseats to ignore, no matter how much they might have wished to do so and to keep going about their business as usual. But business was changing. The rise of industry created a new class of capitalists, whose political outlook did not match that of merchant elites in either Germany or the United States. These upstarts made their money not in circulation, but in production. To be sure, they still needed merchants to facilitate market exchange; but increasingly, this new class of entrepreneurs called the shots economically. Industrialists tended to look inland, not overseas. They depended first on the completion of national markets, not on ties overseas; and the relative fragility of this new economic sector made them look toward strengthened, unitary states for support. States, in turn, depended on industry, not only for a stable fiscal base, but even more so, for the production of the new weapons that promised to decide future international conflicts. In both America and Germany, the creation of national, unitary states was achieved in a coalition between political leaders and captains of industry, in which the mercantile interest was pushed to the side.[8]

These sudden changes shattered Hanseats' political, social, and economic ties. Some Bremish merchants embraced wholeheartedly the new economy of the day,

---

[7] Hamerow, Theodore S., *The Social Foundations of German Unification: Ideas and Institutions*, Princeton, NJ, 1969; Biefang, Andreas, *Politisches Bürgertum in Deutschland, 1857–1868. Nationale Organisationen und Eliten* (Kommission für Geschichte des Parlamentarismus und der politischen Parteien, corp. ed., Beiträge zur Geschichte des Parlamentarismus und der politischen Parteien, vol. 102), Düsseldorf, 1994.

[8] Beckert, *Metropolis*, extensively treats this shift in economic importance, which he describes with Marx' term of the "subsuming of merchant capital under industrial capital" (p. 301). See e.g., 46–77, 87–90, 131–2, 165, 240–8.

and the political options of strengthened national states that seemed to follow from it. Others wished to maintain their accustomed ways while making concessions to changing conditions. Still others hoped to succeed by fighting the changes or hoping to modify the course of events in a way consistent with their customary practices. The central fact, however, is that Hanseats were no longer of one mind when it came to the most important political and economic choices of the day. Whether or not the growing disharmony among their estate was to blame, by 1867 Bremen would cease to be an independent state, and the Hanseats' ability to influence world affairs would be significantly diminished.

The most important of the choices Hanseats had to make during these years were those between opposing parties in wars. The complexities of the developments and opinions that we find in both German and American societies, the endless debates of those weighing in with suggestions and criticisms, and the entire fabric of public debate were reduced to a simple alternative between two mutually exclusive poles the very moment that weapons began to speak. The choice was between North and South in America, and between Prussia and Austria in Germany. On the western shore of the Atlantic, Lincoln played the role as the unifier of the nation; on the eastern end, that role was played by Bismarck. As part of the simplification of the conflicts, choosing sides became equivalent to supporting or opposing the generally accepted figurehead of unification. Moreover, once these conflicts had taken on a military character, discussions appeared moot, and the fate of the nation appeared to be in the hand of generals and great statesmen. Like many contemporaries, Hanseats found themselves standing on the sidelines, watching passively as the forces of history battled it out on the field. The world that resulted from one side's victory was dealt to them ready-made. They had to take it or leave it – and accordingly adjust their ways of doing business, making politics, and forming social bonds. This is not to say that Hanseats did not weigh in with their opinions and interests. During the years under discussion here, the years that remade the two countries that were most important to them, Hanseats did not fail to attempt to shape the world in which they lived and did business – they merely failed in the attempt.

On both sides of the Atlantic, and across the ocean, economic, political, and social developments mutually influenced each other. Nonetheless, these developments must be analytically separated, if we are to do justice to their respective logic and their specific role. It is, therefore, not to assign a privileged role to economic processes, but to isolate their specific effects on Hanseats, that this chapter focuses on political economy, while Chapter 8 treats political and social developments. Only if understood in relation to each other do the political, economic, and social changes of the 1860s add up to explain the demise of that transatlantic community Hanseats had built in the first six decades of the century.

CHANGES IN BUSINESS IN THE 1860S

By the 1860s, Hanseats had begun to change their business practices. The share of their capital that was directly invested in commodities that they traded on their own account decreased precipitously. Instead, Hanseats began to expand their trade on commission, or even in commodity futures. More and more, Hanseats crossed over into the world of finance, handling stocks and bonds and facilitating financial transactions, in general, between Europe and North America.

Most importantly, the link between shipownership and trade became severed. The rise of ocean-going steamships began to siphon off growing numbers of emigrant passengers. In 1860, the bulk of emigrants still traveled by sailing ship. In that year, only 25.6 percent of all passengers between Bremen and New York traveled by steamer.[9] By 1869, the share of passengers embarking in Bremerhaven on steamers had risen to 74.7 percent. In 1873, the steamers' share had climbed further, reaching 85.5 percent (Table 11 and Graph 7).[10] The days in which Hanseats had been able to offer cheap freight rates, because the emigrants on their sailing vessels had already paid for the cost of the entire journey by the time the ship reached America, were over.

Improvements in technology that made steamers more efficient meant that for the first time, ocean liners could compete with sailing vessels on the price of transportation. Screw propellers replaced side-wheels, compound engines reduced the amount of coal burnt, and steel hulls allowed for larger vessels. The combined effect was to increase the amount of space available on steamers. Below deck, where once coal had been bunkered and machinery hulked, now bales of cotton and steerage passengers generated revenue that turned steamers into profitable investments even without heavy government subsidies.[11]

Sailing vessels were still filling a need in the transportation of bulk cargo and hazardous materials. The Bremish firm of Wätjen & Co., for example, became the world's largest sailing-ship owner by initially specializing in petroleum, which was not a well-received cargo on vessels driven by fire and steam.[12] Still, steamers quickly displaced sailing vessels. In 1860, ten of the sixty-eight Bremish vessels to arrive in New York were steamers. These ten steamers, all owned by the North German Lloyd, accounted for 43.6 percent of the total tonnage of these sixty-eight vessels.[13] By 1869, the twenty-six steamers owned by Bremish firms made up 22.1 percent of the total tonnage of Bremen's merchant marine. By 1873, the fleet of Bremish steamers, now expanded to thirty-eight vessels, claimed one-third of the total tonnage (Table 11). The number of sailing ships owned by Bremish firms

---

[9] StAHB 2,B.13.b.3, _Hanseatica. Verhältnisse der Hansestädte mit den Vereinigten Staaten von Nordamerika. Hanseatische diplomatische Agenten, Konsuln usw. bei den Vereinigten Staaten von Nordamerika und Korrespondenz mit denselben._ In New York, 1815–1868; file no. 15, "Consulat zu Newyork, F. W. Keutgen, 1859 Novb. 1–1861; Gustav Schwab 1862. – . Enthält No. 1–89. 1859 Nov. 1–1868 Okt. 28," document no. 15 of 89, "Bericht des Bremischen Consulats zu Newyork für 1860, Juni 1861," 19. Further reference to this document will be as "StAHB 2,B.13.b.3, file no. 15, doc. 15," followed by page numbers. Although dated "June 1861," it is evident from context that consul Keutgen began writing this annual report early in 1861 and finished it only in June.

[10] Handelskammer Bremen, _Berichte der Handelskammer in Bremen für die Jahre 1870–1873, erstattet an den Kaufmanns-Konvent,_ Bremen, 1874, 71.

[11] Gerstenberger, Heide, and Ulrich Welke, _Vom Wind zum Dampf. Sozialgeschichte der deutschen Handelsschiffahrt im Zeitalter der Industrialisierung,_ Münster, 1996. See also StAHB 2,B.13.b.3, file no. 15, doc. 15, 12–16.

[12] Beutin, Ludwig, _Bremen und Amerika. Zur Geschichte der Weltwirtschaft und der Beziehungen Deutschlands zu den Vereinigten Staaten,_ Bremen, 1953, 86–7.

[13] StAHB 2,B.13.b.3, file no. 15, doc. 15, 24.

TABLE 11. *Steamers and Sailing Vessels, 1860–1873*

| | 1860 – to New York | | | |
	Tonnage (tons)	Share (percent)	Passengers	Share (percent)
Sailing Vessels	32,398	56	11,480	74
Steamers	25,000	44	3,948	26
Total	57,398		15,428	

| | 1869 – from Bremerhaven, All Destinations | | | | 1873 – from Bremerhaven, All Destinations | | | |
	Tonnage (Brem. Last)	Share (percent)	Passengers	Share (percent)	Tonnage (Brem. Last)	Share (percent)	Passengers	Share (percent)
Sailing Vessels	92,884	78	16,063	25	78,790	66	9,171	15
Steamers	26,351	22	47,456	75	39,813	34	54,070	85
Total	119,235		63,519		118,603		63,241	

Sources: For 1860, StAHB 2,B.13.b.3, *Hanseatica. Verhältnisse der Hansestädte mit den Vereinigten Staaten von Nordamerika. Hanseatische diplomatische Agenten, Konsuln usw. bei den Vereinigten Staaten von Nordamerika und Korrespondenz mit denselben*. In New York, 1815–68; file no. 15, "Consulat zu Newyork, F. W. Keutgen, 1859 Novb. 1–1861; Gustav Schwab 1862. – . Enthält No. 1- 89. 1859 Nov. 1–1868 Okt. 28," document no. 15 of 89, "Bericht des Bremischen Consulats zu Newyork für 1860, Juni 1861," p. 19 and 24; for 1869 and 1873, Handelskammer Bremen, *Berichte der Handelskammer in Bremen für die Jahre 1870–1873, erstattet an den Kaufmanns-Konvent*, Bremen, 1874, 71.

declined to 195 in 1873. In that year, the tonnage of the average steamer was 2.5 times as high as that of the average sailing vessel.[14]

The rise of steam meant a rapid concentration of capital in the Bremish maritime industry. All but three Bremish steamers were owned by the North German Lloyd. Because those steamers not owned by the Lloyd were small vessels, the dominance by the Lloyd of transatlantic steamship service amounted to a monopoly in the passengers business and to a dominant position even in the cargo business.[15]

[14] Handelskammer Bremen, *Berichte der Handelskammer*, 71. Because the figures for 1869 and 1873 include many small sailing vessels not fit for transatlantic voyages, we can assume that the steamers' share of Bremish-American trade had climbed above the mark of 1860.

[15] Twenty-three of 26 steamers in 1869, and 35 of 38 in 1873, ibid. For the Lloyd's monopoly in transportation, and public criticism thereof in 1869, see Bessell, Georg, *1857–1957: Norddeutscher Lloyd. Geschichte einer bremischen Reederei*, Bremen, 1957, 34–5, 40.

Graph 7. Steamers and Sailing Vessels, Share of Emigrant Traffic from Bremen, 1860–1874.

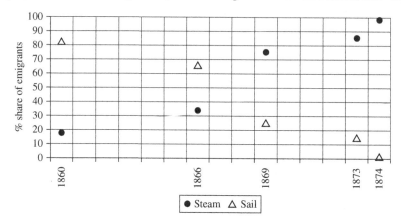

Sources: Bessell, Georg, *1857–1957: Norddeutscher Lloyd. Geschichte einer bremischen Reederei*, Bremen, 1957, 40; Wätjen, Hermann, *Aus der Frühzeit des Nordatlantikverkehrs. Studien zur Geschichte der deutschen Schiffahrt und deutschen Auswanderung nach den Vereinigten Staaten bis zum Ende des amerikanischen Bürgerkrieges*, Leipzig, 1932, 193; also see Table 11.

Friedrich Köper recalled with bitterness that his dreams of carrying on his father's business as an owner of sailing vessels were squashed: "My dream of becoming a great ship-owner was over when big capital, in the shape of joint-stock companies, had taken over steam navigation. It was evident that the great amounts of capital needed for the expensive steamers could not be brought and kept together by private cooperation."[16]

The link between transportation and circulation had been severed, and Hanseats were driven to adopt new business practices.[17] Bremish merchant houses turned from full-scale trading and transportation companies into pure commodity- and money-trading capitalist businesses that handled less and less cargo on their own account. As the opportunities for extraordinary profits in arbitrage and nonequivalent exchange withered (cf. Chapter 1), the margin of profit in trade

---

[16] Köper, Friedrich, "Köper, Lottmann & Cia., Guatemala, Plaudereien über Handelsmarken, Etiquetten, Wappen, etc.," typescript, February 1, 1945, 11, StAHB 7,13, Köper, Friedrich [papers].

[17] Circulation is not synonymous with the movement of objects in space. "A house which A sells to B circulates as a commodity, but it does not take a walk." Similarly, property titles to commodities in storage may change hands repeatedly without the commodities ever being moved. All sales and purchases are acts of circulation, and become activities exclusive to a capitalist form of society. Transportation, by contrast, is a necessity for any society that does not wholly rely on local self-sufficiency. It is tied to the use value of goods. This remains true in capitalism. In order to realize surplus value, a commodity has to meet the need of a solvent consumer, and thus has to be moved to him. While circulation and transportation are synonymous when the merchant owns the commodity he ships, they are severed with trade on commission. Futures trading is only an extreme form, in which promises to buy or sell commodities at a certain place and time appear to take on lives of their own. See Marx, *Capital*, vol. 2, 150–1.

dropped, driving some smaller companies out of business. Herman Henrich Graue, for example, quit his mercantile business to join the manufacturing concern of Wilhelm Wilkens in Baltimore.[18] Other firms stayed in business, but sold their sailing vessels. Oelrichs & Co. took this step in 1862. From that point on, the company specialized in commissions, commodity trading proper, and ticket sales for passenger steamers.[19] Lürman & Co. of Baltimore tried to sail against the wind, without much success. In 1861, the firm's ships earned $23,284.82 on their voyages. In the four years after that, Lürman's vessels lost money as often as they turned a profit. That profit, however, never reached the level seen in 1861 (Table 12).

The balance sheet of Lurman & Co. of Baltimore for 1861 to 1865 shows that commission trade and financial transactions rapidly displaced the trade with commodities owned by the firm and transported on its own vessels. "Adventures" – the journeys of the company's sailing vessels – had been the source of two-thirds of the firm's profits in 1861. In 1862 and 1864, this share dropped to one-third. In 1863 and 1865, the company even lost money on its adventures. By contrast, the importance of commissions for the firm increased. The income from this source, however, could not compensate for the loss of the decline in proper trade. Banking, gold, and stock became more important for Lurman & Co., but the volatility of financial markets rendered these branches of business an unpredictable source of income: a substantial share of the firm's profits from the preceding years was wiped out by losses in the financial markets in 1865. Some of these losses might have represented outstanding debts of Southern planters that had to be written off (Table 12).

Over the course of five years, the firm made a total profit of $33,832.84, just $6,766.57 per year, on average. The associates of the firm were able to extract a total of only $12,188.29 during this time. For two associates, this makes for an annual income of $1,218.82 each (Table 12) – hardly sufficient to sustain a proper Hanseatic lifestyle. In these five years, characterized by the Civil War and the transition of the firm to a modern money- and commodity-trading enterprise, the Lürmans must have lived off their savings, or possibly their income from real estate. Nonetheless, the firm survived these doldrums. Gustav W. Lürman's heirs successfully ran the firm until the turn of the twentieth century.[20]

---

[18] According to Baltimore chronicler J. Thomas Scharf, Graue had been funding Wilkens's manufacturing concern since 1853, and took over his factories after Wilkens's death in the 1870s. Graue's correspondence with his brother, however, suggests that he remained active primarily as a merchant as late as 1860 (see note 18 to Chapter 5). This Wilhelm Wilkens, while also from Bremen, had no relation to the merchant family of Julius Wilkens and his brothers, discussed in Chapter 1. Graue also stepped into Wilkens's shoes in the leadership of the horse-drawn Baltimore and Catonsville Passenger Railroad Company. Wilkens had been the director of this railroad after it was founded in 1860. In 1868, Wilkens stepped down, and Graue became treasurer of the company. See Scharf, J. Thomas, *History of Baltimore City & County*, 2 vols., Philadelphia, 1881, vol. 1, 368, 422–3.

[19] Oelrichs & Co., *Caspar Meier and His Successors*, New York, 1898, 39–48.

[20] See Chapter 1.

TABLE 12. Lurman & Co., Balance Sheet, 1860–1865

US$	1861		1862		1863		1864		1865		1861–5			
	Losses	Profits	Losses	Profits	Losses	Profits	Losses	Profits	Losses	Profits	Share (percent)	Losses	Profits	Share (percent)
Payments to Associates	6,797.20		2,662.68		2,728.41						22	12,188.29		
Adventures	766.08	23,284.82		6,444.95	823.13			4,025.88	2,677.78	2,447.56	8	4,266.99	36,203.21	40
Guarantee		2,695.61											2,695.61	3
Tea a/c[a]		121.26		213.98		262.35		184.70		51.52			833.81	1
Tobacco a/c		453.28		619.73				462.93		23.97			1,559.91	2
Coffee a/c						9,619.79							9,619.79	11
Commissions		8,730.90		1,683.94		2,863.10		5,972.49		1,132.00			20,382.43	23
Charges a/c	2,125.71		5,667.24		6,016.93		5,207.20		7,984.16		48	27,001.24		
Exchange a/c		1,592.00		7,310.45		2,272.36		2,544.91	10,363.28		19	10,363.28	13,719.72	15
Sales of Scrip				2,707.60		1,569.65		100.00					4,377.25	5
Gold a/c								452.09	179.42		0	179.42	452.09	1
Stock a/c									2,011.76		4	2,011.76		
SUM	9,688.99	36,877.87	8,329.92	18,980.65	9,568.47	16,587.25	5,207.20	13,743.00	23,216.40	3,655.05	100	56,010.98	89,843.82	100

[a] "a/c" stands for "account current."

Source: Lurman & Co., Balance Sheet, folder "1830–1867 E.G. Oelrichs and Lurman Company," box 2, MdHS MS.541, Lurman, Gustavus W., 1809–66, Papers and genealogy, 1833–1945.

THE NEW ECONOMY AND THE RISE OF FRIEDRICH WILHELM KEUTGEN

One firm in New York looked like a particularly promising example of Hanseatic adaptation to the changing times. Friedrich Wilhelm Keutgen was the front-runner in a large field of men who hoped to become Bremish consul in New York, after Edwin A. Oelrichs' resignation from that post in 1859. The nature and geographical reach of Keutgen's references, as well as the arguments he and his supporters marshaled in his favor, betray his involvement in the "new economy" of the day.[21]

Keutgen and his non-Hanseatic associates, Gelpcke and Reichelt, were active in banking, both on their own account and as the American agents for the *Dessauer Creditanstalt für Industrie und Handel*. Founded in 1856, and modeled after the French *Crédit Mobilier*, this institution was in the business of providing long-term credit for capital investment, as well as short-term credits for circulation and operation, to manufacturing and transportation concerns.[22] Among these concerns was the North German Lloyd. The *Creditanstalt* controlled 37.5 percent of the steamer line, and by some accounts, it had been for this reason that Gelpcke, Keutgen & Reichelt had been given the Lloyd's agency for New York.[23]

As agents for the *Creditanstalt*, and on their own account, Keutgen and his associates facilitated the investment of German capital in U.S. land, mineral resources, and especially railroads.[24] Keutgen had initially made his name in traditional Hanseatic ventures, trading cotton, sugar, and tobacco from the South. In the 1850s, Gelpcke, Keutgen & Reichelt had heavily extended their interests to include

---

[21] StAHB 2,B.13.b.3, *Hanseatica. Verhältnisse der Hansestädte mit den Vereinigten Staaten von Nordamerika. Hanseatische diplomatische Agenten, Konsuln usw. bei den Vereinigten Staaten von Nordamerika und Korrespondenz mit denselben.* In New York, 1815–1868; file no. 7, "Acta betr. die Resignation des bisherigen bremischen Consuls Edw. A. Oelrichs zu Newyork und die Ernennung des Kaufmanns Friedr. Wilh. Keutgen dortselbst zu seinem Nachfolger, 1859 April 4. – 1860 Jan 14." Further reference to this file will be as "StAHB 2,B.13.b.3, file no. 7," followed by page numbers. Keutgen's, unlike other firms, left a paper trail that allows us to reconstruct its activities much more extensively than is true for any other Hanseatic concern. Because Keutgen's story is instructive for the economic challenges Hanseats faced in the 1860s, a significant part of this account will be devoted to his activities.

[22] Rosenberg, Hans, "Der Weltwirtschaftliche Struktur- und Konjunkturwandel von 1848 bis 1857," in *Probleme der Reichsgründungszeit 1848–1879*, ed. Helmut Böhme, Cologne and Berlin, 1972, 159–92, see p. 181 for the *Dessauer Creditanstalt*. Although originally published in 1934, Rosenberg's essay still provides a definitive overview of the world economy in the third-quarter of the nineteenth century and of Germany's role in it.

[23] See Chapter 1; Vagts, Alfred, "Gustav Schwab 1822–1880. Ein deutschamerikanischer Unternehmer," in *1000 Jahre Bremer Kaufmann. Aufsätze zur Geschichte bremischen Kaufmannstums, des Bremer Handels und der Bremer Schiffahrt aus Anlaß des tausendjährigen Gedenkens der Marktgründung durch Bischof Adaldag 965* (Bremisches Jahrbuch, vol. 50), Bremen, 1965, 337–60.

[24] *C. Winters [sic] Oeder v. Herman Gelpcke*, Consul of the Principality of Dessau, Frederick W. Keutgen, Consul of the City of Bremen at the Port of New York, and Adolphus Reichelt, Case File A-16-387, Admiralty Case Files, United States District Court for the Southern District of New York, Records of the District Courts of the United States, Record Group 21, National Archives – Northeast Region, New York.

midwestern grain, not a commodity usually dealt in by Hanseats at that time.[25] With his associates from the German hinterland, Keutgen had become heavily involved in the continental expansion of the American economy, and had largely exited the business of trading on his own account those staples of slave labor that formed the backbone of other Hanseats' trade interests.[26]

The degree of the firm's involvement with the opening of the American West is demonstrated by Herman Gelpcke's election in December 1860 to the board of the New York Central Railroad.[27] Cornelius Vanderbilt's latest venture was a railroad that had been founded to establish a trunk line from New York to Chicago, with hopes of drawing the exports from the American breadbasket to New York.[28] A relative of Gelpcke's was a banker in Chicago, the center of the midwestern commodity markets.[29] Apparently, Gelpcke, Keutgen & Reichelt had a hand in all stages of the export business from the newly opened West.

Transatlantically, the firm remained tied to Bremen's interests. As agents for the North German Lloyd, the three businessmen represented the transportation concern that was the lifeline for Hanseatic American commercial relations. Rather than buying or selling commodities, however, Gelpcke, Keutgen & Reichelt were increasingly involved in facilitating commerce in a role as pure merchant bankers. For example, between 1858 and 1860, Gelpcke, Keutgen & Reichelt kept an account for Wilhelm E. Quentell of Bremen, a cotton importer, with Henry Rodewald & Co. of New Orleans, a Hanseatic cotton exporter. Relying on the customary trust among Hanseats, Quentell instructed Keutgen's firm to honor Rodewald's drafts up to a line of credit of $50,000 even when not accompanied by a bill of lading for a cotton shipment. The cotton would be shipped directly to Bremen, but the account between the exporter and the importer would be settled by their intermediary in New York. Essentially, Gelpcke, Keutgen & Reichelt were giving long-term circulation credit to Hanseatic merchants.[30]

---

[25] See Keutgen's annual report for 1860. Written in June 1861, this document can be read as an attempt to vindicate himself in the eyes of the *Senat*. StAHB, 2,B.13.b.3, *Hanseatica. Verhältnisse der Hansestädte mit den Vereinigten Staaten von Nordamerika. Hanseatische diplomatische Agenten, Konsuln usw. bei den vereinigten Staaten von Nordamerika und Korrespondenz mit denselben.* In New York, 1815–1868, file 15, "Consulat zu Newyork, F. W. Keutgen, 1859 Novb. 1–1861; Gustav Schwab 1862.–. Enthält No. 1- 89. 1859 Nov. 1–1868 Okt. 28," document 15, "Bericht des Bremischen Consulats zu Newyork für 1860, Juni 1861."

[26] This shift in Keutgen's interests mirrors the shift made by increasing numbers of non-Hanseatic New York merchants. See, e.g., Beckert, *Metropolis*, 131–7, 144; Adler, Jeffrey S., *Yankee Merchants and the Making of the Urban West: The Rise and Fall of Antebellum St. Louis,* Cambridge and New York, 1991.

[27] "Monetary Affairs," *New York Times,* December 8, 1860, 3.

[28] Cronon, William, *Nature's Metropolis: Chicago and the Great West,* New York and London, 1991. According to Hermann Wätjen, the leading Bremish representatives on the U.S. East Coast, Rudolf Schleiden, Edwin A. Oelrichs, and Albert Schumacher, "did not hold Vanderbilt in high esteem. They considered him the typical self-made man, whose chief character traits were a desire for profit, egotism, brutal recklessness, and untrustworthiness." See Wätjen, Hermann, *Aus der Frühzeit des Nordatlantikverkehrs. Studien zur Geschichte der deutschen Schiffahrt und deutschen Auswanderung nach den Vereinigten Staaten bis zum Ende des amerikanischen Bürgerkrieges,* Leipzig, 1932, 60–1. Apparently, Keutgen and his associates did not share this appraisal of Vanderbilt with the minister-resident and the two consuls.

[29] "Law Reports. Rights of Consuls," *New York Times,* August 21, 1861, 3.

[30] "A Long-Litigated Case," *New York Times,* October 23, 1879, 2. Keutgen's name is misspelled in the article.

Its manifold ties to Bremish commerce made Keutgen's firm a part of the Hanseatic network. But the reach of the firm's connections on the German side extended beyond Bremen, as witnessed not only by its connection with the *Dessauer Creditanstalt*, but also by the number of consulships the partners held. Keutgen already represented the Duchy of Hesse-Darmstadt,[31] while Gelpcke was consul for Saxe-Anhalt, the principality in which the city of Dessau was located.[32] These small German states contained some of the most aggressive new investment banks in Germany.[33] Adding the representation of Bremen, the German state most important in transatlantic trade relations, would have rounded off what amounted to a small consular empire.

With this impressive portfolio alone, Keutgen could have become the poster child for the successful transition of Hanseatic merchants to the new economy of banking, stocks, commodity trading, and industrial transportation concerns. But Keutgen also had the requisite, customary background shared by most Hanseatic merchants in the United States. He came from an old Hanseatic family and maintained connections with his relatives who remained active in Bremen. Like other American Hanseats, Keutgen had been an apprentice in a merchant firm in Bremen. Since coming to the United States in 1849, he had acquired American citizenship. Keutgen's connection with Bremish interests had been reaffirmed when his firm had received the New York agency for the North German Lloyd.[34]

Since the inauguration of its New York line, the Lloyd had managed to capture a growing, yet far from overwhelming, market share. The return on the expensive investments, however, was catastrophic. The share price had plummeted from 90 to 28 percent of its nominal value between 1857 and 1859. Since the inception of transatlantic service, shareholders had not seen a single Thaler of dividends. Wrecks of the steamers *Hudson*, *Weser*, and *Bremen* between August 1858 and January 1859 had made investors understandably nervous, and had not helped the company's reputation. On the *Weser* and the *Bremen*, the machinery had failed during storms on the high seas. Their passengers had been extremely lucky to survive the experience, and their stories were a public relations disaster for the Lloyd.[35]

In 1856, the *Dessauer Creditanstalt* had been the only banking institution in Germany willing to extend the considerable funds needed to set up a steamship

---

[31] StAHB 2,B.13.b.3, file no. 7, 29–30.

[32] Brief by the attorneys of C. Wintgens Oeder, August 6, 1861, in the case of *C. Winters* [*sic*] *Oeder v. Herman Gelpcke*, Consul of the Principality of Dessau, Frederick W. Keutgen, Consul of the City of Bremen at the Port of New York, and Adolphus Reichelt, Case File A-16–387, Admiralty Case Files, United States District Court for the Southern District of New York, Records of the District Courts of the United States, Record Group 21, National Archives – Northeast Region, New York.

[33] Cf. p. 344.

[34] StAHB 2,B.13.b.3, file no. 7, pp. 25–6 and G. W. Krüger to Senat der Freien Hansestadt Bremen, New York, September 27, 1861, StAHB 2,B.13.b.3, *Hanseatica. Verhältnisse der Hansestädte mit den Vereinigten Staaten von Nordamerika. Hanseatische diplomatische Agenten, Konsuln usw. bei den Vereinigten Staaten von Nordamerika und Korrespondenz mit denselben. In New York, 1815–1868*; file no. 10, "Acta betr. die Resignation des Consuls Keutgen zu Newyork und Ernennung des Kaufmanns Gustav Schwab daselbst zu seinem Nachfolger, 1861 Mai 27. – Decbr. 18," 35. See also the advertisement by Gelpcke, Keutgen & Reichelt in the *New York Evening Post*, March 4, 1861, 1.

[35] [North German Lloyd Steamship Company, Bremen], *70 Years North German Lloyd Bremen, 1857–1927*, Berlin, 1927, 31–2.

enterprise. The bank now saw its fortune tied to the success of the Lloyd, and the directors of the bank were openly discussing the liquidation of Lloyd assets. The Damrstädter Bank had already dumped its shares on the market at a loss. Although the latter institutions had held only a small share of stock, the sale had sent a message of nonconfidence to financiers.[36] Because the Lloyd was the only Bremish player in the field of steamship travel, its success was increasingly considered coterminous with that of Bremish commerce at large. Hence, Bremen's mercantile elite rallied around the battered steamer line.[37]

In 1859, New York was still the only North American destination for the struggling steamship company, and the line from Bremerhaven to New York was of central importance to its long-term success. The Lloyd trusted Keutgen with an assignment crucial for the company's survival. Keutgen's enthusiasm for Bremen's shipping interests suggests that this trust was well deserved. In early 1861, he admonished the *Senat* to "suitably support an institution [the Lloyd] which is more than any other bound to Bremish blood, and which every Bremish burgher should eagerly support, even if every Thaler he gave to this institution was lost."[38]

In early 1861, it appeared that investors might lose their every last Thaler to the steamer line. Both the Lloyd, and the Bremer Bank – Bremen's contribution to the flurry of bank foundings in the years preceding the Panic of 1857 – were joint-stock companies, and H. H. Meier had been the driving force behind their creation. In 1856, H. H. Meier had managed to overcome traditional Hanseatic hostility to joint-stock enterprises, convincing many of his peers to invest in these companies. After five years of faring miserably, the continued trust of Hanseatic investors in the Lloyd was by no means assured. External stockholders, especially the *Dessauer Creditanstalt*, were pressing for a liquidation of the company. This bank was only 13.6 percent short of a majority of shares. The Lloyd could not afford losing the support of individual Bremish investors. Fortunately, the overwhelming majority of them seem to have shared Keutgen's point of view.[39]

Keutgen and Meier were kindred spirits in their business practices. They enthusiastically embraced the new economic forms that had arisen during the boom of the 1850s, putting them to work for Bremen's trade interest, but expanding its reach and nature in the process. Like Keutgen, Meier had expanded his interests inland. In a strategy of vertical integration, he acquired coal and iron mines, a foundry, and a

---

[36] Ibid., 25–32.

[37] The Bremish Handelskammer, for instance, referred to the Lloyd as a "company which serves the common good." StAHB 2,B.13.b.3, *Hanseatica. Verhältnisse der Hansestädte mit den Vereinigten Staaten von Nordamerika. Hanseatische diplomatische Agenten, Konsuln usw. bei den Vereinigten Staaten von Nordamerika und Korrespondenz mit denselben.* In New York, 1815–1868; file no. 7, "Acta betr. die Resignation des bisherigen bremischen Consuls Edw. A. Oelrichs zu Newyork und die Ernennung des Kaufmanns Friedr. Wilh. Keutgen dortselbst zu seinem Nachfolger, 1859 April 4. – 1860 Jan 14," 33–4. Further reference to this file will be as "StAHB 2,B.13.b.3, file no. 7," followed by page numbers. The phrase "gemeinnütziges Unternehmen," which the Handelskammer used, if taken in its meaning as a legal term, translates as "nonprofit corporation." Here, it is used in its literal meaning, as a "company that benefits the public."

[38] StAHB 2,B.13.b.3, file no. 15, doc. 15, 18.

[39] Bessell, *1857–1957: Norddeutscher Lloyd*, 17–20, shows, among other things, that Meier explicitly emulated the business model of the French Crédit Mobilier in his founding of the North German Lloyd and the Bremer Bank.

brewery to serve as suppliers to the Lloyd.[40] To finance their endeavors, both men made use of financial instruments like joint-stock companies, which constituted a radical departure from the traditional reliance of Hanseats on the family fortune and the resources of their own house. In the enterprises of both men, stockholder value supplanted the welfare of the family as the *raison d'être* of the business. Keutgen and Meier thus no longer functioned as traditional merchant capitalists; they were becoming agents of money- and commodity-trading capital in an industrial world market.[41]

H. H. Meier's words on the occasion of the first transatlantic trip of a Lloyd steamer show his ability to speak with the voice of a national bourgeoisie, as well as with that of a Hanseat:

We are quite aware of the greatness of our mission and the great difficulties of our task – for it is not enough to get the capital together, to build the ships and to start the service, we must also secure a reasonable interest for our capital, otherwise our institution has no *raison d'être* and cannot, in the long run, work with any benefit .... . *In our flag – an anchor crossed by the Bremen key* [the heraldic symbol of the city] *and surrounded by an oak wreath – you see our motto. The anchor is a sign of our hope that the key will open for us the traffic roads which we will hold with German perseverance, loyalty, and manly vigor.*[42]

With the example of men like Meier and Keutgen, Hanseats might well have been led to accept the need for change in the way they did business. If Bremen merchants had overcome their dislike of banking and stock trading for the purpose of founding the Lloyd, maybe they could be brought to accept a banker and stock trader as their consul in New York, especially because he represented the very bank that had made possible the founding of the steamship line. Hence, Keutgen looked like the most promising candidate for the consulship.

FAMILIES OR STOCKHOLDERS?

We can only imagine that H. H. Meier must have been torn in his preferences. After Edwin Oelrichs had stepped down as consul, Rudolf Schleiden had appointed another associate of Oelrichs & Co., Gustav F. Schwab, as consul pro tempore. Family ties would have suggested to Meier convincing Schwab to apply for the job in permanence.[43] Keutgen, by contrast, represented Meier's most important business venture. Meier would not have lacked the leverage to promote Schwab at the expense of Keutgen. He played a leading role in the *Bürgerschaft*. We do not know whether Meier voiced any opinion at all on the succession in the consulate. We can know, however, that as director of the Lloyd, Meier could no longer bring the will of the private individual and that of the agent of capital into congruence.

---

[40] Hardegen, Friedrich, and Käthi Smidt, geb. Meier, *H. H. Meier, der Gründer des Norddeutschen Lloyd. Lebensbild eines Bremer Kaufmanns, 1809–1898*, Berlin and Leipzig, 1920, 152–4, for Meier's strategy of vertical integration. Oelrichs & Co. began in the 1870s to sell directly to manufacturers in the United States. See Oelrichs & Co., *Caspar Meier and His Successors*, 41.

[41] See Introduction.

[42] [North German Lloyd Steamship Company, Bremen], *70 Years*, 30, English in the original, emphasis in the original.

[43] See Chapter 1.

The record suggests that the tensions between traditional forms of family-based, political and personal loyalty, on the one hand, and the demands the new economy and its representatives made of the state, on the other hand, necessitated a discussion process more drawn out than one might have expected in light of the importance of the consulate. Keutgen's competitors paraded in their applications with long lists of references that, combined, read like a Who's Who of the Hanseatic elite.[44]

In the end, Bremen's mercantile establishment was convinced by Keutgen's references. On June 18, 1859, the *Handelskammer*, responding to the *Senat*'s request to give its opinion on the candidates, recommended appointing Keutgen, "who is particularly qualified for the post in question." The chamber's statement specifically endorsed a view Keutgen's supporters from the German hinterland had advanced: "The agency for the *North German Lloyd*, bestowed on [Keutgen's] house, is to be taken into account; in that a closer connection between *that company, which serves the common good*, and the consulate, can be expected to have manifold advantages."[45]

The Commission on Foreign Affairs took another two weeks after receiving the *Kammer*'s vote, before it presented the *Senat* with its recommendation. Only after "manifold interviews and after taking into consideration all circumstances" did the commission come out in favor of Keutgen. The somewhat Byzantine nature of a process that is most of all carried on orally makes it impossible to know what was discussed. Yet it remains significant that it took the *Senatoren* in charge of Foreign Affairs until July 1 to come to a conclusive vote.[46]

The imperative of the new economy won out over the politics of personal acquaintance, and the ties established by stockholdership proved stronger than those between families when the *Senat* finally appointed Keutgen as Bremish consul for New York. None of the competing claims to political office that were based primarily on family ties and personal acquaintance were successful, and the consul's seal was handed over to a man representing a capitalist enterprise of industrial transportation and its financiers.[47]

We can read in the appointment of Keutgen the signs of a spreading general crisis of the mercantile world, of the "subsumption of merchant capital under industrial capital." Instead of the old mercantile nexus of family, business, and local political power, we see at work in Keutgen's successful application, and in the lobbying effort of his friends, the formation of a German national bourgeoisie. Unlike his fellow applicants for the consulship, Keutgen's business partners were not part of the Hanseatic trading network. They did not owe their wealth to the traditional staples of Hanseatic trade, and they had only *ex post factum* established the Bremen connection through their partnership with Keutgen.

---

[44] The other applicants were Carl Lüling (firm of D. H. Wätjen & Co.), Georg Mosle (Pavenstedt & Co.), and John A. Pauli (Caesar & Pauli). See StAHB 2,B.13.b.3, file no. 7, pp. 9–21.

[45] StAHB 2,B.13.b.3, file no. 7, pp. 33–34, my emphasis. See pp. 29–31 of the same file for letters by Adolf Reichelt and Dessau Mayor Aukemann (?), a board member of the *Creditanstalt*, who supported Keutgen.

[46] StAHB 2,B.13.b.3, file no. 7, 35.

[47] Ibid., 13, 17, 21 (applications by Messr. Lüling, Mosle, and Pauli).

The mobilization of political support for Keutgen, likewise, centrally involved men from outside the Hanseatic network. The mayor of Dessau, who wrote to Duckwitz on Keutgen's behalf, was the director of a classical type of venture for this phase of industrialization, the German Continental Gas Company of Dessau, as well as a board member of the *Creditanstalt*.[48] That bank, in turn, was among the few independent sources of "venture capital" in the German states. Chartered by the Grand Duchy of Saxony-Anhalt, the *Creditanstalt* owed its existence to an attempt by a state that lacked the resources to play a military-diplomatic role equal to even Bavaria and Württemberg, let alone Prussia or Austria, to gain political leverage through the fields of industry and finance.

Hesse-Darmstadt – represented by Keutgen in New York – shared the strategic concerns of Saxe-Anhalt. Like the *Creditanstalt*, the *Darmstädter Bank* differed from the older, private banks of Germany in that it was specifically designed to fund daring industrial enterprises. The new Prussian banks that had emerged during the 1850s were too heavily regulated to engage in much investment banking. Moreover, whereas the banks in the smaller states were left to leave their business decisions based purely on free-market considerations, Prussia pressured its banks to serve the military and political aims of the monarchy. When the liberal majority in the Prussian Diet refused funding for a modernization of the army, Bismarck bought new arms with extrabudgetary funds lent to the state by Prussian bankers.[49]

Keutgen and his partners were associated with the increasingly dense network of German bankers and industrialists who had begun to build a nation in the interstices of the morbid framework of the German Confederation. The material wealth, institutions, and infrastructure they created might have rested on the legal framework provided by dynastic states. There was, however, no doubt in the minds of these protagonists of economic change that they were building a new, modern Germany that would eventually sweep away the vestiges of feudal power and replace them with a nation-state.[50]

The cooperation of businessmen cultivated by tradition-minded Hanseats was based on estate consciousness and personal credibility; by contrast, cooperation among the emergent national bourgeoisie was unfolding along the lines of increasingly impersonal financial ties that underwrote the fast-growing industrial sector. Hanseats traditionally did business as cosmopolitans in an Atlantic economy, while men like Keutgen were invested in an industrial world market. The former traded in the produce harvested by slave labor, the latter in the products of wage labor. In Marx's terms, Hanseats represented merchant capital, while Keutgen's firm had made the transition to commodity- and money-trading capital. The former economic role was increasingly outdated, while that of the latter would expand along with industrial production.[51]

---

[48] [Illegible] for Directorium der Deutschen Continental-Gas-Gesellschaft in Dessau to Senat der Freien Hansestadt Bremen, May 23, 1859, in StAHB 2,B.13.b.3, file no. 7, 31.

[49] Rosenberg, "Struktur- und Konjunkturwandel."

[50] Etges, Andreas, *Wirtschaftsnationalismus. USA und Deutschland im Vergleich (1815–1914)*, Frankfurt and New York, 1999.

[51] Marx, *Capital*, vol. 3, 315–16.

CRISES AND THE FALL OF FRIEDRICH WILHELM KEUTGEN

H. H. Meier and Friedrich Wilhelm Keutgen may well have been the Hanseats who had ventured furthest down the road toward the "new economy" when the Panic of 1857 struck. Both men survived that crisis, which annihilated much of the venture capital that had been pumped into the new, industrial economy since 1848. Perhaps they owed the ease with which they had weathered this storm to their location at the center of the Hanseatic network, which, as a whole, had done better in 1857 than many other groups. The persistence of personal credit and trust among one's peers, which Meier and Keutgen also enjoyed, had buffered Hanseats' losses in that crisis and had prevented numerous firms from failing.[52]

In 1860–1, in the economic crisis touched off by the political uncertainty and increasing sectional animosity after Lincoln's election, Keutgen was no longer that lucky. His embrace of new ways of doing business had made him more vulnerable to changes in the market. With inescapable certainty, this market caught up with him in the spring of 1861. The downfall began slowly, and would end with Keutgen's expulsion from Hanseatic circles. Why did this happen?

The more intertwined the world market became, both with regard to the flow of commodities and the links established by bills of exchange, the faster and further such crises spread. In the commercial crisis of 1798, Bremen merchants still managed to avoid a complete crash by treating the unsellable stock of commodities in the city's warehouses as a form of money. Backed by the state, a so-called commodity bank (*Warenbank*) was established. Merchants received bills from the bank after commissioners took stock of their commodities. The value of these bills equaled the precrisis price of the commodities, and was redeemable in specie supplied by the state. Restraint on the part of the merchants within the city, who did not insist on redemption, saved that system, which enabled foreign merchants to call in their outstanding payments, thus saving Bremen's credit at large.[53]

The Panic of 1857, by distinction, took place at a time when Bremen was interlinked with international financial and commodity markets to a much greater extent. This crisis spread further and involved larger sums. The idea of a commodity bank was again considered but was discarded as impracticable. Instead, H. H. Meier's Bremer Bank successfully assumed the role of a guarantor against external demands, while mediating the demands between Bremish firms.[54] In 1798, the commodities stored could be treated as capital, because they were part of the mercantile circuit of capital, exclusively. In 1857, however, capitalist production had already become the general form of social reproduction to such an extent that

---

[52] Beutin, *Bremen und Amerika*, 112–16.

[53] Beutin, "Bremisches Banken- und Börsenwesen," 23–5. To an extent, conceits of this sort can work even in a more fully developed capitalist economy. E.g., in December 1860 New York banks restored liquidity by circulating $5Mio worth of notes backed by deposits in scrip and accepted by the city's merchants for gold. Unlike the Bremish case, in which commodities represented money, here capital stands in for a means of circulation. See StAHB 2,B.13.b.3, file no. 15, doc. 15, 44.

[54] Entholt, Hermann, "Bremens Handel, Schiffahrt und Industrie im 19. Jahrhundert (1815–1914)," in *Die Hansestädte Hamburg/Bremen/Lübeck*, ed. O. Mathies, H. Entholt, and L. Lichtweiss (Die Deutsche Wirtschaft und Ihre Führer, vol. 5), Gotha, 1928, 131–244, here 167.

the stored goods were commodity capital as part of a larger circuit of capital circulation, involving more parties than just Bremen's merchants. A gentlemen's agreement of the sort practiced in 1798 was not easily duplicable under these conditions. Effectively, by treating the stored and unsellable commodities as if they had an "internal value" independent of their finding a buyer, Hanseats had been able in 1798 to pretend among themselves that there really was no crisis. In 1857, they would have had to convince many more people than just themselves to make this conceit work. A capitalist crisis required a capitalist answer, and Meier stood ready to provide one.

Crises such as the Panic of 1857 still appeared as crises of trade, not production, because the connection between trade and production is obscured, among other things, by the fact that the merchant deals in the commodities of many different manufacturers, often located in various different, faraway places. The "external independence" of merchant capital in relation to industrial capital veils the "squeeze" the merchant actually finds himself in, even to himself: "The two limits of the sales price are, on the one hand, the price of production of the commodity, which he [the merchant] does not control; on the other hand, the average rate of profit, which he does not control either."[55]

In 1861, driven by a loss of investor confidence, this squeeze was even more pronounced, especially for firms like Keutgen's, which was invested in both commodities and securities. At first, Keutgen hoped to contain the impact of the crisis on his firm. On May 4, 1861, Keutgen wrote to the *Senat*:

The price-wise conditions at this place have taken such a turn that my house felt itself compelled to suspend payments. This was done with the intention to liquidate accrued assets; even a minimal improvement in the conditions will make this possible, and will enable [my house] to meet all its obligations in full, since these accrued assets are located mainly in the northwestern states, and have lost almost none of their internal value by the present crisis.[56]

Informing Rudolf Schleiden of his misfortune, Keutgen elaborated on the same theme. He hoped that, in the long run, the company's assets would serve to pay all obligations and leave the associates with a "decent fortune." Keutgen claimed that he had been meaning for some time to dissolve the partnership, when "after the fall of Fort Sumter, commercial conditions here took such a sad turn, that all and every

---

[55] Marx, *Capital*, vol. 3, 318.

[56] F. W. Keutgen to Senats-Kommission für die auswärtigen Angelegenheiten, New York, May 4, 1861, StAHB 2,B.13.b.3, *Hanseatica. Verhältnisse der Hansestädte mit den Vereinigten Staaten von Nordamerika. Hanseatische diplomatische Agenten, Konsuln usw. bei den Vereinigten Staaten von Nordamerika und Korrespondenz mit denselben.* In New York, 1815–1868; file no. 10, "Acta betr. die Resignation des Consuls Keutgen zu Newyork und Ernennung des Kaufmanns Gustav Schwab daselbst zu seinem Nachfolger, 1861 Mai 27. – Decbr. 18," 5–6. Further reference to this file will be as "StAHB 2,B.13.b.3, file no. 10," followed by page numbers. Whether viewed as caused by overproduction or underconsumption, the merchant will be the first to feel a crisis. Marx wrote that "the crisis takes place, as soon as the flow [of sales proceeds] from merchants who sell abroad (or whose stocks have accumulated at home, also), become so slow and spare, that banks urge repayments, or bills of exchange drawn on purchased goods become due, before a sale has taken place. Then foreclosures begin, sales in order to pay." This appears to be what happened to Keutgen. See Marx, *Capital*, vol. 3, 317.

resources were cut off, and that it was made impossible for me to pay off our liabilities at their due dates."[57]

Convinced that Keutgen would emerge from the firm's troubles with his Hanseatic honor intact, Schleiden rejected Keutgen's resignation as consul. Writing to the *Senat*, Schleiden asserted that "several private communications by respected New York merchants convince me that this failure was brought about by the political circumstances and the interruption of commerce they caused, and that [this failure] was generally regarded with surprise." In the light of Keutgen's "accomplishments ... diligence, prudence, and competence," Schleiden recommended leaving him in office and giving him a chance to restore his credit.[58]

Schleiden would find his hopes disappointed. Apparently, the three associates had borrowed heavily to meet their obligations during the slump in business. They received funds from the house of J. & J. Stuart & Co. of New York, whom they gave promissory notes due after thirty days to six months. Between February 7 and April 10, they had borrowed a total of $123,000 from the Stuarts. As the notes became due, starting with one of $5,000 on May 10, Gelpcke, Keutgen & Reichelt were unable to pay.[59]

On June 12, confronted with a rising tide of ninety-day promissory notes to the Stuarts becoming due, Gelpcke, Keutgen & Reichelt filed for bankruptcy. The court followed their request to appoint the firm's clerk, Wilhelm Vogel, as trustee. When asked to post a bond of $120,000, however, Vogel refused and withdrew his consent to act as trustee. Apparently, the clerk knew what Keutgen was not ready to admit: the firm would not be able to meet its obligations. Another forty days passed before the court replaced Vogel with the lawyers Morris K. Jessup and Joseph Herzfeld.[60]

During June and July, Gelpcke, Keutgen & Reichelt began liquidating assets. Apparently, they did not stop at their own. Once word of the firm's bankruptcy reached Germany, their clients began to ask for a settlement of accounts. C. Wintgens Oeder of Aachen, an old acquaintance of Reichelt's, asked that he be sent the 361 shares of railroad stock that Gelpcke, Keutgen & Reichelt had bought in trust for him. The firm answered him that they had sold the stock to meet

---

[57] F. W. Keutgen to Rudolf Schleiden, New York, May 6, 1861, manuscript copy, in StAHB 2,B.13. b.3, file no. 10, pp. 7–8.

[58] Extract aus dem Senatsprotokoll de 1861 – Mai 27 – p. 489, Min. Res. Schleiden, No. 58 Washington 9. Mai; no. 1842., StAHB 2,B.13.b.3, file no. 10, pp. 3–4.

[59] *Joseph Stuart v. Herman Gelpcke*, 27 Nov 1861, case 1861#916, Superior Court; *John Stuart v. Herman Gelpcke*, 27 Nov 1861, case 1861#1327, Court of Common Pleas; *Joseph Stuart v. Herman Gelpcke*, 27 Nov 1861, case 1861#1327, Court of Common Pleas; and *James Stuart v. Gelpcke*, 27 Nov 1861, case 1861#851, Superior Court; all in County Clerk, New York County, County Court House.

[60] Bill of Complaint, August 30, 1861; and Answer of Defendants Gelpcke and Keutgen, December 24, 1861, in the case of *Albert Erhard v. Herman Gelpcke and others* [Frederick W. Keutgen, Adolphus Reichelt, William [sic] Vogel, Morris K. Jessup and Joseph Herzfeld], Case File A-16-393, Admiralty Case Files, United States District Court for the Southern District of New York, Records of the District Courts of the United States, Record Group 21, National Archives – Northeast Region, New York.

their own obligations when their value had been around 52 percent of nominal value, and that they were no longer able to produce the money.[61]

The same happened to one Albert Erhard. When his attorney, Louis A. von Hoffmann, demanded that Gelpcke, Keutgen & Reichelt hand over stocks and bonds they held in trust for Erhard, Keutgen told him that they had sold them and that they no longer had the money. When Erhard sued, his complaint implicated not just Keutgen's firm, but also the *Dessauer Creditanstalt*. Apparently, many of the German accounts Gelpcke, Keutgen & Reichelt handled were with German customers of that bank.[62]

Rudolf Schleiden received word of the developing scandal on August 9. He had heard from his acquaintances in New York that Gelpcke, Keutgen & Reichelt had embezzled up to $40,000 in scrip held for Germans. Nonetheless, the letter Schleiden wrote to Keutgen on the same day betrays Schleiden's assumption that both men still operated under the same code of mercantile honor:

Even if you, personally, may be uninvolved in the [embezzlement], I still fear that you will be held co-responsible for the actions of your house; and even though I do not doubt in the least that the alleged misappropriation of the trust funds managed by your house was caused, in the worst case, by a hardly excusable disarray [of your records]; that even this would not be a sufficient excuse. Under these circumstances, I believe I may not hesitate to ask you to inform me without delay of the true facts of the matter with the same candor, with which I, in your own interest, have addressed you.[63]

A betrayal of investors' trust seemed inconceivable, but the mere rumor of such a betrayal threatened the merchant's honor. Keutgen agreed: "the mere fact, that such a rumor is spreading here, suffices to make impossible the continuation of my functions as Bremish consul."[64] Hence, on August 16, Schleiden relieved Keutgen from his post, and appointed Gustav F. Schwab in his stead.[65]

While Keutgen had to admit to Schleiden that "the rumor is not entirely unfounded," he claimed attenuating circumstances in that he had been, "deliberately or inadvertently, most severely deceived by a certain party." Apparently, Keutgen still hoped that he could emerge from the scandal with his honor and credit intact. He pleaded with Schleiden: "Do not judge me too severely, ... and be assured that even in the absence [of such judgment] I am paying a high penalty for that for which I may have to blame myself."[66]

---

[61] Brief by the attorneys of C. Wintgens Oeder, August 6, 1861, in the case of *C. Winters [sic] Oeder v. Herman Gelpcke*, Consul of the Principality of Dessau, Frederick W. Keutgen, Consul of the City of Bremen at the Port of New York, and Adolphus Reichelt, Case File A-16–387, Admiralty Case Files, United States District Court for the Southern District of New York, Records of the District Courts of the United States, Record Group 21, National Archives – Northeast Region, New York.

[62] Bill of Complaint, August 30, 1861, in the case of *Albert Erhard v. Herman Gelpcke and others*, see note 60 to this chapter.

[63] Rudolf Schleiden to F. W. Keutgen, Washington, DC, August 9, 1861, manuscript copy, StAHB 2, B.13.b.3, file no. 10, 15.

[64] F. W. Keutgen to Rudolf Schleiden, New York, August 10, 1861, manuscript copy, StAHB 2,B.13. b.3, file no. 10, 16.

[65] Rudolf Schleiden to Senatskommission für auswärtige Angelegenheiten, n.p. [New York?], August 16, 1861, manuscript copy, StAHB 2,B.13.b.3, file no. 10, 17.

[66] Ibid.

The ripples from Gelpcke, Keutgen & Reichelt's failure spread West as well as East from New York. Not just German investors had been defrauded. In Chicago, the Rock River Bank brought suit against the house of Hoffmann & Gelpcke for a total of $11,800. Hoffmann, like Gelpcke and Keutgen, tried in vain to claim immunity as a consul.[67] Gelpcke, Keutgen & Reichelt, in turn, attempted to collect funds from their own banking costumers. Rodewald & Co. of New Orleans had failed in February 1860, and their trading partner Quentell in Bremen refused to honor a draft of $33,000 Rodewald had made on Quentell's account with Gelpcke, Keutgen & Reichelt. Now, the latter took Quentell to court in New York.[68]

On November 27, the Superior Court ordered Gelpcke, Keutgen & Reichelt to pay $64,089.92 to the Stuarts. On the same day, the three merchants offered the Stuarts another $53,000 plus interest in settling a separate case before the Court of Common Pleas.[69] After these payments, Gelpcke, Keutgen & Reichelt were all the less able to repay their defrauded German customers. By their own estimate, their total liabilities amounted to $400,000. Keutgen and Gelpcke owned up to their responsibility, but argued that the German owners of stock should be paid pro rata along with the firm's other creditors. Reichelt summarily denied all charges, as well as the Admiralty Court's jurisdiction in the case.[70] The verdict of the Admiralty Court in Erhard's case against Gelpcke, Keutgen & Reichelt has not been preserved. Perhaps the court found that it did not have jurisdiction.[71]

No matter the legal resolution of their situation, the reputations of Gelpcke, Keutgen, and Reichelt were ruined. They had had to admit that they had embezzled stock they had held in trust, which sufficed to exclude them from the ranks of the respectable. After Schleiden had taken the consul's seal from Keutgen, there was no further mention of the disgraced merchant in the correspondence.

BREMEN'S INTEGRATION INTO THE INDUSTRIAL-CAPITALIST WORLD MARKET

The man who replaced Keutgen as Bremish consul and Lloyd agent in New York was Gustav Schwab. Schwab's consular reports were much more detailed, and covered more ground than those of any of his predecessors or of consuls in other

---

[67] "Law Reports. Rights of Consuls," *New York Times*, August 21, 1861, 3.

[68] By 1879, the case had gone through three appeals. I was unable to ascertain whether the 1879 decision in Gelpcke, Keutgen & Reichelt's favor stood up to appeal. The court's ruled that Quentell had to pay nearly $70,000. If he did, Gelpcke, Keutgen & Reichelt might have been able, after all, to meet many of their obligations. See "A Long-Litigated Case," *New York Times*, October 23, 1879, 2.

[69] *Joseph Stuart v. Herman Gelpcke*, 27 Nov 1861, case 1861#916, Superior Court; *John Stuart v. Herman Gelpcke*, 27 Nov 1861, case 1861#1327, Court of Common Pleas; *Joseph Stuart v. Herman Gelpcke*, 27 Nov 1861, case 1861#1327, Court of Common Pleas, see note 59 to this chapter.

[70] Answer of Defendants Gelpcke and Keutgen, December 24, 1861; and Demurrer by Adolphus Reed, January 8, 1862, in the case of *Albert Erhard v. Herman Gelpcke and others* [Frederick W. Keutgen, Adolphus Reichelt, William [sic] Vogel, Morris K. Jessup and Joseph Herzfeld], Case File A-16-393, see note 60 to this chapter.

[71] In the case against Gelpcke & Hoffmann of Chicago, the U.S. Supreme Court ruled that Gelpcke did not enjoy immunity as a consul, because his exequatur had been revoked ("Law Reports. Rights of Consuls," *New York Times*, August 21, 1861, 3). Hence, Hermann Gelpcke and F. W. Keutgen would have been unlikely to have enjoyed immunity.

ports. Wilhelm de Voß in Richmond listed in handwritten annual reports broad trends in commodity prices, state bonds, and some railroad stock. Schwab, by contrast, submitted reports of more than twenty pages, some of which were handwritten, but most of which contained statistics clipped from newspapers. These clippings covered in ample detail the entire range of the New York markets for bonds, stocks, and commodities. Evidently, by the 1860s, Hanseats could no longer afford to ignore those kinds of investments that they would have avoided a decade earlier, and which they continued to scorn as "speculation" even as they derived a larger and larger share of their income from them.[72]

The 1860s were still a period of transition, in which many older Hanseats may well have continued to trade in commodities exclusively on their own account. By the 1870s, however, it was evident that Hanseats had embraced their new economic function as commodity-trading capitalists. Ludwig Beuting offers two revealing examples in his accounts of the post-1860s history of Bremish trade in cotton and petroleum.

The clearest sign of the changed times was the opening of the Bremen Cotton Exchange (*Baumwollbörse*) in 1872. Serving as a clearinghouse for the trade in cotton futures, the Cotton Exchange was modeled after similar institutions in New York and Liverpool.[73] The Cotton Exchange was complemented by the *Bremer Lagerhausgesellschaft* (BLG; Bremen Warehouse Company), a state-run institution that stores commodities, founded in 1876. The storage receipts issued by the BLG serve as the foundation for the futures trade at the Stock Exchange and Cotton Exchange.[74] The Cotton Exchange and BLG are continuing success stories for Bremish trade. Both institutions still exist today, and Bremen has remained the largest continental cotton market for decades.[75]

For a while, it looked as if Bremen was going to become the dominant continental market for petroleum as well. The activities of Wätjen & Co. (see p. 377)

---

[72] StAHB 2,B.13.b.3, *Hanseatica. Verhältnisse der Hansestädte mit den Vereinigten Staaten von Nordamerika. Hanseatische diplomatische Agenten, Konsuln usw. bei den Vereinigten Staaten von Nordamerika und Korrespondenz mit denselben.* In New York, 1815–1868; file no. 15, "Consulat zu Newyork, F. W. Keutgen, 1859 Novb. 1–1861; Gustav Schwab 1862. –. Enthält No. 1- 89. 1859 Nov. 1–1868 Okt. 28."; StAHB 2,B.13.b.10, *Hanseatica. Verhältnisse der Hansestädte mit den Vereinigten Staaten von Nordamerika. Hanseatische diplomatische Agenten, Konsuln usw. bei den Vereinigten Staaten von Nordamerika und Korrespondenz mit denselben.* Richmond, Norfolk und Petersburgh 1842–1867, files 12 (annual report for 1854), 16 (1855), 20 (1856), 23 (1857), 27 (1859), 29 (1860), 31 (1861). By 1861, e.g., Schwab had also begun to act as an insurance agent. See Sophie Schwab to Gustav F. Schwab, Stuttgart, April 9, 1861, MSS 434, Schwab Papers, series I, box 2, folder 37.

[73] Schildknecht, Karl-Heinz, Bremen und Baumwolle im Wandel der Zeiten, Bremen 1999; Beutin, Bremen, 99–102; Engelsing, Rolf, "England und die USA in der bremischen Sicht des 19. Jahrhunderts," *Jahrbuch der Wittheit zu Bremen,* 1957, 33–65, here p. 38. Between 1872 and 1877, the institution was formally called "Komité für den Bremer Baumwollhandel," but already served the same purpose. See also Cronon, William, *Nature's Metropolis: Chicago and the Great West,* New York and London, 1991.

[74] Beutin, *Bremen,* 101, 296, note to p. 101. Here, Beutin cites the 1877 Bürgerschaft speech of a master-stevedore who complained that "the main reason [for founding the BLG] was to facilitate speculation in commodities," and adds, "He was quite right." The stevedores' guild-like control of the port was broken by an 1878 law that put the BLG in charge of quayside operations.

[75] See http://www.baumwollboerse.de (accessed September 30, 2005) and Schildknecht, *Bremen und Baumwolle.* Beutin, *Bremen,* 102–5. See also Kellner-Stoll, *Bremerhaven,* 129–31.

had made Bremerhaven and the neighboring Prussian ports of Geestemünde and Nordenham the centers of petroleum importation in Europe. From the beginning, trade in this commodity was characterized by futures trading and the dominance of transportation and retail sale by only a few companies. In 1890, an attempted takeover by Standard Oil of the four German firms trading in petroleum resulted in the creation of the *Deutsch-Amerikanische Petroleum-Actiengesellschaft* (German-American Petroleum Joint-Stock Company) in which Standard Oil held more than one-third of stock, while the rest was shared among Bremish merchants. It is hard to imagine a more telling example of the integration of Hanseatic capital into a global framework of finance and commodity trading than its involvement with this epitome of the trust.

Some Hanseats were successful in making the transition to the new economy, with its increased risks for entrepreneurs. Those Bremish merchants who had survived the 1860s continued to improve their competitive position in the world market. In the process of capital concentration, however, many Hanseats found themselves compelled to abandon trade. A medieval Hanseat might have found familiar much of what he would have seen in Bremen in 1850. In 1870, he would have been bewildered. This was no longer the same mercantile world whose sons had first set out to trade with America.

But business was not the only field in which the Hanseats' customary practices proved increasingly unsustainable. In international politics, the actions of the great powers undermined Bremen's ability to pursue an independent foreign policy that strove to avoid wars, or at least the city's participation in wars. In domestic politics – Bremish and American – Hanseats no longer spoke with one voice. The conflicting political options that presented themselves as nations went to war pitted members of Bremen's elite against each other.

Customarily, Hanseats had responded to economic strains by falling back on their dense network of ties between firms and families. This same network had ensured their political unanimity on the most important questions. Now, as the heads of merchant houses and their sons began to quarrel over "great politics," and as business ties no longer automatically meant family ties, domestic harmony turned increasingly sour, thus shattering the communal nexus of business enterprise, family life, and political power.

8

Decisions and Divisions

Hanseatic Responses to Nation-Making Wars, 1859–1867

In Europe and America, the long decade between 1859 and 1871 was characterized by wars that were qualitatively new. For armaments and supplies, the armies engaged in these wars relied on heavy industry to an unprecedented extent. The mobilization of the masses to join or support these armies encouraged demands for popular participation, and the war aims put forth by the leaders who waged these wars were political and economic, as well as territorial. Bismarck, Cavour, and Lincoln fought for national unity, envisioning the nation-state as the container for a modernized society, one in which industrial capitalism and wage labor would gain dominance.

Bremen's mercantile elite found much to complain about in these wars. The empowerment of the lower sorts, the disruption of trade caused by the hostilities, and the centralization and expansion of state power, ran against all that the Hanseats had held dear. At the same time, a Protestant calling was implicit in the causes championed by Bismarck and Lincoln, and to the extent that industrial development fostered improvement, and that territorial unification furthered commercial relations, many Hanseats found points of commonality with both sides in these conflicts.

Bremen's merchants discovered that the most significant effect of these wars in Germany and America was to disrupt the relations between members of their own group. Bismarck's Prussia and Lincoln's United States considered the interests of the Hanseatic city entirely secondary to their goals, and did not require Bremen's cooperation in their pursuit. Thus, for the first time since the Napoleonic Wars, Bremen's merchants and diplomats became merely passive spectators to world-historical events. In the past, the prospect of collectively influencing policies in America and the German states had put a premium on group unity. With this prospect gone, there was nothing to mitigate the increasingly deep political divisions that began to cut across firms and families and to dissolve the bonds that had made these Hanseats into a cosmopolitan community.

BREMEN AND THE INTERNATIONAL SITUATION, 1859

In international politics, the year 1859 brought a shock to the European system of states. With French support, the Kingdom of Sardinia-Piedmont – under its prime minister, the Count Cavour – set out to conquer the Austrian parts of northern Italy in a first step toward an Italian nation-state. After a defeat at Solferino, Austria ceded Lombardia to Sardinia-Piedmont but held on to the Veneto. Popular movements in the following year resulted in the fall of additional small Italian fiefdoms and the Kingdom of the Two Sicilies. By early 1861, the Sardinian-Piedmontese monarchy had become the Kingdom of Italy – albeit still short of a nation-state, in that it excluded Venice and Rome. In exchange for French support, Sardinia-Piedmont had also ceded its province of Savoy – almost one-third of its initial territory – to France.

German nationalists were outraged. The Bremen *Handelsblatt* had recently come under the editorship of Victor Böhmert, who was to play a central role as publicist and secretary of the *Handelskammer* in scrapping Bremen's guilds.[1] In the pages of his paper, Böhmert fumed:

One of the oldest and most powerful European dynasties [the Habsburgs] . . . gives up, not only one of its richest and most beautiful provinces, but also, and more importantly, the principle of the life of its state, historical right. And this happens at a time when Prussia and Germany advance their armies to the Rhine to divert the enemy's forces. Rather than trusting in its own strength and paying the price that Germany asked [i.e., Prussian command over the joint German forces] for its participation in the struggle against the national enemy and the disturber of world peace [i.e., Napoleon III or France], Austria has readily succumbed to Napoleonism. . . .

Napoleon cunningly conjured up this war, not for the sake of liberty, but for power and for the breach of that international law, on which order and peace in Europe are predicated. . . . In our view, the results of the war are a repeated warning against neutrality and non-activity in the great European questions. . . .

The lofty goal Napoleon talked about [i.e., national unification] was meant to justify the means, but the solution the Italian question found in the peace treaty appears to make a mockery of the wishes and needs of Italian patriots. . . .

For the sake of business, we should be glad about the armistice; but the result of the war is too paltry, when measured against the high stakes and the losses suffered because of the interruption of peace.[2]

The incoherence of Böhmert's argument was characteristic of the confusion in German nationalist circles. On the one hand, they envied Italy for having taken a step toward unification; on the other hand, they resented that it had been achieved with the help of France. Böhmert's editorial remained obscure on the point of who, exactly, was meant by the "national enemy and disturber of world peace," France or its ruler. Napoleon III was associated with dictatorial rule, based on popular acclamation. Hence, as a monarch, he was tainted with the formally democratic mode of his ascent to power; and as a man of the people, he was insufficiently

---

[1] For Böhmert, see Chapter 3 and Biefang, Andreas, *Politisches Bürgertum in Deutschland, 1857–1868. Nationale Organisationen und Eliten* (Kommission für Geschichte des Parlamentarismus und der politischen Parteien, corp. ed., Beiträge zur Geschichte des Parlamentarismus und der politischen Parteien, vol. 102), Düsseldorf, 1994, esp. pp. 53–65, for Böhmert's leading role in the founding of the Kongreß deutscher Volkswirte (Congress of German Economists), an organization with a strong national orientation; and p. 437 for a brief vita, and throughout for his role in the German nationalist movement, including the *Nationalverein*.

[2] Bremen *Handelsblatt*, July 16, 1859, 1–2.

democratic in his exercise of power. With this mix of absolutism and popular sovereignty, Napoleon combined two principles equally detested by German elites.

Moreover, while Böhmert accused Napoleon of insincerely claiming to have fought the war over the principle of nationality, sacred to German nationalists, the editor also found the emperor guilty of violating the opposite principle of legitimacy. On a continent where states and nations were not congruent, national sovereignty[3] and the sovereignty of states were evidently incompatible. Any German attempt at national unification was sure to violate one or the other principle as well. Men like Böhmert were ready to embrace national/popular sovereignty at the expense of violating the rights of smaller German states and their sovereigns. In accusing Napoleon of "disturbing world peace" for doing the same in the Italian case, Böhmert was nourishing the illusion that German unity could be had any other way.

As a newspaper editor dependent for his salary on mercantile subscriptions and advertisement, Böhmert might have been led to this incoherent editorial line by his attempt to satisfy his readers' interests along with their wishes to see the "national" argument made. The practical interest of Hanseats at this time, as we have seen, was to do what was best "for the sake of business"; and the sovereignty of little Bremen, founded not on popular acclaim but on "historical right," was what made possible an independent foreign policy in the interest of business.[4]

Böhmert was an outsider in Bremen. As a new type of professional politician, he led the city's *Nationalverein*. German historians point to men like Böhmert when arguing that Bremen's elite supported national unification under Prussian leadership. Even leading members of the *Nationalverein* among that elite, however, were not willing to give up the benefits of Bremen's independence. The activities of Bremish merchants suggest that they envisioned a strengthened German Confederation that could ensure the security of trade, while leaving extensive leeway to individual member states in most fields of policy, including foreign relations. This German state might be ruled by an emperor and would have a parliament, albeit not necessarily one elected by universal suffrage, but it would not be a unitary, centralized state, thus allowing Bremen to continue its special relations to foreign countries.[5]

The brand of nationalism embraced by the *Nationalverein* could thus be attractive to Hanseats. In the view of many German nationalists, centralism was what characterized the French polity, while the German national character was shot through with the attachment to local particularism. Prussia was the German state most likely to lead the other German states into a firmer union.

---

[3] In German, *Volkssouveränität* implies both the sovereignty of the ethnically homogeneous populace, or *Volk*, and the sovereignty of the people, as opposed to the monarch.

[4] Cf. the *Senat*'s rebuttal in 1872 of the demand by Bremerhaven's representative to increase the size of the port city's delegation in the Bürgerschaft, in which the executive argued that, first, the parliament was based on estates, not numbers, and second, that all subjects of Bremen enjoyed virtual representation in the legislature. Kellner-Stoll, Rita, *Bremerhaven, 1827–1888. Politische, wirtschaftliche und soziale Probleme einer Stadtgründung* (Burchard Scheper, ed., Veröffentlichungen des Stadtarchivs Bremerhaven, vol. 4), Bremerhaven, 1982, 184.

[5] Cf. Biefang, *Bürgertum*.

Unfortunately, Prussia was also the most "French" among the German states; that is, the most centralized and bureaucratic among the members of the German Confederation.[6] When nationalists in the early 1860s said that Prussia had to become German, instead of vice versa, they expressed the hope that Prussia would abandon its bureaucratic centralism in the process of unifying Germany. In this vision of Germany, Hanseats could imagine that there would be a place for Bremish foreign-trade relations independent of and separate from the central government.[7]

PLOTTING A COURSE TOWARD PRUSSIA

In 1861, leading Hanseats began to perceive the need for a German navy that could protect Bremen's trade in the case that France should once more act out of the bounds of international law and legitimacy. German–Danish relations lent additional arguments to supporters of a navy. While the conflict over control of Schleswig-Holstein had been settled in favor of Denmark in 1851, renewed German–Danish hostilities, which would have brought the risk of another blockade of German trade by the Danish fleet, were a distinct possibility.

Two men became the main promoters of a German navy among Hanseats, H. H. Meier and Arnold Duckwitz. Meier joined the *Nationalverein* partly to gain a platform for this project, but also lent his support to the association's other policy initiatives in the *Bürgerschaft*.[8] Burgomaster Duckwitz was not a friend of the *Nationalverein*. He feared that the association's activities would empower the democratic movement. In a letter to Rudolf Schleiden, written in May 1861, Duckwitz complained that

> the old democrats of 1848 make every effort to excite the lower classes and to demand a reinstatement of the 1849 constitution, with universal suffrage and all that, so that the higher estates will be pushed aside and the lower estates will capture government. These people hope that the so-called *Nationalverein* will get a political movement going, to which they then can hitch their cart, just like they did in 1848.[9]

Duckwitz had been the German Minister of the Navy in 1848–9, and still bemoaned the "shameful" auctioning of that fleet in 1852. Meier, too, had kept in touch with his acquaintances from the revolutionary days when he had been a member of the national parliament in Frankfurt.[10] Their differing attitudes toward

---

[6] See Kiesselbach's arguments, Chapter 3.

[7] Biefang, *Bürgertum*; Krieger, Adolf, *Bremische Politik im Jahrzehnt vor der Reichsgründung* (Schriften der Bremer Wissenschaftlichen Gesellschaft, Reihe F [früher A*], Friedrich Prüser, ed., Veröffentlichungen des Archivs der Hansestadt Bremen, vol. 15), Bremen, 1939, 26–7, relates that the association had 500 members in Bremen already in 1860. Remarkably, for a book based on a PhD dissertation written under National Socialist rule (University of Kiel, 1939), Krieger's text avoids a nationalist teleology and acknowledges discontent in the process of German unification.

[8] Krieger, *Politik*, 27.

[9] Arnold Duckwitz to Rudolf Schleiden, Bremen, May 4, 1861, StAHB 7,116 [Rudolf Schleiden Papers], folder "Briefwechsel Rudolf Schleiden mit Senator Arnold Duckwitz, 1854–1879," third of five unnumbered and unlabeled boxes. See also Arnold Duckwitz to Rudolf Schleiden, Bremen, November 22, 1861, ibid., for additional examples of Duckwitz's animosity toward the *Nationalverein*.

[10] Bessell, Georg, *1857–1957: Norddeutscher Lloyd. Geschichte einer bremischen Reederei*, Bremen, 1957, 18, notes that Meier's ties to former members of the Casino faction of the Frankfurt Assembly combined political and business interests.

the *Nationalverein* suggest that the two men had drawn different lessons from 1848. In spite of their disagreement, however, Duckwitz and Meier worked together for a German navy.

Meier envisioned a small flotilla of steamboats for coastal defense as the nucleus of a revived German navy.[11] Duckwitz doubted that it would suffice in case of war, when the protection of vessels on the high seas was as important as the defense of coasts and ports. Nevertheless, he was willing to support Meier's plans, which represented a first step in the right direction.[12] This initial fleet was to be built and maintained jointly by the coastal German states. Due to its size and financial resources, Prussia would have to play an especially important role. Convincing the Hohenzollern monarchy to fill that role was key to the success of this plan.

Even if the plan of building a German fleet appears as a departure from the internationalist foreign policy Bremen had pursued in the 1850s, Hanseats promoted this project with the same means that had been at the core of that foreign policy. Meier and Duckwitz hoped that the tried and true Hanseatic practice of building broad public support to back up a concerted diplomatic effort by mercantile envoys dispatched to foreign capitals would achieve their aims. This approach had worked well in 1846, when it had led to the establishment of the OSNC. As late as 1859, their campaign for the protection of private property at sea had demonstrated that Hanseats could amplify their voice on the international stage by enlisting the support of like-minded elites abroad. Now, Meier and Duckwitz hoped that a similar approach would move Prussia to take up their plan for a German navy.[13] Together, they were to find out about the limits of Prussian statecraft. It was to be a deeply sobering experience.

Laying the groundwork for the publicity campaign for a German navy, *Nationalverein* members introduced a resolution "Concerning Coastal Defense" into the *Bürgerschaft*. Similar resolutions were brought before other German parliaments.[14] The resolution claimed that "the present fragmentation of Germany … prevents the protection of the maritime interests of our fatherland" and "urgently" demanded the *Senat* to build "steam gun-boats" in cooperation with the other German governments.[15]

When the resolution came to a vote on June 19, 1861, it passed with a comfortable majority of sixty-six against eleven votes. Although only slightly less than half of all *Bürgerschaft* members were present for the roll call, two-thirds of the mercantile delegation (Class II) took part in the vote. Every single one of them cast their vote in favor. The only class that surpassed the merchants in its enthusiasm for a German navy was the scholarly estate. Three-quarters of its delegates were present for the vote, and all but one supported the resolution. Opposition to the measure was clustered in the lower rungs of the social order, especially the classes IV.b.

[11] Hardegen, Friedrich, and Käthi Smidt, geb. Meier, *H. H. Meier, der Gründer des Norddeutschen Lloyd. Lebensbild eines Bremer Kaufmanns, 1809–1898*, Berlin and Leipzig, 1920, 173–9.
[12] Krieger, *Politik*, 56, note 1.
[13] Arnold Duckwitz to Rudolf Schleiden, Bremen, August 30, 1861, StAHB 7,116 [Rudolf Schleiden Papers], folder "Briefwechsel Rudolf Schleiden mit Senator Arnold Duckwitz, 1854–1879," third of five unnumbered and unlabeled boxes.
[14] VdBBü 1861/14, June 5, 1861, 230–1 (Dr. Pfeiffer), Hardegen and Smidt, *H. H. Meier*, 174.
[15] VdBBü 1861, 208.

and IV.c., representing residents of the city of Bremen with an annual taxable income below 500 Thaler (Table 9, Chapter 3, and Table 13).[16]

The Hanseatic elite's support for a German navy, however, does not indicate that it supported German nationalism, nor that it endorsed the program of the *Nationalverein*. A separate resolution, signed by roughly the same *Bürgerschaft* members who had introduced the motion for a navy and submitted at the same time, called for the creation of a "German central authority, including a parliament." Although the latter resolution made a concession to the "independence and self-government of the individual states, which to hold in high importance Bremen's happy commonwealth is particularly entitled," those who suspected the spirit of 1848 in the motion could not be fooled. After all, the central demand set forth in the document was the creation of a "universal popular representation" (*Volksvertretung*, or parliament). Other than that, the resolution was replete with empty catchwords: power, security, liberty, respect, and welfare; all of which, it claimed, hinged on the creation of a central authority.[17]

When the resolution for a German central authority came to a vote, a majority of Bürgerschaft members had already left for the night – many of them at the beginning of the debate, in a show of disinterest. Of the remaining ones, the slimmest majority of thirty-six against thirty-five votes supported it. Proponents of the measure considered the outcome a defeat, because nothing short of unanimous endorsement was going to send a powerful message to the German people. There was no possible way of reconciling the rhetoric of the resolution, which claimed that a strengthened nation was in the interest of all social groups, with the obvious disagreement between those very groups about this claim.[18]

Across all classes of *Bürgerschaft* members – with the exception of class VI, representing Bremerhaven, whose delegation was absent for the vote on the navy – the resolution for a central authority received less support than that for a navy. Half of the mercantile delegation was absent for the vote on the central authority. Of those who had cared to take part in the roll-call vote, fifteen voted aye and nine voted nay. Of the total number of mercantile *Bürgerschaft* members, only 31 percent supported the resolution for a central authority. Only among the scholars did the resolution receive the support of half the members of any class (Table 13).[19]

A closer comparison between the two votes reveals a consistent pattern (Table 14). The merchants in the *Bürgerschaft* were split into three main groups: supporters, conditional supporters, and nonsupporters of the *Nationalverein* initiatives. There was a core of strong supporters of the *Nationalverein* among the Hanseatic mercantile elite at this point, but this cadre remained in a minority among its estate. Eight of the forty-eight members of class II had voted for both resolutions, and had signed either one or the other. These can be considered the nationalist hard core (Table 14, category 1). Another seven merchants in the

[16] VdBBü 1861/15, June 19, 1861, 267–8.
[17] VdBBü 1861, 207.
[18] VdBBü 1861/14, June 5, 1861, 229–38.
[19] Ibid., 237–8.

TABLE 13. *Roll-Call Votes on* Nationalverein *Resolutions in the* Bremische Bürgerschaft, *June 1861*

Class		Navy			Central Authority			Total in Class
		Aye	Nay	Absent	Aye	Nay	Absent	
1	Scholars	11	1	4	8	3	5	16
2	Merchants	31		17	15	9	24	48
3	Artisans	8	2	14	3	5	16	24
4.a	Bremen, >500 Thaler	4	1	5	3	3	4	10
4.b	Bremen, >250 Thaler	2	3	5	1	7	2	10
4.c	Bremen, <250 Thaler	4	3	3	2	2	6	10
5	Vegesack	1		4			5	5
6	Bremerhaven			5	2	1	2	5
7	Agriculture	2		8	2	1	7	10
8	Other rural	3	1	6		4	6	10
ALL		66	11	71	36	35	77	148

Sources: *Verhandlungen der Bremischen Bürgerschaft im Jahre 1861*, 14. Sitzung, June 5, 1861, 237–8; 15. Sitzung, June 19, 1861, 267–8; *Staats-Calender der freien Hansestadt Bremen auf das Jahr 1861*, Bremen, 1861, 5–7. Two seats in the *Bürgerschaft* were vacant (one in class 5.c., one in class 6.c.) and were not included in the calculations. Cf. Chapter 3, Table 9.

Bürgerschaft qualify as moderate supporters of the *Nationalverein*. They voted for both resolutions, without having signed either of them (category 2).

The fifteen merchants who were strong or moderate nationalists stood alone among their peers in their support for a central authority. Fourteen merchants joined the supporters of the *Nationalverein* when it came to the navy resolution. These can be considered conditional supporters of the *Nationalverein* (category 3). Of the remaining nineteen merchants, ten were absent for both votes and nine voted against a central authority. Of these nine, only three also voted for a navy. Because support for a navy was not coterminous with support for the *Nationalverein*, as Burgomaster Duckwitz's case shows, we can regard the three mercantile *Bürgerschaft* members who opposed a central authority, but supported a navy, as weak opponents of the *Nationalverein* (category 5), while those six who voted against a central authority without supporting a navy can be considered strong opponents of the *Nationalverein* (category 6).[20]

The difference of opinion between Meier and Duckwitz was thus mirrored by the split among the mercantile delegation in the *Bürgerschaft*. The two men represented conflicting options for dealing with the nation. Meier was willing to join the *Nationalverein*, and considered a democratically elected national parliament as an evil that could be controlled; while Duckwitz stayed away from the association because he saw a greater danger in any expansion of democratic, popular participation in the affairs of the state. They could, however, find common ground in support of a German navy. For some merchants, however, even that project was unpalatable.

[20] Ibid.; and 1861/15, June 19, 1861, 267–8.

TABLE 14. *Categorization of Bürgerschaft Members by Their Response to Nationalverein Initiatives*

Class	Category:	*1* Strong Supporters of Nationalverein	*2* Moderate Supporters of Nationalverein	*3* Conditional Supporters of Nationalverein (Navy only)	*4* Indifferent	*5* Weak Opponents of Nationalverein	*6* Strong Opponents of Nationalverein
1	Scholars	5	3	3	3	1	1
2	Merchants	8	7	14	10	3	6
3	Artisans	1	2	6	11	2	2
4.a	Bremen, >500 Thaler	3	1		3	2	1
4.b	Bremen, 250–500 Thaler			2	3	2	3
4.c	Bremen, <250 Thaler	2		2	3	1	2
5	Vegesack			1	4		
6	Bremerhaven			2	2	1	
7	Agriculture	1		1	8		
8	Other rural				8	2	
ALL		20	13	31	55	14	15

Sources: Verhandlungen der Bremischen Bürgerschaft im Jahre 1861, 207–8; 14. Sitzung, June 5, 1861, 237–8; 15. Sitzung, June 19, 1861, 267–8; Staats-Calender der freien Hansestadt Bremen auf das Jahr 1861, Bremen, 1861, 5–7.

TABLE 14. *(cont.)*
Criteria for the Categorization:

Criterion/Category	1	2	3	4	5	6
Signed one or both of the resolutions	X					
Voted for both resolutions	X	X[a]				
Voted for navy			X		X	
Voted against central authority					X	X[b]
Absent from both votes				X		

[a] Includes one member who was absent for the vote on the navy but signed and voted for the resolution for a central authority.
[b] Includes one member who signed the resolution for a central authority but voted against it, and who did not vote on the navy resolution.

Johann Friedrich Philippi spoke for this group of mercantile antinationalists in the *Bürgerschaft*.

To Philippi, the resolutions amounted to a request for an "endorsement of the program of some association [the *Nationalverein*]." By upsetting the status quo in the European concert, this program amounted to a call for revolution, and hence, Philippi found that the resolutions implicitly "denigrate, mock, and debase all governmental authority." Present nationalist activities directly resembled the democratic movement of 1848: "We have already had something like this some ten years ago, ... and in the end we were glad to have the German Confederation, so that we had at least something to hold on to." Instead of the association's nationalist vision, Philippi advocated an undiluted continuation of the independent and neutral course Bremen had steered in the 1850s. A small republic must keep a low profile and "avoid the field of great politics," where it could run afoul of more powerful states. Advocating measures that challenged the authority of foreign sovereigns could do "more harm ... than good ... because our [state] is too unimportant," Philippi argued. The consequence of the *Nationalverein*'s goals would be Prussian dominance over Germany, a prospect Philippi abhorred. This sentiment put him in line with the majority of Germans. In essence, this Hanseat saw the specter of centralism and democracy in the *Nationalverein*'s initiatives, and he was not going to have any of that.[21]

When it came to national politics, Bremen's elite was deeply divided. In 1861, those who endorsed all-out a program of national unification, as represented by the *Nationalverein*, constituted a minority among mercantile elected officials. Significantly, however, this minority was disciplined and committed. They showed up for the votes that mattered and were able to gain the support not only of members of the *Bürgerschaft* from other voter classes, but also, more importantly, the conditional support of the *Senat* and burgomaster for one of their policy initiatives, the creation of a German navy. The only other group in the *Bürgerschaft* that had a higher share of nationalists among its members at this point was the scholarly estate. The democrats,

[21] VdBBü 1861/14, June 5, 1861, 232.

and especially their leader, Johannes Rösing Sr., however, stayed at a distance from this new brand of respectable, mercantile nationalism.[22] Whatever Philippi's fears about a democratic nationalist movement may have been, the actual democrats were not about to make them come true.

COSMOPOLITANS AND CONFEDERATES

Affairs in the United States looked not much better for Hanseats than they did in Bremen. On the western shore of the Atlantic, as in the city on the Weser, the questions of "big politics" drove a wedge between Bremish merchants. In the biggest political question of the day – slavery – different interests pulled Hanseats in different directions. Their religion might have drawn Bremish merchants toward abolitionism, while the dependence of their trade on slave-economy staples, such as cotton and tobacco, gave them a stake in defending the "peculiar institution."[23] Hanseats' strong involvement in the transportation of immigrants suggested an alliance with the North, the section of the country that attracted an overwhelming share of new Americans, whereas Hanseats shared with Southerners a commitment to a hierarchically ordered society.[24] Individual Hanseats differed in picking their priorities among these conflicting interests, diminishing their chance to influence the American political process as a group. In the past, they had sometimes succeeded in mobilizing American elite opinion in favor of their interests. Now, Hanseats no longer spoke with one voice.

Moreover, the preferred mode of political activities among Hanseatic Americans had been to talk to people who mattered in Washington, New York, or Baltimore. These people were the very merchants and notables whose own influence diminished, the more the sectional conflict drew the mass of the population onto the political stage.[25] With a certain sense of fatalism, Rudolf Schleiden thought in late 1860 that war could only be prevented "by the people itself, if the Dear Lord has mercy," because "there is a complete lack of leaders who could bring the affair [the threat of secession] to a good ending."[26] Hence, Hanseats not only had to make a choice between conflicting political affiliations, but they also had to decide whether to engage in popular politics. While some of them made this step, others continued

[22] Rösing spoke and voted against both measures because he found that only a democratic mass movement, not legislative resolutions, was going to effect change in Germany. See VdBBü 1861/14, June 5, 1861, 233–4.

[23] This dilemma Hanseats shared with their American counterparts. See Abbott, Richard H., *Cotton and Capital: Boston Businessmen and Antislavery Reform, 1854–1868*, Amherst, MA, 1991; McKay, Ernest A., *The Civil War and New York City*, Syracuse, NY, 1990.

[24] Wright, Gavin, *The Political Economy of the Cotton South: Households, Markets, and Wealth in the Nineteenth Century*, New York, 1978, esp. pp. 128–57.

[25] For the reaction of the larger mercantile class of New York to the Civil War, see Foner, Philip, *Business and Slavery: The New York Merchants and the Irrepressible Conflict*, Chapel Hill, NC, 1941; McKay, *Civil War*; and Beckert, Sven, *The Monied Metropolis: New York City and the Consolidation of the American Bourgeoisie, 1850–1896*, Cambridge, MA, 2001, 111–44. Beckert saw the beginnings of the diminishment of mercantile influence in the 1850s.

[26] Rudolf Schleiden to Gustav F. Schwab (in NY), Washington, DC, December 16, 1860, MSS 434, John Christopher Schwab Family Papers, Manuscripts and Archives, Yale University Library, series I, box 2, folder 38.

to rely on political influence through personal ties. Hence, Hanseats' political paths diverged, not just in the choices they made, but also in the ways they worked for their conflicting aims.

In Baltimore, senior Hanseat and Bremish Consul Albert Schumacher decided in 1859 that it was time to leave the countinghouse and the clubhouse and side with the general German population. Nativist violence in the port city had peaked since the election in 1856 of American Party majorities to the state legislature and the city council. Thanks to the strong ties between Baltimore and Bremen that Hanseats had established, one-third of Baltimore's population was German.[27] Reports of Nativist attacks on immigrants were certain to harm Bremen's business interests. Traditionally, Hanseats had relied on charity in American cities and a careful screening of emigrants in Bremerhaven to ensure the respectability and economic independence of those they brought to the United States. In the 1850s, in the face of an antiimmigrant movement of growing strength, this passive strategy of preempting American hostility toward Germans no longer worked.

Together with Pastor Scheib of Zion church, frequented by elite Germans, Albert Schumacher devised a way of making a more active case for Germans' patriotism. Schumacher organized and presided over a parade in honor of Baron von Steuben. In the recollection of an old Hanseat, the parade was an "imposing demonstration ... of the patriotism ... of the German-American element[, and] satisfied all the intelligent native born ... of the sincerity of their political allegiance to their adopted country."[28]

While Nativism in the North drew on the same intellectual fount as abolitionism – the Evangelical churches – Baltimore Nativism resembled that of the South in that it represented a generically racist movement. Baltimore Know-Nothings viewed the numerous free blacks in the city as part of the "vagrant, vicious, and violent element of the population," along with immigrants. Maryland Democrats, who defended the rights of immigrants, went even further in their hostility toward African Americans: their platform in the 1859 election proposed the reenslavement of all free blacks.[29] The only organization that opposed Nativism as well as slavery was the German socialist *Turner* (gymnasts) movement. Armed and militant, they provided immediate self-defense at picnics and other community events. The *Turner* were a tiny minority, however. In 1860, they were the sole political force

[27] Baker, Jean H., *Ambivalent Americans: The Know-Nothing Party in Maryland*, Baltimore 1977, 17–19, 38–9; Browne, Gary Larson, *Baltimore in the Nation, 1789–1861*, Chapel Hill, NC, 1980, 196–215; Evitts, William J., *A Matter of Allegiances: Maryland from 1850 to 1861* (The Johns Hopkins University Studies in Historical and Political Science, 2nd series, vol. 1), Baltimore and London, 1974; Brugger, Robert J., *Maryland, a Middle Temperament, 1634–1980*, Baltimore, 1988; Fields, Barbara Jeanne, *Slavery and Freedom on the Middle Ground: Maryland during the Nineteenth Century*, New Haven, CT, and London, 1985, 59–89.

[28] Louis P. Hennighausen, "Reminiscences of the Political Life of the German-Americans in Baltimore during 1850–1860," in *Seventh Annual Report of the Society for the History of the Germans in Maryland, 1892–1893*, 53–9 (part 1), and *Eleventh and Twelfth Annual Report of the Society for the History of the Germans in Maryland, 1897–1898*, 3–18 (part 2); quote from part 2, pp. 17–18. Hennighausen was president of the Society for the History of the Germans in Maryland, and had served as a Union volunteer. See also the web page of Zion Church at http://www.zionbaltimore. org (accessed January 24, 2005).

[29] Browne, *Baltimore*; Fields, *Slavery*, quote p. 61.

in Baltimore to support Abraham Lincoln, who received only a few thousand votes in the entire state of Maryland.[30]

Hanseats would not have found the *Turner* suitable political allies. Most Hanseatic merchants subscribed to the Democratic newspaper, *Der Deutsche Correspondent*, which defended slavery.[31] At the end of the century, Louis Hennighausen recalled that their vote, "in common defense against the Know-Nothing Party, was solid for the Democratic Party."[32] In 1859, one second-generation Hanseat, John C. Brune, was elected to the state legislature on the Democratic ticket. This election resulted in a landslide victory for the Democrats, leaving only the governor's office to the Know-Nothings. Comprehensive measures of repression against blacks considered by that legislature were on their way to being implemented when the Civil War began.[33]

Brune must have felt that his peers supported his political course. The tone in Baltimore's German elite clubs was overwhelmingly pro-Confederate. When a member of the Concordia choral society expressed an antislavery viewpoint among his fellow singers in 1861, all others left the room in protest. The membership of the Germania Club was equally dedicated to the Confederate cause. The authorities closed the institution in 1862 because, according to the German-American historian, Dieter Cunz, "the president, Frederick Schepeler, a tobacco merchant . . . had been a bit too free in his expression of sympathy for the South." Only when the club elected Schepeler's business partner, Albert Schumacher, as his successor, was the clubhouse allowed to open again.[34]

Some elements of Hanseatic political ideology better lent themselves to an alliance with Confederates than others. On one hand, a cosmopolitan, commercial calling to create world peace did not go well with Confederate politics.[35] On the other hand, Hanseats could understand the idea of States' Rights in terms of their own particularism. They could, furthermore, relate to the ideology of slaveholders who defended a hierarchically ordered society and criticized the foundations of liberalism. Bremen and the South could be perceived of as commonwealths whose way of life was threatened by demands to submit to a larger political entity that threatened to level customary social distinction and to uproot traditional practices. The South argued its case as the defense of the true, traditional constitutional and social order against the fanaticism of a popular movement, not unlike the nationalist movement in Germany that threatened Bremen's independence.[36]

[30] Hennighausen, "Reminiscences"; Cunz, Dieter, *The Maryland Germans: A History*, Princeton, NJ, 1948, 304–9.

[31] Cunz, "Maryland Germans in the Civil War," *Maryland Historical Magazine* 36, no.4 (December 1941); Heinrich to Julius Wilkens, April 20, 1865, MdHS MS.439.

[32] Louis P. Hennighausen, "Reminiscences," quotes from part II, pp. 10, 14. See also Baker, *Ambivalent Americans*, 17–19, 38–9, 128–51; Browne, *Baltimore*, 196–215; Echternkamp, Jörg, "Emerging Ethnicity: The German Experience in Antebellum Baltimore," *MdHM* 86, no. 1 (Spring 1991), 1–22.

[33] Fields, *Slavery*, 63–89.

[34] Cunz, "Maryland Germans in the Civil War," 414–16.

[35] Cf. Fitzhugh, George, *Cannibals All! or, Slaves without Masters*, Richmond, 1857.

[36] Bowman, *Masters*, esp. Chapter 4; Genovese, Eugene, *The Slaveholders' Dilemma: Freedom and Progress in Southern Conservative Thought, 1820–1860*, Columbia, SC, 1992; Wright, Gavin, *The*

Some Hanseats were even willing to make a sacrifice, if not of their life, then at least of their money and of the lives of their children, for the cause of the Confederacy. One of the staunchest supporters of the South among Baltimore Hanseats was Gustav Wilhelm Lürman. His son, also named Gustav, joined the Confederate army and fought until after the surrender of Lee. The elder Gustav W. Lürman, "gave and lost largely his fortune" for the South. He extracted almost $75,000 from his business during the war years. Although no use for these amounts is given in the records, it can be assumed that he invested much of that sum in Confederate war bonds.[37]

The decisions Hanseats made as the Civil War approached split decades-long alliances between firms and families. Gustav W. Lürman was the son of Sophie Charlotte Oelrichs, an aunt of his business partners.[38] Yet blood and money were no longer able to ensure political harmony. Lürman's associate of twenty-two years, Heinrich Oelrichs, could not have disagreed more with the pro-Confederate course of his senior partner. On January 1, 1861, Oelrichs ended his involvement in Oelrichs & Lurman and relocated to New York. There he joined his brother Edwin and Gustav F. Schwab in the firm of Oelrichs & Co.[39]

Relations between the Oelrichs and the Lürmans became outright nasty over the next few years. E. G. Oelrichs, another brother of Heinrich's, and a former associate of Lürman's in Baltimore, had already died in 1857. In 1865, however, the executors of E. G. Oelrichs's will sued Lürman in a British court over payments on Maryland bonds that had been bought by E. G. Oelrichs & Lurman in the 1830s, but had been depreciated in 1842. Lürman argued that the losses had been amicably settled in 1842, but that no record had been kept, because of the confidence and friendship between the partners. Heinrich Oelrichs had already been an associate in Oelrichs & Lurman of Baltimore in 1842, and would have been aware of such a settlement. Because no one had raised the question of the bonds between 1842 and 1865, the Oelrichs's lawsuit against Lürman looks suspiciously like an act of spite. Although ably represented by Severn Teackle Wallis, a Baltimore lawyer associated with the pro-Confederate Maryland elite, Lürman could not prove his innocence, and his opponents had the bonds that suggested his guilt. In 1866, a British court ordered him to pay.[40]

Political Economy of the Cotton South: Households, Markets, and Wealth in the Nineteenth Century, New York, 1978, esp. pp. 128–57.

[37] Heiser, Elinor S., *Days Gone By*, Baltimore, 1940, 90, quoted in Cunz, "Maryland Germans in the Civil War," 416; "Recapitulation of the Business for Statements from 1861 to 1867," folder "1830–1867 E.G. Oelrichs and Lurman Company," box 2, MdHS MS.541. This collection also contains some Confederate war bonds.

[38] Hirschfeld, George W., genealogical overview to "Stephan Lürman, Brief an meine Kinder aus 2. Ehe (1813)," typescript 1977, unmarked, orange binder, StAHB 7,128, Lürman [family papers], box 3. Hirschfeld erroneously dates Stephan Lürman's marriage to Sophie Charlotte Oelrichs in 1818. Stephan Lürman died in 1816, and married Ms. Oelrichs in 1806.

[39] Lürman, Gustav Wilhelm, "History of Oelrichs & Lurman," manuscript 1866, and Lurman & Co., notice of change in partnership, January 1, 1861, both in MdHS MS.541, Lurman, Gustavus W., 1809–66, Papers and genealogy, 1833–1945, box 2, folder "1830–1867 E.G. Oelrichs and Lurman Company."

[40] S[evern], T[eackle], Wallis to Gustav W. Lürman, April 3, 1866; Maynard Sons & Co, London, to G.W. Lurman, February 6, 1865 and December 21, 1865; G. W. Lürman to Maynard & Sons Co.,

For a while, Gustav W. Lürman left the United States to escape the possible consequences of his politics. In a letter to his niece, Augusta, written in Baltimore on May 2, 1865, he referred to an extensive stay in London and Paris, and visits to Switzerland. Lürman returned to Baltimore on March 22, 1865, where he found his son, Gustav, who had "fought to the last," yet was already paroled. Lürman showed clear signs of despair at the new political situation. While still in Europe, he had found "the news from home so depressing that I fell into a certain lethargy." Back in the United States, Lürman thought that "I will find it hard to adapt to the changed conditions but thank God in my house we are all of one opinion." In spite of the consolation this unanimity within his own family offered, Lürman still felt that "I have suffered a bitter disappointment of all the hopes I harbored."[41] Among the casualties of the war was the community of Hanseats on which Lürman had relied in the antebellum years. No longer could he be secure in the knowledge that he was "of one opinion" with a larger group of his peers. Instead, he had to rely for that comfort on his immediate family.

Lürman was not the only Confederate Hanseat to prefer the safety of foreign countries to an active, personal involvement in the war. John C. Brune, who had been a member of the proslavery legislature of 1860, also went abroad, where he died in 1864.[42] It appears that most Hanseats who sided with the South did so cautiously, even if they were firm enough in their convictions to take the defeat of the Confederacy personally.[43]

While most Baltimore Hanseats were pro-Confederate, Heinrich Oelrichs was by no means alone in his Northern sympathies. Julius Wilkens never went on record with any strong statement in support of either side, but he did make sure he was not drafted into military service. In August 1862, and again in July 1863, he obtained legal documents confirming his exemption on the ground that he was not a citizen of the United States. While in Bremen in the summer of 1865, Julius Wilkens became a citizen of Bremen.[44] His brother, Wilhelm Wilkens, was openly in support of the Union. In March 1865, he wrote to Julius, then in Bremen: "Jeff Davis is in discord with his Congress, Richmond will be evacuated and all in the South are at the end of their tether . . . , in short matters look very favorable here at

London, January 21, 1866, folder "1830–1867 E. G. Oelrichs and Lurman Company," box 2, MdHS MS.541. Wallis's correspondence with Lürman suggests that the latter had relied on the customary trust between Hanseats, and was now caught off guard by its revocation. Thus Wallis wrote to Lürman: "I think prudence should have suggested to you both, to have had some written minute of your respective rights and obligations prepared at the time when the partnership was dissolved. As between Mr. Oelrichs and yourself, your confidence in each other and your long personal friendship of course rendered no such precaution necessary, and I presume it was on this account that nothing of the sort was thought of" (Wallis to Lürman, April 3, 1866).

[41] Gustav W. Lürman to Augusta [Lürman?], May 2,1865, folder "1817–1865; n.d. Gustav[us] [W.] Lürman – Correspondence," box 1, MdHS MS.541.

[42] Howard, George W., *The Monumental City, Its Past History and Present Resources*, Baltimore, 1873, 208–10.

[43] There was a strong minority of Northern merchants who continued to support a peace agreement that left slavery intact. See Beckert, *Metropolis*, 127–8.

[44] Passport issued by the Office of the Provost Marshal General, State of Maryland, August 28, 1862; Letter by Justice of the Peace, July 14, 1863; Heinrich to Julius Wilkens, Baltimore, June 9, 1865, MdHS MS.439.

present."[45] He might not have been that frank if he had considered his brother a Confederate.

The firm of Stellmann & Hinrichs took a conspicuous position on the side of the Union. During the parade celebrating the fall of Richmond and Petersburg, they greeted the celebrators with a patriotic display on the front of their three-story building on Baltimore Street, on the parade route. A clerk employed by Geyer & Wilkens wrote the following:

Last night was again a night of excitement the whole city was illuminated. Balto street was one blaze of light. . . . Stellmann Hinrichs & Co. made as fine a display as any; they had the front of their store lit up bottom to top. (600 candles.) in every window an am. flag, and several foreign flags strung across the street; in the doors they had the following transparencies, One country, 1 flag, 1 Constitution, 1 Destiny. the balance of houses were illuminated with candles.[46]

Other businesses in downtown Baltimore apparently showed a high degree of patriotism, too, making Baltimore Street that "blaze of light," fueled by gas candles.

Geyer & Wilkens, located on 22 South Calvert Street, just around the corner from the route of the parade, decided to show only token support for the celebration. Wilhelm Middendorf, another of Geyer & Wilkens's clerks, wrote that "We had (Geyer & Wilkens) a ten cent flag stuck out the 2nd story window."[47] Eventually, even this small amount of adaptation was too much to bear for Eduard Geyer: "Mr. Geyer was so disgusted with the news [of the Confederate defeat] that he would [not] allow the 10 cent rag to hang out the window any longer he put went up and took it down [*sic*]."[48] Middendorf apparently had feelings similar to those of his employer. Having reported the burning of Richmond and Petersburg, which destroyed all of the tobacco stored there, he was pleased that "the Yanks did not get that much after all." After citing the above-mentioned banners on Stellmann & Hinrichs's store front, Middendorf quipped, "something they forgot and that was, *two camps [Zwei Lager]*."[49]

Eduard Geyer's business partner, Heinrich Wilkens, had little sympathy for the Northern cause as well. When he wrote to his brother, Julius, about Lincoln's assassination, he displayed an attitude characteristic for Confederates at that time. He was appalled at the cowardice of the assassin, and thought the attempt on the president's life politically inexpedient:

If the murder had been accomplished a year ago, it might have benefited the Southern Cause, but now it is only spite [*Bosheit*] and revenge. What is worst for the southern states, the new president Johnson will not deal so leniently and conciliatory with the rebel leaders.[50]

[45] Wilhelm to Julius Wilkens, March 24, 1865, MdHS MS.439. The last part of the sentence was written in English in the original letter, which otherwise was in German.

[46] H. C. Roglmann to Julius Wilkens, April 7, 1865, MdHS MS.439. English in the original. If a German author used English in the source, I will mark the citation with the letters "E.o." from here on.

[47] Wilhelm Middendorf to Julius Wilkens, April 7, 1865, MdHS MS.439, E.o.; for shop location: Ferslew, Eugene, *Baltimore City Directory, for 1859–60*, Baltimore, 1859.

[48] H. C. Roglmann to Julius Wilkens, April 7, 1865, MdHS MS.439, E.o.

[49] Wilhelm Middendorf to Julius Wilkens, April 7, 1865, MdHS MS.439, E.o.

[50] Heinrich to Julius Wilkens (in Bremen), Baltimore, April 20, 1865, MdHS MS.439.

Between the Wilkens brothers, disagreement over the Civil War did not lead to the kind of venom that tore apart the Oelrichs and the Lürmans. Still, fraternal harmony was ruined. In a letter to Julius Wilkens, then in Bremen, Wilhelm Wilkens gave an uncharitable account of a Sunday visit to their brother Heinrich's:

Heinrich is still his old self, how else could it be, "cool to the heart." I was there the past Sunday, [it was] even more boring then usually, as the pure genius of Mr. Roeholl, Esq., increased the boredom by his presence. . . . I also had the unspeakable pleasure to see his Highness, Mr. Geyer, with consort. . . . The next two Sundays I will enjoy in blissful freedom, since I have had it with these charming family suppers and dinners and will eat there at most every three weeks.[51]

Personal dislike may well have been to blame for the spoiled family harmony among the Wilkens, but their disagreement about the war did not help for keeping the brothers on good terms.

Perhaps the most ardent Hanseatic supporter of the Republican Party was Gustav F. Schwab. He made his strong opinions on Christian morality the foundation of his politics. A week after Lincoln's inauguration, Schwab lectured a largely hostile audience of German commoners in New York on the benefits of temperance and the evils of slavery. In a letter to his mother, he praised Lincoln's politics, and by the fall of 1861, he was playing a leading role in the "German Union League."[52] In 1864, weeks before the presidential election, Schwab joined a broad coalition of New Yorkers of different backgrounds at a meeting in support of Lincoln's reelection.[53] His wife, too, shared her husband's sentiment and expressed it in a letter to her children: "Yesterday morning we read in the newspaper about Grant's glorious victory near Petersburg and in the evening Mr. Mali came over and told us that Richmond is ours. . . . I should like to tell Uncle Christoph these news myself and see his face brighten up at it."[54] Between Schwab and Lürman, Hanseats embraced the full range of conflicting positions found at the beginning of the Civil War.

Strong opinions on the war were not limited to American Hanseats. In Bremen, the Meier and Noltenius families enthusiastically supported Schwab's politics. Christoph Theodor Schwab and his wife, Emily, neé von Post, happened to be staying with the Meiers in Bremen when Hermann and Amalie Noltenius visited the Meier villa. They brought a fresh letter from Gustav F. Schwab, who had enclosed newspaper clippings reporting on his speech. Christoph Theodor

---

[51] Wilhelm to Julius Wilkens (in Bremen), Baltimore, March 24, 1865, MdHS MS.439. Wilhelm Wilkens cites Goethe's popular poem, "The Fisherman." "Kühl bis an's Herz Hinan," in its context, refers to the unsentimental fisherman who sees in the fish not the fellow creature, but the prey. Metaphorically, the fisherman is the calculating utilitarian, and Wilhelm Wilkens seems to imply the same about his brother, Heinrich.

[52] Sophie Schwab to Gustav F. Schwab, Stuttgart, April 9, 1861 and May 9, 1861, MSS 434, John Christopher Schwab Family Papers, Manuscripts and Archives, Yale University Library, series I, box 2, folder 37; *New York Times*, The Sunday Question, March 11, 1861, 8; and "The German Union League," October 26, 1861, 3. The latter article mentions the participation of a Dr. Dulon, possibly pastor Rudolf Dulon, the exiled leader of the 1848 revolution in Bremen.

[53] "The Union," *New York Times*, September 28, 1864.

[54] E.v.P. (i.e., Eliza von Post) to My Dear Boys (in Stuttgart), Fordham, April 4, 1865, MSS 434, Schwab Papers, series I, box 2, folder 39.

reported to his brother that "we discussed the speech you made in front of the great assembly, and its style and good purpose found applause and universal support."[55]

Although not sympathetic to the Southern cause, other Hanseats in Bremen remained highly skeptical of the prospects of the North. Burgomaster Arnold Duckwitz did not have much trust in the Republicans and their followers. Commenting on a loan by American banks' to the federal government for financing the war, Duckwitz wrote to Rudolf Schleiden: "These 50 Million $ . . . will soon be distilled away, and the raucous rabble that will enlist in the army will run home shortly." Schleiden shared Duckwitz's doubts. Nonetheless, these leading players in Bremish foreign policy cast their lot with the Northern side, refusing to recognize the Confederate States.[56]

The rifts among Hanseats in Bremen, Baltimore, and New York meant that they no longer functioned as a group, politically. Political disagreement even led to the dissolution of more fundamental ties, those between, and even within, families and firms. The basis of this transatlantic community was rapidly giving way under the outside political pressures. The economic crisis, precipitated by the lack of confidence of businessman in the face of the looming division between the sections, added more strains to the already fraying Hanseatic network. The most prominent Hanseatic casualty of the economic crisis that began after Lincoln's election was Consul Keutgen in New York.

Keutgen's shameful departure from office did not bode well for Hanseatic diplomacy. The episode was emblematic for the ineffectiveness of Hanseats' attempts in 1861 to shape "great politics" through their accustomed channels of influencing decision makers. Two episodes illustrate this failure of the mechanisms of Bremish foreign policy. In Washington, Rudolf Schleiden convinced Lincoln to send him on a peace mission to Richmond. In Bremen, Burgomaster Arnold Duckwitz and *Senator* Otto Gildemeister went on a mission to Berlin to convince the Prussian government to build a joint navy with the other German coastal states. Both ended in failure and disappointment. From that point on, Bremen increasingly found itself on the edge of the dance floor, as others set the tune of the concert of powers.

A DINNER WITH LINCOLN AND A MISSION TO RICHMOND

Rudolf Schleiden's attempt to prevent a civil war that would break up the American union began promisingly. On the evening of March 2, two days before

---

[55] Christoph Theodor Schwab to Gustav F. Schwab, Stuttgart, April 9, 1861, MSS 434, John Christopher Schwab Family Papers, Manuscripts and Archives, Yale University Library, series I, box 2, folder 37. Christoph Theodor Schwab attached his letter to the letter by Sophie Schwab of the same date, cited in the previous note. Apparently, on April 9, he had just returned to his home in Stuttgart from his visit to the Meiers in Bremen.

[56] Arnold Duckwitz to Rudolf Schleiden, Bremen, August 30, 1861, StAHB 7,116 [Rudolf Schleiden Papers], folder "Briefwechsel Rudolf Schleiden mit Senator Arnold Duckwitz, 1854–1879," third of five unnumbered and unlabeled boxes; Rudolf Schleiden to Gustav F. Schwab (in NY), Washington, DC, December 14, 1860, MSS 434, John Christopher Schwab Family Papers, Manuscripts and Archives, Yale University Library, series I, box 2, folder 38.

his inauguration as president, Lincoln accepted a dinner invitation to Schleiden's residence. The diplomatic guests at the event included Johannes Rösing, the freshly minted attaché to Schleiden; Albert Schumacher, the Baltimore Consul; and the ministers for Great Britain, the Netherlands, and Austria. Besides the president-elect, the American guests were General Winfield Scott and seven other American politicians, whose selection, according to a newspaper correspondent, "showed the host's understanding of the varying constituents of the incoming administration." The Republican politicians in attendance represented half of Lincoln's future cabinet: William H. Seward (Secretary of State), Samuel P. Chase (Secretary of Treasury), Simon Cameron (Secretary of War), and Montgomery Blair (Postmaster General). Also present were David Davis, an old ally of Lincoln's from his native Illinois, whom he placed on the Supreme Court in 1862, and Senator Charles Sumner.[57]

Arguably, Schleiden was quite adept at the game of identifying influential figures and getting them to listen to Hanseatic concerns. Considering his recently professed unfamiliarity with the leaders of the Republican Party, the diplomat's ability to assemble them at his house was all the more remarkable.[58] The minister-resident drew all registers of diplomatic glamour. The correspondent of the *New York Evening Post* was duly impressed:

The dinner was worthy of the guests and the reputation of the entertainer. Mr. Schleiden has quite a name for the age and excellence of his wines. One of the wines on his list, served in diminutive glasses, . . . dates but four years after the landing of the pilgrims; and the value of a single bottle at compound interest would more than defray our national debt. . . . This dinner has become the town topic of the capital.[59]

Evidently, Lincoln was taken with Schleiden's diplomatic skills and knowledge – enough so to send him on a secret mission to Richmond, to sound out the possibilities of a peaceful resolution of the conflict with Confederate Vice-President Alexander H. Stevens, a personal acquaintance of the Hanseat. Schleiden set out on his errand in the last week of April. He hoped to convince the South to agree to a three-month "suspension of all hostilities" – the Northern blockade and the Southern issue of letters of marquee. At the end of this period, Congress would convene on July 4, and a negotiated solution might be reached.[60]

[57] "The State of the Nation," *New York Evening Post*, March 4, 1861, 2. Baron von Gerolt, the Prussian minister, and a personal friend of Schleiden's late father, had canceled at the last minute to observe the mourning period for the recently departed King Friedrich Wilhelm IV.

[58] Wätjen, Hermann, "Dr. Rudolf Schleiden als Diplomat in Bremischen Diensten, 1853–1866," *Bremisches Jahrbuch* 34 (1933), 262–76, here p. 271.

[59] "The State of the Nation," *New York Evening Post*, March 4, 1861, 2. The correspondent for the *Evening Post* lent additional glamour to the event by making the humble republican Johannes Rösing into a French nobleman, calling him "De Rosigny."

[60] Adams, Ephraim Douglass, *Great Britain and the American Civil War*, London and New York, 1925, 65–72; Lutz, Ralph Haswell, *Die Beziehungen zwischen Deutschland und den Vereinigten Staaten während des Sezessionskrieges*, Heidelberg, 1911; idem, "Rudolf Schleiden and the Visit to Richmond, April 25, 1861," *Annual Report of the American Historical Association for the Year 1915*, Washington, DC, 1917, 209–16. In his fictional account, Gore Vidal ennobles the Minister Resident, as "Baron von Schleiden" (*Lincoln: A Novel*, New York, 1984).

Schleiden met twice with Stevens, the first time for three hours. Stevens listed among his conditions for entertaining an armistice that Maryland be permitted to join the Confederate States. Schleiden attempted to gain a written commitment of a specific list of conditions under which the Confederacy would agree to an armistice, but Stevens refused. In the end, Schleiden returned to Washington on April 27, where he informed Lincoln and Seward that "the leading men of the South are determined to leave the Union."[61]

For Bremish diplomacy in America, Schleiden's failed attempt at reconciling the sections represents both a last hurrah and the first coffin nail. That he believed he might be successful shows that he was used to being heard and being taken seriously by American leaders. At the same time, this belief appears as a grandiose delusion. The forces of popular conviction and sectional competition were not to be contained in deals that reasonable leaders made in secret negotiations. The kind of genteel politics that Schleiden and his Hanseatic allies had conducted so successfully in the preceding decades had reached its limits, and its main representative in the United States had failed to grasp the magnitude of the change and the insufficiency of the means at his disposal.

Schleiden's acquired reputation as a skilled and knowledgeable diplomat still received some recognition during the war, but from the point of view of his American counterparts, his role was strictly that of a consultant, no longer that of a lobbyist. Between 1861 and 1865, the Lincoln administration occasionally asked Schleiden's advice on questions of international law, and he was glad to share it.[62]

Schleiden suggested in his autobiography that he had an input in the making of the Emancipation Proclamation. Already at his first meeting with Lincoln, Schleiden had established his antislavery credentials, based on his involvement with the emancipation of Danish slaves on the Virgin Islands in the 1840s. As a Danish bureaucrat, Schleiden had studied international precedent and legal options for laws that ended slavery in preparation for the Danish decree of 1847. His experience would have made him a valuable advisor on questions like compensation and the integration of freedmen into society, both of which were on the mind of Lincoln's administration. Although Lincoln may well have asked Schleiden's help or opinion on emancipation, there is nothing in the literature on the Emancipation Proclamation that suggests the Hanseat's involvement in the political decision process that led to this document. Even though it is true that Schleiden and Lincoln have in common that they signed proclamations for the emancipation of slaves, Schleiden had done so in a subordinate way; as a bureaucrat who had to countersign a royal decree before it went into effect.[63]

The sporadic activity as an advisor to the cabinet did not fill Schleiden's time. He felt that there was little left for him to do in the American capital. As early as May 1861, under the immediate impression of his failed peace mission, he asked for permission to go on a vacation in Europe. While acknowledging the envoy's powerlessness under wartime conditions, Burgomaster Duckwitz still asked him

[61] Lutz, *Beziehungen*, 30–1.

[62] Ibid., 31–40.

[63] Schleiden, Rudolph, *Erinnerungen eines Schleswig-Holsteiners. Neue Folge, 1841–1848*, Wiesbaden, 1890, 227–32.

to stay on his post, because "the [Bremish] merchants will at least be mollified, if they can be assured by your continued presence in the belief that all that can be done [for their interests], will be done."[64] The remaining function of Bremen's minister-resident was now officially one of merely psychological value. The occasional intervention in disputes over contraband or smuggling still required the involvement of a Bremish representative, but attaché Rösing was able to handle such cases. After several prolonged absences, in 1865 Schleiden left Washington for good to take on the post of Hanseatic minister-resident to the United Kingdom.[65]

DEALING WITH PRUSSIA

Meanwhile, in Germany, *Senatoren* Arnold Duckwitz and Otto Gildemeister, backed by the *Bürgerschaft*'s vote in favor of a German navy, traveled to Berlin to negotiate the terms of such a fleet. They had high hopes, because Prussia had been sending encouraging signals. Count Roon, Prussian Minister of the Navy, had even come to Bremen to talk in private to members of the Hanseatic leadership.[66]

In keeping with the *Bürgerschaft* resolution, Bremen's delegates hoped to convince the Prussians to create a navy based on a treaty between those German states who wished to participate, run jointly by the coastal states, and commanded by Prussian admirals. The city was willing to contribute 50,000 Thaler. As Duckwitz and Gildemeister found out, Prussia had different ideas. The kingdom envisioned a naval convention between the German states as a means of making others pay for an expanded Prussian fleet, in exchange for the promise of protection of all German traders.[67]

Prussia wanted to see financing of the navy apportioned according to the tonnage of the states' merchant navies, rather than by population, as Bremen had proposed. Under Prussia's plan, Bremen would have paid half as much as the kingdom, which had 180 times as many inhabitants as the city, but had only twice as strong a merchant marine. Evidently, Prussia overestimated the fiscal capabilities of the Hanseatic city. While the population of the latter commanded significant fortunes and incomes, the ability of the Bremish state to marshal these resources for public purposes was much more limited than that of the Prussian state.[68]

Negotiations were never formally ended, and fizzled out in the spring of 1862.[69] It had been a thoroughly sobering experience for Arnold Duckwitz. In a letter to Rudolf Schleiden, the burgomaster summed up his disillusionment:

Conditions in Berlin are disconsolate. The gentlemen mean well, are charming and intelligent, but [do not have] a trace of creative genius, [instead they show] an

---

[64] Arnold Duckwitz to Rudolf Schleiden, Bremen n.d. [received May 16, 1861], StAHB 7,116 [Rudolf Schleiden Papers], folder "Briefwechsel Rudolf Schleiden mit Senator Arnold Duckwitz, 1854–1879," third of five unnumbered and unlabeled boxes.

[65] In 1862, Schleiden had become Hanseatic, rather than Bremish, minister-resident in Washington; representing Hamburg and Lübeck in addition to Bremen. Wätjen, "Schleiden," 274.

[66] Hardegen and Smidt, *H. H. Meier*, 177–8.

[67] Ibid., 178–9; Krieger, *Politik*, 27.

[68] Hardegen and Smidt, *H. H. Meier*, 178–9; Krieger, *Politik*, 27.

[69] Hardegen and Smidt, *H. H. Meier*, 179.

inflexibility reminiscent of the old-Prussian general staff; so that it is indeed not at all surprising, if the middling states [of Germany] have no respect for Prussia and do not want to subject themselves to it. It is a sad state of affairs, but this is how it is. . . . The impression of Prussia which I gained in 1848/1849, that the future of a unified Germany with maritime strength will not grow on the sands of the March, has remained the same. . . . At least now we will not put ourselves into a dangerous dependency [on Prussia].[70]

These private words explain the tone of Duckwitz's public address on New Year's Day, 1862:

The right policy for Bremen is to keep a free hand in political questions, and not to do anything that might loosen the band of international law of the German Confederation. As long as the greatest Protestant power [Prussia] moves on the basis of the German Confederation, we will prefer her company over others; but, beyond that [basis], to put ourselves into a dependency on her, and to gain the enmity of other Confederates as a result, is something I cannot condone, and against which I must most earnestly caution.[71]

Duckwitz had seen that the hope for a federal nation-state under Prussian leadership was vain. The kingdom's bureaucracy had a strong centralistic agenda, and was not about to share responsibility with others, nor to consider points of view beyond the limits of the dynastic interests of the Hohenzollern. Weak though it may be, the state of Bremen was still better off alone.

H. H. Meier, however, was undeterred by the experience of the failure of his pet project, the fleet of gunboats. He continued to cast his lot with Prussia, even taking his activities to the "national" level. Prussia's newfound enthusiasm for free trade particularly appealed to Meier. After an offer made in 1861 by Napoleon III, Prussia had secretly negotiated a free-trade agreement with France and presented it to the governments of the German Customs Union for its adoption in 1862. The German bourgeoisie was divided about the merits of this agreement. The German Chamber of Commerce (*Deutscher Handelstag*, or DHT), founded only the previous year as one of the interest groups in the orbit of the *Nationalverein*, split over a motion to voice support for the treaty.[72]

Austria, like Bremen, was not a member of the *Zollverein*, but for opposite reasons. The Habsburg monarchy maintained a stiff protective tariff, while Bremen wished to uphold free trade. Bringing the *Zollverein* into the free-trade camp by way of the treaty with France would have weakened the ties between Austria and the other German states. The Prussian trade policy was thus a brilliant diplomatic move: it gave the German bourgeoisie an incentive for siding with Prussia and isolated Austria, Prussia's main rival.[73]

---

[70] Arnold Duckwitz to Rudolf Schleiden, Bremen, January 17, 1862, StAHB 7,116 [Rudolf Schleiden Papers], folder "Briefwechsel Rudolf Schleiden mit Senator Arnold Duckwitz, 1854–1879," third of five unnumbered and unlabeled boxes. Duckwitz alludes to the sandy soils of Brandenburg, the area surrounding Berlin, also referred to as the March.

[71] Cited in Krieger, *Politik*, 45–6.

[72] Biefang, *Bürgertum*, 207–20.

[73] Ibid., 259–72.

It was evident to the delegates of the 1862 DHT convention that support of the Franco-Prussian treaty meant taking sides in the dualism between the two German Great Powers. DHT president, David Hansemann, a liberal industrialist and railroad promoter from the Prussian Rhineland, opposed an endorsement for this very reason. H. H. Meier spoke in favor of an endorsement. Meier's side won by four votes, and Hansemann resigned.[74]

In 1864, the DHT recognized the importance of Meier's role in bringing the organization in line with Prussian policy and elected him president. Ten days after his election he responded to a letter by Count Itzenplitz, Prussia's Minister of Commerce, who had congratulated him on his election, but had cited concerns that a DHT leader from a state that did not belong to the *Zollverein* might be adverse to Prussian interests. Meier wrote:

I would have to reply [to such concerns] that I have never in my public life been led by my private interests. If needed, however, I do not lack the private interest [to connect me with the *Zollverein*], since I am a *Zollverein* industrialist, having a coal mine and an iron mill on my estate in Brunswick. As a non-Prussian, I deem, if His Excellency will grant me His trust, that I can make felt the presidential influence over non-Prussian members [of the DHT] much more firmly in the interest of a good cause, which His Excellency wishes to see promoted, than I could if I had the honor to be a Prussian.[75]

With this record of ingratiation, Meier might well have been ennobled, if ever Prussia had annexed Bremen, which outlawed titles of nobility.[76]

DOUBTS ABOUT THE NATION

While Duckwitz had the *Senat* and the Bremish consular network to amplify his opinions, and Meier had the nationalist associations like the *Nationalverein* and the DHT to work for his aims, antinationalists among Hanseats lacked similar organizational means. That is not to say that there was not plenty of disagreement with the idea of national unification. Some of this disagreement was merely directed against a united Germany under Prussian leadership, but some was opposed to any

---

[74] Hardegen and Smidt, *H. H. Meier*, 168–9. Biefang, *Bürgertum*, 269–71 and note 43, gives a contradictory account, whereby Meier took a pro-Austrian position and spoke in support of Hansemann. Hardegen and Smidt specifically cite Meier as supporting the claims of the Prussian delegation that *pacta sunt servanda*, directed against Hansemann. The present account follows Hardegen and Smidt, who had at their disposal Meier's personal papers. Although Hansemann was Prussian, he was a leader of the liberal opposition to the monarchy, and for that reason did not identify with the policy of its ministers.

[75] Hardegen and Smidt, *H. H. Meier*, 170.

[76] Biefang, *Bürgertum*, 376, notes that Meier was approached in 1865 by other members of the *Nationalverein* who wished to create a "specifically pro-Prussian party" within that organization, and who considered Meier a potential ally for that cause. It should be noted, however, that even Meier's enthusiasm for the German nation and Prussian leadership had its limits. During the Seven Weeks' War of 1866, as soon as it became clear that Prussia had defeated Austrian ally Hannover, Meier had large amounts of specie, deposited at the mint of Hannover for the Bremer Bank, brought back to Bremen "at the last hour," rather than have them fall into Prussian hands. See Beutin, Ludwig, *Bremisches Bank- und Börsenwesen seit dem 17. Jahrhundert. Von der Wirtschaftsgesinnung einer Hansestadt* (Abhandlungen und Vorträge herausgegeben von der Bremer Wissenschaftlichen Gesellschaft, vol. 10, no. 4, December 1937), 48.

abandonment of Bremish independence. For lack of organization, these voices are more difficult to hear. We can, however, assume that those we can still discern did not stand alone.

Rudolf Schleiden strongly disagreed with Prussian policy in Germany. At the center of this disagreement stood the question of Schleswig-Holstein, by all accounts one of the most tangled messes in European history. Hence, a brief overview of the issue may be in place. The Danish king ruled as duke in Schleswig, Holstein, and Lauenburg. The latter two had been parts of the Holy Roman Empire of the German Nation, and had become parts of the German Confederation in 1815. Based on a fourteenth-century treaty, Schleswig and Holstein were considered "forever indivisible" under international law. While Schleswig had a mixed German and Danish population, Holstein and Lauenburg had overwhelming majorities of ethnic Germans. Ascendant Danish nationalism demanded a unitary, liberal constitution for all parts of the monarchy and promoted a Danization of its ethnically German parts. The majority of the German population in the duchies was royalist and opposed a liberal constitution on that ground, whereas urban Germans opposed Danization, but often favored liberal reforms within the duchies.[77]

After the death of Danish King Frederick VII in 1863, his successor, Christian IX, declared Schleswig-Holstein to be under a unitary constitution for the entire Danish state. From the point of view of Schleswig-Holstein's medieval constitution, this was a breach of right, because the new king had come to the throne in a female line of succession. In response, Prince Frederick of Augustenburg declared his claim to the title of Duke of Schleswig and Holstein, as the legitimate heir in a male line of succession. The German Confederation supported this claim, but Austria and Prussia did not. Jointly, the two great powers went to war with Denmark without the sanction of the confederation, in order to deny Danish rule over the duchies. After their victory over the Danish in 1864, Austria and Prussia ruled jointly over both Schleswig and Holstein and denied Frederick his claim.[78]

Since the 1848 revolution, Denmark had a liberal constitution. While its king had to give up his position as absolute ruler, an extension of this constitution to the duchies would have served his dynastic interest, because it would have done away with the feudal laws that barred him from ruling there. For these reasons, demands for independence from Denmark by Germans in Schleswig-Holstein took the form of a revolt for legitimate succession, against a liberal constitution and, lastly, against Danization. German nationalists outside of Schleswig-Holstein, however, read the struggle as a defense of German soil and nationality against a foreign oppressor.[79]

---

[77] Schleiden, Rudolph, *Erinnerungen eines Schleswig-Holsteiners. Neue Folge, 1841–1848*, Wiesbaden, 1890, 54–76.

[78] Before the Borusso-Austrian intervention, the German nationalist movement had predominantly supported the Augustenburger. H. H. Meier, acting for the *Nationalverein*, had attempted to secure a bank loan for the pretender's government at low interest. See Biefang, *Bürgertum*, 311–56, esp. pp. 340–1 (for Meier).

[79] Schleiden, *Erinnerungen*, 54–76; Biefang, *Bürgertum*.

As an adherent of legitimate succession in Schleswig-Holstein, and as a man who, rumor had it, had entertained hopes of becoming foreign minister in the Ducal government of the Augustenburger contender, Schleiden was incensed. His outbursts against the Prussian minister in London created a diplomatic scandal that led him to ask for his resignation. Schleiden had hoped that Bremen would take the side of the legitimate contender and was disappointed when he learned that the *Senat* had decided to accept the status quo that resulted from the war.[80] Although Schleiden made his peace with the German Empire created in 1871, he never quite reconciled with Prussia or those German nationalists who had disregarded the question of legitimacy in 1864.

In his memoirs, published in the 1880s, Schleiden took great pains to emphasize that legitimate succession, not nationalism, had driven German discontent with Danish policy in Schleswig-Holstein. By the time he wrote these memoirs, Schleiden had embraced the German Empire. He would have had an incentive to cast his earlier role as that of a nationalist martyr, but chose not to. Instead, he had nothing but kind words and admiration for the Danish monarchs, while he scorned the Danish nationalist intellectuals. The latter, to him, were the main culprits in the strife that had destroyed the Danish state. Schleiden's parents had not only been royalists, but also close friends of the Danish royal family. The son partook in this connection, and when Schleiden was incarcerated for dueling, the crown prince in person – the later king Frederick VII – went to Nyborg to bring Schleiden his pardon. This is not a story an ardent German nationalist would tell.[81]

The Danish war led at least some Hanseats to oppose German nationalism. At the height of enthusiasm for a war against Denmark, Wilhelm Knoche, the friend of Baltimore Hanseat Julius Wilkens, voiced derision of the growing nationalist movement:

The Bavarian beer halls multiply daily, that hurts [our] tavern. – Also, our business in the city suffers from the spreading consumption of Mosel- and Rhinewines.... It seems to me that this fad has become an epidemic through the many German rifle-clubs' fairs [*Schützenfeste*], where German humanity works up German courage with German wine, while they really should have that courage when they are sober.[82]

The kind of nationalist festivities Knoche described, most of which were organized by the *Nationalverein*, were a favorite organizational tool for the nationalist movement. In the masses congregated on these occasions, nationalist orators saw a microcosm of the German people and an embodiment of the high ideals to which it subscribed.[83] Knoche just saw a mass of silly drunks.

In spite of his main article of trade, French wine, Knoche subjected nationalism to the gaze of the sober businessman. It hurt his tavern, and the rhetoric that

---

[80] Wätjen, "Schleiden," 275; Krieger, *Politik*, 56 and note 3.

[81] Schleiden, Rudolph, *Jugenderinnerungen eines Schleswig-Holsteiners*, Wiesbaden, 1886, 86, 294; and idem, *Erinnerungen*, 54–76. See also Chapter 5.

[82] Wilhelm Knoche to Julius Wilkens, February 27, 1864, MdHS MS.439.

[83] Langewiesche, Dieter, *Nation, Nationalismus, Nationalstaat in Deutschland und Europa* (Beck'sche Reihe, vol. 1399), Munich, 2000, esp. pp. 82–102, 132–69; and Hettling, Manfred and Paul Nolte, eds., *Bürgerliche Feste. Symbolische Formen politischen Handelns im 19. Jahrhundert*, Göttingen, 1993.

promised that the nation and its unitary state would serve to benefit everyone's interests did not make for sufficient compensation. The language of the "fad" and the "epidemic" suggest that he saw the participants in nationalist spectacles as intoxicated not just by the cheap national beverages, but also by a questionable ideology that overrules even such an inherently individual judgment as that of taste with a collective commitment to the fatherland.

To be sure, principled opposition to the idea of the nation was a rare matter in Hanseatic circles. Many Bremish merchants felt attached to "Germany" in some way or the other, even if just as a matter of shared culture. Nonetheless, only a minority of them was willing to give up Bremish independence for the promise of a bright new future in a unitary German state. This independent role, however, was to come to an end sooner than many of them had expected or wished.

Even as late as 1860, entering into Bremen's foreign service appeared as a good career move for a bright young man with an education. Johannes Rösing Jr. was a successful young lawyer in Bremen. When Arnold Duckwitz called him into the burgomaster's office in early October 1860 and offered him the post of attaché to Rudolf Schleiden in Washington, Rösing was elated. Duckwitz related the following to Schleiden:

I told Rösing I could not make a firm promise, and that he had to accept that he will be fired after a year, if we should come to the opinion that he was unsuitable. He became pale and then red with surprise, the news hit him like lightning from a clear sky. When he came to, he said that this was precisely what he had desired for a long time, without ever stating it openly.[84]

Rösing came from a well-established Hanseatic family, although his father had fallen from grace after a bankruptcy and his subsequent conversion to the cause of democracy, which he championed as a representative for Bremen's lower middle class in the *Bürgerschaft*. Duckwitz did not hold the father's sins against the son. The burgomaster knew that a person could redeem himself for political missteps. After all, he had advocated revolution in 1830 and had soon after been co-opted into the *Senat* by Johann Smidt. Now Duckwitz was playing the role of the political patriarch, and Rösing was honored by the offer of joining the establishment.

No doubt, Rösing's desire to play a part in the glamorous world of diplomacy was shared by many of his peers. Whether or not he regarded the appointment as a stepping-stone to future honors, in 1860 Rösing was willing to give up a successful law practice for an uncertain future in the foreign service of an independent Hanseatic city. If he had considered the future of that independence in danger, he might have been less enthusiastic about the job. At this point, however, Rösing felt that he could bank on Bremen's continued independence.

Moreover, Rösing must have felt confident that his conscience allowed him to represent Bremen's foreign policy abroad. Had he entertained doubts about the *Senat*'s Atlantic orientation, he would not have been as eager to take on this task. The commitment to the traditional Bremish approach to international relations, in

[84] Arnold Duckwitz to Rudolf Schleiden, Bremen December 15, 1860, StAHB 7,116 [Rudolf Schleiden Papers], folder "Briefwechsel Rudolf Schleiden mit Senator Arnold Duckwitz, 1854–1879," third of five unnumbered and unlabeled boxes.

which Germany played a subordinate role, was apparently not limited to the generation of patriarchs like Arnold Duckwitz or Heinrich Smidt.

THE END OF INDEPENDENCE, 1866–1867

The failure of Schleiden's attempt to make peace between the sections in the United States and the failure of Duckwitz's and Gildemeister's mission to Berlin were signs of the diminished effectiveness of the customary venues of Hanseatic foreign policy in the face of self-assured political leaders who pursued programs of national unification in which there was little space for a small, independent city of free traders. In Otto von Bismarck, Bremen was faced with just such a leader. Appointed Prussian chancellor in 1862 by King Wilhelm I, just a little more than a year after the monarch's ascent to the throne, the "Iron Junker" pursued a policy centered on the interests of the Hohenzollern dynasty. In extending his king's rule over all of Germany, to the exclusion of Austria, Bismarck mobilized public opinion in the guise of the nationalist movement, and against the particularistic interests of the rulers of minor German states. Without ever intending to let executive power slip from monarchical control, he offered German liberals a national parliament in a nation-state under a Prussian monarch. By 1871, he had won the struggles for Prussian hegemony, both on the battlefield and in the "hearts and minds" of most middle-class Germans. The end result was a new German Empire. For Hanseats, however, independence came to an end before that.

In 1866, Hanseats found out just how untenable their independence had become. The joint administration of Schleswig and Holstein by Prussia and Austria had been ridden with conflict from the beginning. In 1866, Prussia announced the intention of annexing the duchies. Austria declared war against the rival, and both sides worked feverishly to get the other German states on their side. Prussia countered the Austrian declaration of war with a comprehensive plan for a German union that would exclude the Habsburg monarchy, headed by the Prussian king, and granting a national parliament, elected by universal, male suffrage. At the time, only the United States had voting rights this democratic.

Most middling states – Bavaria, Württemberg, Baden, the Grand Duchy of Hesse, Saxony, and Bremen's neighbor Hannover – joined Austria. Mecklenburg, Oldenburg, and Hesse-Darmstadt sided with Prussia. Bremen had remained silent on the issue, but did withdraw its representative from the seat of the German Confederation in Frankfurt on the Main. Prussia exerted pressure on the Hanseatic cities to take its side. In two notes, dated June 16 and June 20, the Prussian envoy in Hamburg, von Richthofen, had asked Bremen to respond to the offer of an alliance.

Previously, the *Senat* had often tried to sidestep entreaties from either German Great Power by ignoring them for as long as politely possible.[85] Under the impression of the growing urgency of von Richthofen's letters, however, the head of the *Senat*'s Foreign Affairs Commission, Heinrich Smidt, finally replied on June 25:

---

[85] Krieger, *Politik*, 42–3.

The *Senat* is willing ... to collaborate with Prussia's intended reorganization of Germany; it views in [the] outlines of a federal reform a suitable point of departure for negotiations that will have to be conducted with a German parliament; it will work towards convening [such a parliament], as soon as Prussia will convey an invitation thereto. While [the *Senat*] will have to speak on the condition of the constitutionally required consent of the *Bürgerschaft*, it does not doubt in any way that the *Bürgerschaft* will gladly grant its assent.

The content of the reform draft submitted [by you], does, however, give rise to concerns and to wishes for changes, in points specifically relating to Hanseatic interests. The provisions concerning a German navy, specifically, appear impossible to implement without significant modifications.... The *Senat* believes ... that it will remain its prerogative in a future stage of negotiations to see to it that Bremen's interests in these specific questions will be maintained.

In regard to the war that broke out in Germany, Bremen finds itself in a position that makes it the *Senat*'s duty to abstain from a participation in it as long as at all possible. Bremen's situation as a Hanseatic City, its extensive relations with all seafaring nations and to the great industrial districts in Germany, require a restraint, which to explain in more detail to the royal Prussian government will certainly be unnecessary. Therefore, not merely in its own interest, but also in that of German trade and industry, the *Senat* does not doubt that the [Prussian government] ... will make it possible [for the *Senat*] to maintain the neutral position it has taken, and which so far has not been threatened by another party, either.[86]

Smidt further pointed to the departure of Bremen's representative from Frankfurt as proof of Bremen's willingness to conform to Prussian demands, albeit short of joining the war.

This was a less than enthusiastic response to Prussia's offer of an alliance. Bremen was not willing to subscribe wholesale to the proposed changes in Germany's institutions, but wished to negotiate them further. If past attempts at reforming the German Confederation were any guide, Prussia's initiatives might well die in such negotiations. Hence, buying time meant banking on eventually avoiding the proposed reforms, altogether.[87]

Bremen's response to the proposed military alliance reflects that the *Senat* was still in the hands of men who wished to continue the independent foreign policy the city had pursued in the 1850s. Prussia knew that in a war, Bremen's merchant marine was defenseless without a navy. The city was located between two warring parties, Oldenburg and Hannover. Bremerhaven was entirely surrounded by the latter, Prussia's strongest opponent in Northern Germany (see Map 2). The *Senat* hoped that out of consideration for this precarious position, Prussia would recognize Bremen's neutrality. Besides, the outcome of the war was by no means assured, and Bremen wished to avoid picking the losing side.

---

[86] For the Senat Commission on Foreign Affairs, J[ohan] H[einrich] W[ilhelm?] Smidt to Freiherrn von Richthofen (in Hamburg), Bremen June 25, 1866, manuscript copy of the original, in StAHB 7,116 [Rudolf Schleiden Papers], folder "Verschiedenes, 1844–1866," third of five unnumbered and unlabeled boxes.

[87] Duckwitz, Arnold, *Denkwürdigkeiten aus meinem öffentlichen Leben von 1841–1866. Ein Beitrag zur bremischen und deutschen Geschichte*, Bremen, 1877, esp. pp. 150–63.

The *Senat* almost immediately learned that it had entirely misjudged Bismarck's intentions and resolve. The proposed reforms were intended as is, and "a future stage of negotiations" was not part of the plan. The Prussian request for an active Bremish role in the war, likewise, constituted an "offer" much in the same way as that of a mugger offering his client a choice to hand over his wallet voluntarily in exchange for sparing his life. Unlike Austria, Prussia was in a position to back up such an offer with force. Unbeknownst to Smidt, von Richthofen had written yet another, even sharper note to Bremen on the same day that the *Senator* had penned the preceding letter. Under the impression of the thinly veiled threat of Prussian aggression contained in von Richthofen's most recent note, the *Senat* immediately reversed its position. On June 27, Smidt wrote a terse response to von Richthofen, stating that considering the given conditions and Prussian demands, Bremen would follow the "invitation" to mobilize its troops in a joint brigade with Oldenburg, "post haste express."[88]

Following Prussian victory over Austria at Königgrätz on July 3, 1866, Bismarck quickly moved to replace the defunct German Confederation with a new union under Prussian leadership, and excluding Austria. Because the three German states below the Main River – Baden, Württemberg, and Bavaria – refused to join, the new state came to be known as the Northern German Union.[89]

The king of Prussia became head of state of the union, and a parliament, referred to as the Reichstag, was elected by universal male suffrage in single-member, winner-takes-all constituencies. The Prussian cabinet served as the union government. As the spoils of victory, Prussia annexed Hannover, Hesse-Kassel, Frankfurt, Nassau, Schleswig, and Holstein. The governments of the remaining member states of the union were represented in an upper house of parliament. In this house, however, Prussia had an overwhelming majority. *In nuclei*, this was the form of state of the future German Empire. Constitutionally, all it took in 1871 was for the three southern German holdouts to join the existing framework of the Northern German Union and to acclaim Prussian King Wilhelm as German Emperor.[90]

All essential functions of sovereignty devolved upon the Northern German Union. Trade policy, consular matters, foreign relations, shipping regulations, and questions of war and peace were no longer decided in Bremen, but in Berlin. The only field in which Bremen maintained a measure of control was tariffs. Bremen and Hamburg remained, for the time being, outside of the German Customs Union.[91] In America, consulates were transferred into the responsibility of the Northern German Union as

[88] Freiherr von Richthofen to J. H. W. Smidt, Hamburg, June 25, 1866, and For the Senat Commission on Foreign Affairs, J. H. W. Smidt to Freiherrn von Richthofen (in Hamburg), Bremen June 27, 1866, manuscript copies of the originals, ibid. As a leading member of the Bürgerschaft, H. H. Meier was aware of the Prussian conduct. Perhaps this explains why he had the gold stored in the city of Hannover, which belonged to his Bremer Bank, expedited to Bremen before Prussian troops reached Hannover. See Beutin, *Bremisches Bank- und Börsenwesen*, 48.

[89] Siemann, Wolfram, *Gesellschaft im Aufbruch. Deutschland 1849–1871* (edition suhrkamp, Neue Folge, vol. 537; as such: Wehler, Hans-Ulrich, ed., Neue Historische Bibliothek, unnumbered vol.), Frankfurt/Main, 1990, 276–9.

[90] Ibid., 284–9.

[91] Ibid., 289–91. Bremen joined the *Zollverein* only in 1888, again under pressure from Bismarck. See Beutin, *Bremen und Amerika*, 134–7. It is a similar historical curiosity that the Grand Duchy of Luxemburg, which did not become part of the German Empire, nonetheless remained part of the German Customs Union until 1918.

of January 1, 1867. Baron von Gerolt, the Prussian envoy in Washington, D.C., was put in charge of representing the new German state. Bremen's existence as an independent entity had come to an unceremonious end.

Privately, Burgomaster Arnold Duckwitz did not conceal his despair. In a letter to Rudolf Schleiden, he wrote:

I hope that, in the end, the reorganization of Germany will benefit the common good, and will refresh the life of our nation, but for Bremen the happy times of the past 50 years will hardly return, because all that is essential for the statehood of a small trading-state will come under the authority of [the national] parliament, or will become subject to Prussian "guidance." Few [fields of policy] will be left to the jurisdiction of the Hanseatic Cities. A relation of suzerainty is not the most disgusting one, but it is a source of endless humiliations. If this is what [Prussia] is after, I would consider as preferable a total annexation [of Bremen]. I do not gaze into Bremen's future calmly, even if I expect some things to become easier by the attenuation of Hannoverian idiocy [i.e., the obstruction of Bremerhaven's expansion]. Even if Germany will be strengthened and uplifted by removing or softening certain state-entities, and even if Bremen shares in these advantages, nevertheless many things that were our pride will undoubtedly be buried.[92]

The wars that created strengthened, unitary nation-states in America and Germany had politically divided Hanseats. The rise of that industry which financed and outfitted the armies that fought these wars had forever changed the conditions under which Hanseats did business. Under the stress of a hostile political and economic climate, the Hanseatic family network had become threadbare and showed rips in many places. Blank spots, like the expulsion of Friedrich Wilhelm Keutgen from the historical memory of his peers, covered up the damage. Many Bremish firms had fallen along the wayside in this process, ruined by economic failure or personal strife. Where there once had been a vibrant network of independent firms there now lumbered the dominant Lloyd. The losers of the process of change, like Friedrich Köper, saw more clearly, and certainly most resentfully, what received Hanseatic opinion would not admit: the golden days of this transatlantic community were over, and the age of nation-states and industrial capitalism had begun.

---

[92] Arnold Duckwitz to Rudolf Schleiden, Bad Nenndorf July 22, 1866, StAHB 7,116 [Rudolf Schleiden Papers], folder "Briefwechsel Rudolf Schleiden mit Senator Arnold Duckwitz, 1854–1879," third of five unnumbered and unlabeled boxes. Five days after Königgrätz, Duckwitz had left Bremen to visit the spa of Bad Nenndorf, his health affected by the events he deplored. After a brief period of confusion, Prussia, having annexed Hannover, continued the hostile policy toward an expansion of Bremerhaven (see Chapter 9). Consider Wilhelm von Bippen's characterization of Duckwitz' position in 1866: "in the years 1866 and 1870, [Duckwitz] enthusiastically welcomed the fulfillment of the German hopes, for whose realization he had worked in 1848 and 1849." Bippen, Wilhelm von, "Duckwitz, Arnold," in *Bremische Biographie des neunzehnten Jahrhunderts*, ed. Historische Gesellschaft des Künstlervereins, Bremen, 1912, 115–17. The historical record does not support the nationalist teleology Bippen offered, and which has to this day had an effect on our perception of the 1860s.

9

Patriarchs into Patriots

Hanseats in a World of Nation-States, 1867–1945

THE TRANSFORMATIONS OF MEIER AND SCHWAB

Since 1805, the two firms of Oelrichs & Co. of New York and H. H. Meier & Co. of Bremen had been run as a joint, transatlantic enterprise, in which each shared equally in the profits and losses of the other. In the subsequent decades, men from the families that shared an interest in these firms had crossed the ocean for apprenticeships or partnerships on the other shore. Repeatedly, marriage ties woven between Schwabs, Meiers, Oelrichs, and others in the orbit of this "multi-national" business reaffirmed the connection as one that was not just about business but was also about family.[1]

Then, in 1864, the profit-sharing agreement was terminated.[2] It is unlikely that the two senior partners, Gustav F. Schwab and H. H. Meier, did this out of any fundamental disagreement. They had been acquainted since the 1820s, and had shared teachers and masters in the lyceum and in the countinghouse. Schwab had entered the New York firm in 1858, and since 1861 he had been the New York agent for the North German Lloyd, Meier's steamship line. In all likelihood, Schwab was a shareholder in the Lloyd. But the creation of the Lloyd, a joint-stock corporation that relied as much on investment banks from the German hinterland as on the mercantile elite of Bremen, had changed the dynamic between the two houses.[3]

Even as early as 1859, there had been signs that his new role as director of the Lloyd had changed Meier's priorities. The initial holder of the New York agency had been Friedrich Wilhelm Keutgen – the representative of the *Dessauer Creditanstalt für Industrie und Handel*, one of the main financial backers of the steamship line. When Edwin A. Oelrichs's resigned from the post of Bremish consul to New York, which had been held by partners in that firm since 1805, Oelrichs & Co. lost the consulship to Keutgen, as well.[4]

The argument that won the day in Bremen's policy-making circles for making Keutgen, rather than Gustav F. Schwab, consul in New York, was that Keutgen represented the Lloyd. Had Meier wished to keep the consulship in the family, and

---

[1] See Chapter 1.
[2] Oelrichs & Co., *Caspar Meier and His Successors*, New York, 1898, 19–20.
[3] See Chapters 1 and 2.
[4] See Chapter 7.

give it to Schwab, his voice would have carried significant weight – Meier, for all intents and purposes, was the Lloyd. We can assume that he found that the interests of his joint-stock company outweighed those of ancient family bonds.[5] After the Lloyd's New York agency had returned into the hands of Oelrichs & Co. in 1861, it remained there until at least World War I, and thus continued to tie together the family patriarchs, Meier and Schwab. Yet the substance of this shared concern was a joint-stock company, with all the anonymity that entailed; it was no longer a family business.

Even if the separation of the two firms was not a matter of ill feeling, it shows that both sides no longer felt committed to the same degree as before to maintaining an extensive family network that spanned an ocean. With the economic basis of the link between these two men and their clans gone, the two sides began to drift apart. The new home they found for themselves was bourgeois politics in their respective countries. Each stepped out of his countinghouse and faced the challenge of popular politics. In so doing, they stepped out of the family circles that made the Hanseatic network, and into national politics.

In the year that the transatlantic agreement expired, Meier began to look more toward Germany. In 1864, he became president of the German Chamber of Commerce. In that position, he worked to bring that organization in line with Prussian economic policy, and with the German nationalist movement, more generally. In the *Bürgerschaft*, he assumed the role of the mercantile voice for the *Nationalverein*, promoting a more closely united Germany by means of the creation of a navy and a national parliament.[6]

Like Gustav F. Schwab, H. H. Meier answered the challenge of popular participation in politics by becoming a popular politician. Still firmly opposed to democracy, Meier learned to contend with the masses, newly enfranchised for *Reichstag* elections under the constitution of the Northern German Union in 1867. In a speech he gave in 1874, Meier explained to "the workers" that their interests were best served by electing a man of standing, a man who had given them work:

The best representative for the workers is the man who gives much work to many. . . . Every industrious and respectable worker, the one who feels the just pride of the workman, will agree with me in this. . . . In Bremen, it is the trade and shipping interest that provides most work. . . . When [this interest] flourishes, the employer cannot find workers, and he becomes dependent on the worker. A flourishing trade and shipping interest, therefore, is what we in Bremen have to promote, because the welfare of all of us, not just that of the merchants, is most intimately dependent on it. . . . I honor the independence of the worker, and I give him his due as much as any man who might promise them mountains of gold that he cannot deliver. . . . This it has been my wish to make known to the workers, so that they know how I think about these things, and I feel justified in declaring that I am a friend of the workers.[7]

For the next two decades, more often than not, a sufficient number of Bremish voters felt that a merchant was the best representative for them. When a mob

---

[5] Ibid.
[6] See Chapter 8.
[7] [Anon.], "Die Wahrheit über H. H. Meier. Von einem Wähler," Bremen, 1874.

attacked Meier in 1867, after his victory in the election had become known, "a cooper, tall as an oak" served as his personal body guard. What better image could there be for harmony between the classes, which was based on patronage and protection?[8]

H. H. Meier's exit from public life was a short and painful process. On March 15, 1888, he quit his post as chairman of the board of the North German Lloyd, after he had stood alone with his objection to abandoning freight service on Lloyd vessels. Following a brief interregnum, Dr. Heinrich Wiegand, a lawyer, succeeded him. No longer a merchant, but rather a manager now stood at the helm of the Lloyd. A year later, an attempt to corner the world market in cinchona bark left Meier largely ruined. He died in 1898.[9]

Although he never held elected office, Gustav F. Schwab entered into popular politics with as much vigor as H. H. Meier. In the three decades before his death in 1888, Schwab became a fixture of city politics in New York, where he was associated with the Republican Party. As a "liberal" or "independent" Republican, he supported the backlash against popular participation in politics that began in the 1870s.[10] As a Christian, he pushed for the observation of the Sabbath as a day of rest and religious reflection. And as a merchant, he challenged the traditional Hamiltonian bent of the Republican Party by demanding free trade.[11]

Nowhere was the confluence of these three interests of Schwab more complete, than in his hostility to the emerging labor movement. Democratic, infidel, and statist, the masses organized in unions were a thorn in his eye. Schwab used his leading role in the New York City Chamber of Commerce to push for a hard line against the working class. In April 1886, the chamber of commerce was debating a resolution that attempted to steer a course between the legitimate concerns of workers and the interest of business in preventing violence by supporting national institutions that could deliver binding arbitration in labor disputes.

Schwab objected to this approach as too conciliatory: "Men who make disturbances against the public peace are not ready for arbitration. . . . It is foolish to talk of any such remedy. Every citizen must obey the law, and they who do not must be taught their duty by the law's officers." In that spirit, and to the applause of many in the audience, he offered an addendum to the resolution: "Resolved, That this Chamber . . . considers it the paramount duty of every American citizen to uphold and strengthen the hands of the guardians of law and order as the only possible foundation for the prosperity of the employed as well as of the employer."[12]

One speaker who supported Schwab's militant addendum contended that the original resolution, in stating that "there is no conflict between capital and labor"

---

[8] Hardegen, Friedrich, and Käthi Smidt, geb. Meier, *H. H. Meier, der Gründer des Norddeutschen Lloyd. Lebensbild eines Bremer Kaufmanns, 1809–1898*, Berlin and Leipzig, 1920, 196 (quote), 196–8, 224–9. A similar scene was repeated in 1874, after an election Meier lost. That time, police and firefighters were needed to disperse the crowd.

[9] Bessell, Georg, *1857–1957: Norddeutscher Lloyd. Geschichte einer bremischen Reederei*, Bremen, 1957, 60, 65–6; Hardegen and Smidt, *H. H. Meier*, 251–6.

[10] "Large Meeting in Wall Street," *New York Times*, March 9, 1877; "Mr. Grace a satisfactory man," *New York Times*, October 20, 1884; "The citizens' movement," *New York Times*, October 11, 1884.

[11] "Local Miscellany – Business Interests – The Wool Trade," *New York Times*, October 27, 1874; "Discussing the Tariff," *New York Times*, April 14, 1882; "The Burden of Taxation," *New York Times*, January 13, 1887.

[12] "The Merchants' Voice," *New York Times*, April 28, 1886.

ignored the reality of "sullen, vindictive, determined, bloodthirsty men" who make up the bulk of union members. Yet another blamed any labor unrest on "foreign agitators" who "must be taught a lesson even if it takes a cannon to teach it." Schwab's addendum passed.[13]

In the company of such men, Schwab had come a long way from the Christian-mercantile vision of world peace that had been woven into the Hanseatic approach to international politics. We may doubt that his mother would have had much understanding for the call for cannons to use against the people. In 1860, she had written, "I often ponder whether Christianity should not have enough force to repress these diabolical wars. If all who called themselves Christians truly were, how could it not?"[14] The Gustav F. Schwab of the 1880s no longer felt that violence was un-Christian, if applied in a struggle against socialist, infidel foreigners.

That Schwab still considered Christianity essential to his life is evident in his consistent, active support of Sabbatarianism – the movement to make the Sunday a day of rest and edification. Examples of public meetings in favor of a Sabbath free of vice and alcohol, chaired by Schwab, range from 1861 to 1884.[15] The purpose of a meeting in early 1861 was "to relieve the respectable Germans of the City from the odium resulting from the injudicious conduct of a minority of their countrymen. The respectable, order-loving, and Christian Germans of New-York, are determined that the few Socialists and Infidels and general disturbers of the public peace in their midst, shall no longer misrepresent the character and sentiments of their countrymen in this City."[16]

On the basis of his militant Protestantism, Schwab, the American businessman and politician, also found a new foundation for his affinity with Germany. Writing to his brother, Professor John Christopher Schwab, Gustav F. Schwab commented enthusiastically on a speech given by the Württembergian scholar, Gustav Rümelin, a childhood acquaintance of both brothers, delivered on the occasion of the birthday of Emperor William I.[17]

The deep and thoughtful discussion of the perils of the popular franchise, and the sinister designs of the Catholic Church, which Rümelin developed, resonated with Schwab to such an extent that he enlisted Louis C. Tiffany, who dwelled at his house while working on a commission for new stained-glass windows in St. James's church, to help with the translation of the speech into English.[18]

[13] Ibid.
[14] Sophie Schwab to Gustav F. Schwab, Stuttgart, April 1, 1860, MSS 434, Schwab Papers, series I, box 2, folder 36.
[15] "The Sunday Question," *New York Times*, March 11, 1861, 8; "The Sabbath," *New York Times*, August 17, 1861; "The Sabbath in the Army and Navy," *New York Times*, September 25, 1862; "National Sabbath Convention," *New York Times*, July 11, 1863; "To Promote a Sunday of Rest," *New York Times*, May 24, 1884.
[16] "The Sunday Question," *New York Times*, March 11, 1861, 8.
[17] "Eine zeitgemäße Stimme aus dem Süden," *Weserzeitung* (Bremen), April 10, 1874, morning ed. (M), No. 9773, 2–4.
[18] Gustav F. Schwab to John Christopher Schwab, Fordham, May 8, 1874, MSS 434, Schwab Papers, series I, box 2, folder 46.

FAMILY BUSINESS

In turning their attention from upholding a mercantile family network, and toward the creation of the social and political conditions for the success of their new, large-scale enterprises, Schwab and Meier in part merely executed the verdict that economic change had spoken to the viability of the family firm.

During the golden half-century of Bremen's merchant capital, the counting-house had been a family affair. Not only were Hanseatic mercantile operations contained in a nexus of family, firm, and faith – the countinghouse was where young men were made into Hanseats. Whether a young man was the son of a partner in the firm or of a family friend, whether he was a native-born son of Bremen or a foreigner, whether he was to become the son-in-law and future owner of the business, or a combination thereof, this was where he received his socialization into the moral code of mercantile honor, as part and parcel of his introduction to bookkeeping, commodities, and commercial law.

Considering the importance of mercantile apprentices and clerks for the making of this cosmopolitan community, changes in the economic role and function of office labor in the countinghouse can be expected to have an impact on the broader culture of merchants. By the 1890s, this role had not just been deskilled, but proletarianized. As Engels observed: "hundreds of German clerks, who are trained in all commercial operations and acquainted with three or four languages, offer their services in vain in London City at 25 shillings per week, which is far below the wages of a good machinist."[19]

As Engels points out, Marx had forecast this development in 1865:

The commercial worker, in the strict sense of the term, belongs to the better-paid class of wage-workers – to those whose labour is classed as skilled and stands above average labour. Yet the wage tends to fall, even in relation to average labour, with the advance of the capitalist mode of production....

The necessary training, knowledge of commercial practices, languages, etc., is more and more rapidly, easily, universally and cheaply reproduced with the progress of science and public education the more the capitalist mode of production directs teaching methods, etc., towards practical purposes. The universality of public education enables capitalists to recruit such labourers from classes that formerly had no access to such trades and were accustomed to a lower standard of living. Moreover, this increases supply, and hence competition. With few exceptions, the labour-power of these people is therefore devaluated with the progress of capitalist production. Their wage falls, while their labour capacity increases.[20]

For the owner of a Hanseatic firm in the 1850s, employing a young man, or advancing him as partner in the firm, was not just an investment in his firms integration into the Bremish network. It was a sensible business decision, in that it endowed another person with the still-rare skill set required for a mercantile career.

---

[19] Engels, Friedrich, note 39a to Marx, Karl, *Capital*, 3 vols. (Karl Marx and Friedrich Engels, Werke, vols. 23–5), vol. 3, Berlin, 1979 [1894], 312. For an example of a growing body of scholarship on the history of mercantile clerks, see Schniedewind, Karen, *Begrenzter Aufenthalt im Land der unbegrenzten Möglichkeiten: Bremer Rückwanderer aus Amerika, 1850–1914*, Stuttgart, 1994.

[20] Marx, *Capital*, vol. 3, 311–12.

Where these skills can be acquired elsewhere, and where they are no longer as exclusive, the years-long socialization process implicit in a mercantile education becomes a dysfunctional luxury. Especially at a time when the study of modern society and economy became the subjects of university education, the experience and training of the senior partner may no longer have sufficed for giving the protégée the breadth of training needed for success in a changing world economy.

Where a mercantile career had still been an option for Gustav H. Schwab, the son of the Swabian poet, the offspring of *Bildungsbürger* from the German hinterland found economic conditions in the 1860s less favorable. Sophie Schwab reported to her son that his nephew, Carl Klüpfel, had been unable to find a mercantile apprenticeship: "everywhere he is told that they already have so many engagements."[21] Carl's mother, Gustav's sister Sophie, had complained that "I deem that Carl will not be a scholar, Greek is terribly difficult to him, and thinking, in general, is not his strength. Since he is competent and alert in practical matters, though, I strongly wish that he may one day develop into a merchant."[22] Eventually, Gustav H. Schwab picked up the clues and offered the nephew an apprenticeship in New York. Nevertheless, Carl Klüpfel's career seems to have sputtered from then on. Family ties still counted for Schwab, but as an economic decision, hiring the nephew made little sense. In his will, Schwab felt compelled to give Carl the sum of $5,000 to aid him in his economic existence.[23]

In providing for the education of his own children, Gustav F. Schwab employed a private tutor and sent the children to Germany for parts of their education. In the 1860s, his eldest son, Gustav H., known as "Gussy," and his daughter, Henriette, known as "Henny," spent a year in the old Swabian homeland, to be educated at the school where their uncle Christoph Schwab, Gustav F. Schwab's brother, was an instructor. Gussy went on to an apprenticeship with H. H. Meier in Bremen, and a brief stint in Liverpool, before returning to the United States in 1873. With this educational path, Gustav H. had completed the classical instructions of a Hanseatic merchant. And yet, the mercantile business he entered was much changed from the time his father had completed his apprenticeship in the same firm, in 1844. Back in New York, the Schwab's firm of Oelrichs & Co. was dividing its attention almost evenly between the agency for the North German Lloyd, and the business of trading in commission and financial instruments.[24]

By the time John Christopher, Gussy's and Henny's much younger brother, reached school age in 1867, the home-schooling approach had begun to seem anachronistic, as good public schools were now available. John Christopher attended the educational institutions of New York's bourgeoisie, first Gibbons'

---

[21] Sophie Schwab to Gustav F. Schwab, Stuttgart, May 9, 1861, MSS 434, Schwab Papers, series I, box 2, folder 37.

[22] Sophie Klüpfel to Gustav F. Schwab, Tübingen, October 22, 1858 MSS 434, Schwab Papers, series I, box 2, folder 35.

[23] Gustav F. Schwab, Will, New York, April 18, 1877, MSS 434, Schwab Papers, series I, box 2, folder 61.

[24] Henny Schwab (daughter of Gustav Schwab) to Gustav H. Schwab, Fordham April 4, 1865, MSS 434, Schwab Papers, series I, box 2, folder 39; Ralph H. Graves, "Many Duties of Gustav Schwab – Shipper, Trader, Writer, Student, Politician," *New York Evening Post*, June 26, 1909, MSS 434, Schwab Papers, series II, box 20, folder 222 ("Schwab, John Christopher, Scrapbook: family papers, miscellanea, ca. 1860–1914"); Oelrichs & Co., *Caspar Meier and His Successors*, 37, 42.

and Beach's School in New York City, and then Yale. He continued his higher education in Germany. But rather than spending large parts of his youth in the countinghouse of a family member or close friend, as his father had done in the 1830s, he attended the universities of Berlin and Göttingen to study political economy.[25]

John Christopher was a pupil of William Graham Sumner, Yale's first professional sociologist, and a man who shared the political outlook of New York's elites that had emerged in the 1870s. A proponent of a radically free market and a gold standard, Sumner opposed any government intervention in the economy for the purpose of bettering the lot of the masses. In the Schwab family home, this economic policy was so much part of the fabric of life that whenever someone accidentally dropped a piece of silverware from the dining table, the other diners would rhythmically bang their own utensils on the table to a chorus of "Down with Free Silver!"[26]

THE CHILDREN OF SCHWAB AS AMERICAN PATRIOTS

The socialization that the children of Gustav F. Schwab received no longer produced Hanseats, but American patriots. The diary John Christopher kept between 1884 and 1893 shows that during his study years, he perceived America as his intellectual home, whereas German academia struck him as alien. The economist whose lectures he attended at Göttingen, Professor Gustav Cohn, especially became his foil. Initial enthusiasm for the teacher – "walked home with Cohn after his lecture. Very pleasant." – gave way to disappointment.[27] Soon, he complained, "Cohn on the German wheat tariff. Rather weak. The usual threadbare protectionist arguments."[28] After that, the comments grew increasingly exasperated. "Cohn on medieval guilds not very satisfactory. Of course a tirade against modern free competition," Schwab noted on June 4. Then, on June 11, "Cohn in a serio-pathetic [*sic*] tone about the delusions of free competition. Bismarck favors protection etc. hence the world is convinced that free trade is a delusion + is returning to the ways of our forefathers, hence A. Smith was a fanatic."

By June 13, Schwab's mind was made up. Cohn represents a German way of thinking, "the usual attempt of Germans to 'deduce ultimate principles.' What reason they have for ridiculing the 'Englische abstrakt-individualistische Doktrin' while going to such extremes generalizing abstraction, is beyond me."[29] When the professor advocated "the possibility of the (U.S.) federal government becoming the

---

[25] "Guide to the John Christopher Schwab Family Papers, MS 434" (finding aid), http://hdl.handle.net/10079/fa/mssa.ms.0434 (accessed November 5, 2012).

[26] White, Lucy Sophia, née Schwab, *Fort Number Eight. The Home of Gustav and Eliza Schwab. Compiled by their daughter Lucy Schwab White for their Grandchildren and Great-Grandchildren that they may know something of the Rock whence they are hewn*, New Haven, CT, 1925 (in MSS 434, John Christopher Schwab Family Papers, series II, box 17, folder 212); "Too Many Silver Dollars," *New York Times*, January 29, 1886.

[27] Schwab, John Christopher, Diary No. 5, From May 13 1888 to March 26 1889, Diaries, 1884–1893, MSS 434, Schwab Papers, series II, box 9, folder 182, entry of May 15, 1888.

[28] Ibid., May 31.

[29] Ibid., May 28, in discussing "Bulwerings's International Law."

tax collector of the States etc. and distributing the revenue," Schwab calls it "a German standpoint, of course." It did not help that Cohn was a strong proponent of Bismarck's system of social insurance that covered retirement and health care for the working class. This struck John Christopher Schwab as an embrace of "state socialism."[30]

Rather than following in the footsteps of his father, whose death in 1888 found his son in Germany, as a practitioner of capitalism, John Christopher Schwab returned to America for a career as a theorist of that system. As an economic historian at Yale, he published empirically rich studies of the finances of the Confederate States. He concluded that the South had lost the war, in large part, because its economy suffered from an overly activist and coercive Confederate government, whose interventions in the free market − "the negation of normal economic forces" − were as inept as they were ill-advised. Had the Confederacy only stuck to its *laissez-faire*, States Rights guns, they might have beaten the odds.[31]

Not that young Schwab considered a Confederate victory a desirable outcome. His ideal was no longer that of the embedded economy of a mercantile estate whose members assume a patrician role of patronage for the lesser classes, and certainly not an economic system resting on property in persons. It was a full-blown embrace of a free market, conceived as the battleground between self-interested individuals, and completely divorced from any notions of a common welfare.

While his younger brother had chosen an academic career, Gustav H. Schwab took over their father's business. In that capacity, he stuck to the politics of international improvement for the benefit of expanded, free, international trade that antebellum Hanseats had promoted. In addressing the "Southern Industrial Parliament" − a conference of promoters of Southern industrialization − in Washington on May 24, 1905, Schwab struck familiar notes. He recommended that the South, in the interest of promoting its own industrial development, put its full weight behind an abolition of protective tariffs at the national level. At the same time, Southern states should follow policies that encourage immigration: the adaptation of "uniform labor-laws, safe-guarding child and female labor, and fixing hours of employment for such labor," the publication of brochures in foreign languages, and a public distribution of land that followed the example of the *Homestead Act*.[32]

Schwab based these recommendations on the premise of the primacy of international trade for regional economic development:

You no doubt realize that the fullest development of a nation lies in the cultivation and enlargement of its foreign trade.... Foreign trade is entirely dependent upon

---

[30] Ibid., June 13 and 15. A national economist, Cohn was involved in the creation of the regulatory framework for the German financial sector, the Börsengesetz (Stock Exchange Law) of 1896. One of his works (*The Science of Finance*, Chicago 1895) was translated into English by his student, the American Progressive Thorstein Veblen.

[31] Schwab, John Christopher, *The Confederate States of America, 1861–1865*, New York, 1901, esp. pp. 310–12.

[32] Schwab, Gustav H., "Address delivered by Mr. Gustav H. Schwab, of New York, before the Southern Industrial Parliament in Washington on May 24th, 1905," MSS 434, Schwab Papers, series II, box 20, folder 222.

transportation. . . . Many of the ports of the South enjoy an irregular service of so-called tramp steamers that come and go at intervals as opportunity offers, but few maintain the regular lines of steamships that a highly developed trade demands. . . .

When once established, such regular lines unquestionably add greatly to the material development of any country, but to secure them the importing and exporting trade of the section to be served must be a growing one and the country must be attractive to settlers, and thus the steamship line and the commercial interest it ministers to are dependent one upon the other and the welfare of the one reacts upon the other.[33]

This was the essentially same line of reasoning by which Carl Theodor Gevekoht, Rudolf Schleiden, and other Hanseatic lobbyists had sold Bremen's mail-steamer line to Congress.[34] Schwab also pointed to a line established in 1868 as the result of the cooperation between Bremen's former consul, Albert Schumacher, and the Baltimore & Ohio Railroad, of which Schumacher had then been a director:[35]

I have in mind in this connection the regular service inaugurated by one of the largest transatlantic steamship lines between Baltimore and one of the ports of Continental Europe as long ago as 1868 under trade auspices such as I have described. This line, which began as a monthly service, has gradually developed, until it now maintains, and for a number of years has maintained, a weekly service by large and commodious steamers to the advantage of the port of Baltimore and the advancement of a large section of the country tributary to that port.[36]

Finally, in a clear nod to the great deeds of international improvement that the state of Bremen had undertaken in Bremerhaven, Schwab encouraged Southerners to embrace the public financing of major transportation infrastructure. Large steamers required better port facilities, like quays, basins, and cranes; deeper shipping channels, which the public had to create and maintain by continuous dredging; and connecting infrastructure like railway lines.[37]

Unlike his brother, John Christopher, Gustav H. Schwab was not opposed to an active role of government in promoting commercial development. But unlike the theoretical economist, Gustav H. Schwab, the merchant, relied for parts of his business – maintaining the North German Lloyd's New York agency – on a transportation enterprise that continued to require stiff government subsidies by virtue of its nature. Even with modern steamships, which could transport cargo as well as a large number of passengers in three classes, steamship lines were engaged in a potentially ruinous competition, where periods of oligopolic rate

[33] Ibid.
[34] See Chapter 5.
[35] *Addresses of Albert Schumacher, S. Teackle Wallis, John W. Garrett, W. T. McClintock, of Ohio, E. H. Webster, and others: made on the 26th of March, 1868, at the complimentary banquet by the merchants of Baltimore to the officers of the pioneer steamship of the Baltimore and Bremen line*, Baltimore, 1868; Mayer, *Baltimore*; Howard, George W., *The Monumental City, Its Past History and Present Resources*, Baltimore, 1873; Scharf, J. Thomas, *History of Baltimore City & County*, 2 vols., Philadelphia, 1881, vol. I, 306–7.
[36] Schwab, Gustav H., "Address . . . before the Southern Industrial Parliament."
[37] Ibid.

cartels alternated with periods of free competition paired with government subsidies.[38]

In addressing the Southern industrialists, then, Gustav H. Schwab served as a spokesman for this industry, not as the promoter of a particular port town and its trade interest. He framed his appeal in terms of regional economic growth, which had to occur in competition with other regions of the same country, as well as in terms of international competition. One wishes that John Christopher Schwab, in whose papers a copy of his brother's speech was preserved, had annotated the document. We might imagine that he disagreed with his sibling, in that the economist found any government intervention in the economy undesirable. At the same time, we know that both brothers agreed on the question of money – both were advocates of a gold standard.[39]

Rather than as members of a mercantile network, as their father had been, the brothers represented only slightly different visions for the management of a national economy founded on wage labor, capital, and ties to a world market for goods, services, and labor. Both were at home in the Republican Party – Gustav H. Schwab even in official functions. Their primary frame of reference was their shared interest in the success of the United States' national economy – not that of a specific mercantile community. Gustav H. Schwab's obituary in the *New York Evening Post* attested that, "although connected with a foreign shipping line, he always found it easy to treat any question that came up from an impartial point of view, which was invariably that of a patriotic American citizen."[40]

HOLLYWOOD ENDINGS

After the credits of many a Hollywood movie, we will see biographical snippets that satisfy the viewers' curiosity as to what became of the main characters of the story. These snapshots of future happenings are no longer part of the main narrative, and yet they seem to round it off. The same holds true for the post-1867 biographies of the merchants who populated the preceding pages. For lack of a communal nexus that ties their stories together, these endings are but the biographies of individuals. Their fate in the last third of the century might matter for a different story – bourgeois politics in America or the German Empire, colonialism, or even international trade. Nonetheless, the story told here would seem incomplete for their omission.

In the local boosterist literature of late nineteenth-century Baltimore, Albert Schumacher was celebrated as an important businessman. In 1865, he was elected president of the Baltimore Chamber of Commerce. His particular achievement for "Charm City" was to convince the North German Lloyd steamship company to open a line from Bremerhaven to Baltimore in 1868, which put Baltimore on the

---

[38] Hutchins, John G. B., *The American Maritime Industry and Public Policy, 1789–1914: An Economic History* (i.e., Harvard University, inst. ed., Harvard Economic Studies, vol. LXXI), Cambridge, MA, 1941; Tyler, David Budlong, *Steam Conquers the Atlantic*, New York and London, 1939.

[39] Graves, "Many Duties of Gustav Schwab," see note 24 to this chapter.

[40] Ibid.; "Gustav H. Schwab" (Obituary), *New York Herald*, November 13, 1912, and "Gustav H. Schwab Dead – Head of Oelrichs & Company" (Obituary), *New York Evening Post*, November 12, 1912, both in MSS 434, Schwab Papers, series II, box 20, folder 222.

map of modern transatlantic travel. Schumacher had negotiated an agreement between the Lloyd and the Baltimore & Ohio Railroad to sell through tickets from Bremerhaven to points on the railway line. Local notables regarded this agreement as an important victory against New York in the continuing competition for shares of passenger and commodity traffic. In the same year, Schumacher became the Baltimore agent for the Lloyd. He died in 1871, still a bachelor. His tomb is one of the more imposing structures at Greenmount Cemetery.[41]

In 1871, Rudolf Schleiden was elected to the German *Reichstag* from Altona, then still a city in Prussian Schleswig-Holstein. He was a member of the parliamentary delegation present at the coronation of William I as German Emperor, in the Hall of Mirrors in Versaille. After losing a bid for reelection in 1874, Schleiden moved to Freiburg im Breisgau, where he lived with his sister and aged mother. He returned to the United States in 1873 for a railroad trip through the West. The account of this journey was first published in the *Augsburger Zeitung*, to whose pages Schleiden contributed on occasion.[42]

Arnold Duckwitz never fully recovered from the illness that had gripped him in 1866. His handwriting became visibly shaky. He lived out his life in comfort, in his family estate on the Lesum River, close to the Bremish town of Vegesack on the Weser. The death of his wife in December 1877 greatly troubled him. He followed her home in 1878.[43]

In 1898, Oelrichs & Co. commissioned an official company history. Its otherwise sober, anonymous author was moved to enthusiasm by the following example of the stability and continuity of Hanseatic trade relations:

In 1819, the first mention is made of Joh. Bernhard Hasenclever & Sons in Remscheid, manufacturers of a certain grade of steel used chiefly by scythe makers, which they shipped to New York firms regularly until 1886, when they discontinued its production. The last lot was sold to the old scythe manufacturing firm, David Wadsworth & Sons, Auburn, N.Y., the father of whose senior, Jospeh Wadsworth, had begun the business in 1817, and who had used this same German steel from the earliest times. Thus, for sixty-five years or more, this article passed from the same foreign producers through the hands of the same importing merchants into those of the same manufacturing consumers, all three firms in existence to-day, a record which is perhaps unique in the mercantile history of this country.[44]

In his effort to stress continuity, the corporate biographer missed the key point: in all likelihood, handcrafted steel ceased to be competitive in the 1880s, because the commonly available Bessemer process made high-quality steel available for much

---

[41] *Addresses of Albert Schumacher, S. Teackle Wallis, John W. Garrett, W. T. McClintock, of Ohio, E. H. Webster, and others: made on the 26th of March, 1868, at the complimentary banquet by the merchants of Baltimore to the officers of the pioneer steamship of the Baltimore and Bremen line,* Baltimore, 1868; Mayer, *Baltimore;* Howard, *Monumental City;* Scharf, *History of Baltimore,* vol. I, 306–7.

[42] Schleiden, Rudolf, *Reise-Erinnerungen aus den Vereinigten Staaten von Amerika,* New York, 1873.

[43] Arnold Duckwitz to Rudolf Schleiden, Bad Nenndorf, January 15, 1878, StAHB 7,116 [Rudolf Schleiden Papers], folder "Briefwechsel Rudolf Schleiden mit Senator Arnold Duckwitz, 1854–1879," third of five unnumbered and unlabeled boxes; Bippen, Wilhelm von, "Duckwitz, Arnold," in *Bremische Biographie des neunzehnten Jahrhunderts,* ed. Historische Gesellschaft des Künstlervereins, Bremen, 1912, 115–17.

[44] Oelrichs & Co., *Caspar Meier and His Successors,* 28.

lower prices. Precisely because industrialization changed the way Hanseats did business beyond recognition, the owners of old firms felt a need for historical accounts like that of *Caspar Meier and His Successors*.

BOMBING NIGHTS

As British and American bombs rained down on Bremen in the winter nights of early 1945, Friedrich Köper hunkered down in a basement with a typewriter, hammering away at his memoir with an increasing sense of embitterment. He had intended to give an account of old tobacco labels, or so the title of the typescript suggests. Yet he never said a word on this subject, as his mind reconnected with his life as a youth in Bremerhaven and his struggle as a young adult to establish himself in Guatemala, and carried him down a stream of consciousness that gave away a resentment that had had eighty years to grow.

Köper called up the ghosts of past adversaries and long-gone slights, compressed into a hate-filled image of an overbearing and ever-present other by the pounding of the firebombs, the latest incarnation of the incapacitating power of this evil that had never let him enjoy the fruits of what had been, at its height, a quite successful career as an import-export merchant in Central America.

Köper had different names for this evil. Sometimes it was the American, sometimes it was Big Capital, but mostly it was simply the Jew, whom he perceived as the true driving force behind it all. Köper had been the head of the largest German trading house in Guatemala City, and they had taken that away from him, too. He had been a respectable citizen in his new home. He had even become president of the National Socialist Workers Party of Germany – Overseas Organization for Guatemala. Now, in this basement, it all willed out:

The German colony in Guat[ema]la was the largest and most respectable, there were few Americans at that time [1887], some French, English, Dutch, and Belgians. But there were already a number of German Jews who had taken the usual route: Galicia, Breslau, Berlin, Hamburg, New York. In USA they acquired citizenship, back then this was possible after a short residency, and further shortened by Jewish tricks, and then they came to Guatemala and Central America (especially Salvador is completely Jewified these days) in steady proliferation. After they expelled the Germans from Guatemala, they will, with U.S. help, step into the German place, at least in trade. That will be all the easier for them with their German names, and since the Indios and Guatemaltecos cannot tell the difference between the various white European races. For them, it is the same as with us and the colored. The Chinese, for instance, all look the same to us, in spite of their quite different tribes.[45]

The bombing nights of World War II brought to light the completion of the process of nationalization that had remade the Hanseatic merchant class. National Socialism promised to recapture the organic, exclusive, harmonious conditions of

---

[45] Köper, Friedrich, "Köper, Lottmann & Cia., Guatemala, Plaudereien über Handelsmarken, Etiquetten, Wappen, etc.," typescript, February 1, 1945, p. 16, StAHB 7,13, Köper, Friedrich [papers].

the lost community of German hometowns.[46] It wedded this false promise to the anticommercialism that had become the standard feature of any reactionary critique of capitalism. Nineteenth-century Hanseats had played a role both in the making of the modern world market and of its false critique.

As the spirit of Hanseatic cosmopolitanism took its last breath, its most visible symbol vanished. When the Bremen Art Museum was hit by a stray bomb on September 5, 1942, the centerpiece of its collection hung deserted in the main hall. Its companions had been evacuated, but Leutze's monumental canvas was too large to be taken to a safer place. The original version of *Washington Crossing the Delaware* burned in that night.

---

[46] This is the main argument of Walker, Mack, *German Home Towns: Community, State, and General Estate, 1648–1871*, Ithaca, NY, and London, 1971.

Conclusion

Too often in social history, the world market just somehow happens, and it usually happens *to* people.[1] The experience of Hanseats in the nineteenth century shows that the world market was being made. It was made by people with the help of the state. Then, it "happened to" not just *other* people, but to the very people who helped make it. When Bremen's independence ended in 1867, and when the mercantile estate of the city lost its independent economic role vis-à-vis industrial capital, both the state of Bremen and its economic elite had been working for fifty years or more to bring about the conditions that proved their undoing. Bremen's merchant capital was a victim of its own success.

Hanseats had brought Northern and Central Europe in direct connection with an American market. In so doing, they had furthered economic development on both sides of the ocean and had reduced the dependency on Britain of countries that had been peripheries of the British trade empire. As the United States and the German states embarked on their projects of industrialization and national uni-fication, they could build on the rapid economic development both societies had been able to enjoy in the preceding decades, in part thanks to Bremen's mercantile estate.

In establishing commerce and communication between America and Europe, Hanseats had worked hand in hand with governments. In Washington, Berlin, and other power centers in Germany and America, Bremen's merchant diplomats had enjoyed a degree of political influence that reflected the actual economic impor-tance of their role. As the importance of their role was diminished, so was their political influence. Thus at the very moment when these societies came into their own as capitalist nation-states, the little trading city suddenly found itself on the sidelines, unable any longer to influence the actions of much larger states.

Bremen's merchants had been at the cutting edge of the modernization of world trade in the middle third of the nineteenth century. For the purpose of furthering their commercial enterprises, they embraced the most advanced technologies and economic practices of the day. But steamships, railroads, investment banking, and joint-stock corporations served Hanseats as the means for carrying on a pursuit they

---

[1] Cf. Braudel, Fernand, *Civilization and Capitalism, Fifteenth–Eighteenth Century*, 3 vols., Berkeley, CA, 1992 (1982–4).

considered their traditional calling – linking distant places in exchange for the improvement of this world, and for the betterment of man. The moral content these merchants ascribed to their economic activities was not just an ideological smoke screen to hide a naked profit motive. It formed the actual basis of their economic existence.

Hanseats had done business, not simply as individual economic agents, but quintessentially as parts of a community that was cosmopolitan and transnational in character. Extensive kinship networks, established over multiple generations, tied each Bremish firm to many others. The nexus of family, firm, and faith that tethered the countinghouse to a vigilantly upheld moral code was not merely a complement to an otherwise self-interested economic existence; it was the substance of the Hanseat's economic role.

Even as this moral economy of mercantile honor appeared as an anachronism in the nineteenth century, it was a highly functional arrangement on whose basis Bremen's mercantile estate thrived in a rapidly changing global market. Thus, although the loss of political independence to a German nation-state and the loss of economic independence to industrial capital dealt harsh blows to this cosmopolitan community, it was the dissolution of the unity between family and business that truly brought to an end the Hanseatic community of the mid-nineteenth century.

CONSERVATIVE MODERNIZERS

In appreciating the irony that a highly successful group of merchants, with an impressive record of innovation and adaptability, was defined by its traditionalist mores and business practices, this study is an argument against anticommercialism, against reifying the market, and especially the *world* market, as an *agens* without actors. But it is also an argument against a certain voluntarism that explains market relations as completely reducible to the intentions – interests and strategies – of actors. The whole of the market and its logic adds up to more than the sum of its parts.

This study, then, is an argument for taking seriously the dialectic of modern capitalist society: the things actors make take on a life of their own as structures, and they can, and often will, turn against their creators. In experiencing the painful end of this dialectic, Hanseats did not stand alone. Other conservatives on both sides of the Atlantic shared their pain.

On both sides of the Atlantic, conservative political currents contributed in crucial ways to the modernization of societies. Government had a necessary role to play in creating the legal and technological infrastructure that created the conditions of the possibility of the full development of capitalist social relations, specifically of industrial-capitalist commodity production on a large scale. The sense of improvement that animated conservatives, with all the moral overtones of that term, provided the political motive for giving government the power it needed to fill this role.

In Germany as well as America, conservatives were motivated by a wish to uphold a good social order. The foil for their project was the French Revolution. In their view, this event had shown the dangers of democracy and of the moral decay it engendered. Advocating firm Christian values and social hierarchy was a response to these perceived dangers. This response was made all the more urgent by the continuous boost democratic aspirations among the masses received from the disruption caused by the Industrial Revolution.

In both societies, conservatives realized that the Industrial Revolution in Britain changed the conditions of social production everywhere. In Germany and America, the introduction by world trade of industrially manufactured commodities destroyed less efficient modes of production. Conservatives responded to this challenge by emulating the British example. This meant the spread of wage-labor relations, industrial technology, and new forms of business organization. Nonetheless, the conservative project was not a revolution of all social relations. It was the attempt to preserve hierarchy, tradition, and particularity by appropriating the main leveling agent – equality on the market – and, in the process, to defuse its socially disruptive properties. Not, in the words of Charles Sellers, "to make democracy safe for capitalism," but to make capitalism safe for tradition, was the essence of conservative politics.[2]

By combining technological progress with firm values and an insistence on social hierarchy in an ideology of improvement, conservatives hoped to change the world in ways that preserved essential elements of the early-modern order that was quickly disappearing in the nineteenth century. The most important of these elements was not the embeddedness of production and exchange, but rather the shared, binding morality that rested on tight social control. Aware that morality was no longer made binding as a function of immediate personal ties among the members of a community, these modern conservatives put government in charge of exerting social control over the members of a society.

Finally, in responding to events in Britain and France, and in cooperating between Europe and America, conservatism was a transnational political current. Just as the dual challenges of democracy and industrialization were potentially universal in their implications, so was the conservative response to them. International cooperation, and even internationalism, was not the exclusive domain of liberals or democrats. Between Bremen and America, it long remained the exclusive domain of conservative elites.

The resilience they brought to encounters with others and the reluctance they showed as late as the 1860s to abandon the traditions of their estate – the gender arrangements and the barriers to membership in the mercantile estate – demonstrate that Hanseats were not liberals in sheep's clothing. Fundamentally, they remained convinced that society was more than an amassment of equal individuals. They held to the belief that the proper order of the world was one that allowed for distinctions, and they knew that democracy and completely unfettered market relations were leveling agents. It took massive challenges from the outside to uproot and break apart this transnational community, and to cast its members, separately, into the forming national bourgeoisies of Germany and the United States. War-making nation-states, industrial production, and the growing support of democratic popular participation extended by newly empowered, unitary states were the main agents of the Hanseats' downfall. These were forces beyond their control. If left to their own

---

[2] Sellers, Charles, *The Market Revolution: Jacksonian America, 1815–1846*, New York and Oxford, 1991.

devices, they would have lacked a motive to embrace the fundamental social transformation carried out by these nation-states.

Contrary to the anticommercialist imagination that sees merchants as the conscious agents of exploitation and dissolution, these champions of global commerce were at the same time among the most ardent supporters of preserving traditional values and a communal ethos. Not classical merchant capital, represented by Hanseats, but modern industrial capital and its commodity-trading and money-trading branches, together with its political complement, the nation-state, were the main agents of the dissolution and subversion of community. Hence, in the last third of the nineteenth century, the wish of anticommercialists in America and Germany to use monetary and trade policies to end exploitative economic relations by subjecting merchants and other agents of the market to the discipline of a national economy, enforced by the nation-state, did not come true. Capital and the state continue to play their role as "levelers," in spite of their fundamentalist and anticommercialist fans.

COSMOPOLITAN CONSERVATIVES

Stubborn Hanseatic traditionalism was not a matter of provinciality. Both in formulating their ideals and in shaping their responses to social changes, Hanseats incorporated what they learned abroad. France, Britain, and America made appearances in Bremish thought not just as abstract examples. Hanseatic merchants had experienced firsthand political and social life in these countries, especially in the United States. Hence, their ideas differed from the mainstream of German political life. Before the diffuse political currents of the German middle class had congealed into clearly delimited parties, Bremen's elite had found its voice in a Western conservatism. It had thus found a response to the dual challenges of industrialization and democracy that allowed for a supercession of hometown traditions in a political ideology open to translocal alliances.

Like Hanseats, Whigs were engaged in the project of paving the way for capitalist social relations, while attempting to shore up the moral foundations of community eroded by the rise of capitalism. In this approach to modernization, they were located in opposition to democrats on both sides of the ocean, and they were aware that they had a common adversary. Based on this commonality, Hanseats and Whigs embraced steamship technology, which revolutionized international commerce. Unlike Whigs, Hanseats did not promote steamships as a step toward building an industrial-capitalist society. Like their American friends, however, they perceived technological and institutional change as "improvements" upon a fundamentally good social order.

The American Civil War and the German wars of unification of the 1860s rendered Hanseats' multilateral approach to international politics increasingly ineffective. Guns and warships made by modern industry, not mercantile diplomacy, decided the domestic conflicts in the two societies that were most important to Hanseats. The search for a response to their loss of political leeway divided Hanseats. In America, Hanseats-turned-Unionists and their Confederate counterparts dissolved partnerships that had rested on decades-long ties between old families. In Germany, some Hanseats became enthusiastic supporters of a Prussian-led unification of the country, while others continued to detest both the authoritarian Prussian state and the democratic national movement with which it was allying itself. As the masses mobilized to decide political questions with guns and ballots, a fractured elite that faced existential economic changes on top of these political challenges found it increasingly impossible to shape politically its own destiny. Within a few years, Hanseatic politics had ceased to be what Bremen's longtime burgomaster, Johann Smidt, had described as "an extended family life." The hope for an improved society under the careful guardianship of local elites had failed.[3]

In the 1870s and 1880s, many Hanseats continued to do well in business and politics. H. H. Meier and Gustav Schwab became prominent businessmen and influential bourgeois politicians, fighting for free trade and defending Christian morality against socialist infidels. Yet those who, with more or less enthusiasm, had adjusted to the changed political and economic conditions were no longer linked to each other by the same kind of transnational family network that had existed in the previous decades. Ties to the emergent national bourgeoisie in America and Germany, respectively, became more important than those to one's peers on the opposite shores of the Atlantic. Although Hanseats continued to maintain strong trading ties between Germany and America, they relied less and less on their family networks to do so. By the end of the century, as the generation that had built the mid-nineteenth-century Hanseatic world had passed away, the memory of a transnational community replaced the reality.

In becoming agents of a specialized, commodity-trading branch of industrial capital, Hanseats lost much of what had made them cosmopolitan, or even transnational, in the past. Their ability to maintain a separate community across the Atlantic had run up against powerful obstacles: the modern nation-state with its armed forces and its reliance on popular politics and the dynamism of industrial capitalism. Hanseats' traditionalism had been resilient enough to allow them to continue far into the nineteenth century a way of life more typical of the eighteenth century. To continue this way of life, with its insistence on a limited scale of business, antiquated economic practices, and a reliance on the household and the family as the end and starting point of profit, would have meant certain ruin in the global economy of the last third of the nineteenth century.

Hanseats' aloofness from popular politics likewise proved increasingly unsustainable. In Bremen and New York, they had to contend with an invigorated population who insisted on their say in matters of big politics, and who enjoyed the support of central governments in many of their claims. If Hanseats wanted their voice to be heard under these conditions, they had to ask for the trust of the public. The currency of the club and the countinghouse, character and reputation, were no longer sufficient for political purchase. The discourse of popular politics in the new nation-states was increasingly characterized by nationalism and geopolitics. The days when a global class of merchants could believe – with some reason – that they were building a cosmopolitan world beyond war-making states were over.

To mobilize support for the political projects of national capitals now required popular appeal. Imperial expansion and the repression of colonized peoples abroad;

---

[3] Smidt, Johann, *Denkschrift über die Judenfrage in Bremen*, as paraphrased by Baron, Salo W., *Die Judenfrage auf dem Wiener Kongreß*, Vienna and Berlin, 1920, 105.

the pacification of labor at home, by its integration or exclusion; and the mobilization of nationalist sentiment in positioning one's nation in an armed race for global market shares against competing national bourgeoisies, all called for the sustained, large-scale involvement of broad strata of the population in clubs, parties, and, ultimately, armies.

CAPITAL AND COMMUNITY

In following interests that arose from within their existence as a *community*, Hanseats helped transform Germany and the United States into industrial capitalist *societies*. The new economy of industrial capitalism undermined the economic independence of classical merchant capital. In the transition to this new economy, Hanseatic merchant capital does not appear as an exploiter preying upon local communities, but as a community undone by its own success.

As a community that would have held up to Tönnies's criteria for this term, Hanseats did not survive the 1860s. What was left of them after that decade was a rudimentary family network, stripped of the essential economic and political functions it had fulfilled in the past, and reduced by those who had dropped out over political differences or under economic duress. Although many old Hanseatic families still exist today, the essential features of what had made them a community, the organic intertwining of their economic, domestic, and political existence, based on a shared moral economy, does not.

The memory of the golden age of Hanseatic, transatlantic trade of the 1830s through 1850s survives but as an ideology in the self-image of present descendants of the great merchant capitalists of the nineteenth century. Hanseatic chroniclers have helped to make that myth of an unbroken tradition, thus obscuring the cataclysmic nature of the changes of the 1860s. One indicator of this obscuration is the disappearance of Consul Keutgen's name from the historical record (see Chapter 7).

Friedrich Hardegen and Käthi Smidt, in their biography of Smidt's father, H. H. Meier, mention in passing that the first Lloyd agency in New York was the "branch of the *Dessauer Creditanstalt*," whose unnamed owner "failed in 1861."[4] The economic historian Alfred Vagts, having fled to the United States from the National Socialist regime in Germany, called the Lloyd's agents "an American firm," whose failure in 1861 logically resulted from the absence of Hanseatic business ethics from their conduct. In Vagts's account, too, the owners of that firm remain nameless.[5]

---

[4] Hardegen, Friedrich and Käthi Smidt, *H. H. Meier, der Gründer des Norddeutschen Lloyd. Lebensbild eines Bremer Kaufmanns 1809–1898*, Berlin and Leipzig, 1920, 133. The first instance of this practice of omitting the name of the failed firm seems to have been Oelrichs & Co., *Caspar Meier and His Successors*, New York, 1898, 42.

[5] Vagts, Alfred, "Gustav Schwab 1822–1880. Ein deutschamerikanischer Unternehmer," in *1000 Jahre Bremer Kaufmann. Aufsätze zur Geschichte bremischen Kaufmannstums, des Bremer Handels und der Bremer Schiffahrt aus Anlaß des tausendjährigen Gedenkens der Marktgründung durch Bischof Adaldag 965* (Bremisches Jahrbuch, vol. 50), Bremen, 1965, 337–60. The index catalog of the Staatsarchiv Bremen does not contain an entry for Keutgen, either.

Considering the immediate identification of these Hanseatic historians with their subjects, the blind spot suggests a continuous attempt to erase the "speculator" from the record. Hanseatic capital, in their narrative, is dedicated to honestly providing useful services.[6] By definition, the merchant who fails to live up to the standard is not, and has never been, a Hanseat. As an embarrassment to Bremen, Keutgen lost his good name, and the historians who have ignored him conform to the custom of the estate in making his name disappear altogether.

But Keutgen's eradication from memory is not merely a function of conformity to traditional sensibilities. The merchant whose failure drags into the light the dark underbelly of exchange relations and their foundation on dirty self-interest, is the merchant who most unabashedly functions as a subject in a capitalist market. Under attack from anticommercialists, and eventually National Socialist propaganda, the subject participating in the market out of self-interest was othered as an Anglo-American or Jewish type, the counterimage to the German *Unternehmer* and his commercial counterpart, the "royal merchant."[7]

In the anticommercialist imagination, the latter are normatively defined as productive servants of concrete needs and the former as exploiters and hucksters who deceive the honest, hard-working majority with arcane legal and financial sophistry. The former are of one blood with the people, whose fate they share; the latter are outsiders who hide their dealings from plain view. As this anti-commercialist view became the centerpiece of National Socialist economic thought, countinghouse and temple fused into one image of a command central of exploitation.[8]

It is ironic that the silent verdict that placed Keutgen outside of the community, and inside the recesses of the commercial temple, should have been executed against the one Hanseatic merchant in the United States who more than any of his colleagues represented the new, capitalist commercial enterprise – the joint-stock steamship company, North German Lloyd. Hanseats engaged in the new forms of commerce that define a modern, industrial world market, but they were in denial about the fundamental nature of the change in their customary ways this engagement represented. To themselves and to others, they continued to present their activities as part of an unbroken tradition reaching back to the Middle Ages.

---

[6] See note 22 to Chapter 1.

[7] A term coined by Gustav Freytag in his popular novel, *Soll und Haben*, Leipzig, 1855.

[8] Adorno, Theodor W., and Horkheimer, Max, *Dialektik der Aufklärung. Philosophische Fragmente*, Frankfurt, 1969 (New York 1944), 177–217; Postone, Moishe, "Anti-Semitism and National Socialism," in *Germans and the Jews since the Holocaust: The Changing Situation in West Germany*, ed. Anson Rabinbach and Jack Zipes, New York, 1986, 302–14. For the similarities between this type of anticommercialism and a producerist ideology common in the United States, see Beckert, Sven, *The Monied Metropolis: New York City and the Consolidation of the American Bourgeoisie, 1850–1896*, Cambridge, MA, 2001, 63, 148, 168–9. For an anti-Semitic pamphlet by a Hanseat born in the 1860s, see Achelis, Eduard, *Meine Lebenserinnerungen aus 50jähriger Arbeit* (photocopy of typescript), Bremen 1935/1936, StAHB, call number 135.Ai, esp. pp. 30–1, 41, 54–6, 62. Achelis considered the World Economic Crisis of the 1930s as the result of a Jewish conspiracy (pp. 30–1).

NATION, RELIGION, GENDER, AND CLASS

As persons not born in the United States, Hanseats who settled on the western shores of the Atlantic shared with many of the members of general American populace the formal distinction of being immigrants, but not much else. Germans, Irishmen, and Scotsmen who swelled the American wage-labor force, or who established themselves on a farm or in a workshop of their own, moved among those of their own social class, in that they competed and cooperated with them in a shared desire to make a better living in America. In the interaction between Anglo-Americans and the various groups of immigrants from Europe, the pressure to become disciplined, frugal, and sober wage workers was enacted as the demand to become respectable American citizens.

In embracing the demands of a capitalist wage-labor regime, the foreign-born working class often traversed a more strenuous trajectory than a transatlantic passage, one they shared with those who had remained in Europe – the making of a working class. Like in Europe, this social class was forged by capital as much as it was making itself. Like in Europe, this process involved making peasants and artisans, Catholics and Protestants, villagers and townspeople into members of a nation. Whether the nation immigrants to America embraced was the United States, or whether Americanization progressed through the stage of becoming German in the emigration, the end result was an embrace of nationhood, if not nationalism.

But Hanseats did not share this working- and middle-class experience. They were the mongers of the capital and commodities from which the market forces that shaped working-class communities were made. They felt under very little pressure to "become American," even as, in creating an international outlet for a national market in goods and services, they created the real social basis for the nation. Only when the wars of the 1860s forced Hanseats to take sides, did they – but not all chose the same side. And even as they became Germans and Americans – or, in other cases, disgruntled adherents to competing projects, like Confederates in exile and German particularists in an "inner emigration" – they maintained their distance from the common crowd. If democracy did not make people politically equal, and if contracts and markets did not make them economically equal, the mere fact of belonging to the same nation certainly would not erase proper distinctions of station.

Hanseats did share this experience with other members of their social class. Browns, Donnells, Lürmanns, Astors, and Schwabs mingled with Hones, Tappans, Wadsworths, Fishers, and Taneys. It is hard to imagine that the difference in national backgrounds among these families would have been a subject of conversation in their business dealings or political cooperation, let alone a hindrance to either. These Englishmen, Scots, Germans, and Anglo-Americans shared a bond more enduring than nationality – wealth.

They did, to a large extent, also share a Protestant faith, usually of a more Calvinist than Lutheran persuasion. Bremen's merchants, in particular, avoided doing business with Jews, even as German-Jewish businesses were thriving in American port cities. Catholics were less categorically avoided, but still regarded with a certain suspicion. But Protestantism was not a source of identity that competed with the nation. On the contrary, it became a key component to the nationalisms that emerged in the United

States and the German Empire from the 1870s onward; and in both places, public policies on the local level became increasingly anti-Semitic, with Jews being turned away from popular resort towns such as Saratoga and Borkum. Famously, Joseph Seligman, whose efforts in selling U.S. war bonds in Europe were crucial for Union victory in the Civil War, was denied admission to the hotel in Saratoga he had visited for several summers in a row.

Of the Hanseats studied here, Gustav Schwab was perhaps the most "Americanized." When he learned that Bismarck had taken on the power of the Catholic Church in open conflict, he responded with an enthusiasm that betrays an insight into the strong Protestant tint that nationalism had received in Germany and America. If the nation became Protestant, it might just become a suitable source of identity for a man of means.

Just as the entwined stories of migrations and the making of classes and nations change, once we lift our gaze from the lower rungs of society to consider the movers and doers, so the formation of gender roles in the Victorian world looks different among the mercantile elites than it did among the middle class. To be sure, the cult of true womanhood, and the cultivation of a female role as guardian of the home, understood as a safe haven from the rude realities of the marketplace, set the tone for the twentieth century. But the 1950s were likely more true to the nineteenth-century middle-class ideal of gender relations than were the 1850s.

Hanseats were not hostile to the empowerment of women, in absolute terms. Rather, the purpose for which such power was employed made all the difference. Female, Protestant reformers of morals and institutions received warm praise from Schwabs and Meiers. After all, in the literary world of the German *Bildungsbürgertum*, female authors had long played an accepted role. More importantly, Hanseats were keenly aware that their own estate relied to a large degree on the powerful and often economically independent role of the matriarchs of Bremen's merchant elite. To take at face value the pronouncements of principles from Hanseats who voiced opinions on gender relations means to miss the more ambivalent practices of this estate.

To those who study capitalism, and to those who wish to bring it to an end, the story of Bremen's merchants in the nineteenth century presents a lesson. Under a system that subjects every utterance of human life to the logic of exchange, the moral predispositions of its participants are ultimately irrelevant. To the student of capitalism, this means not to put too much stock in the self-image of groups of market participants, but rather to consider as primary the economic basis for the existence of such groups. For those who wish to overcome this system of production and exchange, the lesson is one of avoiding a moralistic approach to the critique of its elites. The example of the Hanseats who were the subject of this study demonstrates that even those most deeply committed to ethical conduct, and opposed to treating others as mere means to an end of profit maximization, can play an economic role that negates the best of intentions. It is not the intention that matters, but the economic conditions of one's actions.

Sources

MANUSCRIPT AND PRINTED SOURCES

Baltimore

Maryland Historical Society Library

Archival Materials (Manuscripts Department)

MS.439, Wilkens, Julius, 1838?–1898, Papers, 1849–83
MS.541, Lurman, Gustavus W., 1809–66, Papers and genealogy, 1833–1945
MS.610, Baltimore. Merchants' Exchange Reading Room, record books, 1832–99, 72 volumes
MS.1921.1, Brune, Frederick W., 1776–1860, Brune Family Papers, 1831–97
MS.2004, Brune, Emily Barton, 1826–1908, Papers, 1782–1972
MS.2826, Graue, Heinrich H., fl. 1834–71, Papers, 1834–71
Vertical File "Geyer & Wilkens"

OTHER HOLDINGS

Lurman, John S., *Genealogy of the Lurman and Allied Families*, Baltimore, 1904

Johns Hopkins University, Milton S. Eisenhower Library, Government Records

HOLDINGS

Congressional Globe, vol. 15, 29th Congress, 1st Session (1845–6)

Bremen

Staatsarchiv Bremen

ARCHIVAL MATERIALS

2,B.13.b.1.a.2.b.I., *Hanseatica. Verhältnisse der Hansestädte mit den Vereinigten Staaten von Nordamerika. Hanseatische diplomatische Agenten, Konsuln usw. bei den Vereinigten Staaten von Nordamerika und Korrespondenz mit denselben. In Washington, Rudolf Schleiden, Ministerresident 1853, Berichte und Korrespondenz desselben, 1856–57*

2,B.13.b.3, *Hanseatica. Verhältnisse der Hansestädte mit den Vereinigten Staaten von Nordamerika. Hanseatische diplomatische Agenten, Konsuln usw. bei den Vereinigten Staaten von Nordamerika und Korrespondenz mit denselben. In New York, 1815–1868*

2,B.13.b.10, *Hanseatica. Verhältnisse der Hansestädte mit den Vereinigten Staaten von Nordamerika. Hanseatische diplomatische Agenten, Konsuln usw. bei den vereinigten Staaten von Nordamerika und Korrespondenz mit denselben. Konsulate Richmond etc.*

2,C.4.g.1.II, *Beitritt der Hansestädte zu den zwischen England und Frankreich zur Unterdrückung des Sklavenhandels abgeschlossenen Verträgen 1837. Generalia et diversa 1836–1868*

4,48.21/5.E.1, *Bremische Gesandtschaft in Washington, Angelegenheiten des bremischen Ministerresidenten Dr. Rudolph Schleiden (1845) 1853–1862*

7,116, [Rudolf Schleiden Papers]

7,128, *Lürman* [family papers]

7,13, *Köper, Friedrich* [papers]

NEWSPAPERS

Handelsblatt
taz [Die Tageszeitung] Bremen
Weser-Zeitung, Mikrofim FB 311

OTHER HOLDINGS

Achelis, Eduard, *Meine Lebenserinnerungen aus 50jähriger Arbeit* (photocopy of typescript), Bremen 1935/1936

[Freie Hansestadt Bremen], *Bremischer Staatskalender auf das Jahr 1861*, Bremen 1861

[Freie Hansestadt Bremen], *Bremischer Staatskalender auf das Jahr 1866*, Bremen 1866

Verhandlungen der Bremischen Bürgerschaft

New Haven

Yale University Library, Manuscripts and Archives

ARCHIVAL MATERIALS

MSS 434, John Christopher Schwab Family Papers

New York

New York Public Library, Research Library, Special Collections Department

ARCHIVAL MATERIALS

U.S. Army – Quartermaster's Department – Copy Book – Virginia Merchants – Tobacco Claims – 1865 May–June

NEWSPAPERS

New York Evening Post
New York Times

National Archives – Northeast Region, New York

Archival Materials

Admiralty Case Files, United States District Court for the Southern District of New York, Records of the District Courts of the United States, Record Group 21,
-Case File A-16–387, C. Winters [*sic*] Oeder v. Herman Gelpcke, Consul of the Principality of Dessau, Frederick W. Keutgen, Consul of the City of Bremen at the Port of New York, and Adolphus Reichelt.
-Case File A-16–393, Albert Erhard v. Herman Gelpcke and others [Frederick W. Keutgen, Adolphus Reichelt, William [*sic*] Vogel, Morris K. Jessup and Joseph Herzfeld].

County Clerk, New York County, County Court House

Archival Materials

1861#851, Superior Court, *James Stuart v. Gelpcke*, 27 Nov 1861
1861#916, Superior Court, *Joseph Stuart v. Herman Gelpcke*, 27 Nov 1861
1861#1327, Court of Common Pleas, *John Stuart v. Herman Gelpcke*, 27 Nov 1861
1861#1327, Court of Common Pleas, *Joseph Stuart v. Herman Gelpcke*, 27 Nov 1861

Other Sources

Internet and Telecommunication

Adams, Willi Paul, "German Translations of the American Declaration of Independence," http://chnm.gmu.edu/declaration/adams2.html (accessed June 7, 2004)
Baumwollbörse Bremen, http://www.baumwollboerse.de (accessed September 30, 2005)
Dippel, Horst, "Die Unabhängigkeitserklärung in Deutschland: Betrachtungen über politische Kultur und gemeinsame Werte," http://www.dhm.de/mag azine/unabhaengig/dippel_d.htm (accessed June 7, 2004)
Evangelische Landeskirche Schaumburg-Lippe, http://www.ekd.de/schaum burg/ (accessed April 17, 2001)
Evangelische Landeskirche in Württemberg, http://www.elk-wue.de/lande skirche/zahlen-und-fakten/geschichte-der-landeskirche/ (accessed November 16, 2005)
Hamid Hussain, "The Story of the Storm – 1857," *Defence Journal* (India) May 2002 (online edition), http://www.defencejournal.com/2002/may/storm. htm (accessed January 15, 2005)
"History Disproved?" *Deccan Herald*, June 30, 1953; i.e., "From our Files, 50 Years Ago," *Deccan Herald*, June 30, 2003, http://www.deccanherald.com/ deccanherald/jun30/files.asp (accessed January 15, 2005)

Telephone interview by the author with Edward Gieske, February 2, 2001

Touro College Law Center, Project P.A.T.C.H., http://www.tourolaw.edu/patch/Scott/Campbell.asp (accessed October 1, 2005)

Zion Church Baltimore, http://www.zionbaltimore.org (accessed January 24, 2005)

Bibliography

Abbott, Richard H. *Cotton and Capital: Boston Businessmen and Antislavery Reform, 1854–1868*. Amherst, MA, 1991.

Abelshauser, Werner, et al. *Wirtschaftliche Integration und Wandel von Raumstrukturen im 19. und 20. Jahrhundert*, ed. Josef Wysocki (Schriften des Vereins für Socialpolitik, Gesellschaft für Wirtschafts- und Sozialwissenschaften; N.F., vol. 232). Berlin, 1994.

Adams, Ephraim Douglass. *Great Britain and the American Civil War*. London and New York, 1925.

Addresses of Albert Schumacher, S. Teackle Wallis, John W. Garrett, W. T. McClintock, of Ohio, E. H. Webster, and others: made on the 26th of March, 1868, at the complimentary banquet by the merchants of Baltimore to the officers of the pioneer steamship of the Baltimore and Bremen line. Baltimore, 1868.

Adler, Jeffrey S. *Yankee Merchants and the Making of the Urban West: The Rise and Fall of Antebellum St. Louis*. Cambridge and New York, 1991.

Adorno, Theodor W., and Horkheimer, Max. *Dialektik der Aufklärung: Philosophische Fragmente*, Frankfurt, 1969 (New York, 1944).

Ahrens, Gerhard. "Staatsschuld und Anleihenpolitik der hanseatischen Stadtrepubliken im frühen 19. Jahrhundert," *Blätter für Deutsche Landesgeschichte* 134 (1998): 361–406.

Altvater, Elmar, and Birgit Mahnkopf. *Grenzen der Globalisierung: Ökonomie, Ökologie und Politik in der Weltgesellschaft*. Münster, 2007.

Altvater, Elmar, ed. *Der Sound des Sachzwangs – Der Globalisierungs-Reader*. Berlin, 2006.

Anbinder, Tyler G. "Fernando Wood and New York City's Secession from the Union: A Political Reappraisal," *New York History* 68 (January 1987): 67–92.

Anderson, Benedict. *Imagined Communities: Reflections on the Origin and Spread of Nationalism*. London and New York, 1983.

Andree, Rolf, and Ute Rickel-Immel. *The Hudson and the Rhine: Die amerikanische Malerkolonie in Düsseldorf im 19. Jahrhundert*, Kat. Ausst. [Exhibition Catalog]. Düsseldorf, Kunstmuseum, 1976.

[Anon.], "Die Wahrheit über H. H. Meier. Von einem Wähler." Bremen, 1874.

Apelt, Hermann. "Friedrich List und die Hanseaten," *Der Schlüssel, Bremer Beiträge zur Deutschen Kultur und Wirtschaft* 6, no. 8 (1941): 133–43.

Archdeacon, Thomas. *Becoming American: An Ethnic History*. New York and London, 1983.

Armgort, Arno. *Bremen-Bremerhaven-New York. Geschichte der europäischen Auswanderung über die Bremischen Häfen (A history of European emigration through the ports of Bremen)*. Bremen, 1991.

Arnell, J. C. *Steam and the North Atlantic Mails: The Impact of the Cunard Line and Subsequent Steamship Companies on the Carriage of Transatlantic Mails*. Toronto, 1986.

Ashworth, John. *Slavery, Capitalism, and Politics in the Antebellum Republic*, 2 vols., vol. 1: *Commerce and Compromise, 1820–1850*. Cambridge, 1995.

"Agrarians" and "Aristocrats": Party Political Ideology in the United States, 1837–1846. London and Atlantic Highlands, NJ, 1983.

Baasch, Ernst. "Hamburg und Bremen und die deutschen wirtschaftlichen Einheitsbestrebungen von der Begründung des Zollvereins bis zum Anschluß Hannovers (1854)," *Hanseatische Geschichtsblätter* 47 (1922): 115–69.

Baker, Jean H. *Ambivalent Americans: The Know-Nothing Party in Maryland.* Baltimore, 1977.

Bailyn, Bernard, and Patricia L. Denault, eds. *Soundings in Atlantic History: Latent Structures and Intellectual Currents, 1500–1830.* Cambridge, MA, 2009.

Barber, Benjamin. *Jihad vs. McWorld: How Globalism and Tribalism Are Reshaping the World.* New York, 1995.

Barclay, David E., and Elisabeth Glaser-Schmidt, eds. *Transatlantic Images and Perceptions: Germany and America since 1776.* Cambridge and New York, 1997.

Baron, Salo. *Die Judenfrage auf dem Wiener Kongress.* Vienna and Berlin, 1920.

Beard, Charles. *An Economic Interpretation of the Constitution of the United States.* New York and London, 1965 (1913).

Becker, Frank. "Konfessionelle Nationsbilder im Deutschen Kaiserreich," in *Nation und Religion in der deutschen Geschichte*, ed. Heinz-Gerhard Haupt and Dieter Langewiesche. Frankfurt and New York, 2001, 389–418.

Beckert, Sven. "Merchants and Manufacturers in the Antebellum North," in *Ruling America: A History of Wealth and Power in a Democracy*, ed. Gary Gerstle and Steve Fraser. Cambridge, MA, 2005, 92–122.

The Monied Metropolis: New York City and the Consolidation of the American Bourgeoisie, 1850–1896. Cambridge, MA, 2001.

Bender, Thomas. *A Nation among Nations: America's Place in World History.* New York, 2006.

Bessell, Georg. *1857–1957: Norddeutscher Lloyd. Geschichte einer bremischen Reederei.* Bremen, 1957.

Best, Heinrich. *Interessenpolitk und nationale Integration 1848/49. Handelspolitische Konflikte im frühindustriellen Deutschland*, ed. Helmut Berding, Jürgen Kocka, and Hans-Ulrich Wehler, Kritische Studien zur Geschichtswissenschaft, vol. 37. Göttingen, 1980.

Beutin, Ludwig. *Bremen und Amerika: Zur Geschichte der Weltwirtschaft und der Beziehungen Deutschlands zu den Vereinigten Staaten.* Bremen, 1953.

Bremisches Bank- und Börsenwesen seit dem 17. Jahrhundert. Von der Wirtschaftsgesinnung einer Hansestadt (Abhandlungen und Vorträge herausgegeben von der Bremer Wissenschaftlichen Gesellschaft, vol. 10, no. 4, December 1937). Bremen, 1937.

Von 3 Ballen zum Weltmarkt. Kleine Bremer Baumwollchronik 1788 bis 1872. Bremen, 1934.

Bevan, Edith Rossiter. "Willow Brook, Country Seat of John Donnell," *Maryland Historical Magazine* 44, no. 1 (March 1949): 33–41.

Biebusch, Werner. *Revolution und Staatsstreich. Verfassungskämpfe in Bremen, 1848–1854* (Veröffentlichungen aus dem Staatsarchiv Bremen, vol. 8). Bremen, 1974.

Biefang, Andreas. *Politisches Bürgertum in Deutschland, 1857–1868: Nationale Organisationen und Eliten* (Kommission für Geschichte des Parlamentarismus und der politischen Parteien, corp. ed., Beiträge zur Geschichte des Parlamentarismus und der politischen Parteien, vol. 102). Düsseldorf, 1994.

Bippen, Wilhelm von. *Johann Smidt, ein hanseatischer Staatsmann.* Stuttgart and Berlin, 1921.

"Duckwitz, Arnold," in *Bremische Biographie des neunzehnten Jahrhunderts*, ed. Historische Gesellschaft des Künstlervereins. Bremen, 1912.

"Rösing, Johannes (I.)," in *Bremische Biographie des neunzehnten Jahrhunderts*, ed. Historische Gesellschaft des Künstlervereins. Bremen, 1912.

Blackbourne, David, and Richard J. Evans, eds. *The German Bourgeoisie: Essays on the Social History of the German Middle Class from the Late Eighteenth to the Early Twentieth Century.* London and New York, 1991.

Bluestein, Gene. "The Advantages of Barbarism: Herder and Whitman's Nationalism," *Journal of the History of Ideas* 24, no. 1 (1963): 115–26.

Blumin, Stuart M. *The Emergence of the Middle Class: Social Experience in the American City, 1760–1900.* Cambridge and New York, 1989.

Boch, Rudolf. *Grenzenloses Wachstum? Das rheinische Wirtschaftsbürgertum und seine Industrialisierungsdebatte, 1814–1857* (Bürgertum. Beiträge zur europäischen Gesellschaftsgeschichte, vol. 3). Göttingen, 1991.

Böhme, Helmut, ed. *Probleme der Reichsgründungszeit 1848–1879.* Cologne and Berlin, 1972.

Böhmert, [Karl] Victor. "Die Stellung der Hansestädte zu Deutschland in den letzten drei Jahrzehnten," *Vierteljahrsschrift für Volkswirthschaft und Cultur* 1 (1863): 73–115.

Beiträge zur Geschichte des Zunftwesens (Preisschriften, gekrönt und herausgegeben von der fürstlich Jablonowski'schen Gesellschaft zu Leipzig, IX.). Leipzig, 1862 (1859).

Bohner, Theodor. *Der deutsche Kaufmann über See.* Hamburg, 1956.

Bolster, W. Jeffrey. *Black Jacks: African American Seamen in the Age of Sail.* Cambridge, MA, and London, 1997.

Bondi, Gerhard. *Deutschlands Außenhandel 1815–1870* (Deutsche Akademie der Wissenschaften zu Berlin, Schriften des Instituts für Geschichte, Reihe I: Allgemeine und Deutsche Geschichte, vol. 5). Berlin (DDR), 1958.

Borries, Bodo von. *Deutschlands Außenhandel 1836 bis 1856. Eine statistische Untersuchung zur Frühindustrialisierung* (Knut Borchardt et al., eds., Forschungen zur Sozial- und Wirtschaftsgeschichte, vol. 13). Stuttgart, 1970.

Brandes, Erika. "Der Bremer Überseekaufmann in seiner gesellschaftsgeschichtlichen Bedeutung im 'geschlossenen Heiratskreis,'" *Genealogisches Jahrbuch* 3 (1963): 25–48.

Bratranek, F[ranz] Th[omas], ed. *Goethe's Briefwechsel mit den Gebrüdern von Humboldt (1795–1832),* Im Auftrage der von Goethe'schen Familie herausgegeben von F. Th. Bratranek (Neue Mittheilungen aus Johann Wolfgang von Goethe's handschriftlichem Nachlasse, part 3). Leipzig, 1876.

Braudel, Fernand. *Civilization and Capitalism, Fifteenth–Eighteenth Century,* 3 vols. Berkeley, CA, 1992 (1982–4).

Bringmann, Michael. *"Pecht, Friedrich," Neue Deutsche Biographie* 20. Berlin, 2001: 156–7.

Browne, Gary Larson. *Baltimore in the Nation, 1789–1861.* Chapel Hill, NC, 1980.

Brubaker, Rogers. *Citizenship and Nationhood in France and Germany.* Cambridge, MA, 1992.

Bruford, Walter Horace. *The German Tradition of Self-Cultivation: "Bildung" from Humboldt to Thomas Mann.* Cambridge, 1975.

Brugger, Robert J. *Maryland, a Middle Temperament, 1634–1980.* Baltimore, 1988.

Burke, Edmund. *Reflections on the Revolution in France.* London, 1986 (1790).

Buruma, Ian, and Avishai Margalit. *Occidentalism: The West in the Eyes of Its Enemies.* New York, 2004.

Burwick, Fred L. "The Göttingen Influence on George Bancroft's Idea of Humanity," *Jahrbuch für Amerikastudien* [West Germany] 11 (1966): 194–212.

Bushman, Richard. *The Refinement of America: Persons, Houses, Cities.* New York, 1992.

Cannadine, David. *Ornamentalism: How the British Saw Their Empire.* London, 2001.

Chalfant, Randolp W. "Calvert Station: Its Structure and Significance," *Maryland Historical Magazine* 74, no. 1 (March 1979): 11–22.

Chandler, Alfred D., Jr., *Strategy and Structure: Chapters in the History of the American Industrial Enterprise.* Cambridge, MA, 1962.

Chapman, Stanley D. *Merchant Enterprise in Britain from the Industrial Revolution to World War I.* Cambridge, 1992.

The Rise of Merchant Banking. London, 1984.

Chitwood, Oliver Perry. *John Tyler: Champion of the Old South.* New York and London, 1939.

Christadler, Martin. "Romantic Landscape Painting in America: History as Nature, Nature as History," in *American Icons: Transatlantic Perspectives on Eighteenth- and Nineteenth-Century American Art*, ed. Thomas W. Gaehtgens and Heinz Ickstadt (Julia Bloomfield, Kurt W. Forster, and Thomas F. Reese, eds., Issues and Debates. A Series of the Getty Center Publication Program, vol. 2). Santa Monica, CA, 1992, 93–117.

Chused, Richard H. "Married Women's Property Law, 1800–1850," *Georgetown Law Journal* 71, no. 5 (June 1983): 1359–1426.

Cronon, William. *Nature's Metropolis: Chicago and the Great West*. New York and London, 1991.

Cunz, Dieter. *The Maryland Germans: A History*. Princeton, NJ, 1948.

"Maryland Germans in the Civil War," *Maryland Historical Magazine* 36, no. 4 (December 1941): 394–419.

A History of the Germania Club of Baltimore City, Maryland, 1840–1940. Baltimore, 1940.

Davidoff, Leonore and Catherine Hall. *Family Fortunes: Men and Women of the English Middle Class, 1780–1850*, rev. ed. London and New York, 2002.

Dippel, Horst. *Die amerikanische Verfassung in Deutschland im 19. Jahrhundert. Das Dilemma von Politik und Staatsrecht*. Goldbach, Germany, 1994.

Ditz, Toby. "Shipwrecked; or, Masculinity Imperiled: Mercantile Representation of Failure and the Gendered Self in Eighteenth-Century Philadelphia," *Journal of American History* 81, no. 1 (June 1994): 51–80.

Dörner, Andreas. *Politischer Mythos und symbolische Politik. Sinnstiftung durch symbolische Formen am Beispiel des Hermannsmythos*. Opladen, 1995 (also PhD diss., Universität Essen, 1994).

Drayton, Richard. *Nature's Government: Science, Imperial Britain, and the "Improvement" of the World*. New Haven, CT, and London, 2000.

Duckwitz, Arnold. *Denkwürdigkeiten aus meinem öffentlichen Leben von 1841–1866. Ein Beitrag zur bremischen und deutschen Geschichte*. Bremen, 1877.

Echternkamp, Jörg. "Emerging Ethnicity: The German Experience in Antebellum Baltimore," *Maryland Historical Magazine* 86, no. 1 (Spring 1991): 1–22.

Eley, Geoff and David Blackbourn. *The Peculiarities of German History*. Oxford and New York, 1984.

Engelsing, Rolf. *Massenpublikum und Journalistentum im 19. Jahrhundert in Nordwestdeutschland* (Wolfram Fischer et al., eds., Studien zur Wirtschafts- und Sozialgeschichte, vol. 1). West Berlin, 1966.

Bremen als Auswandererhafen, 1683–1880 (Karl H. Schwebel, ed., Veröffentlichungen aus dem Staatsarchiv der Freien Hansestadt Bremen, vol. 29). Bremen, 1961.

"Bremisches Unternehmertum. Sozialgeschichte 1780/1870," *Jahrbuch der Wittheit zu Bremen* 2 (1958): 7–112.

"England und die USA in der bremischen Sicht des 19. Jahrhunderts," *Jahrbuch der Wittheit zu Bremen* 1 (1957): 33–65.

Entholt, Hermann. "Bremens Handel, Schiffahrt und Industrie im 19. Jahrhundert (1815–1914)," in *Die Hansestädte Hamburg/Bremen/Lübeck*, ed. O. Mathies, H. Entholt, and L. Lichtweiss (Die Deutsche Wirtschaft und Ihre Führer, vol. 5). Gotha, 1928, 131–244.

Equiano, Olaudah. *The Interesting Narrative of the Life of Olaudah Equiano, or, Gustavus Vassa, the African*. New York, 2004.

Etges, Andreas. *Wirtschaftsnationalismus. USA und Deutschland im Vergleich (1815–1914)*. Frankfurt and New York, 1999.

Evans, Richard J. "Family and Class in the Hamburg Grand Bourgeoisie 1815–1914," in *The German Bourgeoisie: Essays on the Social History of the German Middle Class from the Late Eighteenth to the Early Twentieth Century*, ed. David Blackbourne and Richard J. Evans. London and New York, 1991, 115–39.

Evans, Richard J., and Hartmut Pogge von Strandmann, eds. *The Revolutions in Europe, 1848–1849: From Reform to Revolution*. Oxford, 2000.

Evitts, William J. *A Matter of Allegiances: Maryland from 1850 to 1861* (The Johns Hopkins University Studies in Historical and Political Science, 2nd series, vol. 1). Baltimore and London, 1974.

Fein, Isaac M. "Baltimore Jews during the Civil War," *American Jewish History Quarterly* 51, no. 2 (1961–2): 67–96.

Ferslew, Eugene. *Baltimore City Directory for 1859–60*. Baltimore, 1859.

Fields, Barbara Jeanne. *Slavery and Freedom on the Middle Ground: Maryland during the Nineteenth Century*. New Haven, CT, and London, 1985.

Fink, Georg. "Diplomatische Vertretungen der Hanse seit dem 17. Jahrhundert bis zur Auflösung der Hanseatischen Gesandtschaft in Berlin 1920," *Hanseatische Geschichtsblätter* 56 (Lübeck, Germany, 1932): 112–55.

Fischer, Fritz. "Der deutsche Protestantismus und die Politik im 19. Jahrhundert," in *Probleme der Reichsgründungszeit 1848–1879*, ed. Helmut Böhme. Cologne and Berlin, 1972, 49–71.

Fischer, Hermann. "Schwab, Gustav [Benjamin]," *Allgemeine Deutsche Biographie* 33, Munich 1891: 153–5.

Fitzhugh, George. *Cannibals All! Or, Slaves without Masters*. Richmond, VA, 1857.

Flacke, Monika. "Deutschland. Die Begründung der Nation aus der Krise," in *Mythen der Nationen. Ein Europäisches Panorama*, ed. Monicka Flacke. Munich and Berlin, 1998, 101–28.

Flacke, Monika, ed. *Mythen der Nationen. Ein Europäisches Panorama*. Munich and Berlin, 1998.

Foner, Philip. *Business and Slavery: The New York Merchants and the Irrepressible Conflict*. Chapel Hill, NC, 1941.

Formisano, Ronald P. "The 'Party Period' Revisited," *Journal of American History* 86, no. 1 (June 1999): 93–120.

The Transformation of Political Culture: Massachusetts Parties, 1790s–1840s. New York and Oxford, 1983.

The Birth of Mass Political Parties, Michigan 1827–1861. Princeton, NJ, 1971.

Förster, Stig, and Jörg Nagler, eds. *On the Road to Total War: The American Civil War and the German Wars of Unification, 1861–1871*. Washington, DC, 1997.

Fox, Steven. *Transatlantic: Samuel Cunard, Isambard Brunel, and the Great Atlantic Steamships*. New York, 2003.

Fremdling, Rainer, and Richard H. Tilly, eds. *Industrialisierung und Raum. Studien zur regionalen Differenzierung in Deutschland des 19. Jahrhunderts*. Stuttgart, 1979.

Freytag, Gustav. *Soll und Haben*. Leipzig, 1855.

Friedman, Thomas L. *The World Is Flat: A Brief History of the Twenty-First Century*. New York, 2005.

Gaethgens, Barbara. "Fictions of Nationhood: Leutze's Pursuit of an American History Painting in Düsseldorf," in *American Icons*, ed. Thomas W. Gaehtgens and Heinz Ickstadt. Santa Monica, CA, 1992, 149–54.

Gaehtgens, Thomas W., and Heinz Ickstadt, eds. *American Icons: Transatlantic Perspectives on Eighteenth- and Nineteenth-Century American Art* (Julia Bloomfield, Kurt W. Forster and Thomas F. Reese, eds., Issues and Debates. A Series of the Getty Center Publication Program, vol. 2). Santa Monica, CA, 1992.

Gall, Lothar, and Dieter Langewiesche, eds. *Liberalismus und Region. Zur Geschichte des deutsche Liberalismus im 19. Jahrhundert*. Munich, 1995.

Garlich, Inge. *Das Leben einer Bremer Kaufmannsfamilie im 19. Jahrhundert, beschrieben nach dem Tagebuch der Engel Maria Thiermann von 1847–1858* (Hausarbeit zur ersten Staatsprüfung für das Lehramt an öffentlichen Schulen, University of Bremen), 1982.

Gathen, Antonius David. *Rolande als Rechtssymbole: Der archäologische Bestand und seine rechtshistorische Deutung.* West Berlin, 1960.

Gatter, Nikolaus. *"Schwab, Gustav Benjamin," Neue Deutsche Biographie 23.* Berlin, 2007: 772–4.

Gebel, Thomas. "Schwachhausen und die SWAPO," *taz* [Die Tageszeitung] *Bremen* 6639 (January 2, 2002): 23.

Genovese, Eugene D. *The Slaveholders' Dilemma: Freedom and Progress in Southern Conservative Thought, 1820–1860.* Columbia, SC, 1992.

The World the Slaveholders Made: Two Essays in Interpretation. New York, 1969.

Gentz, Friedrich von. *The French and American Revolutions Compared,* translated by John Quincy Adams (1800), in Three Revolutions, ed. Stefan T. Possony. Chicago, 1959.

Gerstenberger, Heide, and Ulrich Welke. *Vom Wind zum Dampf. Sozialgeschichte der deutschen Handelsschiffahrt im Zeitalter der Industrialisierung.* Münster, 1996.

Gesellschaft für Wirtschaftsförderung Bremen, ed. *Bremen – Bremerhaven. Häfen am Strom – River Weser Ports.* Bremen, 1966.

Gilroy, Paul. *The Black Atlantic: Modernity and Double Consciousness.* Cambridge, MA, 1993.

There Ain't No Black in the Union Jack: The Cultural Politics of Race and Nation. London, 1987.

Gosewinkel, Dieter. *Einbürgern und Ausschließen. Die Nationalisierung der Staatsangehörigkeit vom Deutschen Bund bis zur Bundesrepublik Deutschland* (Helmut Berding, et al., eds., Kritische Studien zur Geschichtswissenschaft, vol. 150). Göttingen, 2001 (Habilitationsschrift, Freie Universität Berlin).

Graßmann, Antjekathrin. "Hanse weltweit? Zu den Konsulaten Lübecks, Bremens und Hamburgs im 19. Jahrhundert," in *Ausklang und Nachklang der Hanse im 19. und 20. Jahrhundert,* ed. Antjekathrin Graßmann (Hansischer Geschichtsverein, ed., Hansische Studien, vol. 12). Trier, Germany, 2001: 43–66.

Graßmann, Antjekathrin, ed. *Ausklang und Nachklang der Hanse im 19. und 20. Jahrhundert* (Hansischer Geschichtsverein, ed., Hansische Studien, vol. 12). Trier, Germany, 2001.

Grant, Clement Lyndon. "The Public Career of Cave Johnson," PhD diss., Vanderbilt University, 1951.

Grießinger, Andreas, and Reinhold Reith. "Obrigkeitliche Ordnungskonzeptionen und handwerkliches Konfliktverhalten im 18. Jahrhundert. Nürnberg und Würzburg im Vergleich," in *Deutsches Handwerk in Spätmittelalter und Früher Neuzeit,* ed. Rainer S. Elkar (Göttinger Beiträge zur Wirtschafts- und Sozialgeschichte, vol. 9). Göttingen, 1983: 117–80.

Grier, Katherine C. *Culture and Comfort: Parlor Making and Middle-Class Identity, 1850–1930.* Washington, DC, 1997.

Groseclose, Barbara S. *Emmanuel Leutze, 1816–1868: Freedom Is the Only King,* Exhibition Catalog, National Collection of Fine Art, Smithsonian Institution, 1976, Washington, DC, 1976.

Gustafsson, Heinz. *Namibia, Bremen und Deutschland. Ein steiniger Weg zur Freundschaft.* Delmenhorst, Germany, 2003.

Habermas, Jürgen. *The Structural Transformation of the Public Sphere: An Inquiry into a Category of Bourgeois Society.* Cambridge, MA, 1989.

Halttunen, Karen. *Confidence Men and Painted Women: A Story of Middle-Class Culture in America, 1830–1870* (Yale Historical Publication, Miscellany, vol. 129). New Haven, CT, and London, 1982.

Hamerow, Theodore S. *The Social Foundations of German Unification: Ideas and Institutions.* Princeton, NJ, 1969.

Hamilton, Alexander, James Madison, and John Jay. *The Federalist Papers.* New York, 1961 (1787–8).

Hancock, David. *Citizens of the World: London Merchants and the Integration of the British Atlantic Community, 1735–1785.* Cambridge and New York, 1995.

Handelskammer Bremen. *Berichte der Handelskammer in Bremen für die Jahre 1870–1873, erstattet an den Kaufmanns-Konvent.* Bremen, 1874.

Handlin, Lilian. "Harvard and Göttingen, 1815," *Massachusetts Historical Society Proceedings* 95 (1983): 67–87.

Harada, Tetsushi. *Politische Ökonomie des Idealismus und der Romantik. Korporatismus von Fichte, Müller und Hegel* (Volkswirtschaftliche Schriften, vol. 386). West Berlin, 1989.

Hardegen, Friedrich, and Käthi Smidt, geb. Meier, *H. H. Meier, der Gründer des Norddeutschen Lloyd. Lebensbild eines Bremer Kaufmanns, 1809–1898.* Berlin and Leipzig, 1920.

Hartog, Hendrik. *Man and Wife in America: A History.* Cambridge, MA, 2000.

Harvey, David. *The Condition of Postmodernity: An Inquiry into the Origins of Cultural Change.* Cambridge, MA, and Oxford, 1990.

Haupt, Heinz-Gerhard, and Dieter Langewiesche, eds. *Nation und Religion in der deutschen Geschichte.* Frankfurt and New York, 2001.

Hegel, G. W. F. *Elements of the Philosophy of Right,* translated by H. B. Nisbet. Cambridge, 1991.

Heine, Heinrich. *Deutschland: A Winter's Tale,* translated by T. J. Reed. London, 1986.

Heiser, Elinor S. *Days Gone By.* Baltimore, 1940.

Hennighausen, Louis P. *History of the German Society of Maryland.* Baltimore, 1909.

"Reminiscences of the Political Life of the German-Americans in Baltimore during 1850–1860," *Seventh Annual Report of the Society for the History of the Germans in Maryland, 1892–1893,* 53–59 (part I), and *Eleventh and Twelfth Annual Report of the Society for the History of the Germans in Maryland, 1897–1898,* 3–18 (part II).

Herzstein, Robert Edwin. "New York City Views the German Revolution 1848: A Study in Ethnicity and Public Opinion," in *Consortium on Revolutionary Europe 1750–1850: Proceedings 1976,* 102–20.

Hettling, Manfred and Paul Nolte, eds. *Bürgerliche Feste. Symbolische Formen politischen Handelns im 19. Jahrhundert.* Göttingen, 1993.

Heyde, Ludwig, "Böhmert, Karl Victor," *Neue Deutsche Biographie* 2. Berlin, 1955: 394–5.

Hibbert, Christopher. *The Great Mutiny: India 1857.* New York, 1978.

Hidy, Ralph W., *The House of Baring in American Trade: English Merchant Bankers at Work, 1763–1861* (Harvard Studies in Business History, vol. 14). Cambridge, MA, 1949.

Hobsbawm, Eric J. *Nations and Nationalism since 1780: Programme, Myth, Reality.* Cambridge and New York, 1992.

The Age of Capital, 1848–1875. London, 1975.

Hobsbawm, Eric J., and Terence Ranger. *The Invention of Tradition.* Cambridge and New York, 1983.

Hoerder, Dirk, and Jörg Nagler, eds. *People in Transit: German Migrations in Comparative Perspective, 1820–1930.* Washington, DC, 1995.

Holt, Michael F. "The Primacy of Party Reasserted," *Journal of American History* 86, no. 1 (June 1999): 151–7.

Political Parties and American Political Development from the Age of Jackson to the Age of Lincoln. Baton Rouge, LA, and London, 1992.

Howard, George W. *The Monumental City, Its Past History and Present Resources.* Baltimore, 1873.

Howat, John K. "Washington Crossing the Delaware," _Metropolitan Museum of Art Bulletin_ 26, no. 7 (March 1968): 289–99.

Howe, Daniel Walker. _American History in an Atlantic Context: An Inaugural Lecture Delivered before the University of Oxford on June 3 1993._ Oxford, 1993.

The Political Culture of the American Whigs. Chicago and London, 1979.

Hübinger, Gangolf. _Kulturprotestantismus und Politik. Zum Verhältnis von Liberalismus und Protestantismus im wilhelminischen Deutschland._ Tübingen, 1994.

Hundt, Michael. "Die Vertretung der jüdischen Gemeinden Lübecks, Bremens und Hamburgs auf dem Wiener Kongreß," _Blätter für Deutsche Landesgeschichte_ 130 (1994): 143–90.

Huntington, Samuel P. _The Clash of Civilizations._ New York, 1996.

Hutchins, John G. B. _The American Maritime Industry and Public Policy, 1789–1914: An Economic History_ (Harvard University, inst. ed., Harvard Economic Studies, vol. lxxi). Cambridge, MA, 1941.

Hutton, Ann Hawkes. Portrait of Patriotism: _"Washington Crossing the Delaware."_ Philadelphia and New York, 1959.

Irving, Washington. _The Alhambra._ Philadelphia, 1832.

James, Bessie Rowland. _Anne Royall's U.S.A._ New Brunswick, NJ, 1972.

Johnson, Paul E. _A Shopkeeper's Millennium: Society and Revivals in Rochester, New York, 1815–1837._ New York, 1978.

Kamphoefner, Walter D., and Wolfgang Helbich, eds. _Germans in the Civil War: The Letters They Wrote Home,_ translated by Susan Carter. Chapel Hill, NC, 2006.

German-American Immigration and Ethnicity in Comparative Perspective. Madison, WI, 2004.

Kamphoefner, Walter D., Wolfgang Helbich, and Ulrike Sommer, eds. _News from the Land of Freedom: German Immigrants Write Home._ Ithaca, NY, 1991.

Kant, Immanuel. Zum ewigen Frieden _(1795), in_ Kant's Gesammelte Schriften "Akademieausgabe," Königlich Preußische Akademie der Wissenschaften, vol. 8, _Abhandlungen nach 1781,_ Berlin 1923, 341–86.

Kellner-Stoll, Rita. _Bremerhaven, 1827–1888: Politische, wirtschaftliche und soziale Probleme einer Stadtgründung_ (Burchard Scheper, ed., Veröffentlichungen des Stadtarchivs Bremerhaven, vol. 4). Bremen, 1982.

Kelly, Robin D. G. "How the West Was One: The African Diaspora and the Re-Mapping of U.S. History," in _Rethinking American History in a Global Age,_ ed. Thomas Bender. Berkeley, CA, 2002: 123–47.

Kiesselbach, Wilhelm. _Der amerikanische Federalist. Politische Studien für die deutsche Gegenwart,_ 2 vols. Bremen, London, and New York, 1864.

Socialpolitische Studien (Nach den in der Deutschen Vierteljahrsschrift veröffentlichten Aufsätzen des Verfassers zusammengestellt und neu durchgearbeitet). Stuttgart, 1862.

Der Gang des Welthandels im Mittelalter. Bremen, 1860.

Klüpfel, Karl [and Sophie Klüpfel]. _Gustav Schwab. Sein Leben und Wirken._ Leipzig, 1858.

Knobel, Dale T. _America for the Americans: The Nativist Movement in the United States._ New York, 1996.

Kocka, Jürgen, and Allen Mitchell, eds. _Bourgeois Society in Nineteenth-Century Europe._ Oxford and Providence, RI, 1993.

Kohl, Lawrence F. _The Politics of Individualism: Parties and the American Character in the Jacksonian Era._ New York, 1989.

Kramer, Paul. _The Blood of Government: Race, Empire, the United States, and the Philippines._ Chapel Hill, NC, 2006.

Krieger, Adolf. _Arnold Duckwitz, hanseatischer Staatsmann und Reichshandelsminister von 1848 im Kampf für eine deutsche Wirtschaftsordnung. Wirtschaftspolitische Aufsätze_

(Abhandlungen und Vorträge herausgegeben von der Wittheit zu Bremen, vol. 15, no. 1, August 1942). Bremen, 1942.

Bremische Politik im Jahrzehnt vor der Reichsgründung (Schriften der Bremer Wissenschaftlichen Gesellschaft, Reihe F [früher A*], Friedrich Prüser, ed., Veröffentlichungen des Archivs der Hansestadt Bremen, vol. 15). Bremen, 1939.

Kuhlemann, Frank-Michael. "Pastorennationalismus in Deutschland im 19. Jahrhundert – Befunde und Perspektiven der Forschung," in *Nation und Religion in der deutschen Geschichte,* ed. Heinz-Gerhard Haupt and Dieter Langewiesche. Frankfurt and New York, 2001: 548–86.

Langewiesche, Dieter. *Nation, Nationalismus, Nationalstaat in Deutschland und Europa* (Beck'sche Reihe, vol. 1399). Munich, 2000.

Lee, Robert, ed. *Commerce and Culture: Nineteenth-Century Business Elites* (Modern Economic and Social History, unnumbered vol.). Farnham, UK, 2011.

Lemnitzer, Jan Martin, "'A few burghers in a little Hanseatic town' – Die Bremer Seerechtskampagne von 1859," *Bremisches Jahrbuch* 83 (2004): 87–111.

Levine, Bruce. *The Spirit of 1848: German Immigrants, Labor Conflict, and the Coming of the Civil War.* Urbana, IL, 1992.

Levinger, Matthew. *Enlightened Nationalism: The Transformation of Prussian Political Culture, 1806–1848.* Oxford, 2000.

Liebeschütz, Hans, and Arnold Paucker, eds. *Das Judentum in der deutschen Umwelt, 1800– 1850. Studien zur Frühgeschichte der Emanzipation.* Tübingen, 1977.

Lippe, Pauline, Fürstin zur. *Eine Fürstin unterwegs. Reisetagebücher der Fürstin Pauline zur Lippe, 1799–1818,* ed. Hermann Niebuhr (Lippische Geschichtsquellen, vol. 19). Detmold, Germany, 1990.

Lipset, Seymour Martin, and Earl Raab. *The Politics of Unreason: Right-Wing Extremism in America, 1790–1977.* Chicago and London, 1978 (1970).

List, Friedrich. *The National System of Political Economy,* translated by Sampson S. Lloyd. London, 1928 (1841).

"Longfellow, Henry Wadsworth," *Dictionary of American Biography 6.* New York, 1933: 239–40.

Loose, Hans-Dieter, "Nutzbares Erbe oder belastende Relikte einer glorreichen Vergangenheit? Der hanseatische Umgang mit dem Londoner Stahlhof und dem Antwerpener Haus der Osterlinge in der ersten Hälfte des 19. Jahrhunderts," in *Ausklang und Nachklang der Hanse im 19. und 20. Jahrhundert,* ed. Antjekathrin Graßmann (Hansischer Geschichtsverein, ed., Hansische Studien, vol. 12). Trier, Germany, 2001: 31–42.

Lührs, Wilhelm, "Kiesselbach, Wilhelm (1867–1960)," *Neue Deutsche Biographie 11.* Berlin, 1977: 599–600.

Lutz, Ralph Haswell. "Rudolf Schleiden and the Visit to Richmond, April 25, 1861," in *Annual Report of the American Historical Association for the Year 1915* (Washington, DC, 1917), 209–16.

Die Beziehungen zwischen Deutschland und den Vereinigten Staaten während des Sezessionskrieges. Heidelberg, 1911.

"Mann, Ambrose Dudley," *Dictionary of American Biography 6.* New York, 1933: 239–40.

Marschalek, Peter. "Der Erwerb des bremischen Bürgerrechts und die Zuwanderung nach Bremen um die Mitte des 19. Jahrhunderts," *Bremisches Jahrbuch* 66 (1988): 295–305.

Marshall, Helen. *Dorothea Dix, Forgotten Samaritan.* Chapel Hill, NC, 1937.

Marx, Karl, *Capital,* 3 vols. (Karl Marx and Friedrich Engels, Werke). Berlin, 1979.

"Theses on Feuerbach," in *The Marx-Engels Reader,* ed. Robert C. Tucker. New York and London, 1978: 143–5.

Marx, Karl, and Friedrich Engels. "Manifesto of the Communist Party," in *The Marx-Engels Reader*, ed. Robert C. Tucker. New York and London, 1978: 473–500.

Mayer, Brantz. *Baltimore, As It Was and As It Is: A Historical Sketch of the Ancient Town and Modern City from the Foundation, in 1729, to 1870*. Baltimore, 1871.

McBride, David, Leroy Hopkins, and C. Aisha Blackshire-Belay, eds. *Crosscurrents: African Americans, Africa, and Germany in the Modern World*. Columbia, SC, 1998.

McCormick, Richard P. *The Second American Party System: Party Formation in the Jacksonian Era*. Chapel Hill, NC, 1966.

McGerr, Michael. "The Price of the 'New Transnational History,'" *American Historical Review* 96, no. 4 (1991): 1056–67.

McGrane, Reginald Charles. *William Allen: A Study in Western Democracy*. Columbus, OH, 1925.

McKay, Ernest A. *The Civil War and New York City*. Syracuse, NY, 1990.

Meinecke, Friedrich. *Weltbürgertum und Nationalstaat* (Hans Herzfeld, Carl Hinrichs and Walther Hofer, eds., Friedrich Meinecke, Werke, vol. 5). Munich, 1962 (1911).

Mensching, Günther. *Das Allgemeine und das Besondere. Der Ursprung des modernen Denkens im Mittelalter*. Stuttgart, 1992.

Mintz, Steven. *Moralists and Modernizers: America's Pre–Civil War Reformers* (Stanley I. Kutler, ed., The American Moment Series, unnumbered vol.). Baltimore, and London, 1995.

Mitchett's Baltimore City Director [sic] for 1849–50. Baltimore, 1849.

Mitchett's Baltimore City Director [sic] for 1855–56. Baltimore, 1855.

Möller, Kurt Detlev. "Zur Politik der Hansestädte im Jahre 1806," *Zeitschrift des Vereins für Hamburgische Geschichte* 41 (1951) (Festschrift für H. Reincke): 330–52.

Molineux, Catherine. "The Peripheries Within: Race, Slavery, and Empire in Early Modern England," PhD diss., Johns Hopkins University, 2005.

Moltmann, Günter. *Atlantische Blockpolitik im 19. Jahrhundert. Die Vereinigten Staaten und der deutsche Liberalismus während der Revolution von 1848/49*. Düsseldorf, 1973.

Mueller, Henry R. *The Whig Party in Pennsylvania* (Columbia University Studies in the Social Sciences, vol. 230). New York, 1969 (1922).

Müller, Adam Heinrich, and Ritter von Nitterdorf. *Die Elemente der Staatskunst*, 3 vols. Meersburg am Bodensee, Germany, and Leipzig, 1809.

Müller, Karin. *Die Freie Hansestadt Bremen – Zentrum des Baumwollhandels in Mitteleuropa*. Nürnberg, Germany, 1985 (Diplomarbeit, Friedrich-Alexander-Universität Erlangen-Nürnberg, Fachbrereich Betriebswirtschaftslehre).

Mustafa, Sam A. *Merchants and Migrations: Germans and Americans in Connection, 1776–1835* (Derek H. Aldcroft, ed., Modern Economic and Social History Series, unnumbered vol.). Aldershot, UK, 2001.

"The Role of the Hanseatic Cities in Early U.S. – German Relations," *Maryland Historical Magazine* 93, no. 3 (Fall 1998): 265–87.

Nadel, Stanley. *Little Germany: Ethnicity, Religion, and Class in New York City, 1845–80*. Urbana, IL, 1990.

Nelson, Elizabeth White. *Market Sentiments: Middle-Class Market Culture in Nineteenth-Century America*. Washington, DC, 2004.

Niebuhr, Hermann, ed.: See Lippe, Pauline, Fürstin zur.

Niehoff, Lydia. *550 Jahre Tradition der Unabhängigkeit. Chronik der Handelskammer Bremen*, ed. Handelskammer Bremen. Bremen, 2001.

"Niles, John M." *Dictionary of American Biography* 7. New York, 1934: 522–3.

Nolte, Paul. *Gemeindebürgertum und Liberalismus in Baden, 1800–1850. Tradition – Radikalismus – Republik* (Kritische Studien zur Geschichtswissenschaft, vol. 102). Göttingen, 1994.

[North German Lloyd Steamship Company, Bremen]. *70 Years North German Lloyd Bremen, 1857–1927.* Berlin, 1927.

Novick, Peter. *That Noble Dream: The "Objectivity Question" and the American Historical Profession.* Cambridge and New York, 1988.

Oberg, Jan. "Strange Sailors: Maritime Culture in Nineteenth-Century Bremen," in *Bridging Troubled Waters: Conflict and Co-operation in the North Sea Region since 1550,* ed. David J. Starkey and Morten Hahn-Pedersen (7th North Sea History Conference, Dunkirk 2002) (Fiskeri- og Sofartsmuseets Studieserie, vol.17). Esbjerg, Denmark, 2005: 113–33.

Oelrichs & Co. *Caspar Meier and His Successors.* New York, 1898.

O'Rourke, Kevin H., and Jeffrey G. Williamson. *Globalization and History: The Evolution of a Nineteenth-Century Atlantic Economy.* Cambridge, MA, and London, 1999.

Osterhammel, Jürgen, and Niels P. Petersson. *Globalization: A Short History.* Princeton, NJ, and Oxford, 2005.

Pecht, Friedrich. *Südfrüchte: Skizzen eines Malers,* 2 vols. Leipzig, 1854.

Perkins, Edwin J. *Financing Anglo-American Trade: The House of Brown, 1800–1880.* Cambridge, MA, 1975.

Pessen, Edward. *Jacksonian America: Society, Personality, and Politics.* Homewood, NJ, 1969.

Pitsch, Franz Josef. *Die wirtschaftlichen Beziehungen Bremens zu den Vereinigten Staaten von Amerika bis zur Mitte des 19. Jahrhunderts* (Karl H. Schwebel, ed., Veröffentlichungen aus dem Staatsarchiv der Freien Hansestadt Bremen, vol. 42). Bremen, 1974.

Porter, P. Glenn, and Harold C. Livesay. *Merchants and Manufacturers: Studies in the Changing Structure of Nineteenth-Century Marketing.* Baltimore, 1971.

Postone, Moishe. "Anti-Semitism and National Socialism," in *Germans and the Jews since the Holocaust: The Changing Situation in West Germany,* ed. Anson Rabinbach and Jack Zipes. New York, 1986: 302–14.

Prüser, Friedrich. "Gildemeister, Otto," *Neue Deutsche Biographie* 6. Berlin, 1964: 395–6.

Quaife, Milo Milton, ed. *The Diary of James K. Polk during His Presidency, 1845 to 1849,* 4 vols. Chicago, 1910.

Rabinbach, Anson, and Jack Zipes, eds. *Germans and the Jews since the Holocaust: The Changing Situation in West Germany.* New York, 1986.

Rediker, Marcus B., and Peter Linebaugh. *The Many-Headed Hydra: Sailors, Slaves, Commoners, and the Hidden History of the Revolutionary Atlantic.* Boston, 2000.

Richardson, Heather Cox. *The Death of Reconstruction: Race, Labor, and Politics in the Post–Civil War North, 1865–1901.* Cambridge, MA, and London, 2001.

Riehl, Wilhelm Heinrich. *Die bürgerliche Gesellschaft.* Stuttgart, 1861.

Riesman, David. *The Lonely Crowd: A Study of the Changing American Character.* New Haven, CT, 1950.

Roberts, Earl, Field-Marshal. *Letters Written during the Indian Mutiny.* London, 1924.

Roberts, Timothy M. *Distant Revolutions: 1848 and the Challenge to American Exceptionalism.* Charlottesville, VA, 2009.

Roberts, Timothy M., and Daniel W. Howe. "The United States and the Revolutions of 1848," in *The Revolutions in Europe, 1848–1849. From Reform to Revolution,* ed. R. J. W. Evans and Hartmut Pogge von Strandmann. Oxford, 2000: 157–80.

Rockman, Seth. *Welfare Reform in the Early Republic: A Brief History with Documents* (Bedford Series in History and Culture, unnumbered vol.). Boston and New York, 2003.

Rodgers, Daniel. *Atlantic Crossings: Social Politics in a Progressive Age.* Cambridge, MA, and London, 1998.

Rosenbaum, Julia B., and Sven Beckert, eds. *The American Bourgeoisie: Distinction and Identity in the Nineteenth Century* (Palgrave Studies in Cultural and Intellectual History, unnumbered vol.). New York, 2010.

Rosenberg, Hans. "Der Weltwirtschaftliche Struktur- und Konjunkturwandel von 1848 bis 1857," in *Probleme der Reichsgründungszeit 1848–1879*, ed. Helmut Böhme. Cologne and Berlin, 1972: 159–92.

Rösing, Johannes. "Schleiden, Rudolf," *Allgemeine Deutsche Biographie* 54, Munich 1908: 33–41.

Rössler, Horst. *Hollandgänger, Sträflinge und Migranten. Bremen-Bremerhaven als Wanderungsraum*. Bremen, 2000.

Rüthnick, Richard. *Bürgermeister Smidt und die Juden (Bremens Judenpolitik 1803–1848)*. Bremen, 1934.

Sardar, Ziauddin. *Postmodernism and the Other: The New Imperialism of Western Culture*. London and Chicago, 1998.

Scharf, J. Thomas. *History of Baltimore City & County*, 2 vols. Philadelphia, 1881.

Schildknecht, Karl-Heinz. *Bremen und Baumwolle im Wandel der Zeiten*. Bremen, 1999.

Schiller, Friedrich. *On the Aesthetic Education of Man: In a Series of Letters*, translated by Elizabeth Wilkinson and L. A. Willoughby. Oxford, 1967 (1793–5).

Schivelbusch, Wolfgang. *The Railway Journey: Trains and Travel in the Nineteenth Century*. New York, 1979.

Schleiden, Rudolf. *Erinnerungen eines Schleswig-Holsteiners. Neue Folge, 1841–1848*. Wiesbaden, 1890.

Jugenderinnerungen eines Schleswig-Holsteiners. Wiesbaden, Germany, 1886.

Schlesinger, Arthur M., Jr. *The Age of Jackson*. Boston, 1945.

Schnelle, Albert. *Bremen und die Entstehung des allgemeinen deutschen Handelsgesetzbuches (1856–1864)* (Wilhelm Lührs, ed., Veröffentlichungen aus dem Staatsarchiv der Freien Hansestadt Bremen, vol. 57). Bremen, 1992.

Schniedewind, Karen. *Begrenzter Aufenthalt im Land der unbegrenzten Möglichkeiten. Bremer Rückwanderer aus Amerika, 1850–1914*. Stuttgart, 1994.

Scholl, Lars U. *Bremen und Amerika. Die Verbindung der Hansestadt mit den Vereinigten Staaten* (Jahrbuch der Wittheit zu Bremen, 2008/2009). Bremen, 2009.

Schramm, Percy E[rnst]. "Hamburg – Brasilien: Die Forderung einer Dampferverbindung, 1854 verwirklicht," *Vierteljahrschrift für Sozial- und Wirtschaftsgeschichte* 52, no. 1 (1965): 86–90.

Schramm, Percy Ernst. *Hamburg, Deutschland und die Welt. Leistung und Grenzen hanseatischen Bürgertums in der Zeit zwischen Napoleon I. und Bismarck. Ein Kapitel deutscher Geschichte*. Munich, 1943.

Schulz, Andreas. *Vormundschaft und Protektion. Eliten und Bürger in Bremen 1750–1880* (Stadt und Bürgertum, vol. 13). Munich, 2002 (also Habilitationsschrift, University Frankfurt am Main, 2000).

"Liberalismus in Hamburg und Bremen zwischen Restauration und Reichsgründung (1830–1870)," in *Liberalismus und Region. Zur Geschichte des deutsche Liberalismus im 19. Jahrhundert*, ed. Lothar Gall and Dieter Langewiesche. Munich, 1995: 135–60.

"Weltbürger und Geldaristokraten. Hanseatisches Bürgertum im 19. Jahrhundert," *Historische Zeitschrift* 259 (1994): 637–70.

Schwab, Gustav Benjamin. *Wanderungen durch Schwaben* (Das malerische und romantische Deutschland, vol. 2). Leipzig, 1837.

Der Bodensee und das Rheinthal bis Luciensteig. Stuttgart, 1826.

Schwab, John Christopher. *The Confederate States of America, 1861–1865*. New York, 1901.

Schwarzwälder, Herbert. *Geschichte der Freien Hansestadt Bremen*, 4 vols. Hamburg, 1987.

Schwebel, Karl H., *Bremer Kaufleute in den Freihäfen der Karibik. Von den Anfängen des Bremer Überseehandels bis 1815* (Adolf E. Hofmeister, ed., Veröffentlichungen aus dem Staatsarchiv der Freien Hansestadt Bremen, vol. 59). Bremen, 1995.

"Bremen Merchants throughout the World," in *Bremen – Bremerhaven. Häfen am Strom – River Weser Ports*, ed. Gesellschaft für Wirtschaftsförderung Bremen. Bremen, 1966.

Sellers, Charles. *The Market Revolution: Jacksonian America, 1815–1846*. New York and Oxford, 1991.

Siemann, Wolfram. *Gesellschaft im Aufbruch: Deutschland 1849–1871* (edition suhrkamp, Neue Folge, vol. 537; as such: Hans-Ulrich Wehler, ed., Neue Historische Bibliothek, unnumbered vol.). Frankfurt, 1990.

Die deutsche Revolution von 1848/49 (edition suhrkamp, Neue Folge, vol. 266; as such: Hans-Ulrich Wehler, ed., Neue Historische Bibliothek, unnumbered vol.). Frankfurt, 1985.

Sloan, Edward. "Collins versus Cunard: The Realities of a North Atlantic Steamship Rivalry, 1850–1858," *International Journal of Maritime History* 4, no. 1 (June 1992): 83–100.

Stanley, Amy Dru. *From Bondage to Contract: Wage Labor, Marriage, and the Market in the Age of Slave Emancipation*. New York, 1998.

Stein, Rudolf. *Klassizismus und Romantik in der Baukunst Bremens*, 2 vols. (Senator für das Bildungswesen, ed., Forschungen zur Geschichte der Bau- und Kunstdenkmäler in Bremen, vols. 4 and 5). Bremen, 1964–5.

Steinsdorfer, Helmut. "Zur Erinnerung an Rudolf Schleiden (1815–1895) – Diplomat, Politiker und Publizist aus Schleswig-Holstein," *Die Heimat* [Husum, Schleswig-Holstein] 102, no. 9–10 (September–October 1995): 201–15.

Struve, Walter. *Germans & Texans: Commerce, Migration and Culture in the Days of the Lone Star Republic*. Austin, TX, 1996.

Stürmer, Michael, ed. *Herbst des Alten Handwerks. Meister, Gesellen, und Obrigkeit im 18. Jahrhundert*. Munich, 1986.

Taylor, John. *An Inquiry into the Principles and Policy of the Government of the United States*. London, 1950 (1814).

Thompson, E. P. *The Making of the English Working Class*. London, 1965.

Tiffany, Francis. *Life of Dorothea Lynde Dix*. Boston and New York, 1890.

Tönnies, Ferdinand. *Community and Civil Society*, translated by José Harris and Margaret Hollis (Cambridge Texts in the History of Political Thought, unnumbered vol.). Cambridge, 2001 (1887).

Toury, Jacob. "Die Revolution von 1848 als innerjüdischer Wendepunkt," in *Das Judentum in der deutschen Umwelt, 1800–1850. Studien zur Frühgeschichte der Emanzipation*, ed. Hans Liebeschütz and Arnold Paucker. Tübingen, 1977: 359–76.

Trefousse, Hans L. *Carl Schurz: A Biography*. Knoxville, TN, 1982.

Trommler, Frank, and Joseph McVeigh, eds. *America and the Germans: An Assessment of a Three-Hundred-Year History*. Philadelphia, 1985.

Twain, Mark. *The Innocents Abroad*. New York, 1996 (1869).

Tyler, David Budlong. *Steam Conquers the Atlantic*. New York and London, 1939 (also PhD diss., Columbia University).

Tyrrell, Ian. "American Exceptionalism in an Age of International History," *American Historical Review* 96, no. 4 (1991a): 1031–55.

"Ian Tyrell Responds," *Journal of American History* 96, no. 4 (1991b): 1068–72.

Vagts, Alfred. "Gustav Schwab 1822–1880. Ein deutschamerikanischer Unternehmer," *1000 Jahre Bremer Kaufmann. Aufsätze zur Geschichte bremischen Kaufmannstums, des Bremer Handels und der Bremer Schiffahrt aus Anlaß des tausendjährigen Gedenkens der*

Marktgründung durch Bischof Adaldag 965 (Bremisches Jahrbuch, vol. 50). Bremen, 1965: 337–60.

Vidal, Gore. *Lincoln: A Novel.* New York, 1984.

Walker, Mack. *German Home Towns: Community, State, and General Estate, 1648–1871.* Ithaca, NY, and London, 1971.

Walters, Ronald G. *American Reformers, 1815–1860.* New York, 1997 (1978).

Wätjen, Hermann. *Der deutsche Anteil am Wirtschaftsaufbau der Westküste Amerikas.* Leipzig, 1942.

"Dr. Rudolf Schleiden als Diplomat in Bremischen Diensten, 1853–1866," *Bremisches Jahrbuch* 34 (1933): 262–76.

Aus der Frühzeit des Nordatlantikverkehrs. Studien zur Geschichte der deutschen Schiffahrt und deutschen Auswanderung nach den Vereinigten Staaten bis zum Ende des amerikanischen Bürgerkrieges. Leipzig, 1932.

White, Lucy Sophia, née Schwab, *Fort Number Eight. The Home of Gustav and Eliza Schwab. Compiled by their daughter Lucy Schwab White for their Grandchildren and Great-Grandchildren that they may know something of the Rock whence they are hewn.* New Haven, CT, 1925 (MSS 434, John Christopher Schwab Family Papers, series II, box 17, folder 212; see preceding: Sources – 1. Manuscript and Printed Sources – New Haven – Yale University Library, Manuscripts and Archives – Archival Materials.

Wilentz, Sean. *Chants Democratic: New York City and the Rise of the American Working Class, 1788–1850.* New York and Oxford, 1984.

Wippermann, Wolfgang. *Jüdisches Leben im Raum Bremerhaven. Eine Fallstudie zur Alltagsgeschichte der Juden vom 18. Jahrhundert bis zur NS-Zeit* (Burchard Schepeler, ed., Veröffentlichungen des Stadtarchivs Bremerhaven, vol. 5). Bremerhaven, 1985.

Wittke, Carl F. *Refugees of Revolution: The German Forty-Eighters in America.* Philadelphia, 1952.

Wooster, Ralph A. "Sidelights – The Membership of the Maryland Legislature of 1861," *Maryland Historical Magazine* 56, no. 1 (March 1961): 94–102.

Wright, Gavin. *The Political Economy of the Cotton South: Households, Markets, and Wealth in the Nineteenth Century.* New York, 1978.

Young, Linda. *Middle-Class Culture in the Nineteenth Century: America, Australia and Britain.* New York, 2003.

Zimmerman, Andrew. *Alabama in Africa: Booker T. Washington, the German Empire, and the Globalization of the New South* (America in the World, unnumbered vol.). Princeton, NJ, 2010.

Index

Printed in the United States
by Baker & Taylor Publisher Services